GRANT CASTNER

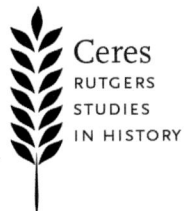

Ceres: Rutgers Studies in History

Lucia McMahon and Christopher T. Fisher, Series Editors

New Jersey holds a unique place in the American story. One of the thirteen colonies in British North America and the original states of the United States, New Jersey plays a central, yet underappreciated, place in America's economic, political, and social development. New Jersey's axial position as the nation's financial, intellectual, and political corridor has become something of a signature, evident in quips about the Turnpike and punchlines that end with its many exits. Yet, New Jersey is more than a crossroad or an interstitial "elsewhere." Far from being ancillary to the nation, New Jersey is an axis around which America's story has turned, and within its borders gather a rich collection of ideas, innovations, people, and politics. The region's historical development makes it a microcosm of the challenges and possibilities of the nation, and it reflects the complexities of the modern, cosmopolitan world. However, far too little of the literature recognizes New Jersey's significance to the national story, and despite promising scholarship done at the local level, New Jersey history often remains hidden in plain sight.

Ceres books represent new, rigorously peer-reviewed scholarship on New Jersey and the surrounding region. Named for the Roman goddess of prosperity portrayed on the New Jersey State Seal, Ceres provides a platform for cultivating and disseminating the next generation of scholarship. It features the work of both established historians and a new generation of scholars across disciplines. Ceres aims to be field shaping, providing a home for the newest and best empirical, archival, and theoretical work on the region's past. We are also dedicated to fostering diverse and inclusive scholarship and hope to feature works addressing issues of social justice and activism.

For a complete list of titles in the series, please see the last page of the book.

GRANT CASTNER

THE LOST ARCHIVE

Nicholas P. Ciotola
and Gary D. Saretzky

Foreword by Margaret M. O'Reilly

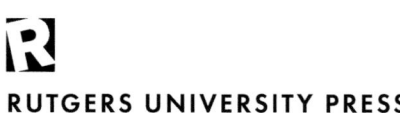

RUTGERS UNIVERSITY PRESS

New Brunswick, Camden, and Newark, New Jersey
London

Rutgers University Press is a department of Rutgers, The State University New Jersey, one of the leading public research universities in the nation. By publishing worldwide, it furthers the university's mission of dedication to excellence in teaching, scholarship, research, and clinical care.

978-1-9788-4520-6 (cloth)
978-1-9788-4521-3 (epub)
Cataloging-in-publication data is available
from the Library of Congress.
LCCN 2025019361

A British Cataloging-in-Publication record for this book
is available from the British Library.

References to internet websites (URLs) were accurate at the time of writing. Neither the author nor Rutgers University Press is responsible for URLs that may have expired or changed since the manuscript was prepared.

♾ The paper used in this publication meets the requirements of the American National Standard for Information Sciences—Permanence of Paper for Printed Library Materials, ANSI Z39.48-1992.

rutgersuniversitypress.org

All the images in this book, unless otherwise credited, are part of the New Jersey State Museum's Grant Castner Collection (CH2019.6), a Gift of Robert R. Jones in Memory of William R. Paquin.

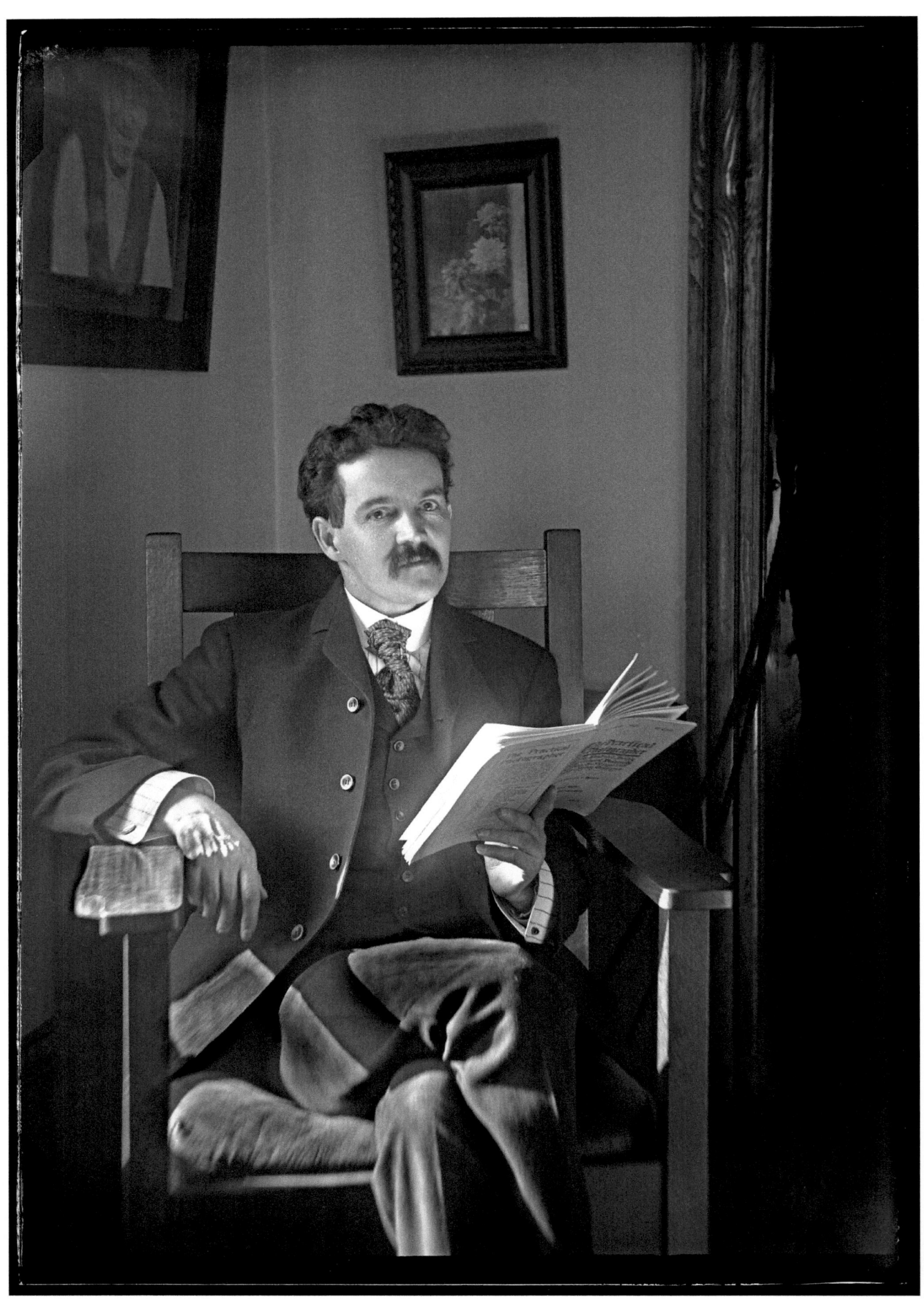

Frontispiece. Grant Castner self-portrait, Trenton, New Jersey, 1906. Digital positive from 5 x 7 in. glass plate negative. CH2019.6.898.

Contents

Foreword

It is with great pride that I introduce this collection of photographs by Grant Castner, a remarkable yet once overlooked photographer whose work captures the essence of New Jersey life in the late nineteenth and early twentieth centuries. Born in Belvidere, New Jersey, in 1863, and later a resident of Trenton from the 1880s onward, Castner's passion for photography found its expression across a wide array of subject matter, including bustling city streets, tranquil rural landscapes, portraits that speak to the character of their subjects, and scenes of transportation and industry that reflect the era's pulse of progress. His still-life compositions also reveal a deep appreciation for the artistry in everyday objects.

For decades, Castner's contributions to photography were largely forgotten, his legacy buried in time. It wasn't until the New Jersey State Museum's major retrospective, held from February to September 2024, that his work was finally given the recognition it deserves. This exhibit marked a pivotal moment in the rediscovery of Castner's art, providing a new generation the opportunity to see the world through his lens.

Thoughtfully organized by New Jersey State Museum's curator of cultural history, Nicholas P. Ciotola, and consulting curator Gary D. Saretzky, the retrospective featured one hundred carefully selected prints and a digital presentation of one hundred additional images drawn from the larger collection of more than one thousand recently discovered glass plate negatives. These were exhibited alongside social and cultural history artifacts from the museum's own collection, many of which had never before been displayed, offering a richer context to Castner's visual narratives. The exhibition's success, highlighted by a feature on *State of the Arts* (NJ TV), demonstrated the public's passionate enthusiasm for, and understanding of, Castner's vision. Many visitors asked if a book was available to take home a piece of this newly revived legacy—and this publication is the answer to that call.

Within these pages, you will find 120 of Castner's photographs, including those showcased in the exhibition. The book is more than a collection of images; it is a testament to Castner's eye for the beauty of the ordinary and the significance of the everyday moments that shaped the life and landscapes of New Jersey over a century ago. We owe a debt of gratitude to the New Jersey State Museum Foundation for their support in bringing this project to life, and to the dedicated museum staff and constituents who worked tirelessly to restore Castner's reputation as one of Trenton's finest photographers.

It is my hope that this book will serve as a lasting tribute to Grant Castner's work and a source of inspiration for all who encounter his images, and that it will offer a window into a world that is both long past and yet enduringly familiar.

Margaret M. O'Reilly
Executive Director,
New Jersey State Museum

Preface

I will always remember the first moment that I heard the name Grant Castner. It all started with a mid-summer 2019 call to my office at the New Jersey State Museum. A man named Robert R. Jones left a voicemail message that he had something that might be of interest to us. In more than twenty-five years as a museum curator, I have fielded thousands such calls. Sometimes, these so-called "leads" are offers to donate a non-working household appliance, a rusty iron tool unearthed in a backyard garden or some other common household item that does not warrant addition to our museum collection, requiring a return phone call and a polite decline. Other times, the subject of a "leads call" turns out to be a true treasure of New Jersey history that perfectly fits into the museum's preservation mission and eventually becomes the newest addition to our ever-growing collection of more than 2 million artifacts, artworks and specimens.

I returned the call within an hour of getting the message. A friendly voice thanked me for calling, expressing some surprise that he heard back from me so quickly considering that it was two days before the Fourth of July holiday. Bob Jones quickly got around to the reason for his call. He was in possession of more than one thousand glass plate negatives depicting people and places in New Jersey dating to a forty-year period from the 1880s to the 1910s. Most were made by one photographer—a native New Jerseyan and Trenton resident named Grant Castner. Moreover, all were still housed in their original sleeves, complete with handwritten notes by the photographer containing information about the name, location, and date of the subject depicted. Immediately intrigued, I asked him to send visual examples of the collection so that I might gauge their historical content and artistic merit. He sent a small selection of images by email right away. To my surprise, he also included a detailed inventory of all of the negatives that provided a full scope of the subjects, locations, and dates covered in each.

When we met in person just a few days later at a storage locker in southern Hunterdon County, Bob shared more details on the collection and its history. His stepson, William R. Paquin, had purchased the glass plate negatives sometime in the 1990s or early 2000s. A Lambertville resident with a passion for antiques and collectibles, Paquin found the glass plates at one of the region's many antique stores that he regularly frequented in search of his main collecting interest—vintage record albums. Bill Paquin's fondness for the Castner collection was immediate and profound. With help from his stepdad, he used a 35mm camera mounted to a copy stand to take reference photographs of all of the negatives. He also spent many hours compiling an inventory of the full collection, numbering and categorizing the individual glass plates and arranging them in groups based on the general subject matter depicted in each. Sadly, Bill's ambitious, multiyear project was cut short when he died unexpectedly in 2016. Three years after his passing, Bill's stepfather called me in hopes of finding a suitable permanent home for the collection so that he could donate it in memory of his stepson.

As we talked, I took a closer look at the glass plates. They were in remarkably good condition considering their age and inherently fragile nature, the original paper sleeves protecting them from a century of storage. Some of them were even packed inside the original boxes in which the glass plates had first been sold to the photographer. Also included in the collection was a small number of silver gelatin prints, cyanotypes and other pieces of paper ephemera about Grant Castner. As I started to pull individual glass plates from their sleeves and hold them up to the light, I got an even better sense of the quality and breadth of this long-forgotten New Jersey photographer's work. One image was a bustling, turn-of-the-twentieth-century streetscape taken on East State Street, just a few blocks from the New Jersey State Museum, in which pedestrians in bowlers and fedoras, horse-drawn carriages and streetcars were framed beneath the iconic spire of historic First Presbyterian Church. Another was a reverential profile portrait view of an elderly African American woman mending a garment while seated in front of a Milford, New Jersey, home, a wall of blooming flowers behind her. Another depicted throngs of happy-faced, woolen suit–clad bathers along the boardwalk in Atlantic City with piers, bathing houses, hotels, and amusements stretching as far as the photographer's lens could reach. Within minutes, I realized that our museum would be the proper home for this remarkable collection. The work was historically important in its depiction of "everyday life in New Jersey," one of the core elements of our collecting policy. It also held artistic merit because of the obvious talents of the photographer, who had a wonderful eye for composition, light, and framing. I called an emergency meeting of our Collections Committee, the internal body that meets once every other month to approve all new donations to the museum, and presented my colleagues with a proposal arguing for its acquisition. The decision to accept was unanimous.

There was one question about the collection for which Bob did not have an answer: How had the collection become separated from the Castner family? To find an answer, I conducted "reverse genealogy" to see if I could locate a relative who might offer some insight on this question. Starting with Grant Castner's lifespan of 1863–1941, I used genealogical resources to work forward in time to find some of his descendants. It did not take too long to trace the family history from Grant Castner to the lives of his two children, Theodore and Eleanor, and on to the next generation and beyond. This research soon unearthed the name of a man who, as best as I could determine, might be a grandson of Grant Castner. I first reached out to John Castner on social media, hoping that I had selected the correct individual amid the numerous online presences of people who shared that not-too-uncommon name combination. On the very first attempt, I received a return message confirming that he was indeed the youngest grandson of Grant Castner. After a lengthy follow-up phone call during which we got to know one another, John graciously invited me to his home and enthusiastically shared family stories and other genealogical materials, including original photographic prints that matched up to the glass plate negatives in our collection. Although John provided a wealth of information about the life and times of his grandfather, he did not know how the glass plate negatives became separated from the family. The most likely scenario, we concluded, was that at some point in time after Grant Castner's death in 1941, a family member made the decision to keep only printed photographs—the medium that could be easily stored in family history albums and framed for display in a home—and felt that the antiquated and unwieldy glass negatives were just no longer needed. How they made it to an antique store and not a landfill remains unknown.

Over the next few years, I worked with my associate, Paula Bisson, to process the Grant Castner Collection (CH2019.6) into the State Museum permanent collection. Paula worked diligently to examine, dust, rehouse, number, catalog, and scan every glass plate slide in the collection, systematically producing a high-resolution digital image of each and arranging for safe and secure, long-term museum storage. Using the donor's original inventory as a basis, I examined the content of each image; conducted research on the people, places, and events depicted; and added the descriptive data into the entries in our museum collections management database. This work made it possible to implement the next stage of the project—a 3,500 square foot exhibition on the first floor of the State Museum that celebrated the life and works of this long-forgotten Trenton artist. For this project, I reached out to my colleague Gary D. Saretzky, a local expert on the history of photography and the definitive scholar of New Jersey's nineteenth-century photographers. As the consulting curator for the exhibition, Gary brought the experiences of a fifty-year-long career as an archivist, historian, and photographer to the project, providing numerous insights on Castner's style, techniques, and influences within the larger scope of American photographic history. Gary and I worked together to assess the full breadth of the Castner collection and selected what we believed to be the very best of Castner's images, both from an aesthetic standpoint and for their ability to convey interesting and unknown stories of New Jersey history. Consisting of two hundred images drawn from Castner's original negatives augmented by seventy-five three-dimensional artifacts from the museum collection relating to the historical content of the images, *Discovering Grant Castner: The Lost Archive of a New Jersey Photographer* opened on February 3, 2024, on the first floor of the New Jersey State Museum and ran through September 15, 2024. The content of this book is drawn from our research and writing for the exhibition.

Numerous individuals aided Gary and me in making this book a reality. William R. Paquin and Robert R. Jones deserve special praise for their early work on the collection and entrusting the New Jersey State Museum as its permanent home. John Castner and his daughter Jennifer Castner provided a wealth of family history information that helped piece together the details of Castner's early life in Belvidere and Trenton. Wilden Munsen and Ed Castner, two additional Castner descendants, shared useful genealogical materials, family history stories, and research leads. New Jersey State Museum Executive Director Margaret M. O'Reilly shepherded this partnership with Rutgers University Press through the complex machinations of state government. The New Jersey State Museum Foundation provided underwriting for this publication through the Beulah L. Brinker Fund, as well as financial support for the exhibition from which the book was created through the Lucille M. Paris Fund. The staff and board of the foundation should be commended for their continuing support of the museum and its initiatives.

My day-to-day colleagues at the State Museum, chiefly Paula Bisson, Henry Hose, Elizabeth Beitel, Susan Greitz, Karen Klink, and Beth Cooper, brought expertise and excitement to the project as it evolved from initial idea to implementation. The following individuals also generously shared their time and assistance at various stages of this project: Linda Barth, Ron Becker, Barbara Bower, Colt Bower, Lynne Calamia, Veronica Calder, David Crum, Pedram Daneshgar, Catherine Denning, Joseph Donnelly, Dana Ehret, Regina Fitzpatrick, Erica Freeman, Karl Flesch, Nicole Jannotte, Albert King, Joseph Klett, Sally Lane, William McKelvey, Joanne Nestor, Gregory Lattanzi, Christopher Loos, Jenny Martin-Wicoff, William Nutter, Susan Orr, Mark Osterman, Rocky Palmetto, Rod Pellegrini, Laura Poll, Kenneth R. Rosen, Alexander Saretzky, Kathlinda Saretzky, Eric Schaum, Susan Taylor, Rebecca Urban, Jenaro Vazquez, Marianna Vertullo, Sarah Vogelman, Nicholas Wood, Joseph Zemla, and Clifford Zink. In the media world, Susan Walner, David Matthau, Ilene Dube, Anne Levin, and Laura Ward used their writing and production talents on their respective platforms to bring popular exposure to the life and works of Grant Castner. Kerin Shellenbarger has long been a creative confidant and fastidious editor for my exhibits, publications, and other museum projects, and this endeavor proved to be no different.

Finally, I would like to extend special thanks to longtime Editor Peter Mickulas and his entire team at Rutgers University Press. A true proponent of New Jersey history who has worked marvels to promote the research of the state's history practitioners, Peter enthusiastically supported this book from the beginning and was the leading force in establishing a long-overdue relationship between New Jersey's flagship university and its state museum—a relationship that is poised to reap many more rewards in the years to come.

Nicholas P. Ciotola
Curator of Cultural History
New Jersey State Museum

GRANT CASTNER

Introduction

It was a chilly, early winter day in the year 1900. A short, thin man with a youthful face and well-groomed, chevron-style mustache slowed his bicycle to a halt near the bustling intersection of State and Broad streets in downtown Trenton. In an age of fedoras, bowlers, and top hats, the man sported a casual, woven cap most commonly associated with "newsies," the young boys who earned their living selling newspapers. His headwear was less a fashion choice and more a statement of identity. News was this man's life. He earned his comfortable, middle-class living as a distributor of newspapers and magazines with the Union News Company, the agency that had a lucrative contract to supply the newsstands of the famed Pennsylvania Railroad with reading material for its passengers. The man's journalistic sensibilities, coupled with an inherent appreciation of the arts, also inspired him to pursue a second career as a photographer.

Quickly yet methodically, he dismounted his bicycle and carefully unpacked the contents of the leather bags strapped to the seat, frame, and handlebars. The bags contained the

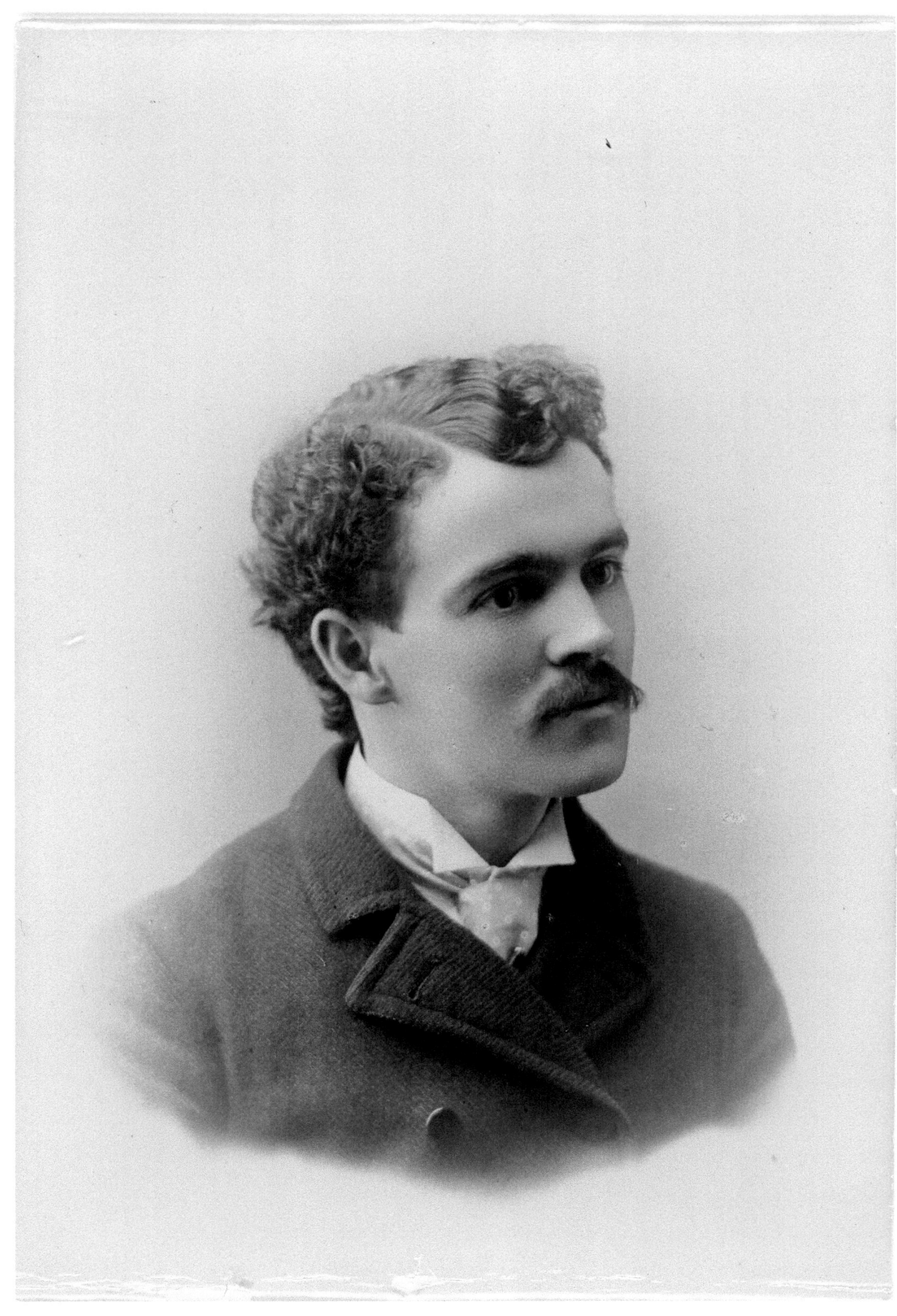

Figure 1. Grant Castner in his early twenties, c. 1885, 5.5" x 3.75". New Jersey State Museum, CH2019.6.1134.

tools of his true passion—a box camera, several lenses, and an ample supply of gelatin dry plate negatives, easily breakable because they were made of glass. Scanning the busy street around him, he took into account the light and shadows, the buildings, trees, skyline, and the positioning of streetcars, carriages, and pedestrians in order to frame a visually appealing scene that told a story. Then he waited, as long as necessary, and, when the moment was just right, clicked the shutter to capture and preserve a pinpoint moment in time.

Quiet, cerebral, and introspective, yet also affable and actively involved in community affairs, the newsman-turned-photographer spent a lifetime taking pictures in Trenton and all across the Garden State. His collective body of work spanned a wide array of subjects, from buzzing city street scenes to the tranquil beauty of nature to intimate portraits of his fellow New Jerseyans at home and at work. His images were greatly admired among his peers within the city's fledgling photographic circles and hailed by the general public for their documentary quality and artistic merit. Well-known among the residents of turn-of-the-twentieth-century Trenton but since lost to history, the name of this talented New Jersey photographer was Grant Castner.

Grant Castner was born on December 6, 1863, in Belvidere, New Jersey, a quaint and picturesque Delaware River town that served as the county seat of rural Warren County. His distant ancestors featured heavily in the early immigrant history of the Garden State, specifically the often-overlooked Palatine German settlements in Morris, Hunterdon, Somerset, and Sussex Counties. In the first decades of the 1700s, Germans living in the Palatinate—an agrarian region in southern Germany along the Rhine River—emigrated from their homeland by the thousands. Facing economic and societal upheaval caused by years of warfare and severe winters that completely destroyed their agrarian way of life, Palatine Germans realized that their only hope for survival lay in the promise of the

American colonies. The largest numbers of these German immigrants settled in New York and Pennsylvania. However, north central New Jersey also developed a notable German immigrant population during this period.[1]

Grant Castner's fourth great-grandfather, Johannes Peter Kastner, was one of these immigrants. Born in Elsenz, Germany, in 1678, Castner first came to New Jersey around 1717 and settled along the headwaters of the Raritan River in Bedminster, where he died in 1756.[2] As an immigrant wishing to assimilate, Johannes was probably the family member who first changed the spelling of the surname. The German word *kastner* refers to a joiner or maker of furniture, suggesting an early occupation of one of the family's distant ancestors in Germany.

Grant Castner's grandfather, the Reverend Jacob Randolph Castner, was also significant to the German American history of New Jersey. Born in Liberty Corner (Somerset County) on July 24, 1785, he played an important role in converting German Americans in central New Jersey to Presbyterianism. Castner was an opinionated thinker, gifted orator, and man of unflappable moral conviction. Licensed as a pastor by the Presbytery on January 15, 1812, he passionately spread his beliefs throughout the German American community—a community that was historically affiliated with the Lutheran and Reformed religions. In 1813, Castner's influential sermons played a key role in convincing several German churches in north central New Jersey to apply to the Presbytery of New Brunswick to enter Presbyterianism. Reverend Castner first found work preaching to Presbyterians in German Valley (now Long Valley), Fairmount, and Chester. He went on to serve as the longstanding pastor at Mansfield Presbyterian Church in Washington, New Jersey, until his death in 1848.[3]

Grant Castner's family history is also intertwined with one of the most notorious cases in the crime annals of the

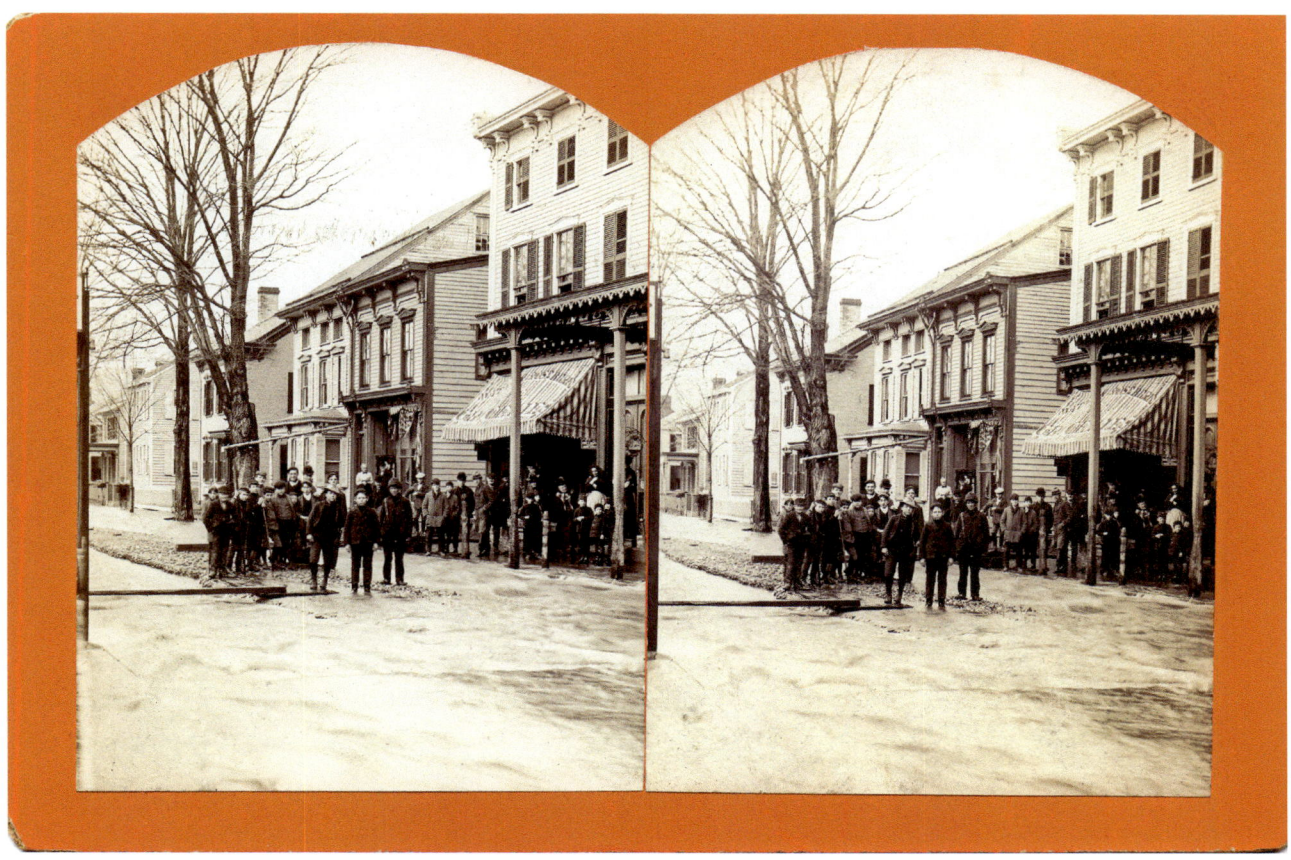

Garden State: the Changewater murders. On the morning of May 2, 1843, a farmer on his way to work in the southern Warren County community of Changewater stumbled across the murdered body of a local resident named John Castner. Further investigation found that the victim's wife, Maria Castner, their daughter, Maria Matilda Castner, and brother-in-law, John Parke, had also been slaughtered. Their bodies were discovered in a nearby home that they all shared. A boarder was found seriously injured inside the house, but the Castners' two young sons miraculously survived unscathed as they were sleeping in a place undiscovered by the assailants. The owner of the home, John Parke, was a wealthy man, and robbery was quickly suspected to be the motive for the heinous killings that shocked and saddened central New Jersey. Due to its sheer brutality, news of the crime traveled well beyond the state's borders.[4]

Figure 2. Stereoview, Belvidere, New Jersey, by Peter D. Ketchledge, active in Belvidere, 1868–1910. Courtesy of Kenneth H. Rosen.

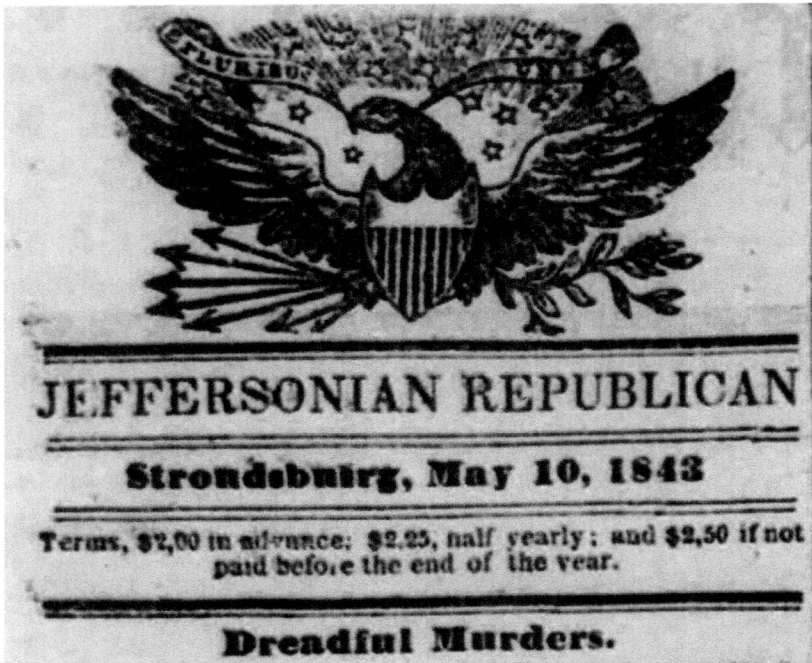

JEFFERSONIAN REPUBLICAN

Stroudsburg, May 10, 1843

Terms, $2,00 in advance; $2,25, half yearly; and $2,50 if not paid before the end of the year.

Dreadful Murders.

One of the most shocking murders which ever occurred in New Jersey, was perpetrated on Monday night, the 1st inst. at Change Water, ten miles from Belvidere, in Warren county, when *four* persons were killed in cold blood, and a fifth beaten almost to death. The victims were, Mr. JOHN B. PARKE, an elderly bachelor, who was reputed to be very wealthy. Mr. JOHN CASTNER, his brother-in-law, who lived with him and farmed his place; his wife, Mrs. Castner, and their child, a little girl about *two years* of age.

Figure 3. Newspapers throughout the mid-Atlantic chronicled the gruesome 1843 murders at Change-water, Warren County, that claimed the lives of Grant Castner's distant relatives. Library of Congress.

Reverend Jacob Randolph Castner—Grant Castner's grandfather—took a great interest in the murders because he shared a surname with the victims, who were distant cousins. The crimes also took place just a few short miles south of his home in Washington and within the sphere of influence of the church where he preached. At the funeral of John Parke, Castner delivered a powerful, hours-long sermon in which he invoked the vengeance of God and implored the grief-stricken mourners to find the guilty parties and bring them to justice. In part because of Reverend Castner's influential involvement, the crimes received front-page attention in the press, and the public clamored for officials to solve the case of the "murders along the Musconetcong" as quickly as possible. Two local men, Joseph Carter and Peter W. Parke, were ultimately tried, convicted, and hanged at Belvidere for the murders, despite the fact that one of them had been acquitted in a first trial due to lack of evidence.[5]

Grant Castner never knew his bombastic grandfather, but he surely learned about his reputation from his father, John Calvin Knox Castner. John Calvin Knox Castner was a well-read local businessman who owned a bookstore in Belvidere. He and his wife, Ellen (née Lowry), raised five children, including Grant. Born in the 1850s, the two oldest children, Mary and Annie, worked as clerks in the family bookstore in their teen years. A third child, Theodore, was born in 1860 but died at a young age from typhoid fever. When Grant Castner arrived in 1863, his parents appear to have been undecided on their newborn son's name. His official birth record actually lists him as John, suggesting that the couple may have first considered naming the boy after his father before finally settling on Grant in time for his baptismal ceremony four months later.[6] Considering that his date of birth came at the height of the American Civil War, Grant Castner is believed to have been named for famed Union general Ulysses S. Grant, whose exploits in the seminal, mid-1863 Vicksburg campaign traveled far and wide. A fifth child, Ida, was born in 1866.[7]

Very little is known about Grant Castner's early years. His hometown of Belvidere was small but held regional importance for two reasons: It was the seat of government for Warren County and served as the northern terminus of the Bel-Del Railroad.[8] Constructed between 1850 and 1855, the Bel-Del ran along the east shore of the Delaware River connecting

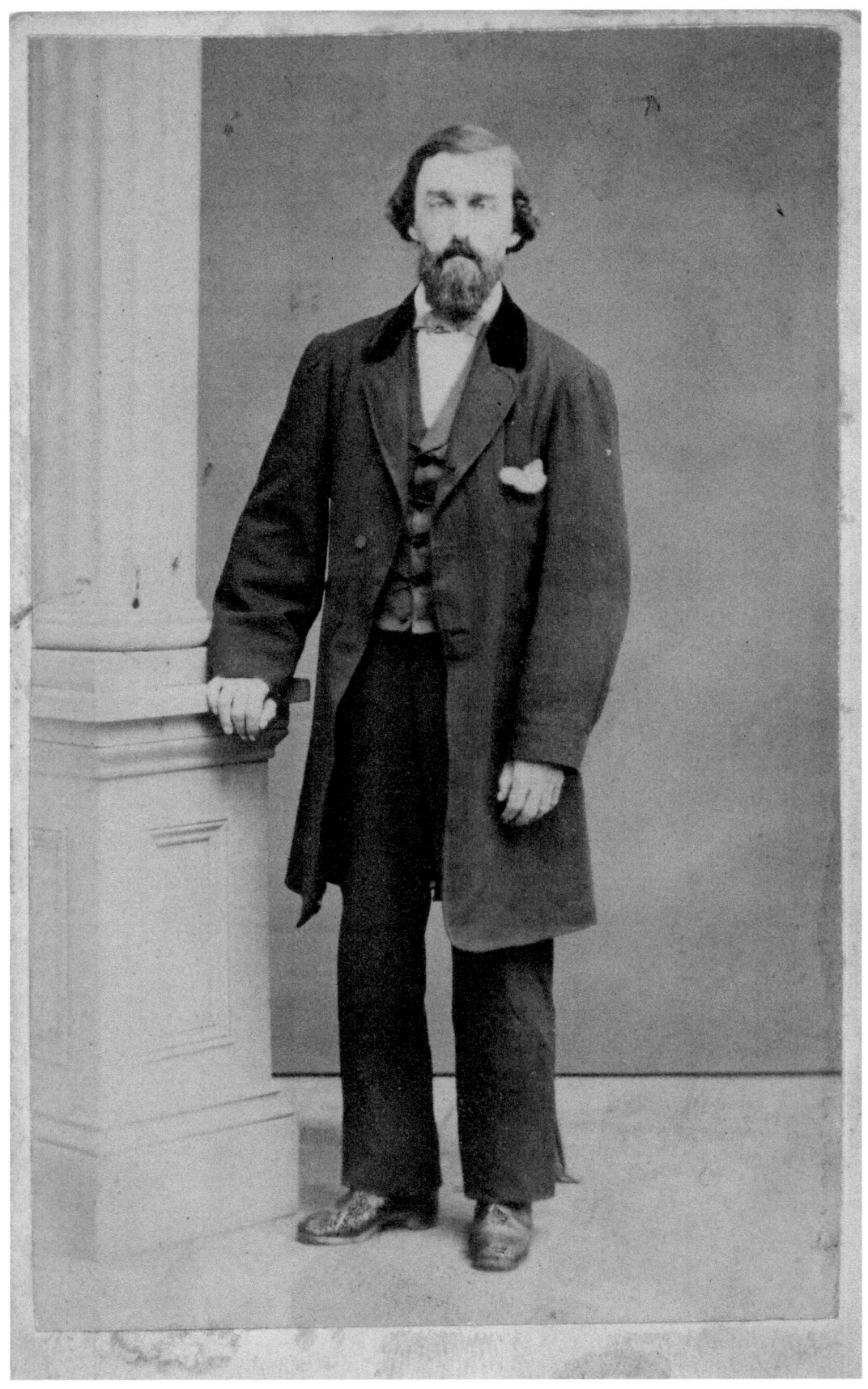

Figure 4. John Calvin Knox Castner (1822–1895), father of Grant Castner, who owned a bookstore in Belvidere, New Jersey. Image by George H. Auxer, Belvidere, New Jersey, 1862, carte-de-visite, 4" x 2.5". New Jersey State Museum, CH2019.6.1100.

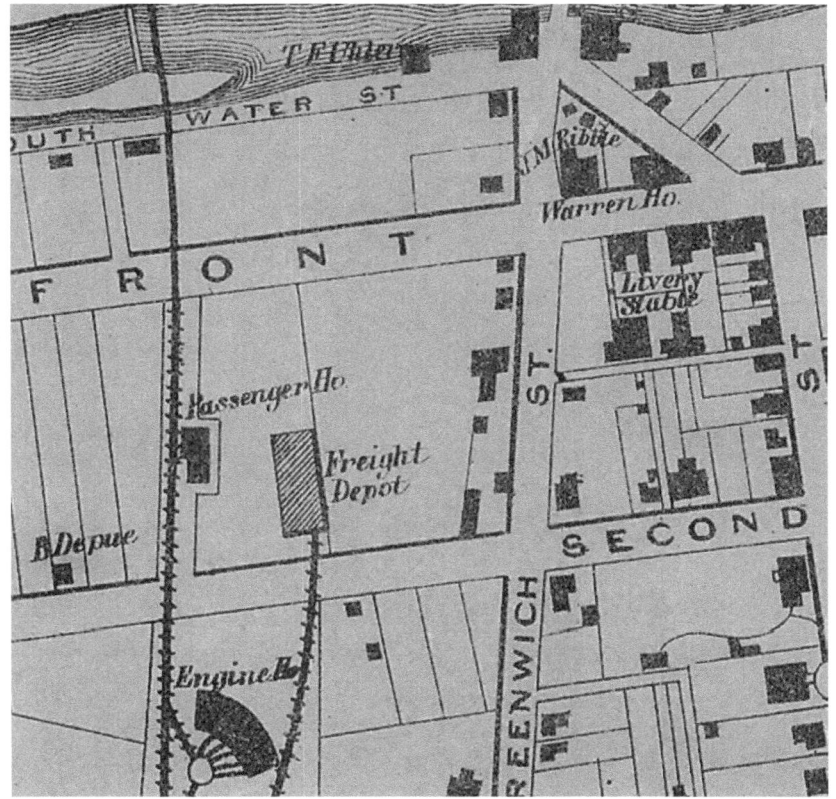

Figure 5. H.F. Walling's 1860 Map of Warren County, New Jersey, showing the passenger station, freight depot, and engine house of the Bel-Del Railroad near Front Street in Belvidere. Library of Congress, G3813.W3 1860.

Belvidere to Trenton, with an extension north to Manunka Chunk added in 1864 to connect it with the Delaware, Lackawanna, and Western Railroad to Scranton. The arrival of the railroad spurred a population boom that doubled the town's population by 1870. Possibly because of the ensuing housing boom, Castner's family changed residences several times during his youth, and he lived in homes on Market Street, Wall Street, and Front Street. Given the learned household of voracious readers in which he was raised, he probably excelled at school. He also developed a profound interest in journalism at a very early age. In 1879, the fifteen-year-old began publishing his own small-format, four-page newspaper titled *The Starry Flag*. Prominently listing himself as editor and publisher, the ambitious teenager wrote and compiled local news stories, obituaries, humorous anecdotes, poems, and other general interest content. He funded the entire endeavor by charging for subscriptions and selling advertising space to local businesses.[9]

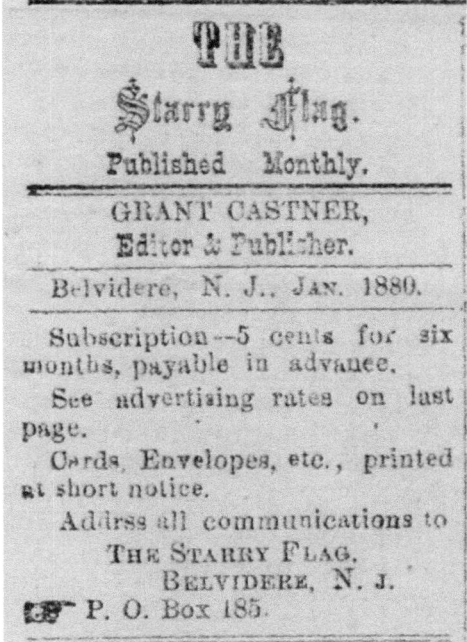

Figure 6. January 1880 issue of *The Starry Flag*, Grant Castner's Belvidere newspaper. Courtesy of American Antiquarian Society.

In 1884, Grant Castner decided to leave Warren County in search of a new career. He first considered a move to the western United States to join a friend but ultimately sought his fortunes closer to home. Taking the Bel-Del Railroad from Belvidere to New Jersey's capital city, the twenty-year-old enrolled in a class at Trenton Business College, the forerunner of Rider University. He also sought job opportunities in both Trenton and Philadelphia, eventually securing a six-month-long job as a clerk in the latter city.[10] By 1885, however, he decided to return to Trenton—this time for good. Grant's tightly knit family played a role in the decision. His older sister Annie and husband Frederick Kampen were already well established in Trenton and welcomed Grant to reside with them. Soon, younger sister Ida joined him as a second boarder in their sibling's home. Grant lived with his older sister at homes on Hudson and Bayard Streets for approximately eighteen years. During this time, he worked briefly as a clerk before embarking on his long-term employment as a news dealer—first with the Union News Company, which supplied Pennsylvania Railroad newsstands, and later with the Curtis Publishing Company, the distributor of *Ladies Home Journal*, *Saturday Evening Post*, and *Country Gentleman* magazines. Following his January 12, 1903, marriage to Sarah Frances Karr, Castner finally moved into a home of his own. The modest, two-story row house was located at 329 Tyler Street, just a few short blocks from the bustling Clinton Street Station that held one of the many newsstands that he serviced. He lived at 329 Tyler Street for the rest of his life.[11]

It is not known exactly when Grant Castner took his first photograph, but it was likely sometime between 1885 and 1889 when he was in his mid-20s. Gainfully employed, boarding with a relative, and still without a family of his own, Castner had enough disposable income to afford the not insignificant expenses of being a photographer in the 1880s: cameras, lenses, tripods, developing chemicals, printing papers and,

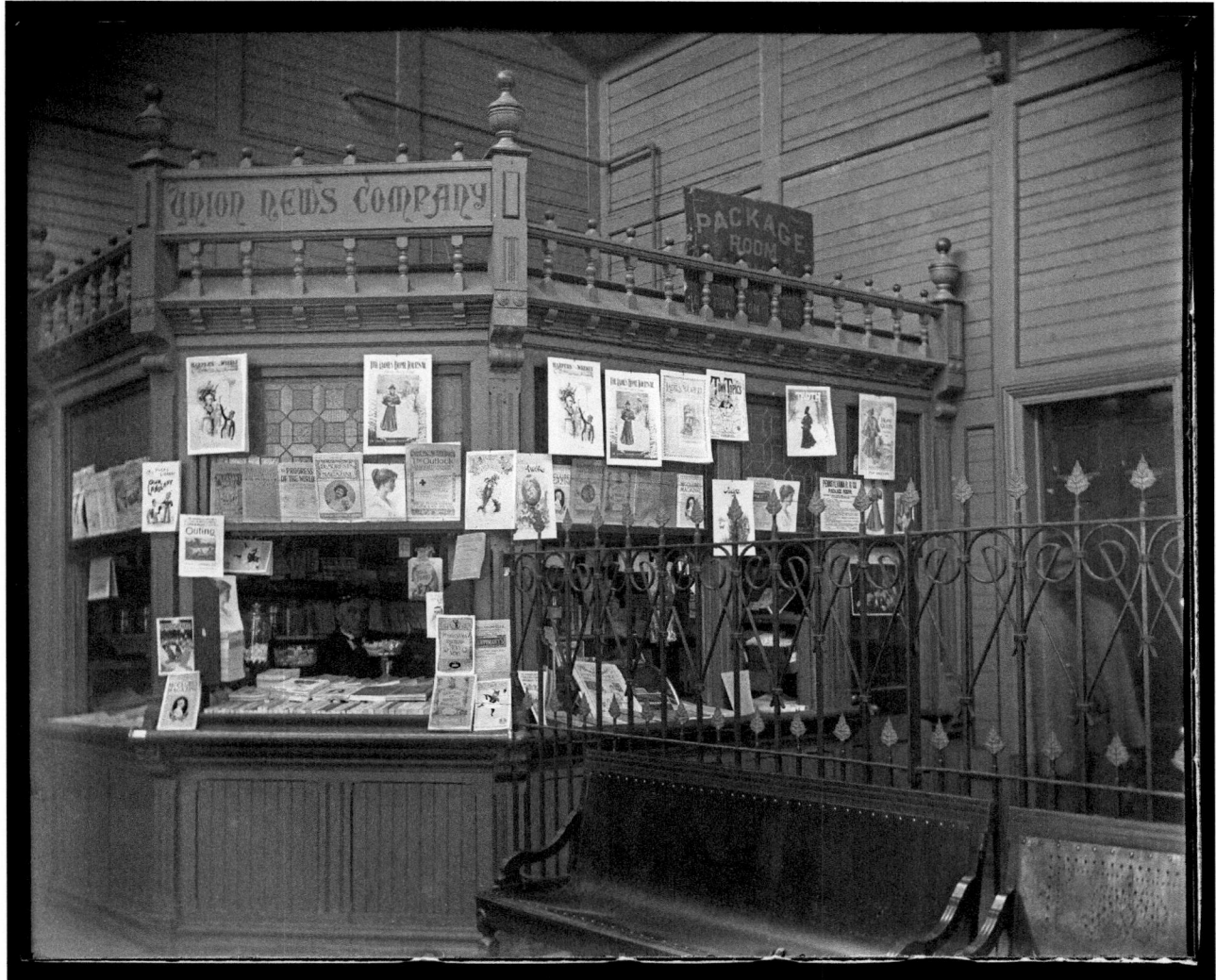

most importantly, an ample supply of glass plate negatives. Glass plate negatives superseded daguerreotypes in the 1850s. Introduced in 1839, daguerreotypes recorded a single positive image on a silver-coated copper plate. But photographers sought a practical way to make a negative on a transparent support so that they could produce multiple positive prints. Although William Henry Fox Talbot's 1841 negative/positive process used semitransparent paper negatives, photographers aspired to a process using glass. When printed on glossy albumen paper, glass negatives would provide finer detail than those on paper. Introduced by Frederick Scott Archer in 1850, wet plate collodion was the first widely used glass plate negative process and remained popular until around 1880. Preparing the negative required coating the plate with potassium

Figure 7. Grant Castner, Union News Company newsstand, Market Street Ferry, Philadelphia, 1896, one of those Castner supplied in his work as a distributor. Digital positive from 4" x 5" glass plate negative. New Jersey State Museum, CH2019.6.96.

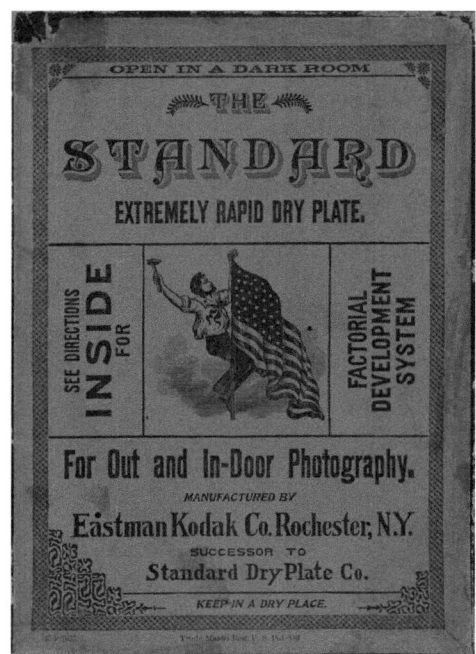

Figure 8. Eastman Kodak Company box that contained "The Standard: Extremely Rapid Dry Plates" purchased and used by Grant Castner. New Jersey State Museum, CH2019.6.1330 a,b.

iodide and collodion, a clear, sticky liquid, and, in the dark, dipping it in silver nitrate, which sensitized it to light. The photographer had to expose and develop the image before it dried. To take pictures in the field, the photographer needed a portable darkroom.[12]

Common from 1880 to the 1920s, gelatin dry plates supplanted collodion for making negatives. They came ready-to-use and were ten times more light sensitive, facilitating stop action photos. Outdoor photographers could put the exposed negatives in a light-tight box and develop them later. Dry plates provided photographers with a newfound freedom of movement. No longer tied to studios or mobile darkrooms, they documented their friends and neighbors where they lived, worked, and played. To be certain, photography after 1880 was still a challenge, as photographers working outdoors still had to transport heavy glass negatives and, after their return, develop and print them.[13] Although Grant Castner may have done some wet plate collodion photography in his very first years as a photographer, the vast majority of his extant work consists of gelatin dry plates.

Grant Castner became a photographer when most camera users were satisfied to capture what they saw and try to reproduce it accurately. Generally absent from his known compositions are active edges, also called "packing the frame."[14] That style has been favored by many later street photographers such as Joel Meyerowitz (b. 1938) to imply that the scene continues outside the image borders and to create geometric forms along the edges.[15] Instead, like most of his contemporaries, Castner usually centered the main subject in his compositions and left space around it with calm edges. He consistently sought detail to tell a visual story, taking advantage of sunlight and shadow and using a sharply focused lens to reveal textures in faces, clothing, nature, architecture, objects and other subjects.

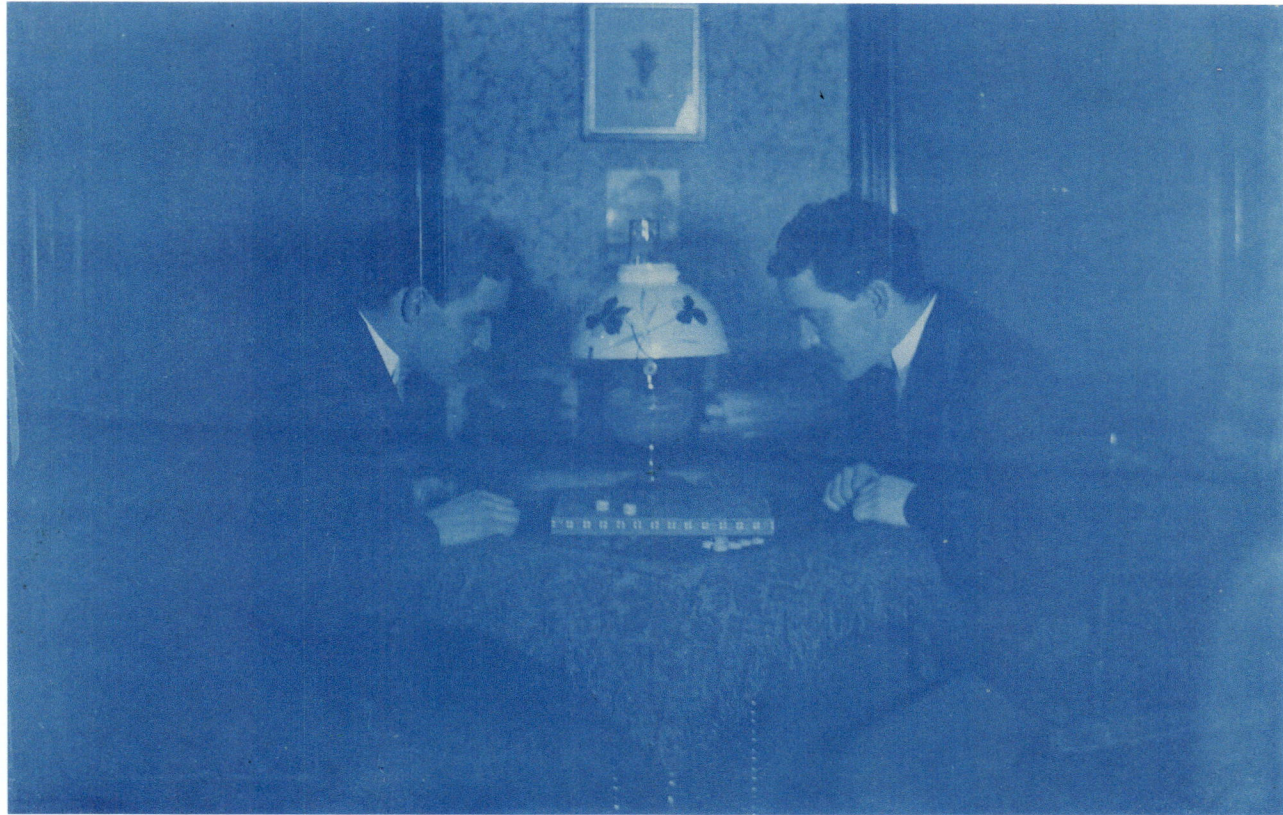

Although Castner did some trick shots, such as a double-exposed self-portrait in which he appears playing checkers with himself, he did not indulge in art photography devices that began to be seen in amateur work in the late 1890s. Castner, as far as known, did not dress up Caucasian sitters in Japanese clothes, as New Jersey-born Eva Watson-Schütze (1867–1935) did, nor did he make extreme close-ups of the face or place the head in an individual portrait near the edge of the frame like Elias Goldensky (1867–1943), both prominent Philadelphia photographers of that era.[16] While some photographers by 1900 were striving for "individuality" to draw attention to their artistry, Castner is more invisible: His photographs are like transparent windows into the past.[17]

In portraiture, Castner did not photograph celebrities, the wealthy, or their residences but portrayed his own social class, such as small business owners and skilled workers, or those of more modest means, in an environment with which he was

Figure 9. Self-portrait, Grant Castner playing checkers with himself. Cyanotype, 4.5" x 6.5". New Jersey State Museum, CH2019.6.1235.

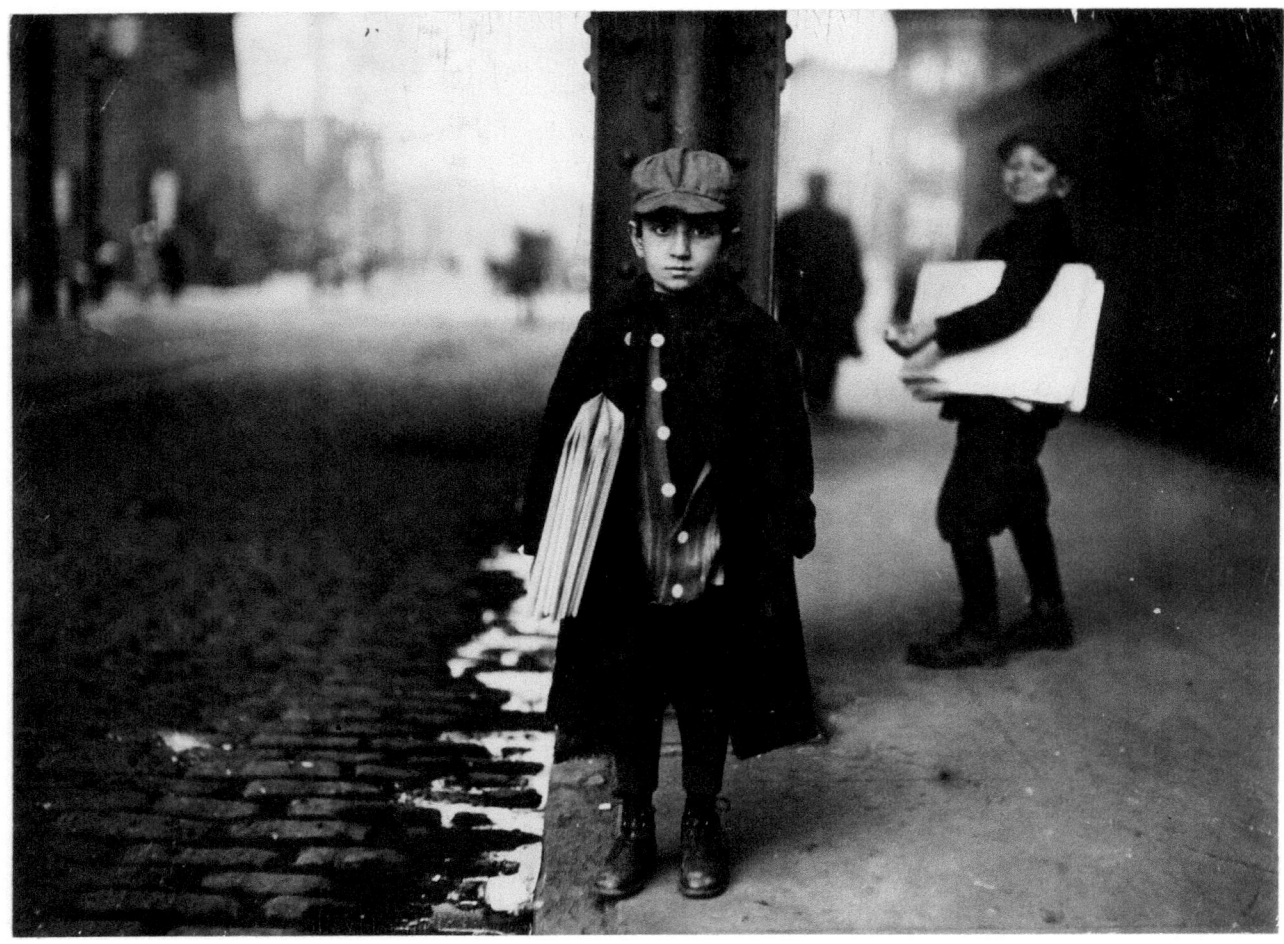

Figure 10. *Seven years old, Tony - 4:15 P.M.* Newark, NJ, 1912. Photograph by Lewis W. Hine (1874–1940). Library of Congress, Hine no. 3227.

familiar. Like the now celebrated Lewis Hine (1874–1940), who extensively photographed early twentieth-century immigrants and child labor practices in New Jersey and other locales nationwide, Castner persuaded those whom he encountered in public, including children, to pose on city streets.[18] Hine photographed strangers while Castner's subjects usually look back at him with recognition of a prior relationship, perhaps only of brief duration. Hine also often used a wide aperture on his lens to isolate figures and throw the background out of focus, while Castner used a smaller aperture to maximize depth of field, allowing us to see all the details of the subject's environment.

Castner's work is more distinguished by what he chose to photograph than how he photographed. Collectively, his work comprises a visual history of how he responded to people,

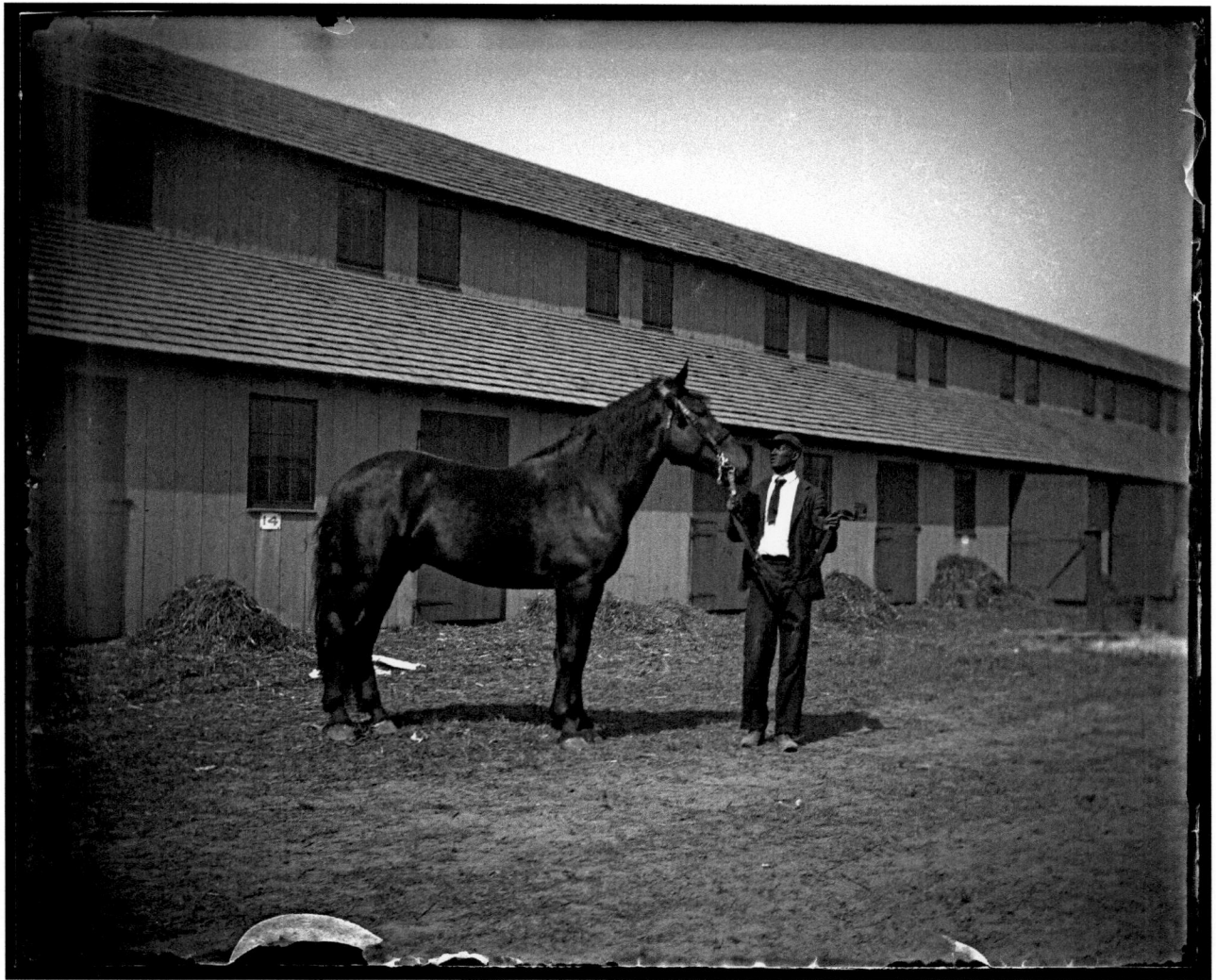

places, and events, especially in Trenton and its environs. Some of his subjects were those that probably appealed more to men than women photographers in that era, such as his portrait of firefighters with their new engine (**plate 42**). But his sensitive portraits of children, for example, could have been taken by a woman.[19] What is consistent about his work is its clarity of expression and directness. The viewer of his photographs can immediately grasp what he wanted to convey, and he achieves this aim primarily through orderly compositions enabled by careful placement of his tripod and, when people were moving, the right moment to trigger the shutter. He would have agreed with the quotation by Francis Bacon that legendary New Jersey-born photographer Dorothea Lange (1895–1965)

Figure 11. Grant Castner, stable hand tending horse, Inter-State Fair, Hamilton Township, NJ, 1895. Digital positive from 4" x 5" glass plate negative. New Jersey State Museum, CH2019.6.357.

kept on her darkroom door: "The contemplation of things as they are, without error or confusion, without substitution or imposture, is in itself a nobler thing than a whole harvest of invention."[20]

While it is not known how Grant Castner came to use photography in this way, perhaps it began through his experience being photographed as a child by a portrait photographer. In the 1860s and 1870s, couples did not take their own photographs of their progeny but went to a local portraitist. Families kept very popular card-mounted photos, usually cartes-de-visite and the larger cabinet cards, in albums and exchanged copies with friends and relatives.[21] Two surviving cartes-de-viste depicting Grant Castner's mother and father were made by George H. Auxer (c. 1825–c. 1869), a photographer who worked in Belvidere in 1862 before moving on to Hackettstown and Hightstown. The Castner family is also known to have patronized the Belvidere photography studio of George K. Marriner (c. 1822–1869).[22] Shortly before Castner's birth, the Merrion Castner & Co. photo gallery was also in business in Belvidere, likely operated by an extended family member who might have captured Grant as a baby.[23] In the 1870s, the Castner family also likely had cartes-de-visite or cabinet cards made by the town's longstanding photographer, Peter Ketchledge (c. 1838–1914), who operated in Belvidere from 1871 to at least 1910.

Castner's family no doubt had a stereographic viewer and a collection of views, which were ubiquitous during his youth in the 1870s. He probably enjoyed some by Ketchledge, who produced stereoviews around 1880 of Belvidere streetscapes with bystanders in front of stores, a flooded street, a large steamboat at the dock, and nearby rural scenes. Castner may have also seen stereoviews by other New Jersey photographers, for example, John P. Doremus (1827–1890), who produced numerous examples around Paterson and its impressive Passaic Falls; Gustavus Pach (1845–1904), the prolific

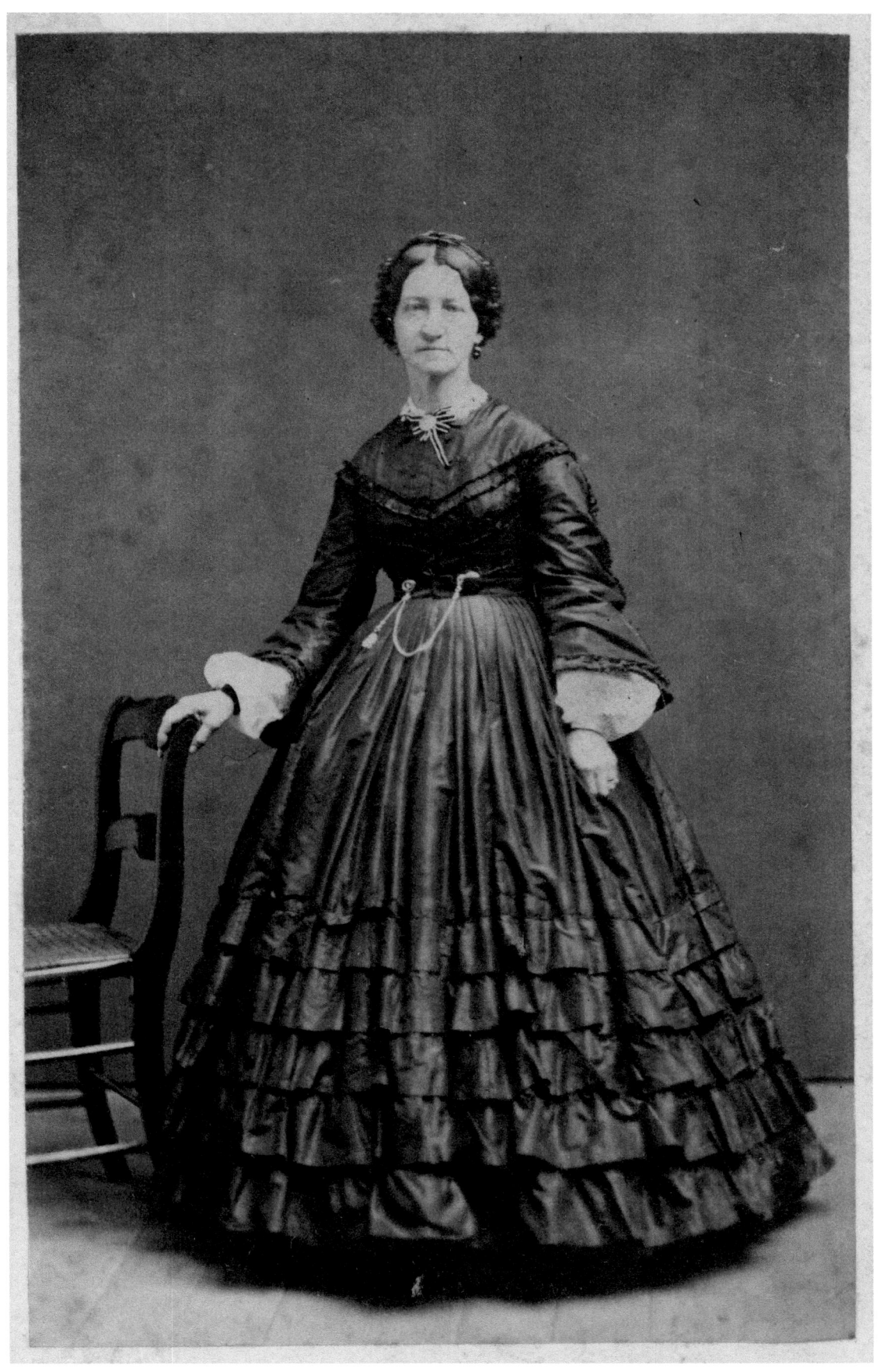

Figure 12. Grant Castner's mother, Ellen Lowry Castner (1831–1897), George H. Auxer, Belvidere, New Jersey, 1862, carte-de-visite, 4" x 2.5". New Jersey State Museum, CH2019.6.1101.

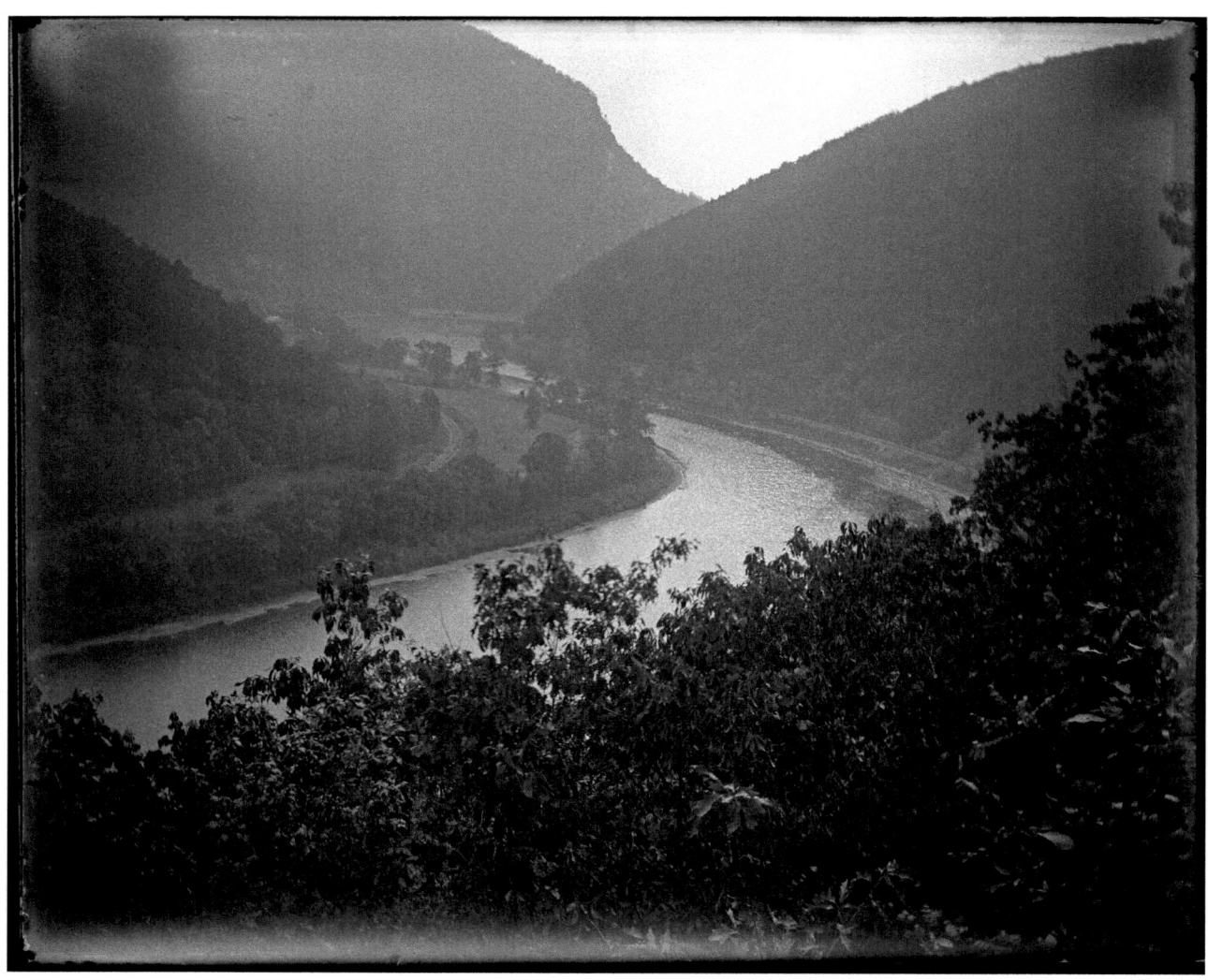

Figure 13. Grant Castner, Delaware Water Gap, 1894, view to the southeast of Mt. Minsi (right) and Mt. Tammany (left) from the Pennsylvania side of the Delaware River. Digital positive from 4" x 5" glass plate negative. New Jersey State Museum, CH2019.6.295.

view maker of the Jersey shore in Long Branch and Ocean Grove; and Plainfield's Guillermo Thorn (1837–1920), who photographed extensively along New Jersey railroad lines.[24] He could easily have been familiar with views by Jesse A. Graves (1835–1895)[25] of the Delaware Water Gap—a New Jersey landmark that Castner also photographed—and perhaps depictions of more remote wonders, from European tourist sites to Niagara Falls. It is also possible that Castner and family visited the 1876 Centennial International Exhibition, the impressive world's fair held in Philadelphia, which was easily accessible from Belvidere via the Bel-Del Railroad to Trenton and points south. The experience would have exposed him to the high-quality landscape and portrait photography of 287 exhibitors in the Photographic Arts Building.[26]

However he first acquired an interest and appreciation for photography, Castner had become an active amateur photographer by the late 1880s and would soon go on to play a leading role in bringing together other Trenton residents who shared his avocation. With the widespread adoption of the convenient, ready-to-use gelatin glass plate negatives in 1880 that became Castner's modus operandi, camera clubs began to proliferate, such as the Boston Society of Amateur Photographers (now the Boston Camera Club) in 1881. A group of camera clubs formed the American Slide Exchange in 1885 so that work in the form of lantern slides could be conveniently shared among these organizations.[27] By 1895, the number of photographic societies and camera clubs in the United States increased from 4 to 109.[28] Exhibitions planned by these clubs began in the 1880s and promoted high standards for a range of photographic genres. Held in 1886, the International Exhibition of Photography in the United States opened under the auspices of the Photographic Society of Philadelphia, with 1,700 prints by 114 photographers from seventeen countries. It would have been a fine opportunity for Castner to see this venue in which both amateurs and professionals participated.[29]

A decade later, Castner became a charter member of the first known Trenton camera club, formed on June 6, 1897, and led by younger men. As reported by a local newspaper, "Last evening a number of camera owners met at the rooms of the Y.M.C.A. and organized The Association Camera Club of Trenton." The officers elected were as follows: president, Oliver Kemp (1876–1934), the son of Trenton professional photographers Frederick and Emma Kemp[30]; vice president, Henry K. Naar (1875–1957), bookkeeper for his father Joseph L. Naar's newspaper, the *True American*[31]; and Secretary Treasurer, Grant Castner. Also appointed was a "committee on rooms, Messrs. Kimble, Applegate and Castner. The association has placed at the disposal of the club two rooms, one

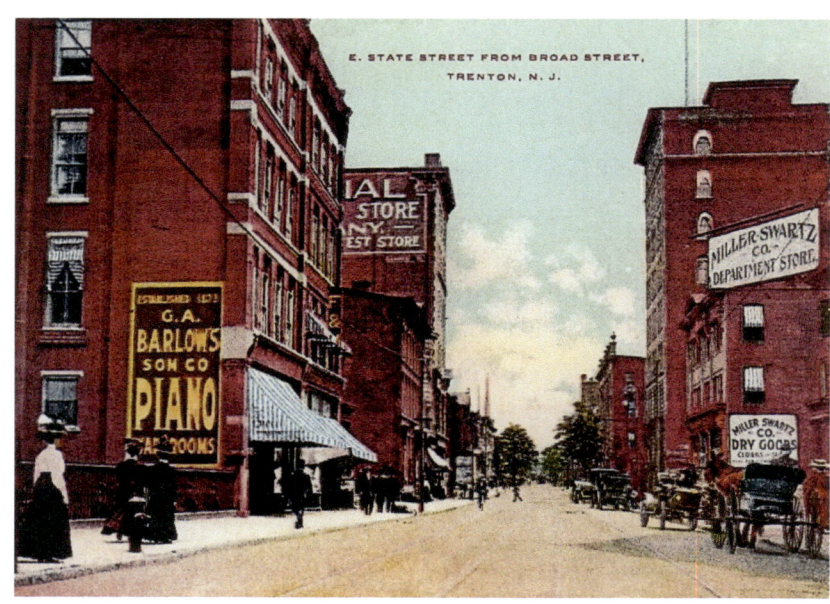

Figure 14. Postcard, Scott Building (left), East State Street, Trenton, with piano and music store at ground level and the headquarters of the fledgling Trenton Photographic Society on the third floor, John C. Voigt Post Card Company, Jersey City, New Jersey, c. 1905. Private Collection.

for the dark room and one for the meetings, etc."[32] Following its official incorporation in 1899 as the Trenton Photographic Society, the growing organization moved its headquarters to a three-room suite on the third floor of the arts-centric Scott Building on East State Street that housed a piano and sheet music store on its ground level. The space was designed to provide members with all of the needs of their photographic hobby, including electric lights, running water, a darkroom, a projector for lantern slides, and an enlarging apparatus. Photographers were expected to purchase their own chemicals, but use of the space and equipment was a gratis benefit for membership in the organization.[33]

While the photography of Castner is the largest and best-known collection of images made by those associated with the Trenton Photographic Society, it is likely that his fellow members photographed some of the same kinds of subjects. Indeed, Castner's photographs document that he went out photographing with friends, including fellow camera enthusiast John S. Neary (1864–1935), who became business manager at the State Teachers College, now The College of New Jersey.[34]

Photographers like Castner enjoyed the social aspect of these organizations, consisting of dedicated lens workers with a like-minded commitment to making photographs that rose

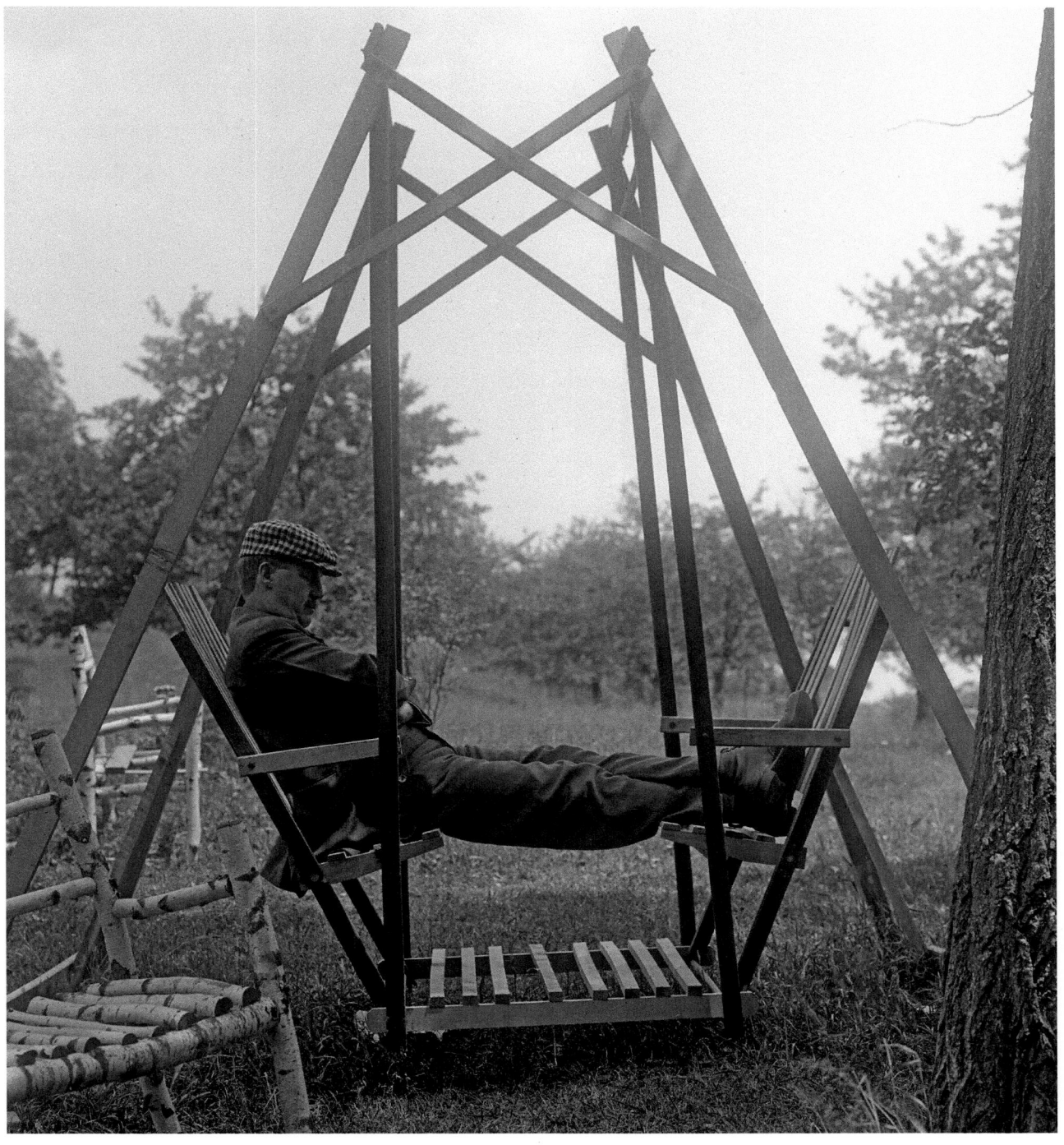

above the quality made by casual snap shooters who used hand-held cameras loaded with roll film, which Eastman Kodak had introduced in 1888. They shared the results of their efforts with each other in lantern slide shows and print exhibitions, which were also open to the general public. Well covered by the local press, these popular events took place at the organization's headquarters in the Scott Building, as well

Figure 15. Grant Castner, John Neary catching a nap during the pair's photographic excursion to Buck Hill Falls near Canadensis, Pennsylvania, in 1910. Digital positive from 6.5" x 8.5" glass plate negative [Detail]. New Jersey State Museum, CH2019.6.851.

as other city venues, including downtown department stores, the YMCA, and the School of Industrial Arts.[35] Cameras, glass plate negatives, chemicals, and other equipment and supplies for these amateurs were readily available from E. & H.T. Anthony, Eastman Kodak and other firms, as well as local shops operated by professional photographers.[36]

Castner loved to read. His lifelong affinity for books and magazines likely began during his childhood as the son of a bookstore owner. As an adult, he worked as a distributor of popular illustrated magazines like the *Saturday Evening Post* and headed a "photographic literature" sub-committee of the Trenton Photographic Society.[37] He also had a fond appreciation for the art and aesthetics of books, inspiring him to study bookbinding at the School of Industrial Arts.[38] His self-portraits often show him holding a book or photography journal, and he no doubt learned about developments in photography through photographic manuals, periodicals, and annuals, some of them published by Flemington, New Jersey, native, Edward L. Wilson (1828–1903), who settled in Philadelphia.[39] For example, *Wilson's Photographics: A Series of Lessons*, contained more than two dozen chapters on the technical aspects of photography.[40]

By the mid-1890s, in photographic magazines, Castner had seen numerous reproductions of photographs illustrating the articles by leading photographers, as well examples of other art media in mass market magazines. After 1900, he probably read profiles of noted photographers by the prolific critic Sadakichi Hartmann (1867–1944), who sometimes used the *nom de plume* Sidney Allan or other pseudonyms.[41] As analyzed in depth by Peter Buse, photography magazines were a major source of inspiration and technical advice for "aspirational amateurs" like Grant Castner . . . photographers who may also have sold photographic literature.[42]

In his reading, Castner would have learned about a key influencer in the development of landscape photography in this period, the English amateur, Peter Henry Emerson (1856–1936), who published the landmark book, *Naturalistic Photography for Students of the Art* (1889).[43] Emerson, who specialized in rural scenes, encouraged photographers to pursue what in the early 1900s came to be called "straight" or "naturalistic" photography as an art medium. In this context, straight photography contrasted with those photographic artists like Henry Peach Robinson (1830–1901), who collaged studio shots of people into landscape photos, or Robert Demachy (1859–1936), who beginning in the 1890s crafted highly manipulated prints that mimicked graphic art processes.[44]

Like Emerson, Castner became skilled in natural, outdoor compositions. In his photograph of an old man walking along the now largely forgotten Trenton Water Power Canal (**plate 60**), he showed his awareness of the Golden Section and, while he did not often use form metaphorically, he did in his view of four pairs of hugging trees along a Monmouth County waterway (**plate 116**).[45] The few prints Castner made from his glass plate negatives in the New Jersey State Museum's collection are conventionally produced silver gelatin or cyanotype contact prints, not highly manipulated bromoil, oil prints, or other hand-crafted media that mimic graphic art, as produced by some *fin de siècle* and early twentieth century art photographers who sought exhibition opportunities to validate their artistic practice.[46] But the best indication of Castner's printing preferences are his lantern slides that he copied from his prints. For example, his *Evening at the Docks*, taken at Cooper's Point, Camden, in 1900 (**plate 82**), is a study of two docked tall-masted sailing ships taken in low light. There is just a hint of detail in the velvety shadows, and the clouded sky has a brighter spot at the right, suggesting that Castner photographed toward the west. As also evidenced by his other lantern slides, Castner here shows his mastery of tonal control without indulging in highly manipulative printing techniques.

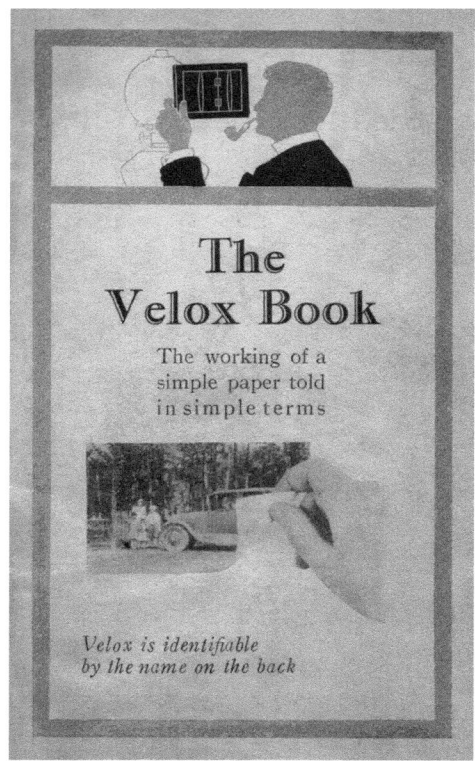

Figure 16. *The Velox Book*, Eastman Kodak Company, undated. 36 pages. 3 1/4" x 5 1/4". Courtesy of Gary D. Saretzky.

Castner sometimes noted the type of paper used for printing on his negative envelopes. For example, for *In Camp*, taken on Eagle Island in the Delaware on September 4, 1896, (**plate 91**) with a Stanley dry plate manufactured by Eastman Kodak, he printed on Velox, a popular silver gelatin paper popular around that time that could be printed with artificial light in a darkroom. These "gaslight papers" were convenient for amateurs who had jobs during the day, unlike albumen paper, the most widely used printing paper before 1895 that required printing in sunlight.[47] Instructions for using Velox were included in the 1898 manual, *Modern Photography in Theory and Practice: A Handbook for the Amateur*, which Castner may have had, and in *The Velox Book*, a pamphlet published by Eastman Kodak.[48] After its inventor, Leo Baekeland, sold his rights to George Eastman in 1899, Eastman Kodak manufactured it in two surfaces, velvet and glossy, in four grades of contrast, and in both single weight and double weight. Kodak also sold Velox postcard paper for printing postcards, a popular practice among photographers from the early 1900s to the 1920s.[49]

Castner no doubt read about the major exhibitions of photography, consisting primarily of work by amateurs, that began in the 1880s. In the 1890s, with both naturalistic and manipulative techniques, Pictorialists—photographers with artistic ambitions—submitted work to photographic salons modeled after those for paintings.[50] The 1891 Vienna Salon featured six hundred photographs chosen by a group of painters and sculptors from more than four thousand submitted; the judging criteria was aesthetic rather than merely technical quality.[51] Closer to Castner, the Photographic Society of Philadelphia, which had participated in rotating exhibits from 1887 to 1892 with the camera clubs in Boston and New York, organized the 1898 Salon at the Pennsylvania Academy of Fine Arts, the first photography show in the United States at an art institution.[52]

One of the judges for the 1898 Salon was Alfred Stieglitz (1864–1946) of the Camera Club of New York. Through his photographs, publishing, and, in later years, gallery management, Stieglitz became one of the most influential photographers of his generation. In the 1890s, he became renowned for his innovative urban scenes, some taken in inclement weather. Stieglitz's photographs from the 1890s and early 1900s often depicted railroads, streetcars, and commercial watercraft, as did Castner's. Ten of Stieglitz's photographs were on display in the 1898 Philadelphia Photographic Salon that Castner might well have visited on a day trip with his fellow camera club members. On May 5 of that year, Castner's fledgling Trenton Photographic Society held a stereopticon exhibition intended to expose local amateurs to the work of photographers of national note, including William D. Murphy, William A. Fraser, and Alfred Stieglitz.[53]

Castner may have been influenced by Stieglitz, although perhaps, despite their very different upbringings, they both were just attracted to the same subjects. Castner's photograph of an incoming steam locomotive (**plate 69**) is rather similar in composition and subject to Stieglitz's well known, *The Hand of Man* (1902).[54] A significant distinction between the two photos is that Stieglitz's print, with its muted midrange tones and slight soft focus, epitomizes the Whistlerian veil popular among Pictorialist photographers around 1900. Since Castner's print has not been found, it is not known how he rendered it. But in any case, if Castner consciously emulated Stieglitz, it was only early on, for the Trenton photographer did not follow Stieglitz, beginning around 1910, into modernism with its emphasis on abstract form and the exploration of the fourth dimension in art.[55]

While Stieglitz led the effort in the United States for photography's acceptance as a fine art medium by the early 1900s, there were many other excellent photographers whose work resonated with Castner's and whose pictures he may have

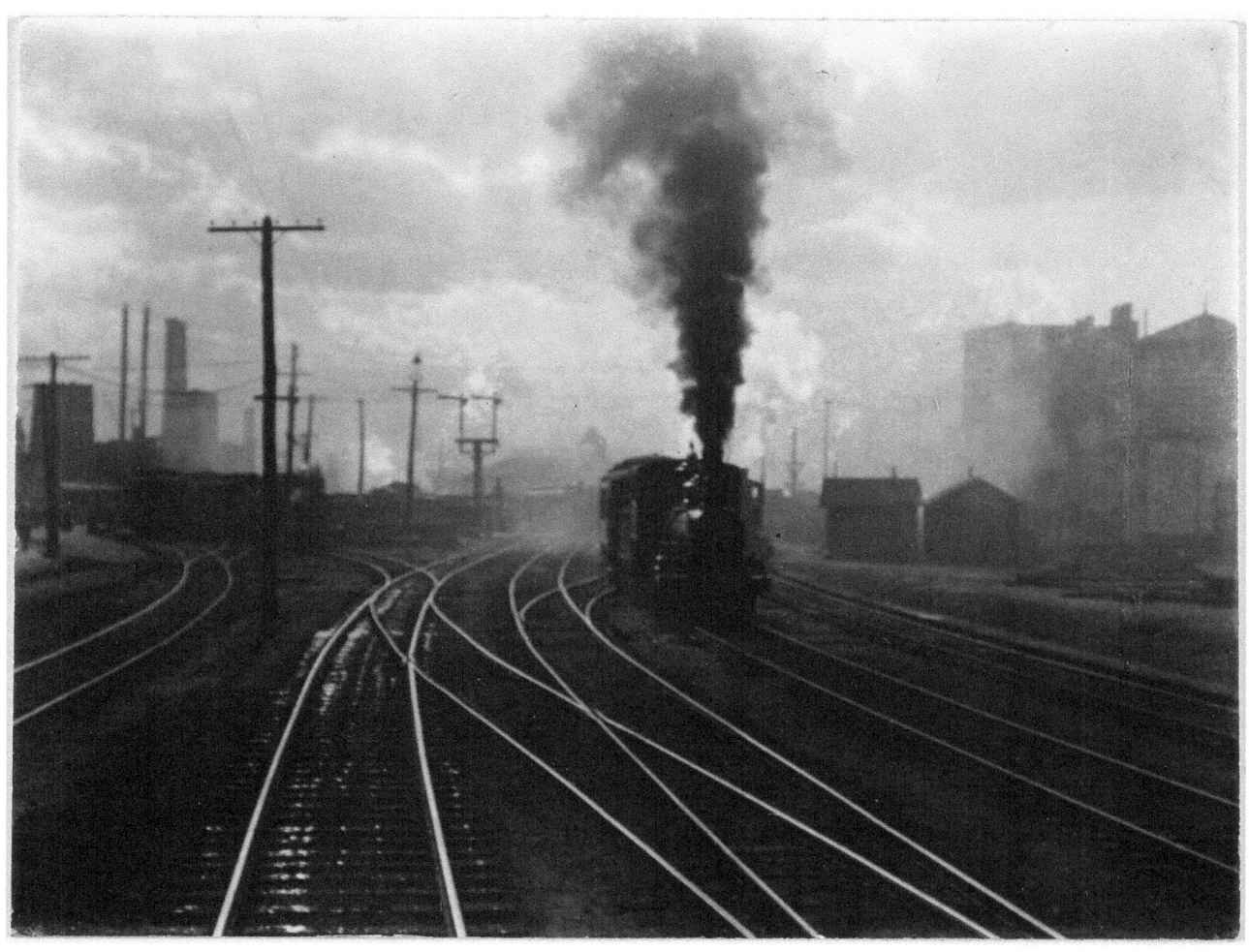

Figure 17. Alfred Stieglitz (1864–1946), *The Hand of Man*, 1902, printed 1920/39. The Art Institute of Chicago, 1949.703.

seen. His contemporary, the versatile Rudolf Eickemeyer Jr. (1862–1932), a native of Yonkers, excelled in both portraiture, which he did for a living in Manhattan, and landscape photos. Eickemeyer was a pioneer in producing affordable large format books of aesthetically motivated photographs reproduced in half-tone, quite different from contemporary photographically illustrated books of such subjects as town architecture and military history.[56] His first, *Down South* (1900), was a sympathetic portrayal of African Americans, a subject that also attracted Castner, who in the 1890s portrayed people of color at home, at school, and at the state fairgrounds near Trenton. The ease of both Black and Caucasian subjects in Castner's portraits provides evidence of his skill at interpersonal relations.[57]

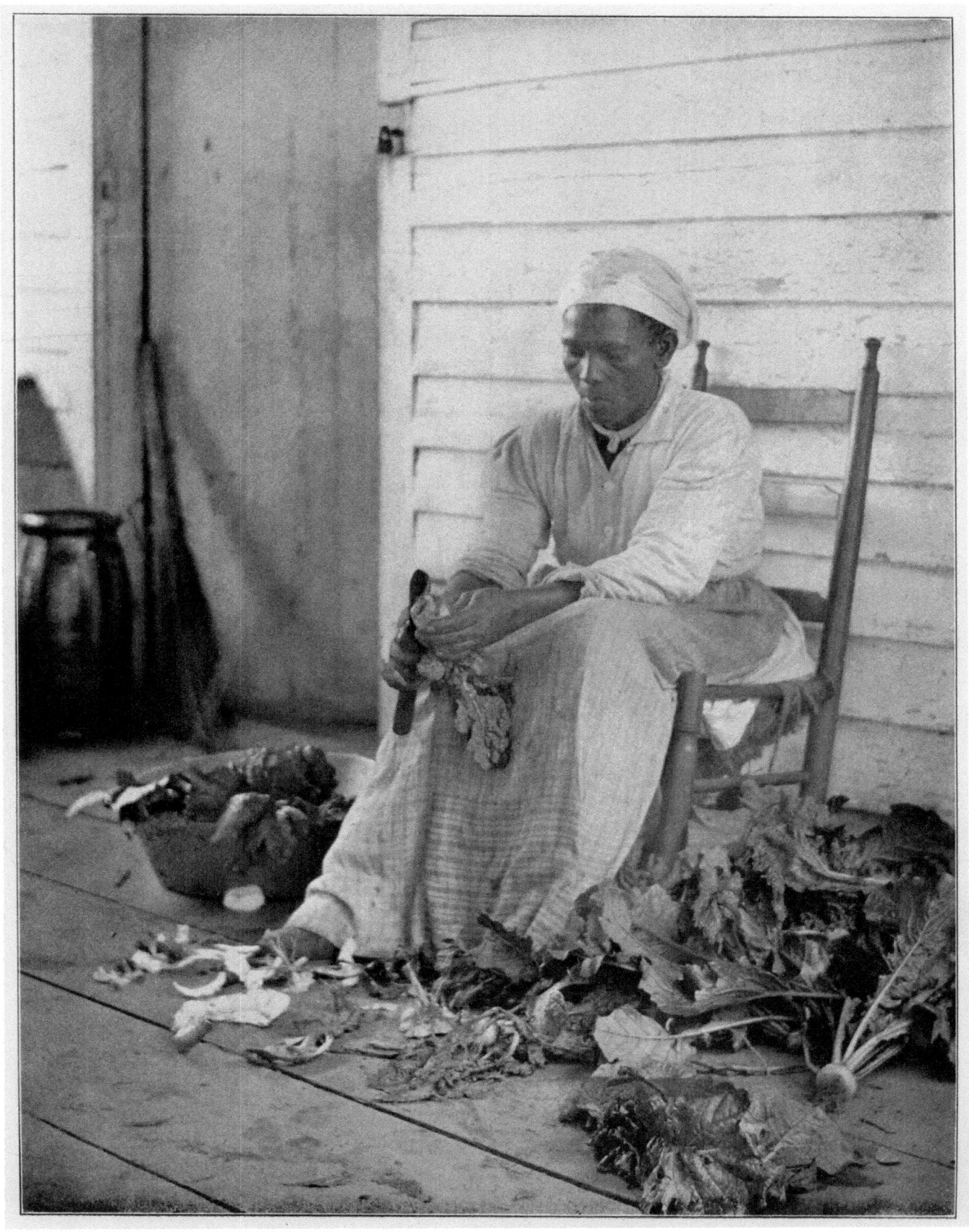

Figure 18. Rudolf Eickemeyer, Jr., "Aunt Chloe Preparing Dinner," from *Down South* (New York: R.H. Russell, 1900), unpaginated. Courtesy of Gary D. Saretzky.

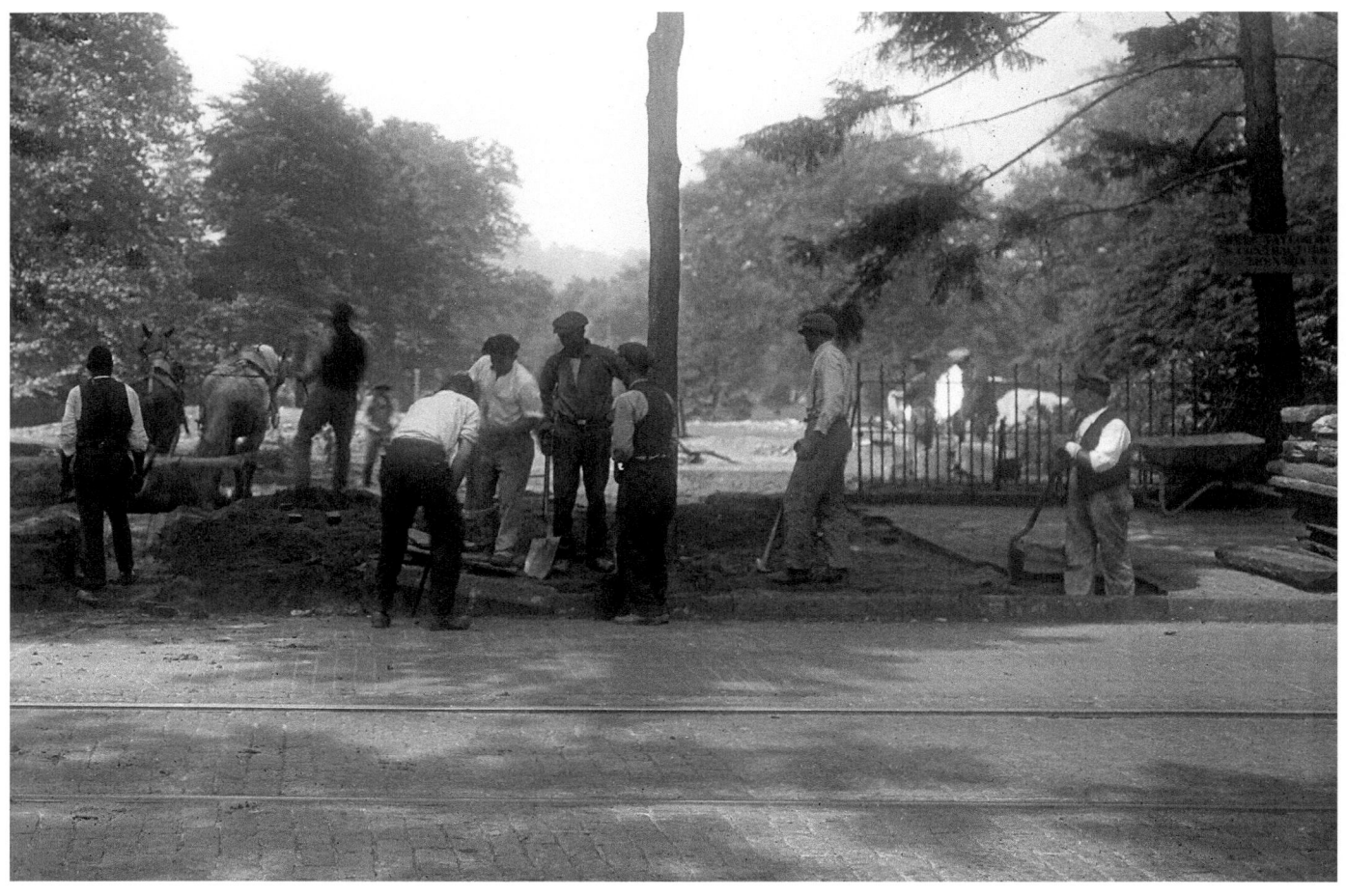

Figure 19. Grant Castner, work crew employed by Rees, Taylor and Company Contractors in brick sidewalk construction, Parkside/ Berkeley Square, Trenton, New Jersey, c. 1915. Digital positive from 6.5" x 8.5" glass plate negative [Detail]. New Jersey State Museum, CH2019.6.617.

With his background in journalism, it is not surprising that Castner also used his lens to document social conditions and events, including the aftermath of natural disasters such as blizzards, floods, and tornados and the Inter-State Fair, the precursor of the New Jersey State Fair.[58] Perhaps surprising is the extent to which he photographed employees at work, or stopping to pose from their labor, such as railroad engineers, locomotive repairmen, fishermen, shoe shiners and construction workers. Portraiture of the working class was an uncommon subject for amateur photographers before the 1890s, and even then it was unusual. Castner would have been unlikely to have seen John Thomson's *Street Life in London*, issued monthly beginning in 1876, or the innovative work in Paris of Eugene Atget, who photographed street professions in the 1890s but whose work was not published in book form until 1930.[59]

Jacob Riis's renowned *How the Other Half Lives* (1890), with woodcut illustrations of poverty-stricken New Yorkers from photographs, also could not have served Castner as a precedent.[60] Riis portrayed immigrants in New York slums to arouse the public to social reform. Castner, by contrast, showed a prospering Trenton working class in a more positive way. He might have taken inspiration from Sigmund Krausz, who published *Street Types of Great American Cities* in 1891, with portraits of people engaged in various occupations and looking at least reasonably satisfied with their lot.[61] Krausz included several photographs of boys and a girl selling newspapers and a shoe shiner. Similarly, Castner posed children who worked for him distributing magazines and at least one whom he encountered shining shoes on the streets of Trenton. Castner's portrait of a barefoot Italian American boy seated on his shoeshine box (**plate 36**) was probably inspired by *Boy with Thorn*, a well-known Greco-Roman bronze sculpture of a lad withdrawing a thorn from the heel of his foot, now in the Palazzo dei Conservatori in Rome. His carefully composed portraits of men in their work clothes looking directly into the camera lens, such as the three Trentonians named Hopkins, Stout, and Swem, each holding their vests in the same way (**plate 20**), anticipates the social documentary photography of photographers such as Milton Rogovin (1909–2011) but without the political agenda that underlay some of these photographers' work.[62]

In addition to urban scenes in Trenton, Castner took his camera to more rural settings, using streetcar, railroad, or bicycle. Except for his summer vacations at the Jersey Shore, he does not seem to have done much overnight travel with his camera, but he did take it with him on day trips.[63] His negatives include views taken at the stone arch bridges over Stony Brook near Princeton, which in those days was connected by streetcar lines from Trenton, as well as many images taken along the Delaware River north of Trenton along the route of

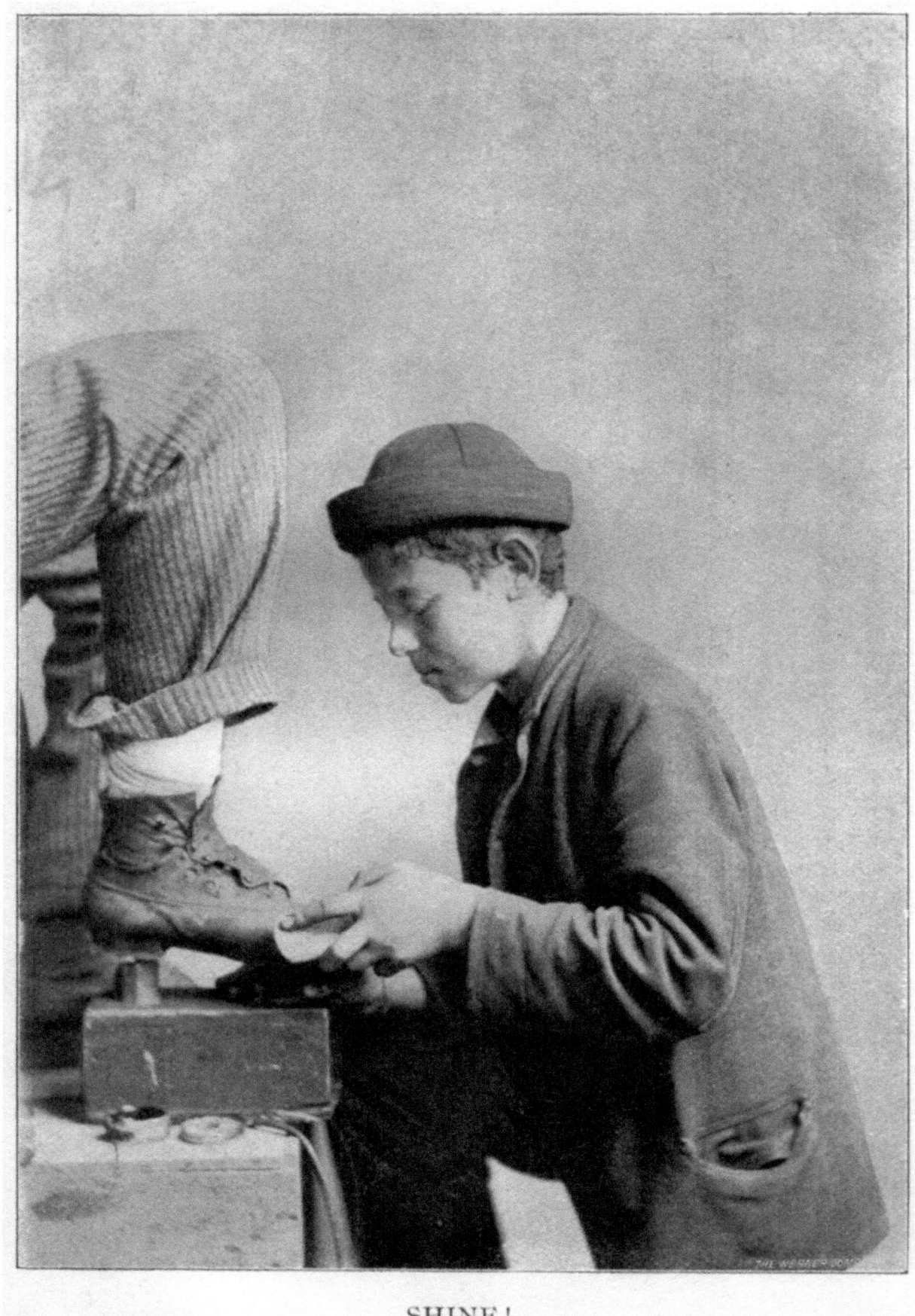

SHINE !

Figure 20. Sigmund Krausz, "Shine!" *Street Types of Great American Cities* (Chicago & New York: The Werner Co., 1891, 1896), page 187. Courtesy of Gary D. Saretzky.

the Bel-Del Railroad to Belvidere, as well as on the Pennsylvania side. With his camera-toting companions in 1904, he took the train to the little station at Tennent, New Jersey, and photographed the historic Old Tennent Church, where the Revolutionary War martyr Joshua Huddy was buried in an unmarked grave. His lovely image of the church in dappled sunlight was one of nine images that he selected to show at the 1907 exhibition of the Trenton Photographic Society[64] (**plate 76**). In the summer, he took his family to the Jersey Shore, also easily accessible by railroad, where he depicted sand dunes, beach bathers, the fishing industry, and harbors filled with sailboats, yachts, and other pleasure and working watercraft.

More locally, Castner probably used his "safety bicycle" to perambulate for camera work. Superseding the velocipede, these now commonplace bikes with two pneumatic tires of equal size became widespread beginning in the late 1880s, and production exploded in 1890s. Far less expensive to maintain than a horse, they afforded freedom of movement that enabled Trenton photographers like Castner to go on excursions, such as up and down the roads and canal towpaths on both sides of the Delaware. Many of Castner's photographs depict scenes along these waterways, some including groups of picnickers with bicycles. One of his photographs depicts Anna Cross with her bicycle in front of a cornfield (**plate 17**), reminding us of how liberating these vehicles were for women and how many became enthusiastic snapshooters, if not serious amateurs.[65] Susan B. Anthony concluded in 1896 that the bicycle "has done more to emancipate women than anything else in the world."[66] But of course bicycles also were beneficial for men's local travel. The Castner collection includes a photo (**plate 34**) of Castner with his bike, strapped with boxes for his glass plate negatives, portraying an intrepid, committed photographer. In the 1920s, Castner owned an automobile and likely started to use it as a replacement for the bicycle on his photographic excursions.[67]

At home, Castner used window light to make carefully composed still life photographs of fruit, including one of a dish on a table holding a bunch of grapes with three quinces (**plate 114**). These still life studies are similar in composition to oil paintings by such artists as Cezanne, for example, his *Still Life with Compotier*, circa 1880, with the difference that Castner captured his subject straight on while Cezanne's is from above and to the side. Castner also made lovely still-life photographs of roses, chrysanthemums, carnations, goldenrod, cosmos, and other flowers (**plate 113**), producing work in a photographic genre pioneered by Adolph Braun (1812–1877) in the 1850s.[68]

Inspired and influenced by the work of both his predecessors and contemporaries, Castner continuously worked hard at improving his skills, evolving into a talented, versatile photographer with a wide range of subjects in his impressive portfolio. From simple, candid portraits of his neighbors to the most artfully composed still life vignettes, Castner's astute vision, meticulous process, and innate eye for composition created images that resonated with his viewers. In addition to the praise that he garnered for his exhibitions and magic lantern shows, Castner also won awards for his work and had his images published in notable periodicals. In 1891, *Frank Leslie's Illustrated Newspaper* published Castner's photograph of the General George B. McClellan monument at Riverview Cemetery in Trenton.[69] Castner had submitted the image to one of the newspaper's many photo contests—contests in which nationally known photographers such as Alfred Stieglitz also competed. In 1898, Castner's image of the marshlands southeast of Trenton was named the "most artistic" entry in that year's exhibition of the Trenton Photographic Society.[70] In 1902, he earned a prize for "amateur photographic views, enlarged" in a contest sponsored by the Inter-State Fair.[71] Eight years later, he won second place for "best collection, 10 pictures, contact or enlargement" in the same competition.[72] His crowning achievement, perhaps, came in 1916. In December of that year, Castner's serene winter scene depicting barren trees along an ice-covered Crosswicks Creek, entitled *Reflections and Shadows*, was published in *Photo Era* magazine[73] (**plate 118**). A leading American magazine for amateur photographers—a publication that had once served as a teaching tool for Castner in the early years of his photographic journey—was now publishing the seasoned artist's work.

Grant Castner's career as a photographer stretched from the late 1880s when he took his first photograph until his death on January 30, 1941, a period of more than fifty years. The decision to move to Trenton was a key component of his transformation from a small town–born son of a bookstore owner into a talented artist with an eye for composition who mastered a relatively new artistic medium. At the turn of the twentieth century, New Jersey's capital city was known principally as a seat of government and a manufacturing powerhouse. However, its close proximity to Philadelphia and New York placed Trenton well within the sphere of influence of those art centers. During Castner's lifetime, Trenton opened theaters, music halls, libraries, museums, and even an art school of its own. It also sustained a growing artistic-minded community that initiated several art clubs. Castner both benefitted from, and contributed to, Trenton's emerging status as an upstart arts hub. His long and productive career was primarily as a passionate amateur, but he did take on some commercial projects, and even promoted himself as a photographer in Trenton's city directories over a twelve-year period from 1912 until 1924. Later in life, Castner experimented with other types of cameras, films, and photographic technologies but remained loyal to glass plates long after most other photographers gave them up, probably because of the clarity and detail that they provided and his comfort, familiarity, and mastery of the medium. Nevertheless, in the 1920s he probably switched to the more convenient, but less stable, film negatives, only a small handful of which have survived.

There is no way to know for certain how many glass plate images Castner took over his lifetime, but it surely numbered in the thousands. From ethereal portraits of his family members in the pleasant sunshine of a backyard, to churning, smoke-filled urban scenes of railway yards and city streets, to candid photographs of the faces of people from all walks of life in their places of work, Castner's impressive body of images, at the time, represented a journalistic exploration of the rapidly changing world in which he lived. Today, looking back, they represent a rare and multifaceted window through which we can explore numerous stories of Garden State history and embark on a visual journey into our collective past as New Jerseyans.

1

Family

Grant Castner was born in Belvidere, New Jersey, in 1863. The county seat of Warren County was a small, bustling Delaware River town. It was also a key northern stop on the Belvidere-Delaware (Bel-Del) Railroad from Trenton. His father, John Calvin Knox Castner, owned a bookstore. His mother, Ellen Lowry Castner, was a homemaker. His two older sisters, Mary and Annie, worked as clerks in the family store. A younger sister, Ida, was nearer to Grant in age. The two developed a close relationship that would last a lifetime.

In the early 1880s, Grant Castner left Belvidere and moved to Trenton in search of work. He took up residence as a boarder in the home of his sister Annie and her husband. Soon afterward, Ida joined him in the capital city. Over the next forty years, Grant Castner began a career as magazine distributor, got married, bought a modest row home on Tyler Street, and started a family of his own. Through it all he pursued his lifelong passion for photography. Some of his finest images are heartfelt portraits of his nearest, dearest relatives.

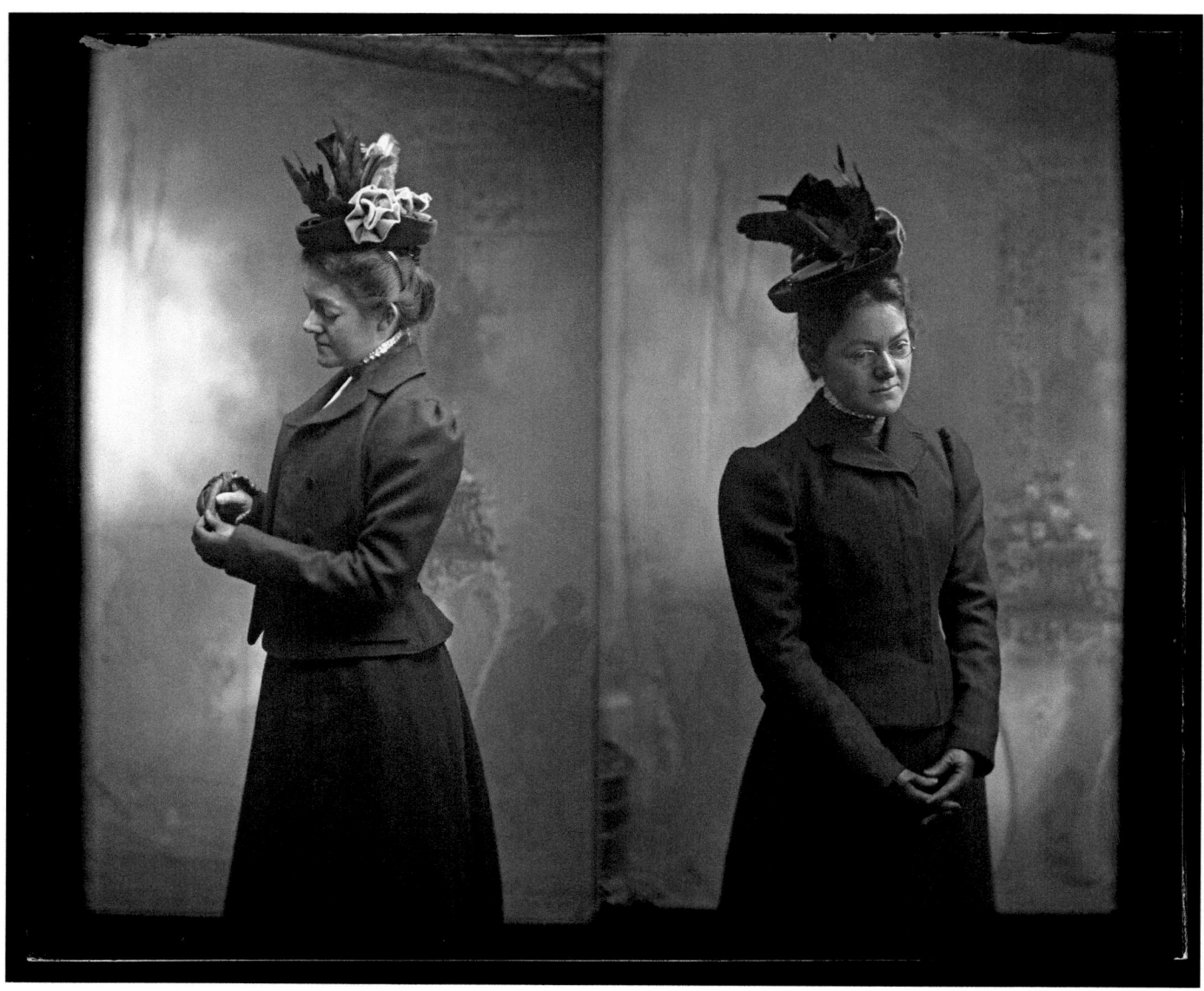

Plate 1. Ida B. Castner, younger sister of Grant Castner, Trenton, New Jersey, c. 1910. Digital positive from 4" x 5" glass plate negative. CH2019.6.180

Ida Castner was a frequent muse for her brother's photography. In **plate 1** Grant Castner produced two exposures on a single plate to capture his sister in two poses side-by-side. She is depicted wearing a hat made of bird feathers. Feather fashion was in vogue at the turn of the twentieth century. The widespread harvesting of wild birds for women's hats gave rise to bird conservation societies named after the famed artist/ naturalist John James Audubon. Their efforts led to the Migratory Bird Treaty Act of 1918 that protected numerous species from so-called "plume hunters."

Grant Castner and his sister Ida were very close. During her lifetime, Ida held a number of jobs, including domestic worker, cook, and salesperson. Her portrait in **plate 2**

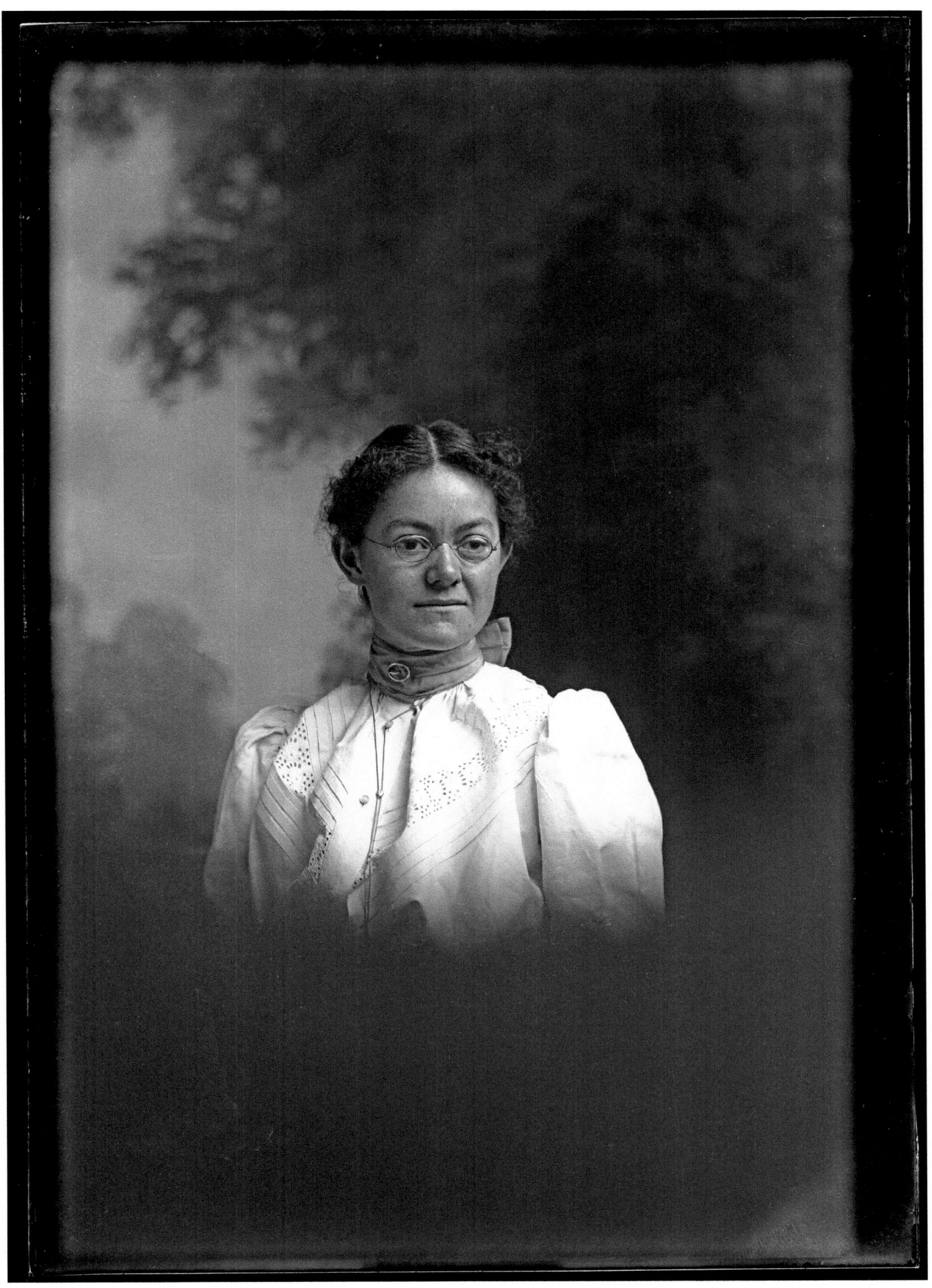

Plate 2. Ida B. Castner, younger sister of Grant Castner, Trenton, New Jersey, c. 1910. Digital positive from 5" x 7" glass plate negative. CH2019.6.452.

captures the demeanor of a strong, independent woman and conveys the obvious respect that the artist had for his sister. Castner enhanced this portrait by placing a painted backdrop behind Ida. Available for purchase from photographic suppliers, these backdrops were often used by professional photographers, but it was uncommon for amateurs to have them, and Castner began photography as an amateur. By the 1910s, he began to take on commercial work and advertise his photographic services. This transition may have led to a need for more professional accessories.

Grant Castner married Sarah Frances Karr in 1903. Known as "Fannie," Sarah Frances was a friend of Grant's sister, Ida. The couple had two children—a boy, Theodore Grant, born in 1904, and a girl, Eleanor, born in 1907. Theodore may have been named after his father's brother Theodore, who had died young. As might be expected, Castner's glass plate collection contains many images of his firstborn child, identified as "Grantie" on the negative sleeves. Mother, father, and three-year-old son are seen in **plate 3** in the backyard of the family home on Tyler Street in Trenton.

Grant Castner and family members pose for a group portrait in a backyard in **plate 4**. The photo was made in 1906 or 1907 before the birth of his second child. The three women are wearing hats typical for the time. Castner is wearing his favorite cap that also appears in other photos of him. Castner's wife Fannie is the only one smiling. Around this time, candid photos often showed people smiling, but they usually looked serious when having a formal portrait made.

Then, as now, Christmas morning was a time for photographs. Grant Castner set up his camera on December 25, 1905, to forever preserve memories of his son Grantie's first Christmas tree. The large number of toys suggests a certain degree of family affluence. From the photographer's notes that accompany the plate in **plate 5**, we know that Castner used

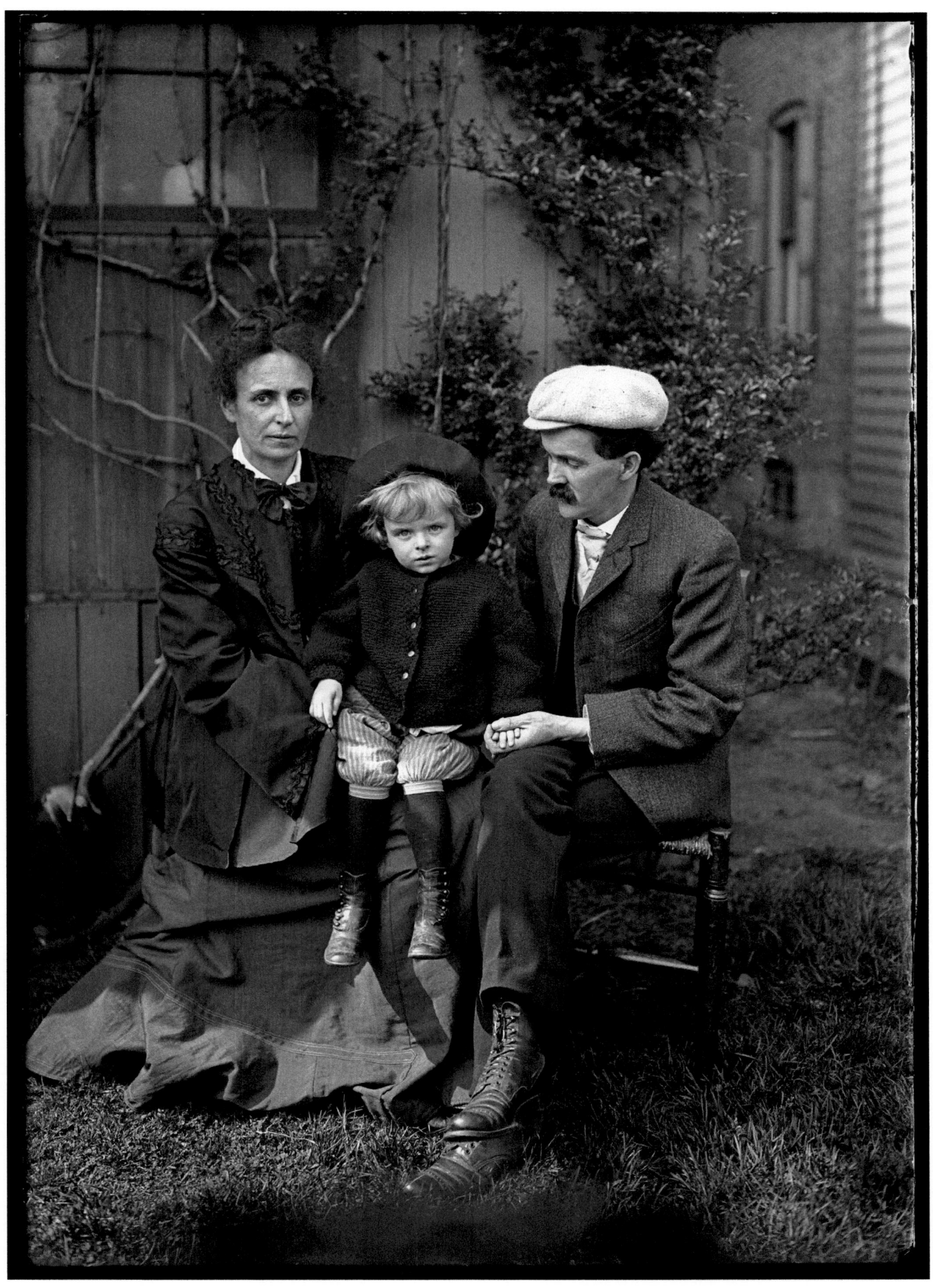

Plate 3. Grant Castner with wife Sarah Frances Castner and son Theodore Grant Castner, Trenton, New Jersey, 1907. Digital positive from 5" x 7" glass plate negative. CH2019.6.877

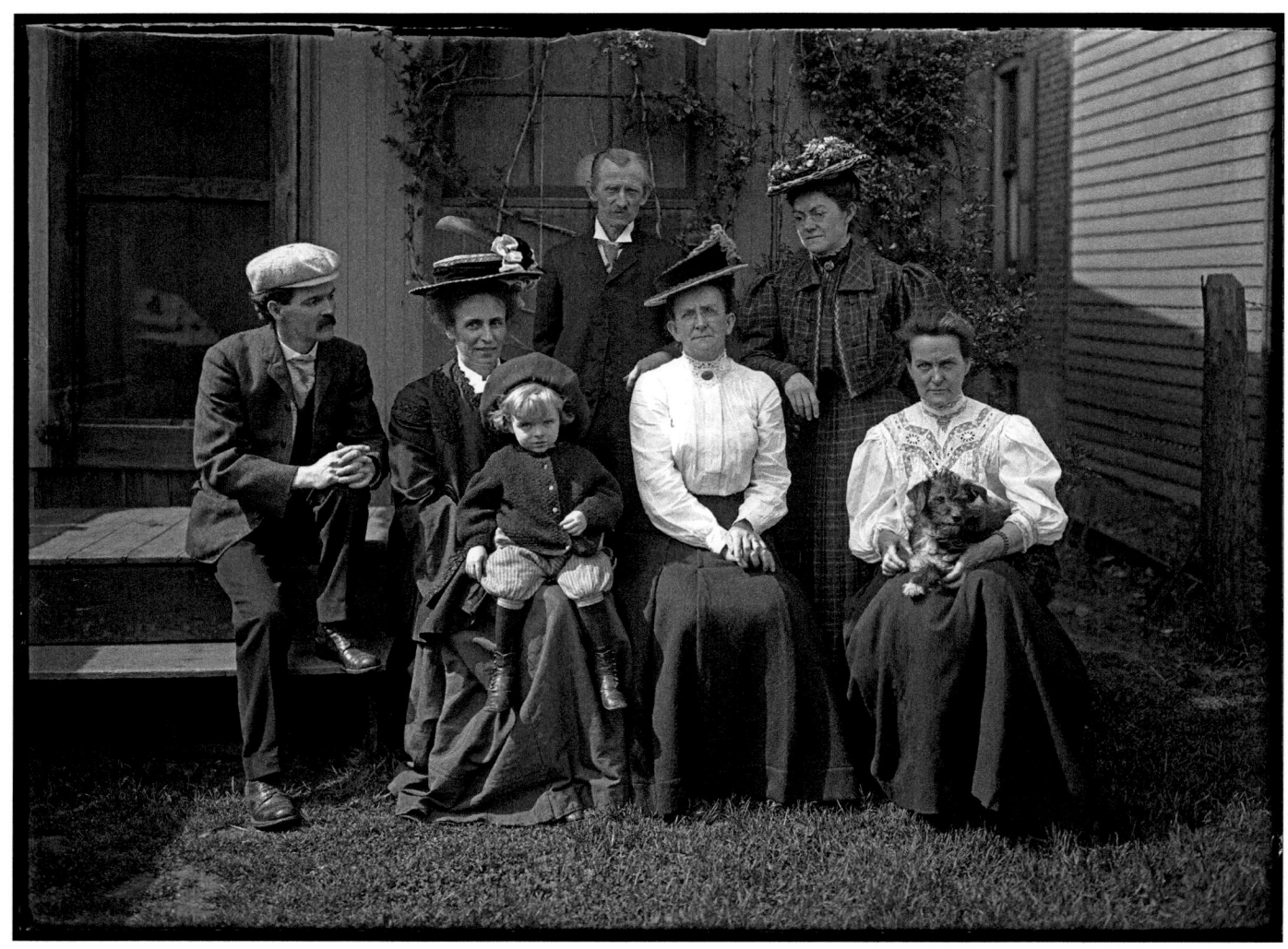

Plate 4. Castner family, Trenton, New Jersey, c. 1907 [From left to right] Grant Castner; wife, Sarah Frances "Fannie" Castner; son, Theodore Grant Castner; Frederick Kampen and his wife Annie Kampen (sister of Grant Castner); Ida B. Castner (sister of Grant Castner); and unidentified woman holding dog (possibly Mary Castner, sister of Grant Castner). Digital positive from 5" x 7" glass plate negative. CH2019.6.885

an Eastman Flash Sheet to take this indoor photograph. Patented in 1897, the Eastman Flash Sheet was a flammable piece of paper that was mounted on a white piece of cardboard twice its size and fixed in a vertical position. Standing at arm's length, the photographer lighted one corner of the sheet with a thin stick at least two feet long. The sheet burst into flame, creating a flash that provided enough light for a photograph in low light or even at night.

In **plate 6**, Grant Castner may have seen the whimsy in this juxtaposition of his diminutive, two-year-old son, with the mammoth leaves of the elephant ear plants that he grew in his backyard on Tyler Street. The child acknowledges the presence of his father by pointing curiously toward the

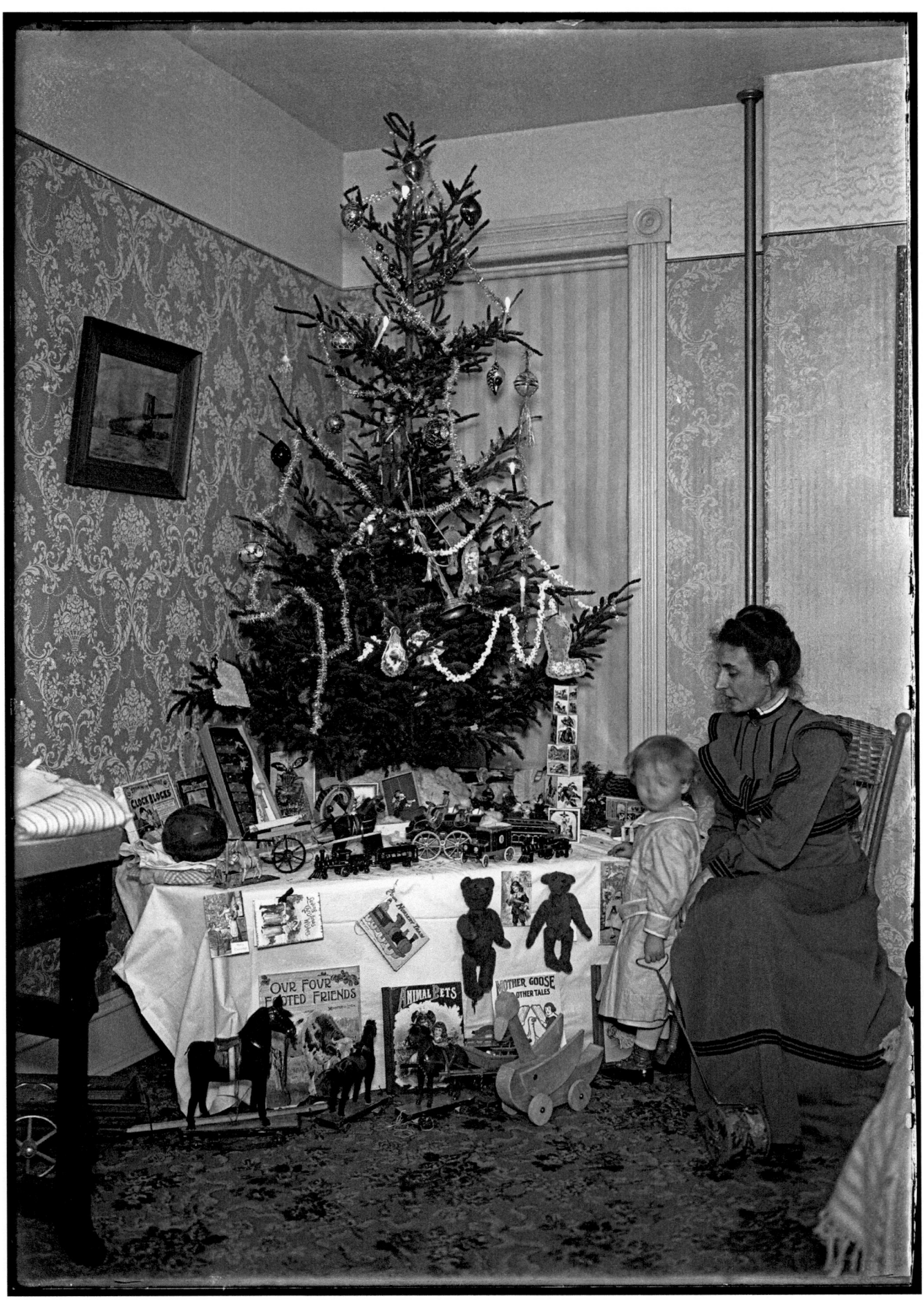

Plate 5. Grant Castner's wife and child, Sarah Frances Castner and Theodore Grant Castner, on Christmas Morning, Trenton, New Jersey, 1905. Digital positive from 5" x 7" glass plate negative. CH2019.6.903

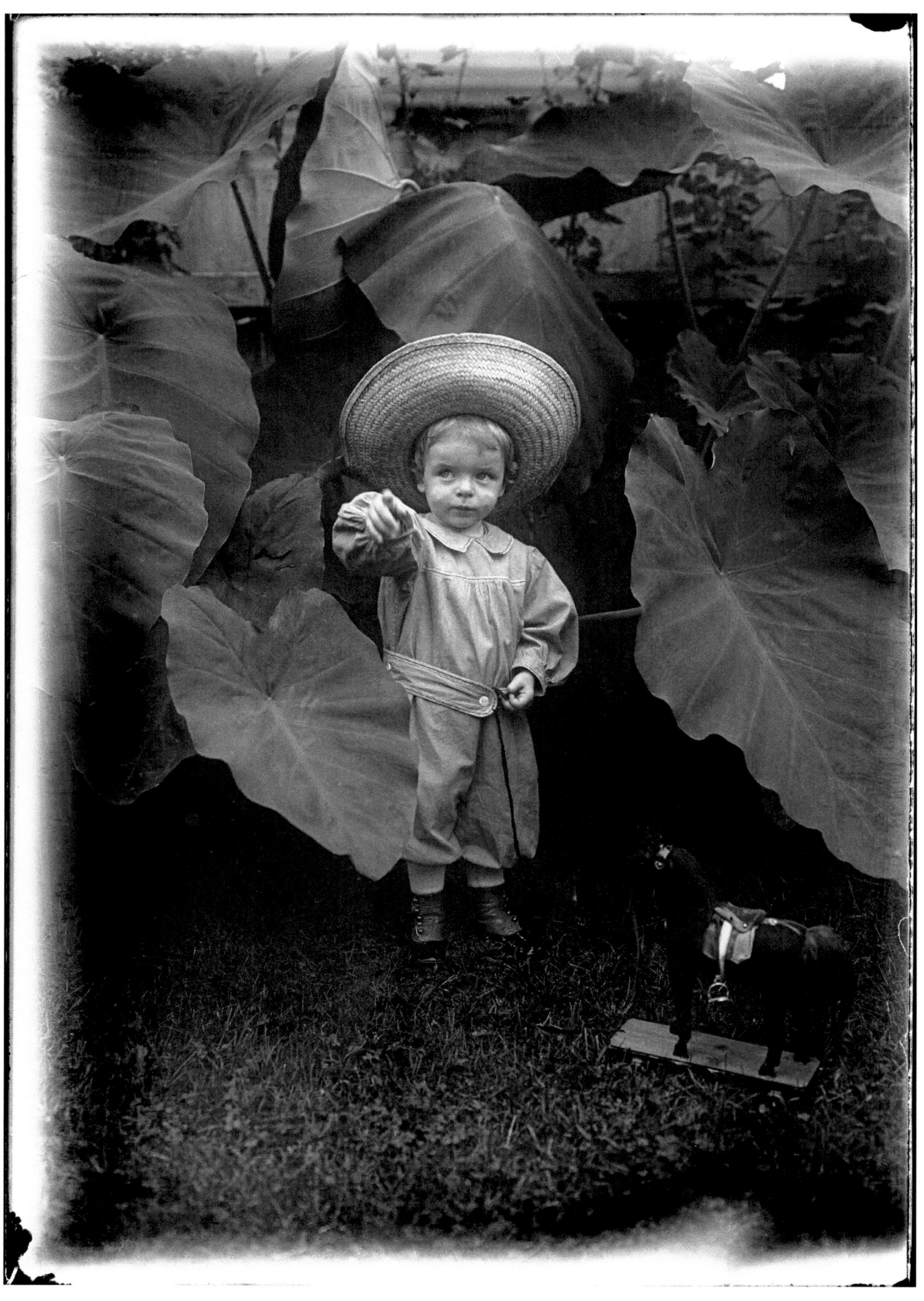

Plate 6. Theodore "Grantie" Castner, son of Grant Castner, Trenton, New Jersey, 1906. Digital positive from 5" x 7" glass plate negative. CH2019.6.701

camera. His oversize straw-hat, halo-like, is reminiscent of the rings of reverence used around the heads of deities and saints throughout art history, perhaps suggesting a father's adoration for his firstborn. The horse pull toy, a favorite Christmas gift from the year before, underscores the simple pleasures of youth. It can be seen in a photograph that Castner took of the family Christmas tree on December 25, 1905. Castner often used contrast as a key element in his compositions, and in this image he contrasted large and small. In other photos, he contrasted such elements as motion and stasis. Castner greatly enjoyed this photograph, so much so that he copied a cropped print to make a lantern slide and shared it with the Trenton Photographic Society in magic lantern slideshows promoting his recent work.

In 1912, Castner set up a fabric backdrop on a wall in his home to take portraits of his two growing children. In **plate** 7, eight-year-old Theodore Grant is depicted with a small, handheld American flag. At the time, these were often referred to as "parade flags" because of their popular use by spectators attending parades and other patriotic events. Castner is known to have taken many pictures on holidays, and this image may have been made in celebration of the Fourth of July. In 1912, the United States admitted the territories of New Mexico and Arizona as the forty-seventh and forty-eighth states. On July 4 of that year, the country officially transitioned from its previous forty-six-star flag to a new forty-eight-star flag with added stars symbolizing the new states.

Born on May 28, 1907, Grant Castner's daughter Eleanor is seen in **plate 8** lovingly clutching a doll that closely resembles those made later by the Fulper Pottery Company of Flemington, New Jersey. Made of unglazed ceramic known as bisque, Fulper doll heads are known for their open mouths and prominent, molded teeth. Fulper based the design of its

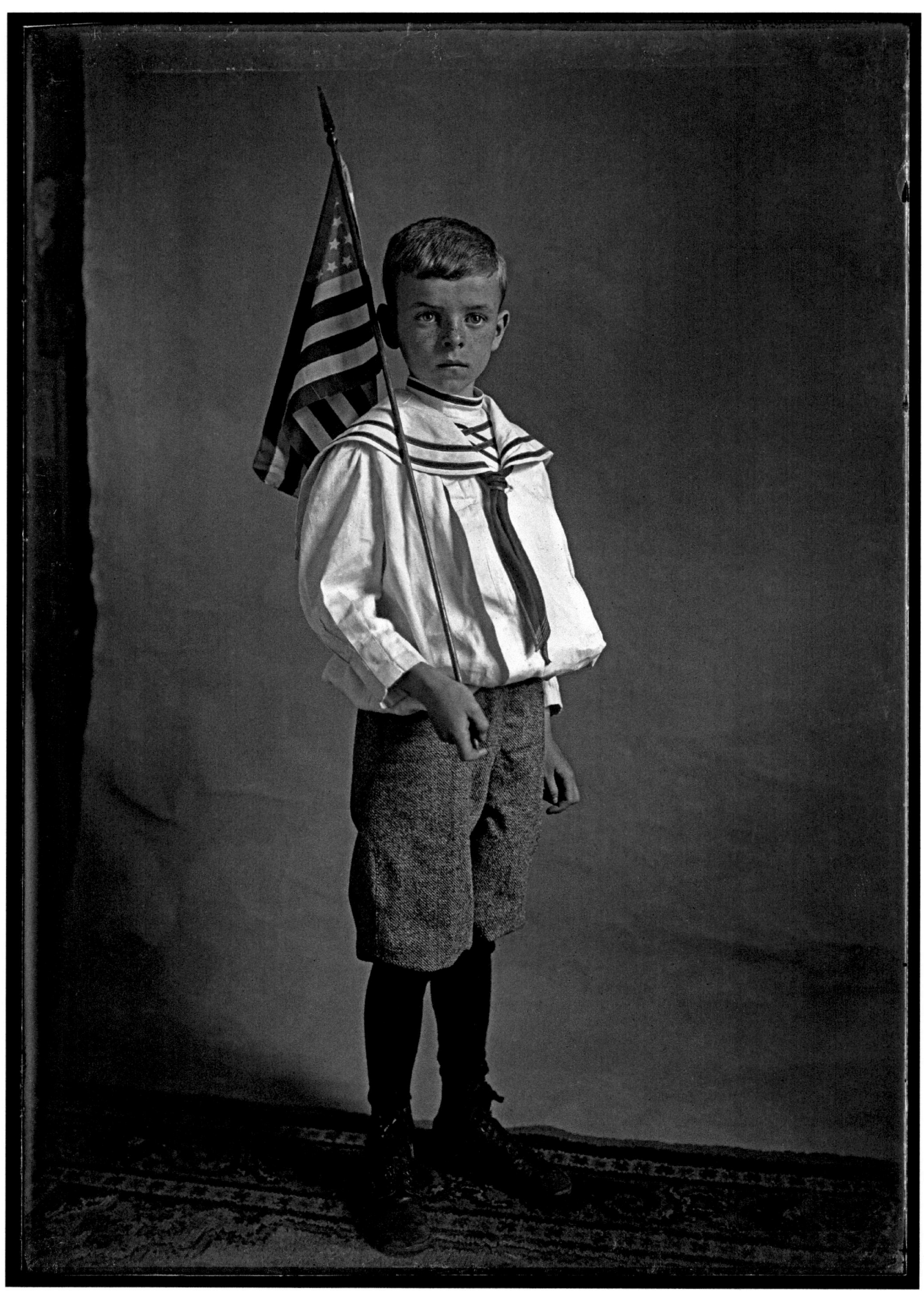

Plate 7. Theodore Grant Castner, son of Grant Castner, Trenton, New Jersey, 1912. Digital positive from 5" x 7" glass plate negative. CH2019.6.910

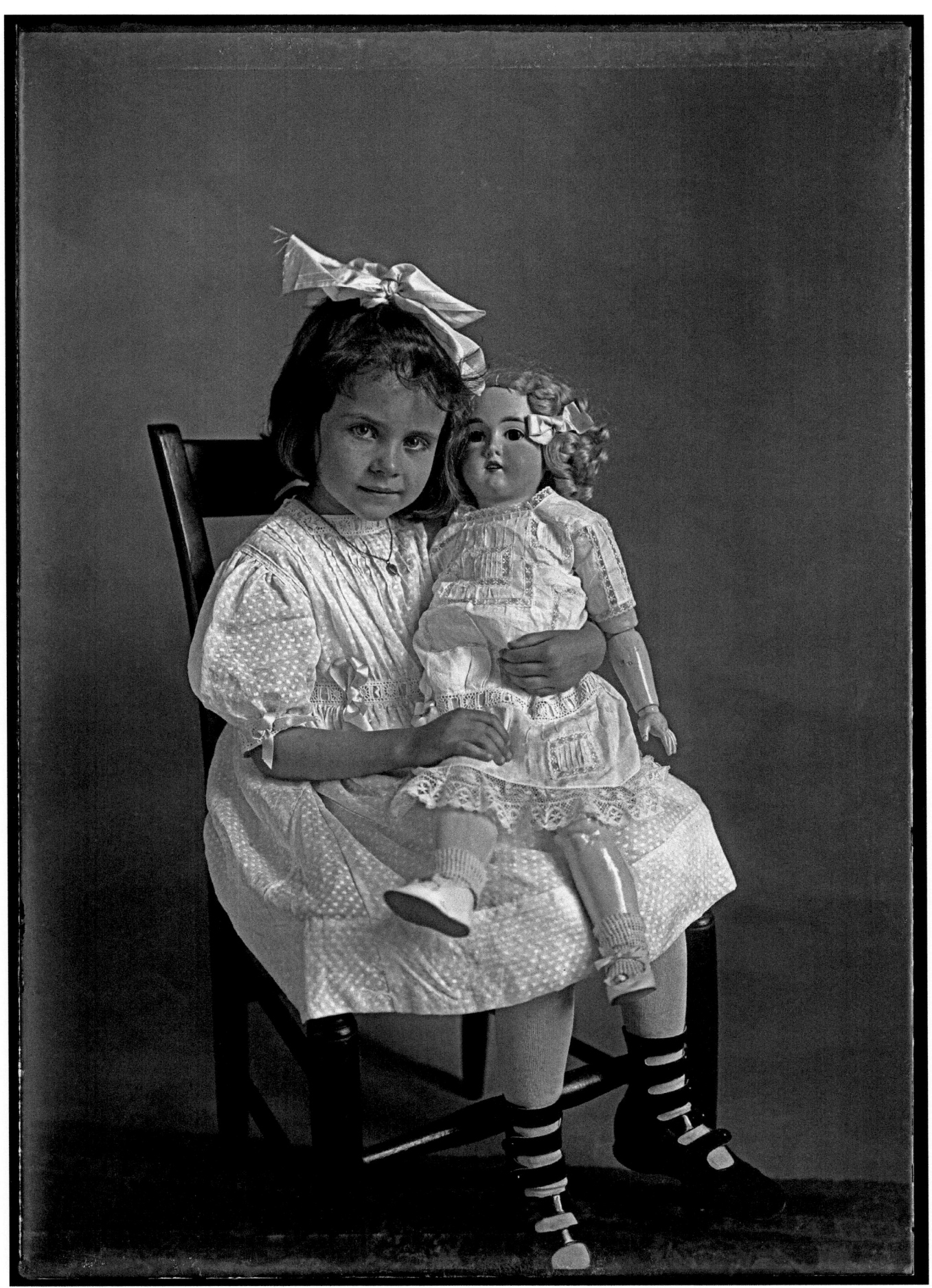

Plate 8. Eleanor Castner, daughter of Grant Castner, Trenton, New Jersey, 1912. Digital positive from 5" x 7" glass plate negative. CH2019.6.912.

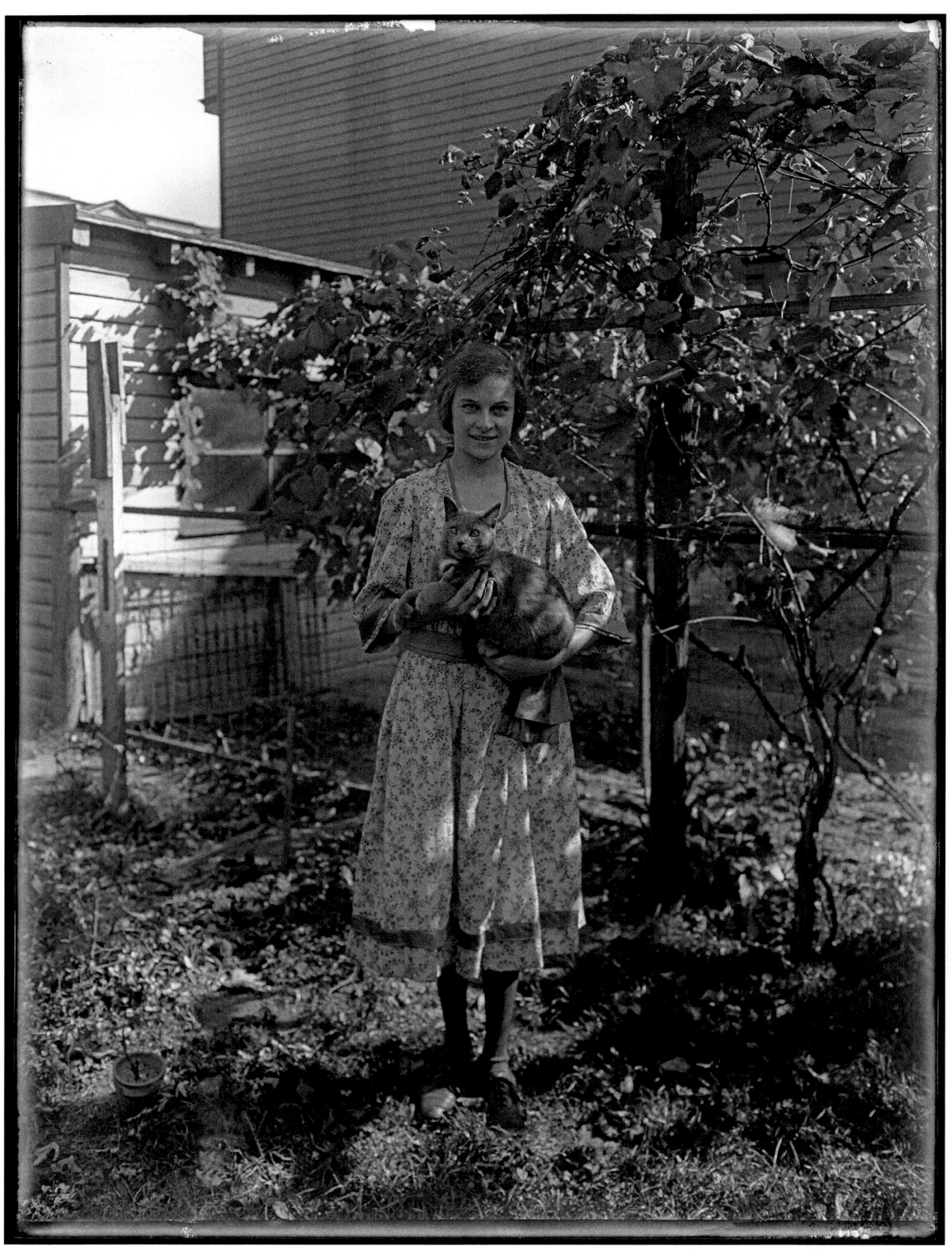

Plate 9. Eleanor Castner, daughter of Grant Castner, Trenton, New Jersey, 1920. Digital positive from 6.5" x 8.5" glass plate negative. CH2019.6.927.

doll heads on molds from German makers and other American doll makers such as Horsman and Amberg. Since Fulper is believed to have manufactured doll heads only between 1918 and 1921, Eleanor's doll was most likely was made by one of the companies that Fulper later copied.

Taken in the backyard of the family home, **plate 9** captures a delicate moment shared between Grant Castner's teenaged daughter Eleanor and the beloved family pet. Pleasant shadows and dappled sunlight through climbing vines give the image an overall feel of peace and happiness. The extreme detail that glass plate negatives could capture in contact prints is evident in the lush, warm fur of the cat; its texture can almost be felt by the viewer. This notable characteristic of glass plate photography prolonged its use by many serious photographers even after the introduction of more convenient, smaller-format roll film from which the negatives could be enlarged with a moderate loss in clarity.

To Lyman Menagh (**plate 10**), the photographer who visited his home was no stranger. It was Cousin Grant. In 1900, thirty-two-year-old Lyman resided on Summer Avenue in Newark with his parents, Joseph and Mary. Mary Menagh, Grant Castner's first cousin, and her family were frequent subjects for Castner's camera. The floral fabric of a Japanese export–style folding bamboo screen provides an attractive visual backdrop for the pleasant portrait of Lyman, who is well dressed for the camera. Known to have visited the family in Newark, Castner probably took the picture inside the Menagh home. Portraits of people with disabilities in wheelchairs from this era are quite rare.

Castner's oldest sister, Mary, moved from New Jersey to Philadelphia in the late nineteenth century. In 1898, she married fireman John G. Richards, and the couple took up residence in a modest row home on North 21st Street. Castner may have taken the photograph in **plate 11** of his

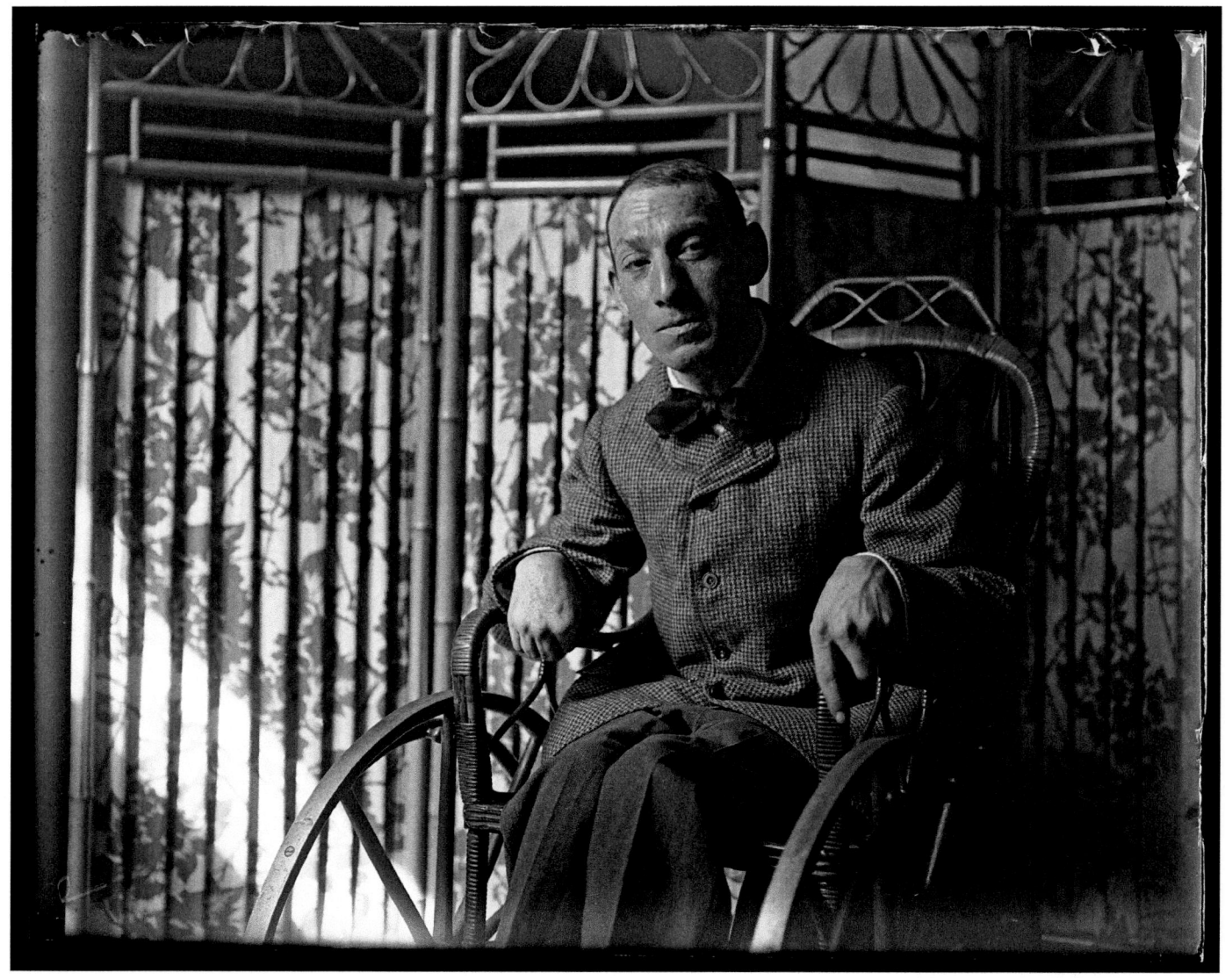

Plate 10. Lyman Menagh, Newark, New Jersey, c. 1901. Digital positive from 4" x 5" glass plate negative. CH2019.6.52.

new brother-in-law somewhere in Trenton, possibly in the backyard of his home on Tyler Street. It is also possible that he took the photograph at the Richards' home during one of his visits to Philadelphia. His smiling subject is well dressed in a jacket, vest, and tie, and the background is a verdant, midsummer backdrop of vines and potted plants. It is not known why Castner chose to photograph Richards alone and not seated next to his new bride.

Castner's glass plate archive contains many examples of self-portraits. He took the photographs either by using a camera timing device or having someone else trip the shutter

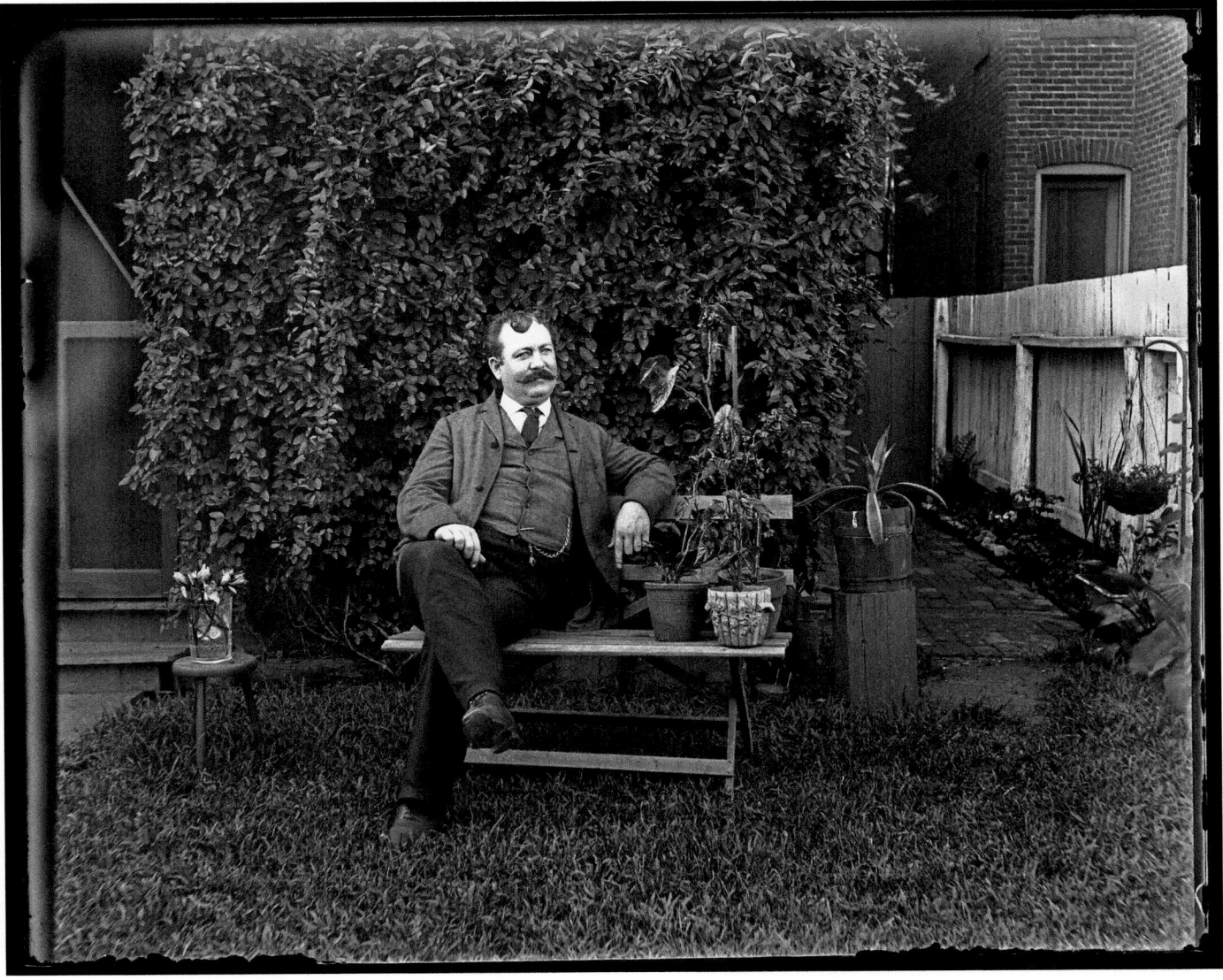

while he posed. A sunny window proved to be the perfect setting for the portrait in **plate 12**, with the natural light dreamily illuminating the scene. Castner is reading a magazine entitled *The Practical Photographer*. This illustrated, monthly publication consisted of detailed articles on the technical aspects of the photographic medium. It was one of the many periodicals available to photographers around the turn of the twentieth century. Choosing to photograph himself with this particular magazine in hand underscores Castner's passion for photography and the centrality of the art form to his identity.

Plate 11. John Richards, Trenton, New Jersey, 1898. Digital positive from 4" x 5" glass plate negative. CH2019.6.175.

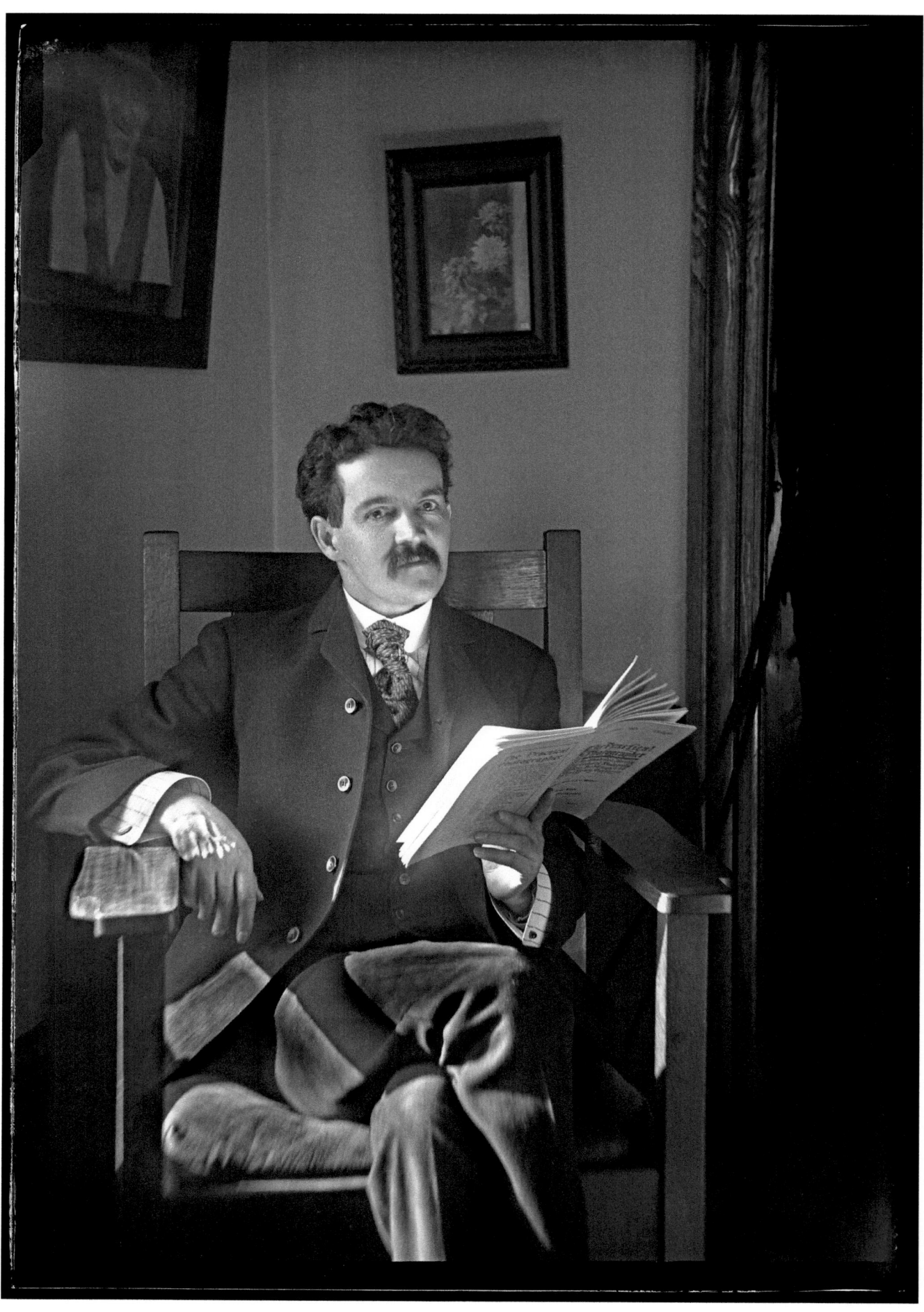

Plate 12. Grant Castner self-portrait, Trenton, New Jersey, 1906. Digital positive from 5" x 7" glass plate negative. CH2019.6.898.

2

Neighbors

While reserved and introspective by nature, Grant Castner also had a clear affection for people. His active involvement in the city's civic, political, and religious life put him in close personal contact with many of his fellow Trentonians. One of his gifts as an artist was the ability to capture the personalities of his friends and neighbors. Some of his subjects were people he knew well. Their familiarity is evident in the comfortable, candid expressions. Other subjects were people he encountered in his travels around the state.

Before Castner's time, having a portrait taken was a very special event. Early photographs usually depict middle-class people wearing their "Sunday best" in a portrait studio. Castner took most of his photographs not in a studio, but out in his community. As a result, his recently discovered images are now a lasting historical record of the faces and attire of everyday New Jerseyans.

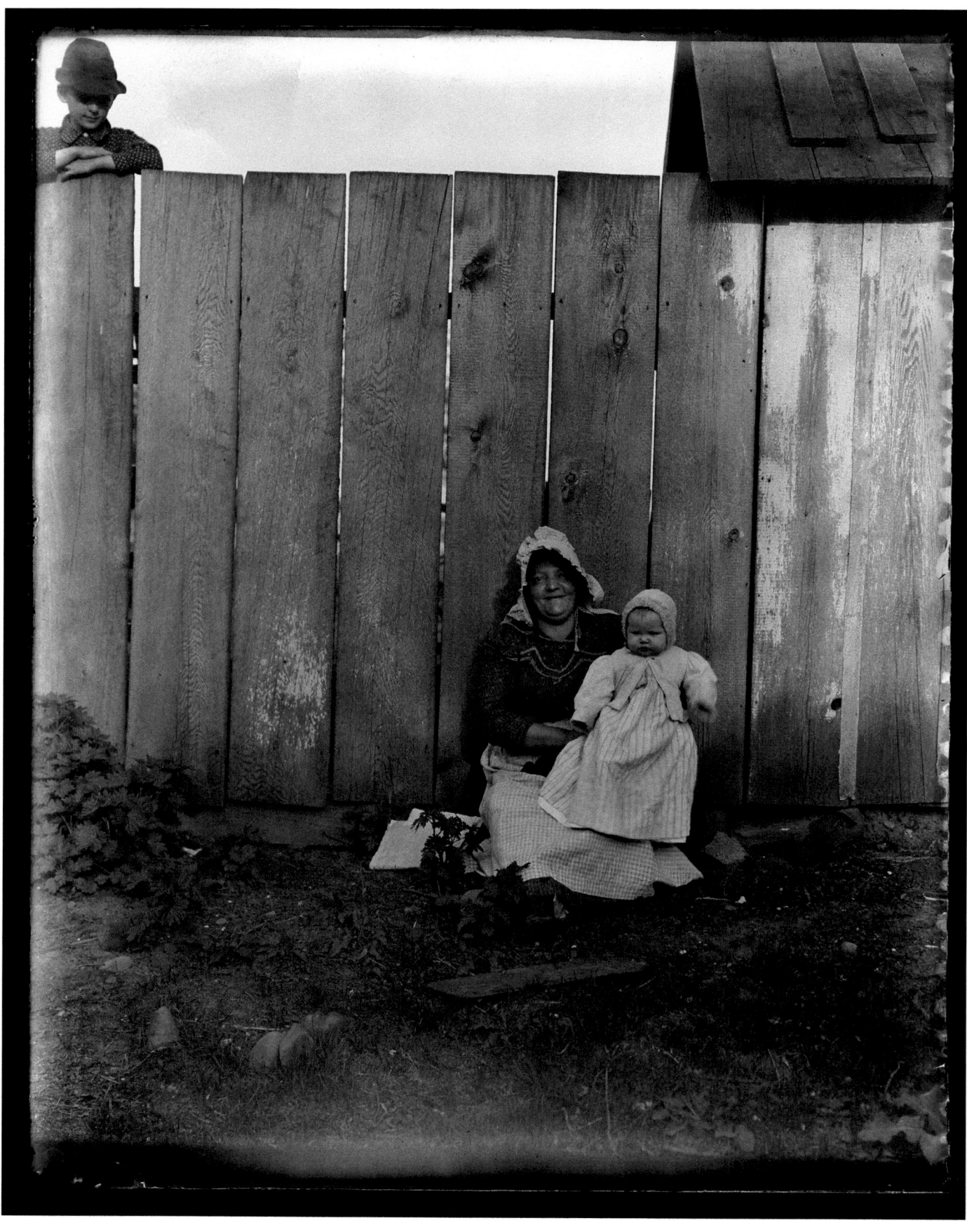

Plate 13. *Mother and Babe*. Mrs. William Holloway with child, White Horse, Hamilton Township, New Jersey, 1901. Digital positive from 4" x 5" glass plate negative. CH2019.6.75.

Castner's sense of humor is apparent in this whimsical view (**plate 13**) of a young, possibly uninvited guest observing a jovial mother and her newborn infant. The boy's attention is on the woman, not the camera, suggesting that Castner snapped the picture when the curious youngster first popped over the fence to observe the ruckus in his neighbor's backyard. Perhaps referencing the Christian imagery of the Madonna and child, Castner titled this image *Mother and Babe*. Although wearing a dress, the baby could either be female or male. In Castner's day, children of both sexes commonly wore long white dresses until they began to walk. As toddlers, their gender can often be identified in portraits by how the hair is parted: on the side for boys and in the middle for girls.

Found on some of the sleeves of his negatives, Castner's handwritten notes are always brief. For the negative in **plate 14**, he only provides a surname, Dillon; a place, Jacobs Creek; and a year, 1899. The U.S. Census for 1900 reveals added details about these individuals. In 1900, forty-two-year-old Thomas Dillon, a peddler originally from Pennsylvania, resided in a rented home in Ewing Township with his New Jersey–born wife, Susan, and four daughters, Rachel, Eva, Julia and Susie. Thomas's warm, welcoming expression suggests familiarity and comfort—possibly even friendship—with the photographer. Needle and thread in hand, Susan does not let the visiting photographer distract her from her work: the making or mending of a family quilt. One of the oldest forms of artistic expression among African American women, quilt making often involved the creative reuse of existing materials such as discarded woolen suits, for the quilt tops, and burlap grain bags, for the quilt filling, or batting.

Castner's portrait of nine-year-old Susie Dillon in **plate 15** is an evocative tour de force that conveys the pure, unadulterated joy of youth. The youngest daughter and namesake of Susan Dillon smiles exuberantly. Castner captured a moment of genuine laughter and happiness, not a forced expression for

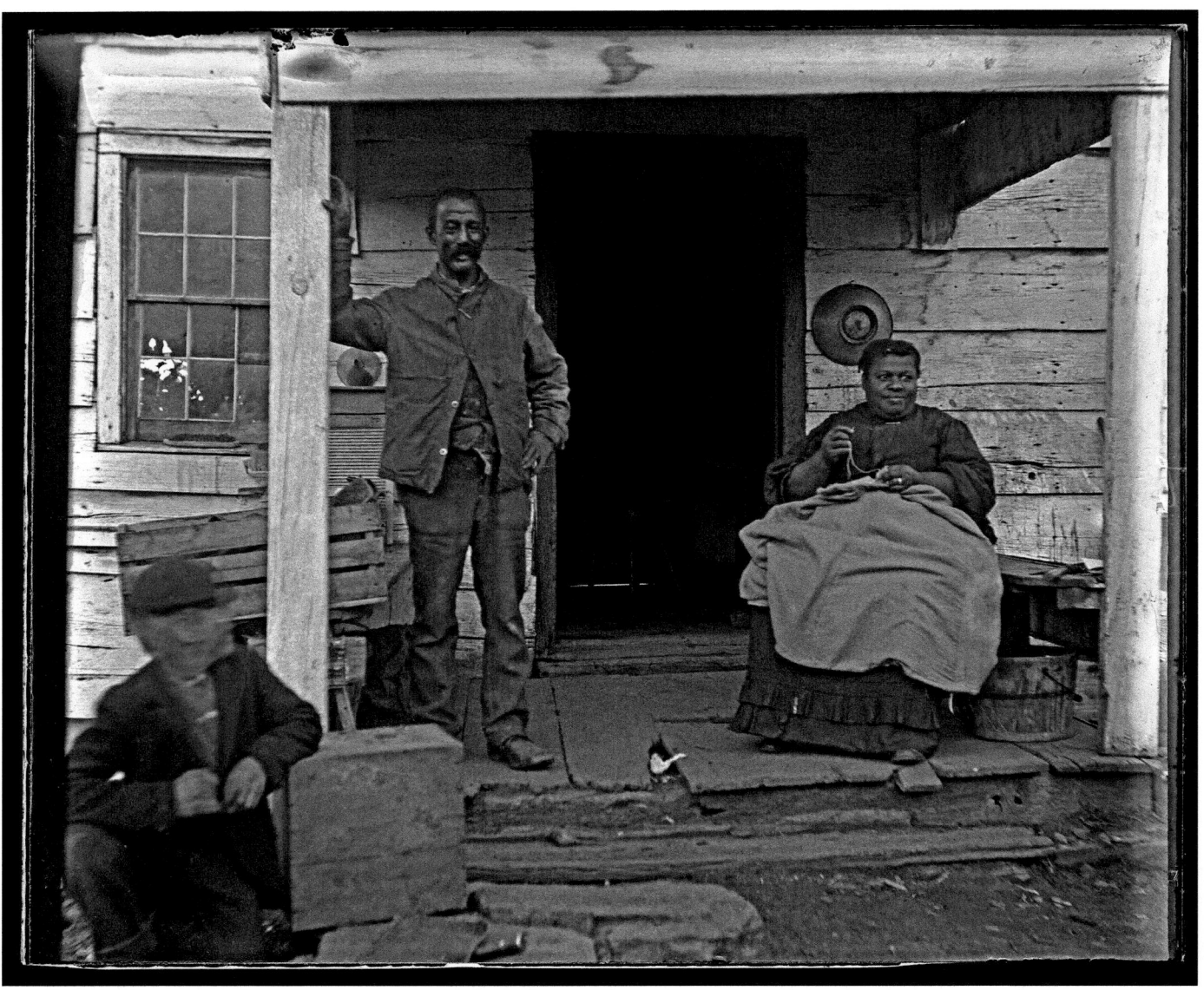

Plate 14. *The Dillons*. Thomas and Susan Dillon, near Jacobs Creek, Ewing Township, New Jersey, 1899. Digital positive from 4" x 5" glass plate negative. CH2019.6.132.

the benefit of the cameraman. The front porch setting suggests a modest, even hardscrabble, life in Ewing Township at the waning years of the nineteenth century. Susie sits next to a washboard and bucket that she likely used to wash clothes under her mother's direction. Nearby is a crate labeled Armour & Co. Founded in Chicago in 1863, it was one of the leading meat packing companies in the United States.

The reverential aura of **plate 16** suggests that Castner knew that he was not photographing an ordinary New Jerseyan but an extraordinary one. His title for the image is *Dinah*, a term that was commonly used as a generic reference for an African American woman. The subject is likely Dian

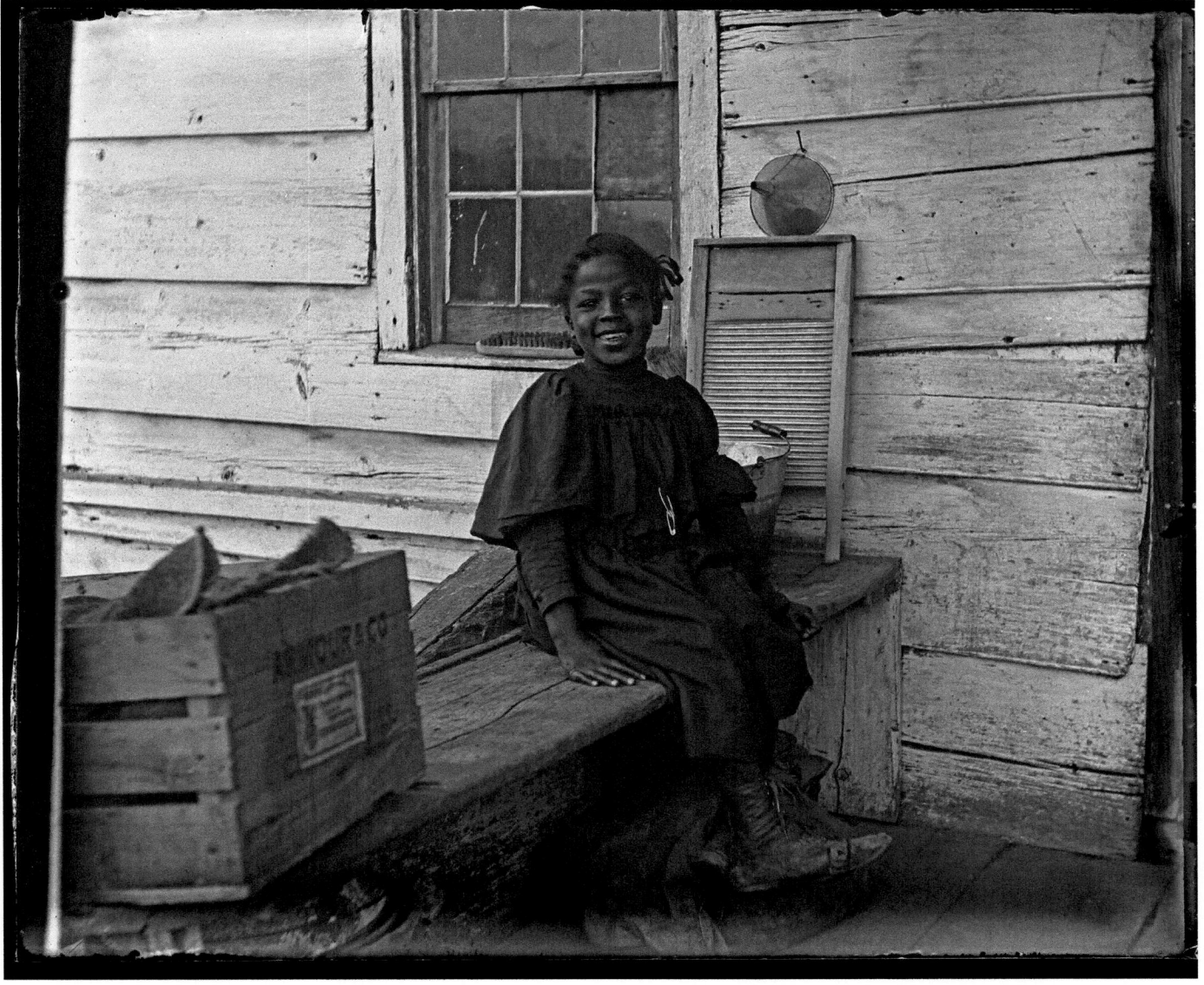

Hartman (1822–1914), a long-standing resident of Milford, New Jersey, who worked as a live-in nanny/domestic worker with numerous local families. Photographed by Castner when she was in her seventies, Hartman died in Milford at the age of 91. An extended obituary in the *Milford Leader* recounts that she spent her early childhood residing with the family of George Carpenter, a white man, in Carpentersville (Warren County). She traveled with the family by raft down the Delaware River to Milford when they relocated there in 1830. Her large and prominent gravestone in Milford Union Cemetery suggests that she commanded a great degree of respect and admiration as a community elder. In his photographs of African

Plate 15. *Susie*. Susie Dillon, near Jacobs Creek, Ewing Township, New Jersey, 1899. Digital positive from 4" x 5" glass plate negative. CH2019.6.131.

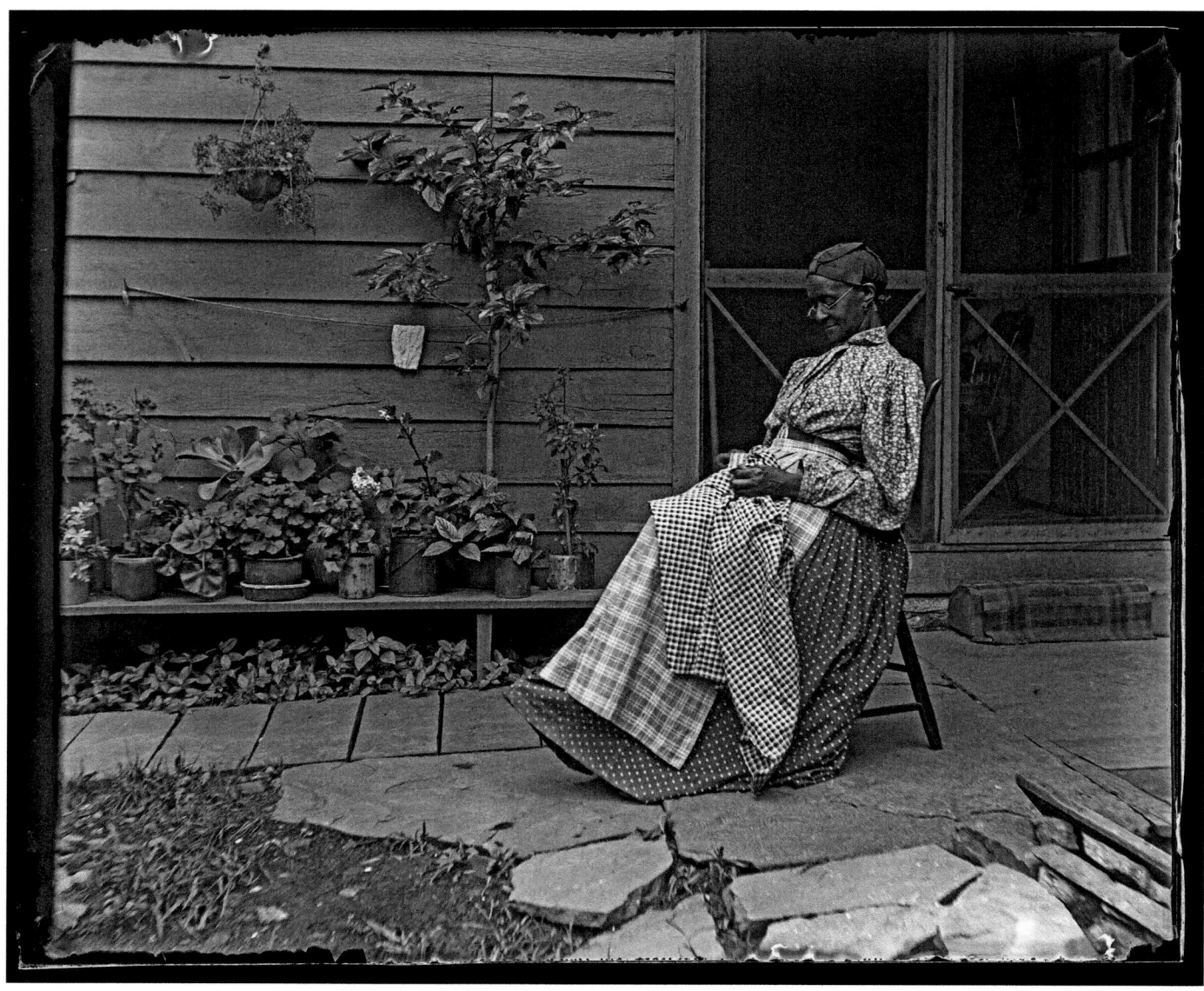

Plate 16. *Dinah*. Dian Hartman mending a garment, Milford, New Jersey, 1898. Digital positive from 4" x 5" glass plate negative. CH2019.6.177.

Americans at home, Castner anticipated *Down South* (1900), the large format photo book by the well-known photographer Rudolf Eickemeyer, Jr., who portrayed agrarian Black life in positive and respectful images. In his composition, Castner juxtaposed his subject with flourishing plants that imply that, despite her modest dress and station in life, she was thriving.

Originally a male-dominated sport characterized by dangerous, difficult-to-ride "high wheel" or "penny-farthing" bikes, bicycling in the 1890s became ubiquitous across social classes for children and adults of all genders. Having two wheels of the same size, safety bicycles were marketed as being much safer and easier to ride than their predecessors.

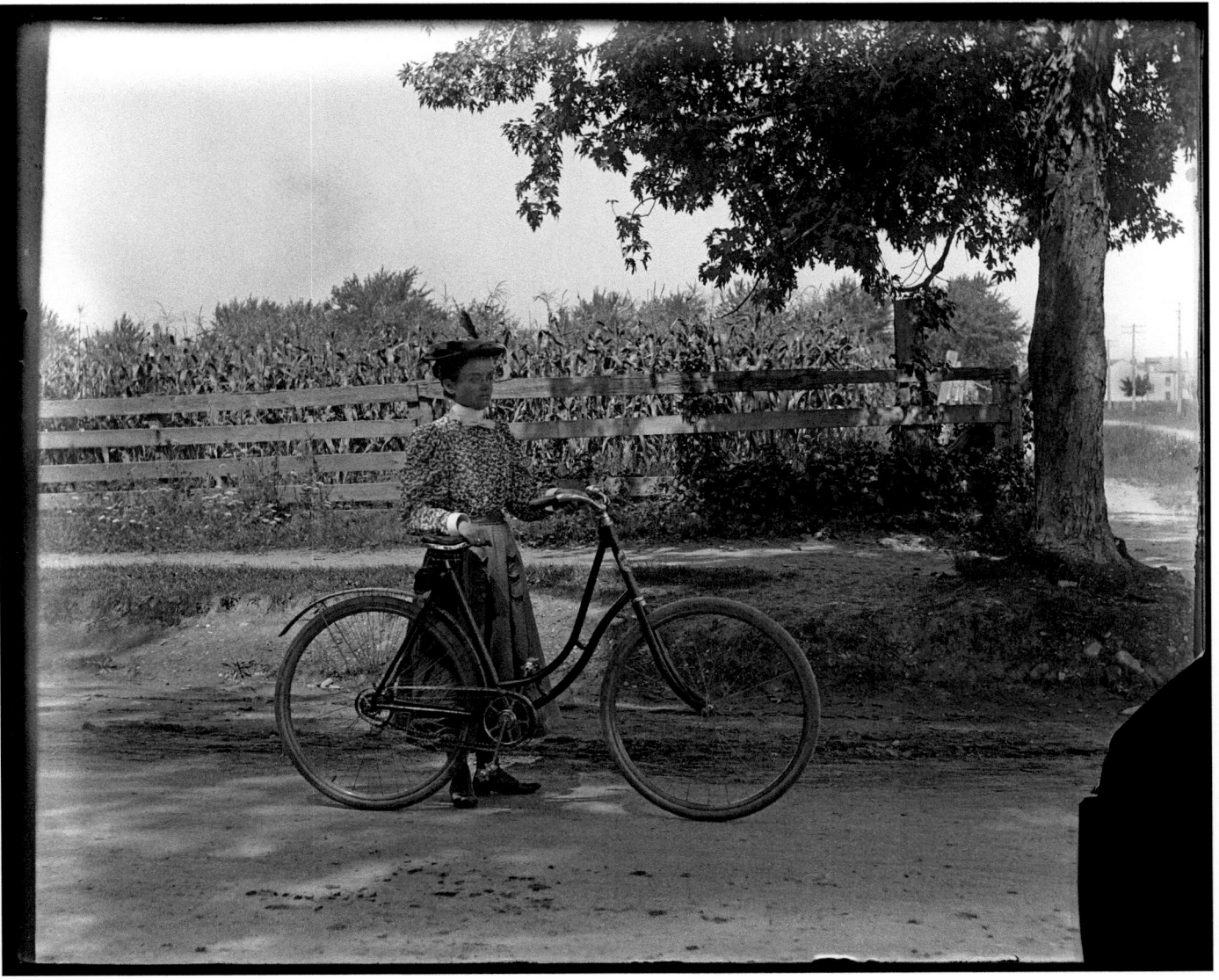

Twenty-seven-year-old schoolteacher Anna Cross, pictured in **plate 17**, lived on Elmer Street in Trenton. Castner may have photographed her while she was on a leisurely ride outside of town. The long skirts characteristic of women's fashion at that time proved to be highly impractical for the cyclist. Such clothing flapped about annoyingly in the wind and could easily get caught in the pedals and spokes. In response, many women advocated for sports clothes that would encourage, not hinder, the freedom of movement of an active, modern woman. This, in turn, influenced a larger movement that challenged traditional gender mores over what women should be wearing. Published in 1897, the popular publication *Lady*

Plate 17. Anna Cross with safety bicycle, New Jersey, 1897. Digital positive from 4" x 5" glass plate negative. CH2019.6.404.

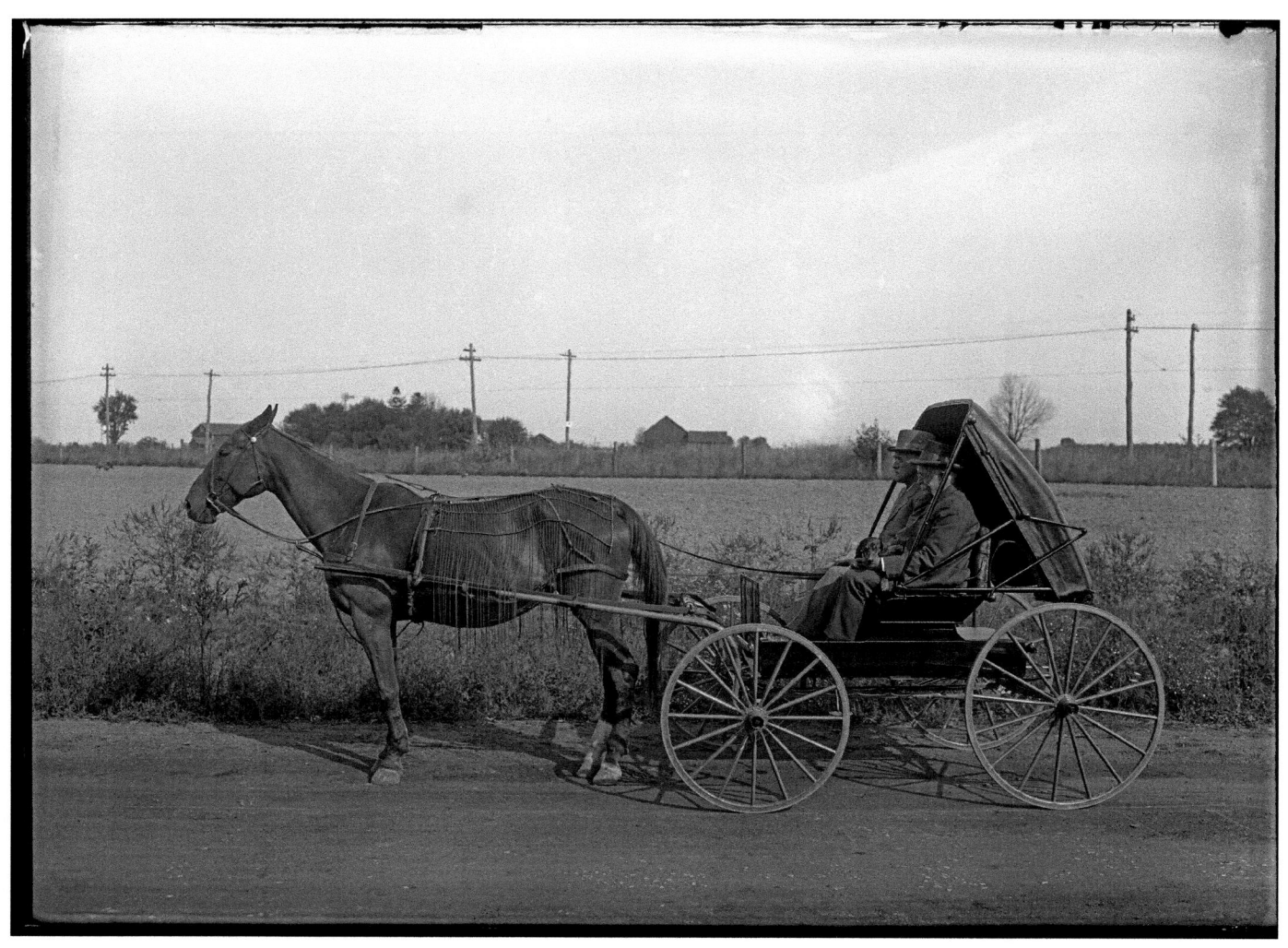

Plate 18. Men and dog in surrey, New Jersey, 1913. Digital positive from 5" x 7" glass plate negative. CH2019.6.468.

Cycling: What to Wear and How to Ride offered practical, how-to advice for the aspiring female cyclist.

Castner lived through a revolutionary period in transportation history—a period when both horse-drawn carriages and automobiles traveled the state's roadways at the same time. Castner's glass plate negatives document these waning years of carriage travel. With names like *surrey, phaeton, brougham,* and *rockaway,* carriages came in a wide array of sizes and styles. New Jersey was home to several carriage manufacturers of national recognition. These included James H. Birch Carriages in Burlington and the New Brunswick Carriage Works. Named for a county in England where they were first made, the surrey was a door-less, four-wheeled conveyance popular in the United States around 1900. The names of the two men in the carriage in **plate 18**, as well as that of their sleepy dachshund, are unknown.

Nothing is known about the young woman who posed for the portrait photograph in **plate 19**. A youthful face and innocent expression suggest that she is probably quite young, perhaps in her late teens or early twenties. At first glance, it might seem that she is wearing a hat trimmed in what appears to be some kind of animal fur. However, fur hats were usually small and close-fitting on the head due to the excessive warmth, weight, and bulk of the fur. In an oversized hat such as this, the material is more likely the downy feathers of an African stork called a marabou. Marabou feathers were a commonly used material on women's hats and stoles at the turn of the twentieth century. The soft, fluffy white feathers came from the underside of the bird's wings and tail.

Written on the negative sleeve, Castner's title for **plate 20** undoubtedly records the surnames of the three individuals posing for his camera. Dressed in a crisp, clean suit and tie and wearing a popular straw hat known as a "boater," the taller man at the rear is likely a clerk, store owner, or other white-collar worker. The soiled boots, work clothes, and accessories of the man on the left suggests that his is blue collar work—perhaps that of a railroad worker. Castner's handwritten notes also read "exp. 8 seconds / prints in 6 minutes." Castner used "gaslight paper" to make prints of this image. Introduced in the 1880s, these gelatin-coated papers sensitized to light with silver chloride could be printed using gaslight and later electric light. Castner placed the negative over the paper in his darkroom and exposed it to light for eight seconds to create an invisible, "latent" image. He then placed it in a tray with a developer solution. The image began to appear and was ready to be taken out after six minutes and stabilized in a fixing bath, then washed to remove residual chemicals.

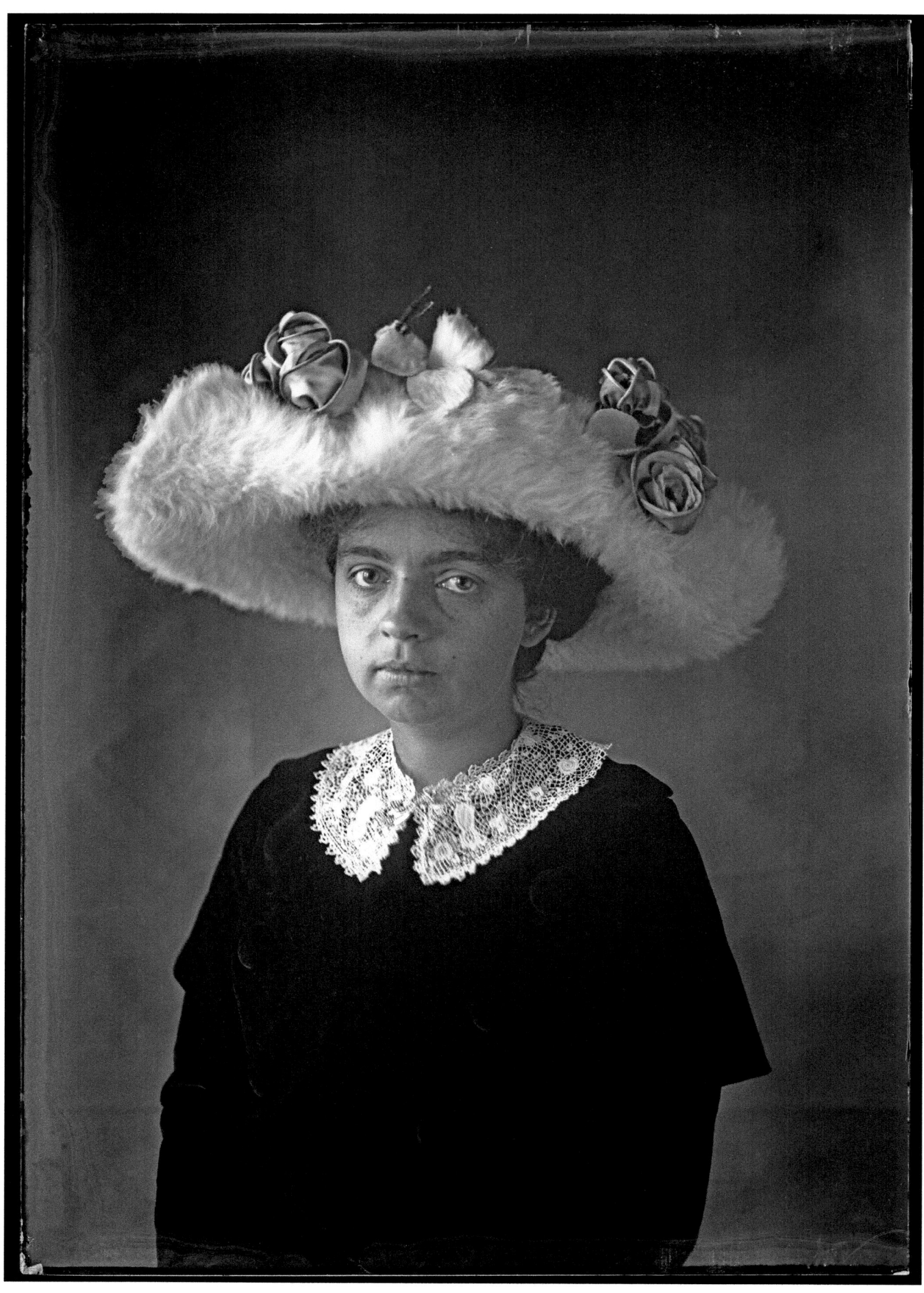

Plate 19. Portrait of an unidentified woman, New Jersey, c. 1900. Digital positive from 5" x 7" glass plate negative. CH2019.6.545.

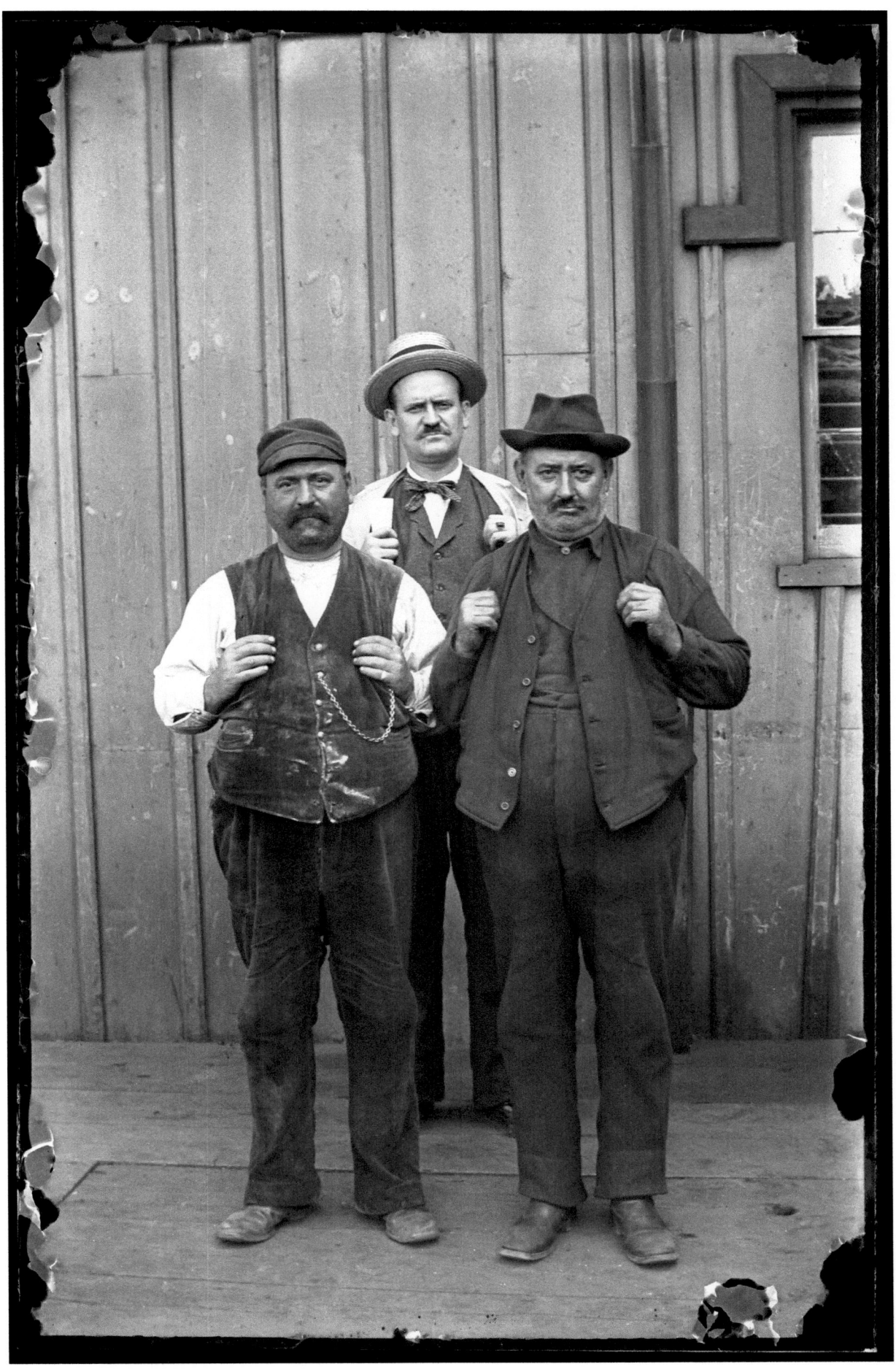

Plate 20. *Hopkins, Stout, Swem*. Men in hats, Trenton, New Jersey, 1890. Digital positive from 4.5" x 6.5" glass plate negative. CH2019.6.639.

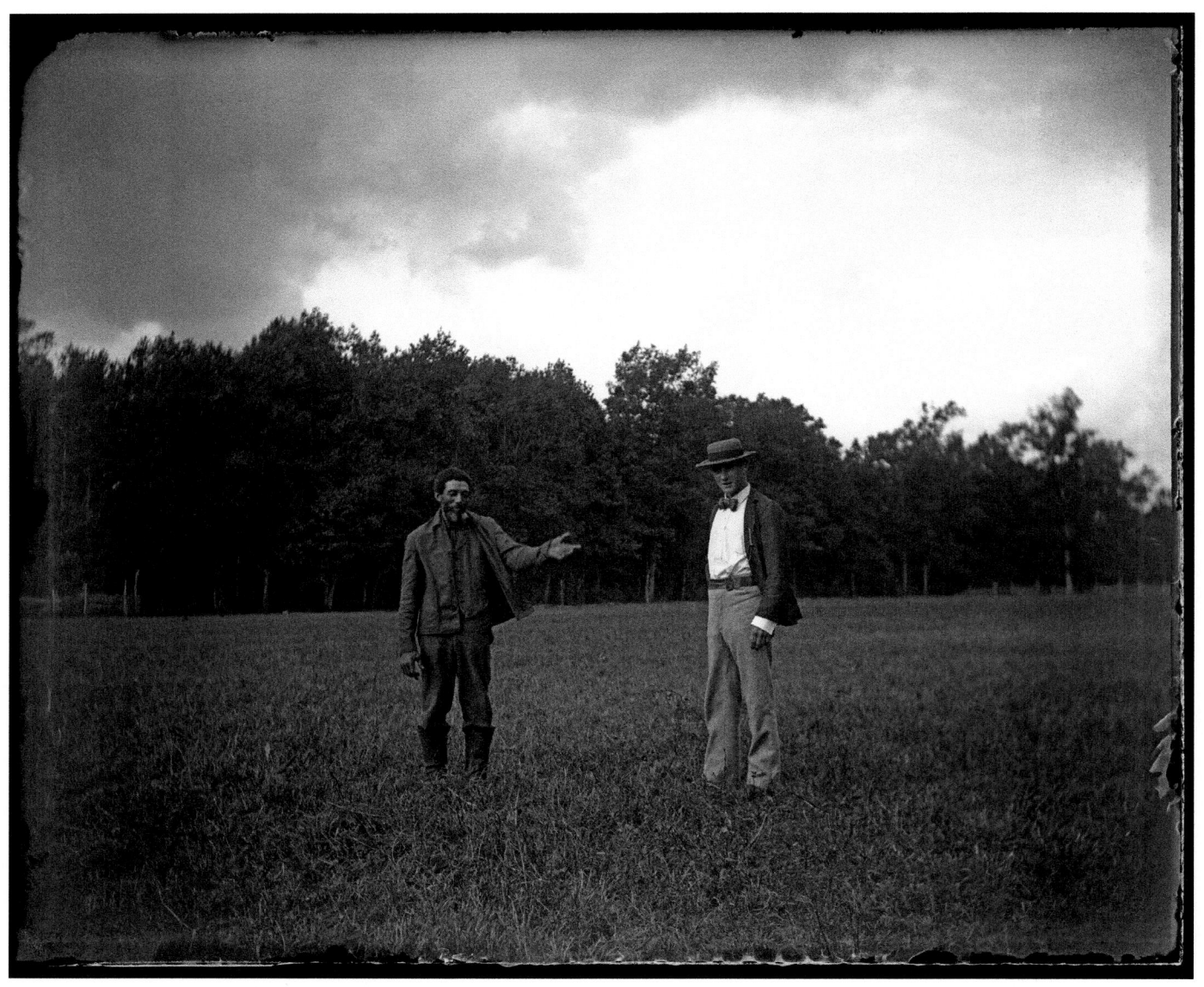

Plate 21. *Take Me As I Am.* Two unidentified men in a field, Ellisdale, New Jersey, 1896. Digital positive from 4" x 5" glass plate negative. CH2019.6.225.

Taken in a small village in Upper Freehold Township in rural Monmouth County near the border of Burlington County, **plate 21** is titled *Take Me as I Am.* The meaning is unclear. Was there some disagreement between these two individuals, causing one to turn, stern-faced, toward the camera and the other to outstretch an arm as if offering peace? Is the man on the left a farmer discussing the price of something, such as a piece of land, with a potential buyer? Or are the two individuals, one Black and one white, meeting for the first time and the title is Castner's commentary on race relations? Many of Grant Castner's photographs are straightforward, documentary artifacts that record people and places. Others,

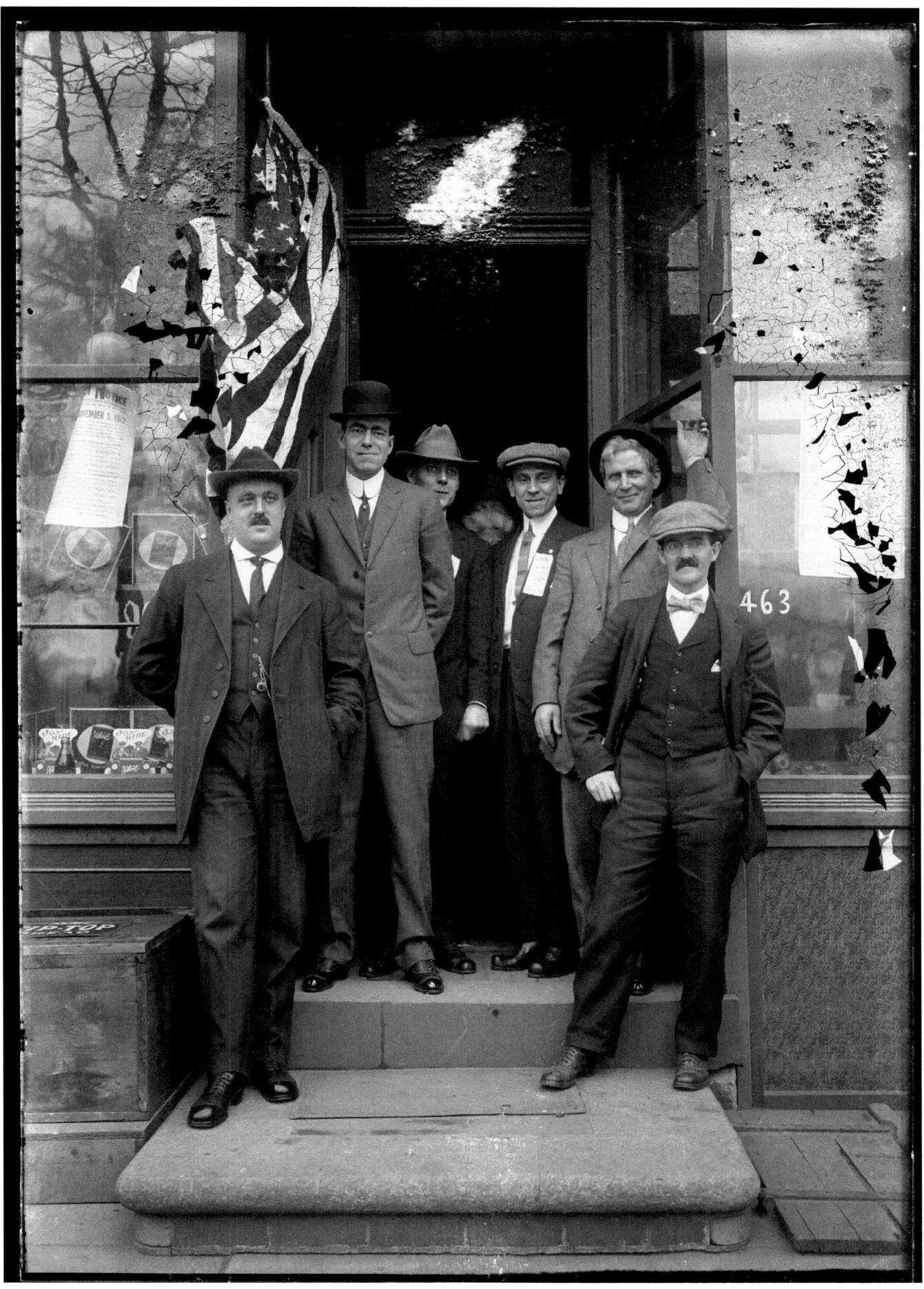

Plate 22. Grant Castner (front right) and associates, Trenton, New Jersey, 1912. Digital positive from 5" x 7" glass plate negative. CH2019.6.754.

like this and artworks in general, are subject to the interpretation of the viewer.

In the early twentieth century, men could choose from an array of popular headwear, but they usually wore some kind of a hat, at least outdoors. What they wore sometimes depended on the occasion; top hats, for example, were often reserved for formal affairs. Other times, a person's occupation or personal preferences determined their choice of head covering. Seen in **plate 22** at the front right, Castner preferred the "newsboy cap" because of its frequent use by newspaper delivery boys. His journalistic career as a news agent and magazine distributor probably influenced this fashion decision. Castner's friends wear two other popular men's hats of the day: a soft-brimmed, indented-crown fedora and a rounded-top bowler, also known as a derby. The lapel ribbon worn by the man at the center states that he is an "official challenger" for the Republican Party. The group may have been members of a Republican political club gathered in support of their candidate on Election Day 1912.

3

City

Tall buildings. Bustling streets. Churning industries. Vibrant civic life. When Grant Castner moved to Trenton in the 1880s, the capital city was just beginning a remarkable transformation into an energetic, urbanized metropolis. Trenton was the political hub for the entire state. It also served as a cultural and commercial center for central New Jersey and neighboring Bucks County, Pennsylvania. Major industrial manufacturers such as Roebling and Lenox called Trenton home. In 1880, the city's population totaled a mere thirty thousand people. By 1920, its population had exploded four-fold to one hundred twenty thousand.

The sights and sounds of the burgeoning city inspired Castner's photography. He often bicycled the city's streets in search of his next photographic subject. Trenton's vibrant cultural sector also helped Castner grow as an artist. The booming city gave rise to several arts and photography clubs. Castner was a founding member of the Trenton Photographic Society and held officer positions, including secretary and treasurer, for more than fifteen years. He also shared his photographs with the public in exhibitions and magic lantern slideshows. Many of these popular events took place at Trenton's premier arts academy, the School of Industrial Arts (now Mercer County Community College).

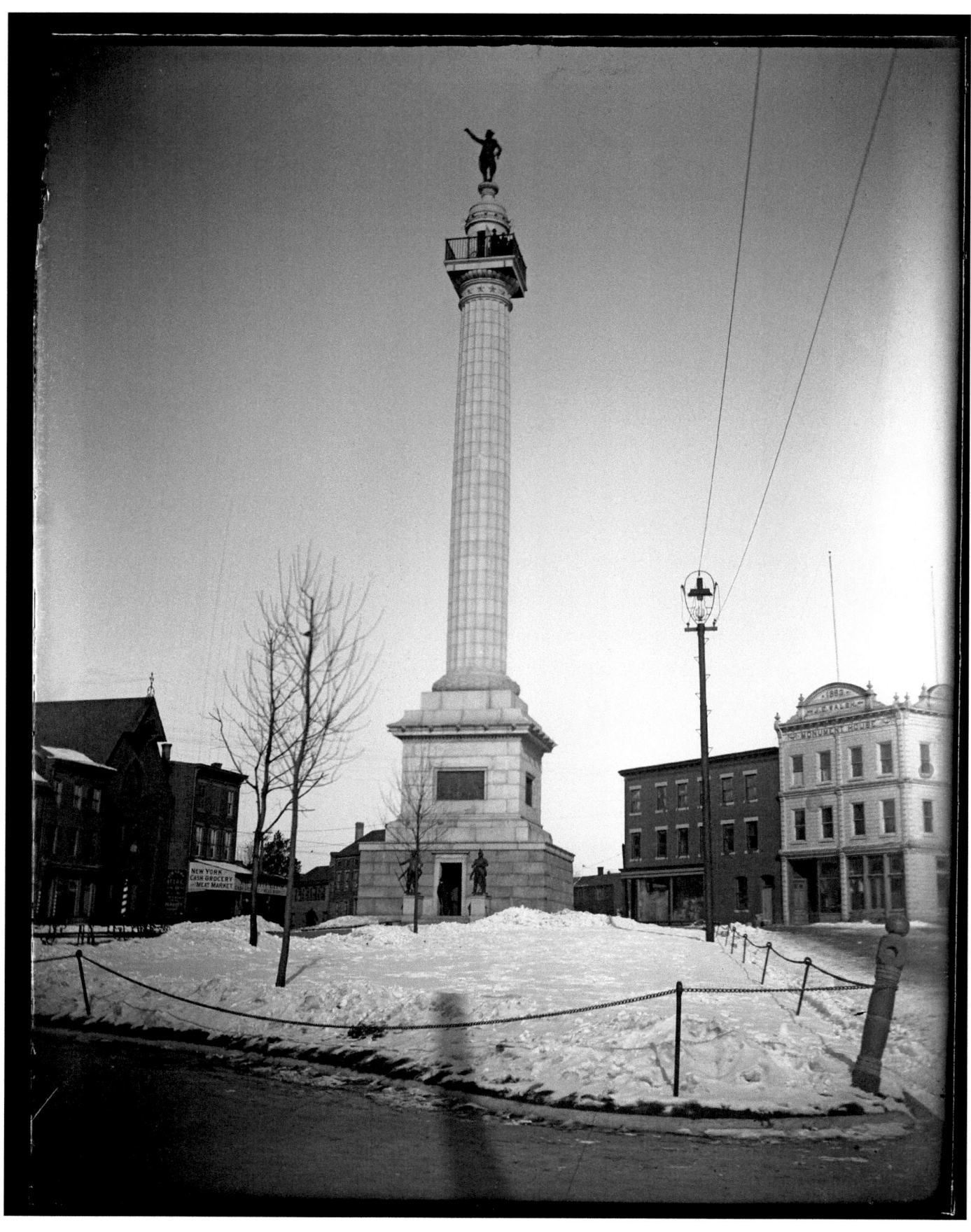

Plate 23. Trenton Battle Monument on Christmas Day, Trenton, New Jersey, 1896. Digital positive from 4" x 5" glass plate negative. CH2019.6.151.

For Castner, the 148-foot-high Trenton Battle Monument (**plate 23**) was more than a patriotic tribute to George Washington and the American victory at the December 26, 1776, Battle of Trenton. It was a photo-op spot with a unique, birds-eye vantage point from which he could record the growth and expansion of his city. The Battle Monument's cornerstone was laid on December 26, 1891, and a formal dedication of the completed granite, statue-capped column took place almost two years later, in October 1893. But it was not until late 1896 that engineers finally completed the elevator designed to take people to the observation platform at the summit. Members of the public were first invited to ride the new elevator at 9:00 a.m. on Christmas Day of 1896. Castner was among the many who visited the monument on that very day, taking a series of photographs of the monument and views of Trenton in all directions.

In **plate 24**, Castner's camera recorded the curving route of the Trenton Branch of the Philadelphia and Reading Railroad that emanated from passenger and freight depots located near the Battle Monument. The historic Philadelphia and Reading Railroad freight depot, seen in the foreground of Castner's photograph, was added to the National Register of Historic Places in 1979 and later became a recreational center for Trenton senior citizens. In the middle distance stands what was one of the city's marquee winter recreational facilities: Prospect Skating Park. Every winter, the park was filled with water and transformed by frigid temperatures into a popular community ice skating rink. The venue also hosted skating races, ice hockey games, bands, carnivals, and other activities all winter long. As might be expected, only a small number of people have left the comfort of their homes to enjoy the park on this cold Christmas Day.

The towering, 50-foot-tall, slate-lined spire of the Cathedral of Saint Mary of the Assumption in **plate 25** nicely frames Castner's view to the south from the summit of the

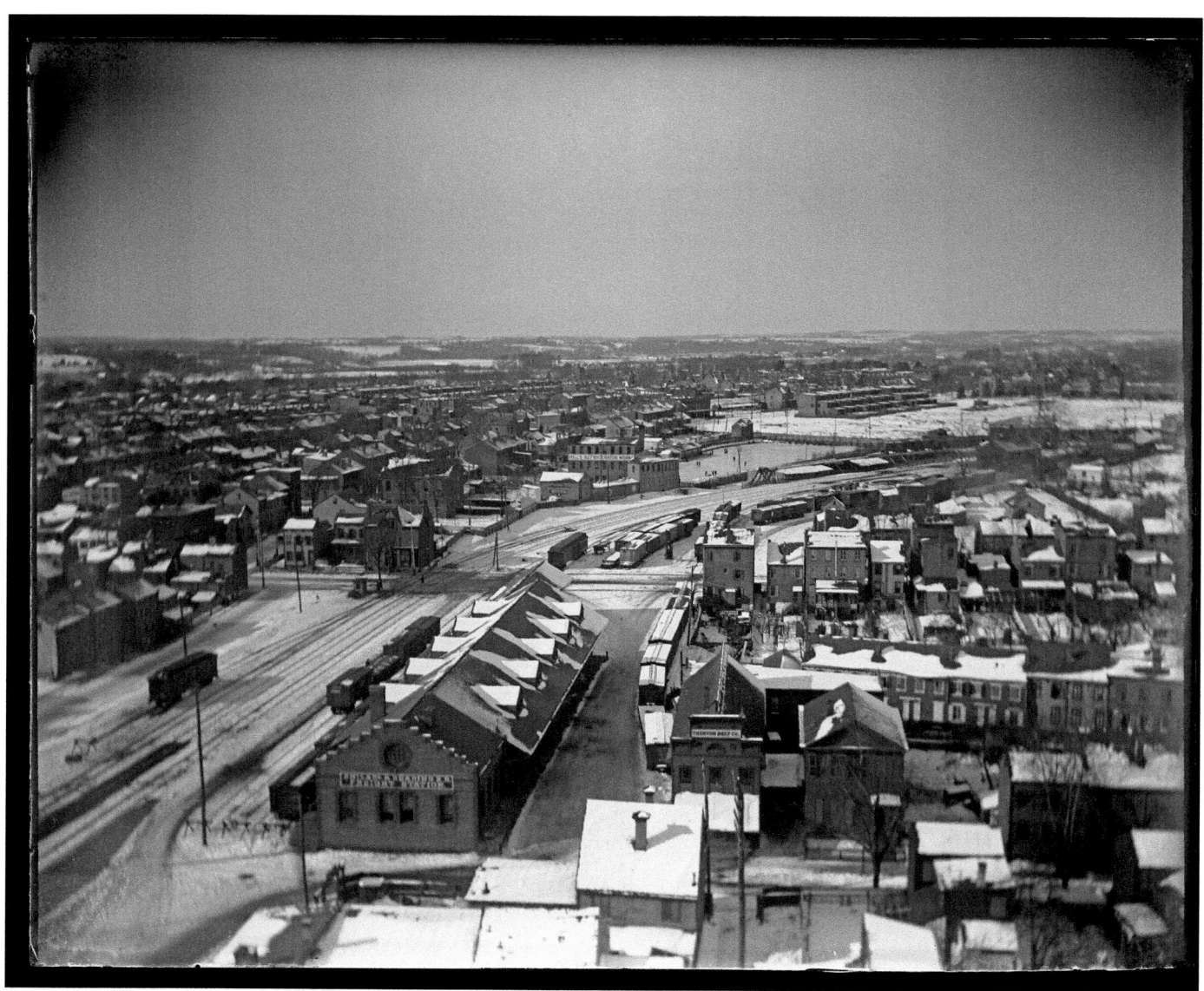

Plate 24. Bird's eye view of Trenton, looking west from the Battle Monument, Trenton, New Jersey, December 25, 1896. Digital positive from 4" x 5" glass plate negative. CH2019.6.152.

Battle Monument. This magnificent Roman Catholic Church, which stood at the corner of Warren Street and Bank Street, was destroyed by fire in 1956. A rebuilt church stands at the same location today. The other prominent landmark in the photograph is the New Jersey State House, the dome of which can be seen against the backdrop of an icy Delaware River and the farms and fields of rural Bucks County, Pennsylvania. In the foreground is a long-gone passenger depot for the Bel-Del Railroad line that connected Trenton with Castner's hometown of Belvidere.

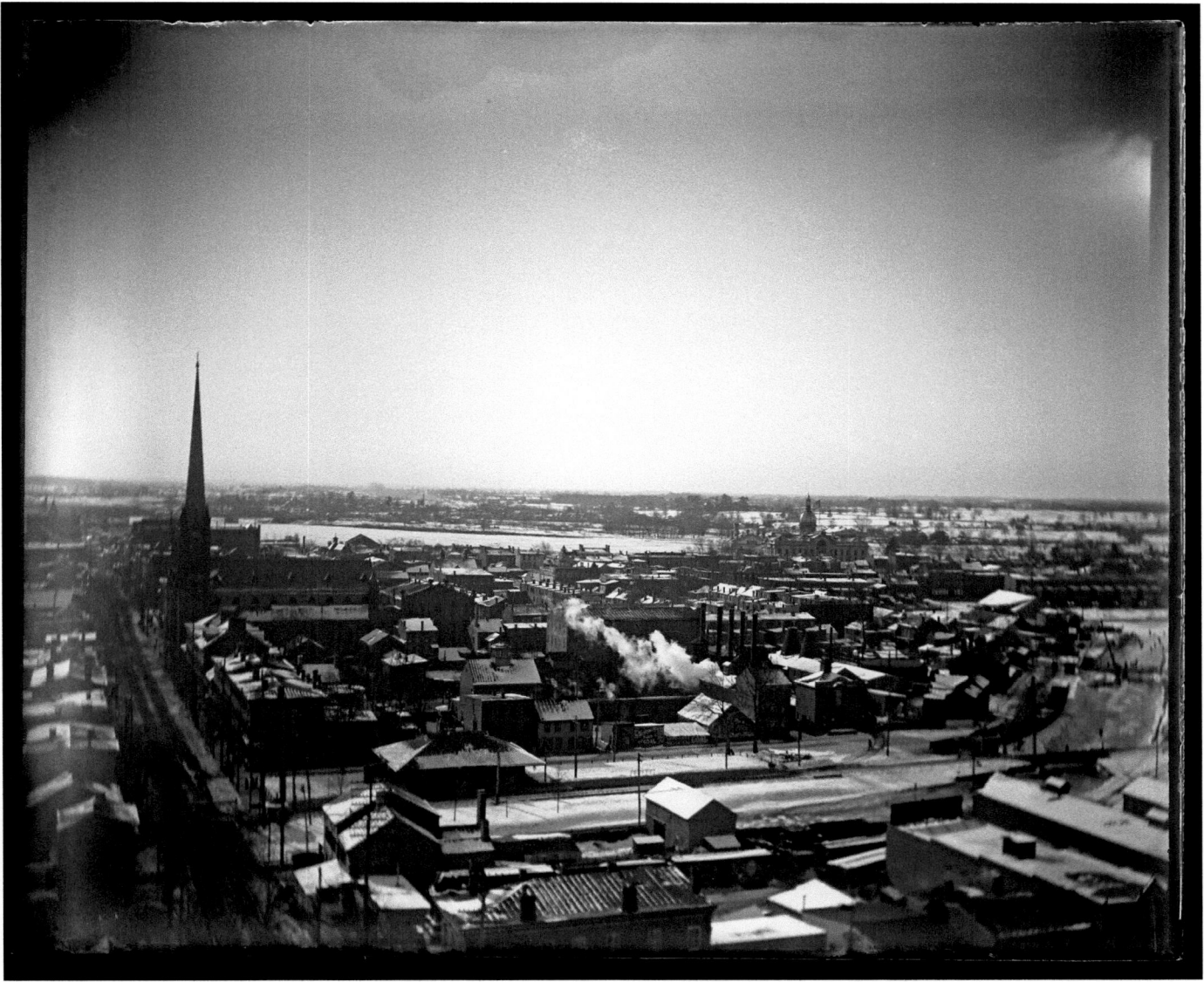

Castner trained his camera along the length of Princeton Avenue (now Martin Luther King, Jr. Blvd.) and the streetcar rails that it once held in **plate 26**. Prominently visible on the east side of Princeton Avenue are the Trenton Wagon Works and Fifth Presbyterian Church behind it. In the right foreground, one can espy the sign for Trenton Carriage and discern the stables behind the building. The wagon works building no longer exists, but the church stands to this day. In 1958, it became the home of Galilee Baptist Church.

Plate 25. Bird's eye view of Trenton, looking southwest from the Battle Monument, Trenton, New Jersey, December 25, 1896. Digital positive from 4" x 5" glass plate negative. CH2019.6.153.

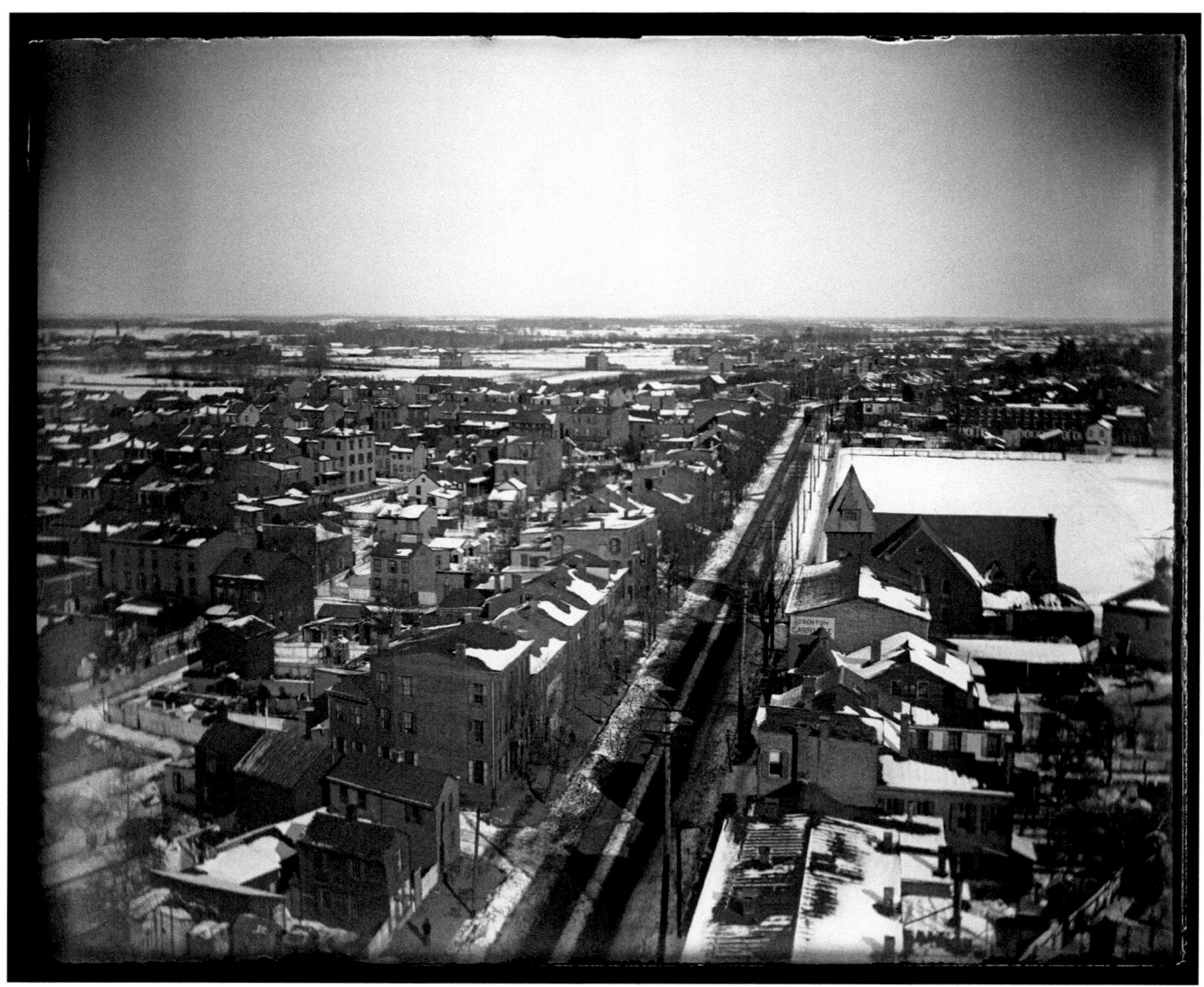

Plate 26. Bird's eye view of Trenton, looking north from the Battle Monument, Trenton, New Jersey, December 25, 1896. Digital positive from 4" x 5" glass plate negative. CH2019.6.154.

When Castner turned his camera to the east, he captured a panoramic view of the city's rapidly growing industrial zone (**plate 27**). In the right foreground are the bottle-shaped kilns of the Trenton Potteries Company (Crescent Works), one of the many ceramics production firms in the so-called "Staffordshire of America." Behind it is the sprawling, multi-story pottery complex and towering smokestack of Thomas Maddock and Sons, a noted national maker of plumbing fixtures. Like many of the city's ceramic manufacturers, these two prominent potteries sat along the Delaware and Raritan Canal and adjacent railroad lines that bisect the center of the photograph. The curved building at the center is a railroad

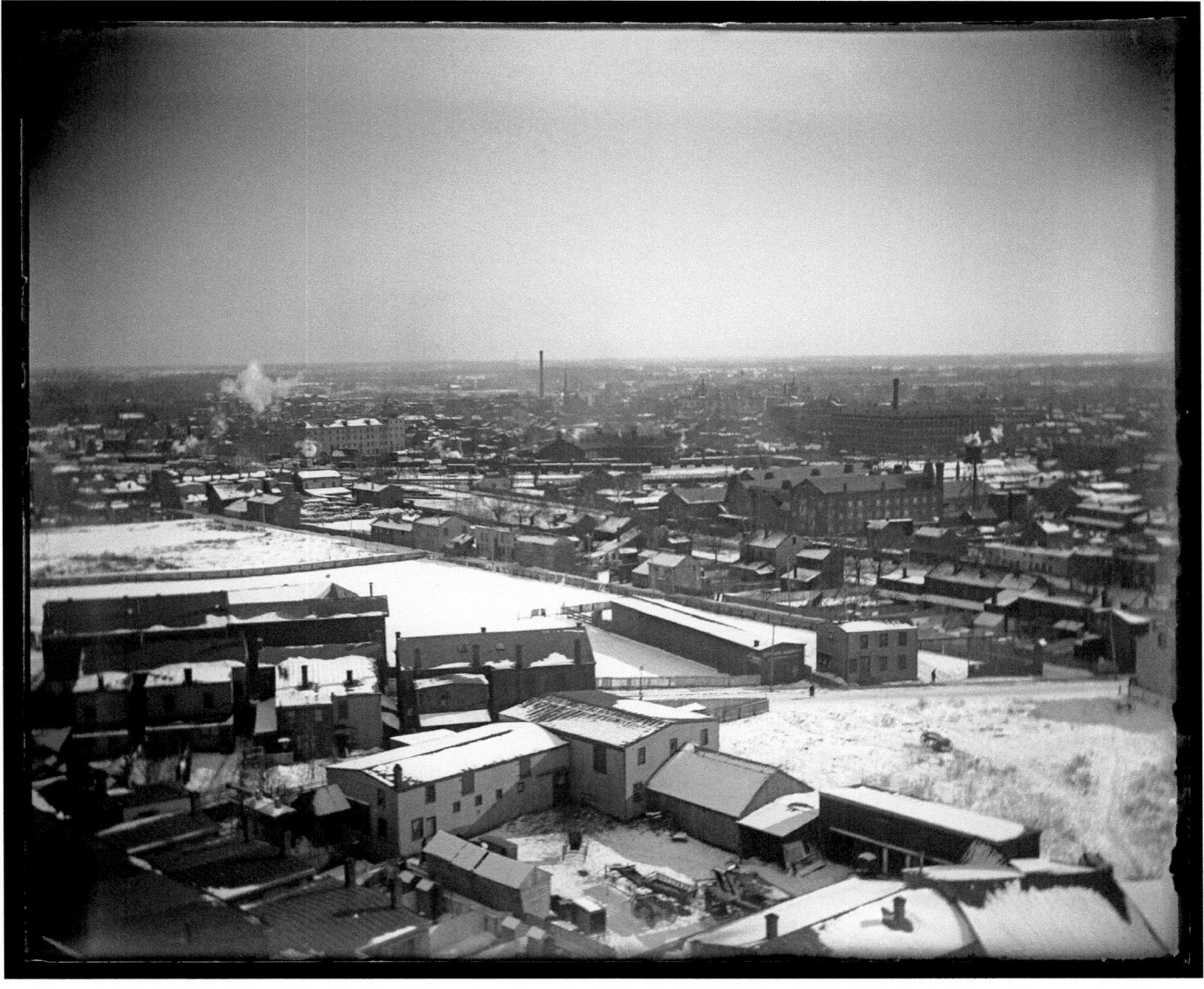

roundhouse, a structure for repairing and storing locomotives. Behind it, barely visible through the smoky haze, are the twin, domed buildings of the New Jersey State Normal School. This historical educational institution was the first teacher training school in the state and the forerunner of The College of New Jersey (TCNJ).

Around 4:30 p.m. on August 10, 1902, a powerful tornado (**plate 28**) swept through Trenton, tearing the roof and front wall off an entire block of six brick row houses on Perry Street. One survivor equated the deafening sound to "the sizzling of a large sky rocket." Castner was on the scene to record the aftermath of the disaster, which also destroyed the nearby Heath

Plate 27. Bird's eye view of Trenton, looking east from the Battle Monument, Trenton, New Jersey, December 25, 1896. Digital positive from 4" x 5" glass plate negative. CH2019.6.155.

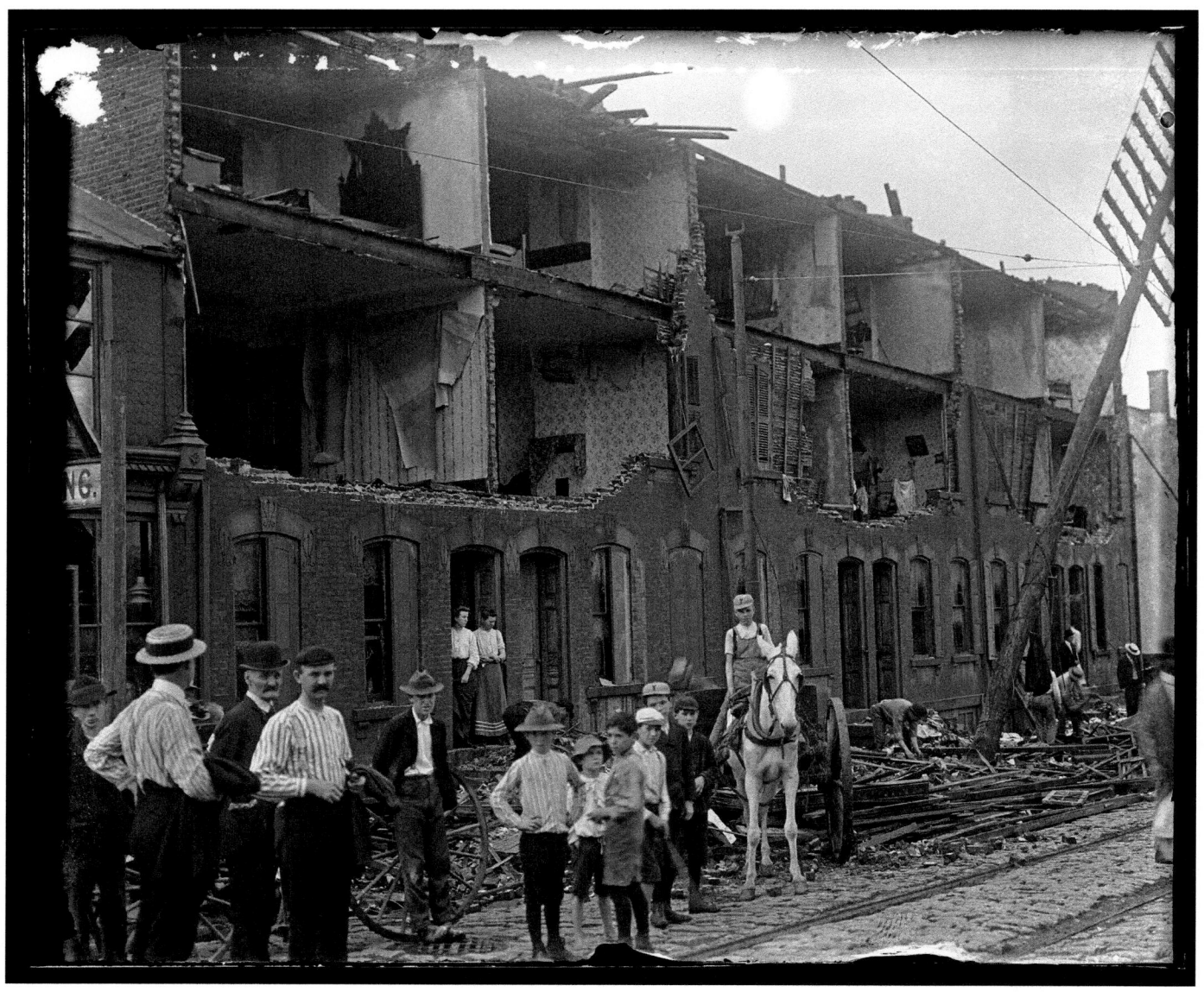

Plate 28. Tornado aftermath, Perry Street, Trenton, New Jersey, 1902. Digital positive from 4" x 5" glass plate negative. CH2019.6.431.

Lumber yard, a long running firm that now does business on Olden Avenue. His camera captured the astonished faces of the residents and relief workers as they observe the unbelievable scene that has just unfolded. The wallpaper, paintings, and furniture of each home are now on full view—a window into the lives of those affected by nature's wrath. Castner's newspaper distribution business likely fostered his interest in documenting newsworthy events. He was probably also familiar with the "real photo" postcards that were immensely popular at the time. Hoping to cash in on the public's fascination with death and destruction, photographers would rush to the

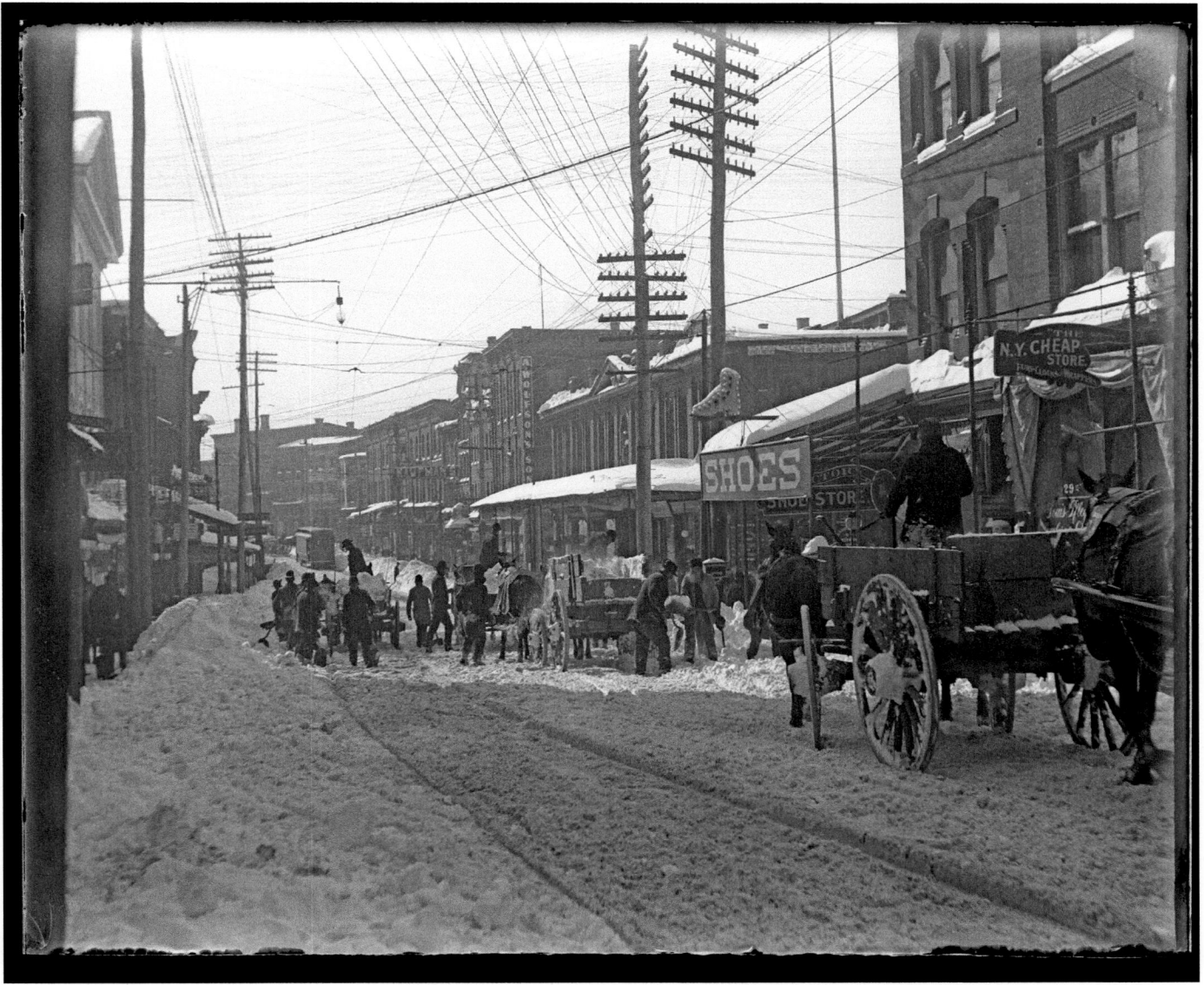

scene of disasters, take pictures of the aftermath, and then sell the images in postcard format.

Often associated with farms and fields, the horse was of equal importance to growing cities. In **plate 29**, horse-drawn wagons transport workers down a snow-covered South Broad Street in an effort to reopen the busy thoroughfare following a blizzard. Newspaper reports recounted how the city's modern, electric streetcar system became paralyzed by the heavy snow. The simple, time-tested technology of the horse helped to get the tracks cleared and the city moving again. The importance of South Broad Street as a commercial center is on full view in

Plate 29. Snow removal on South Broad Street, view to the south from Front Street, Trenton, New Jersey, 1899. Digital positive from 4" x 5" glass plate negative. CH2019.6.439.

Castner's photograph. Large signs advertise some of Trenton's popular retailers, including Kaufman's Department Store, A. Wolfson's Sons Clothiers, and the Factory Shoe Store.

In the pre-dawn hours of March 21, 1885, a policeman patrolling West State Street caught sight of flickering light in a first-floor window of the New Jersey State House. When he drew nearer, he also detected the acrid smell of smoke. The seat of New Jersey government was on fire. The conflagration quickly tore through multiple stories in the front of the building as firefighters raced to the scene to control the blaze. At the time of the fire, the state's Geological Museum (forerunner of the New Jersey State Museum) was located on the third floor of the State House, but fortunately its collections were on view at the world's fair in New Orleans. This section of the building also housed the state's Civil War flags, which were displayed in large glass cases. Police officers and firemen on the scene, some of them former soldiers, quickly realized what was at stake and rushed inside the burning building to save the treasured military relics. **Plate 30** captures the exhausted faces of community members and first responders posing with a steam-powered fire engine that helped battle the blaze.

Four means of wheeled travel in the modern city are documented in Castner's view of the hustle and bustle of South Broad Street: horse-drawn carriage, bicycle, electric streetcar, and automobile (**plate 31**). The view is up Broad Street from the intersection with East Front Street, the sign for which is seen in the foreground. The famed Taylor Opera House is on right. This landmark city theater hosted lectures, concerts, and theatrical productions, as well as the inaugurations of many New Jersey governors, including George B. McClellan and Woodrow Wilson. Across the street is the prominent tower of First Methodist Church. Now known as Turning Point United Methodist Church, the structure still stands. Most of the other

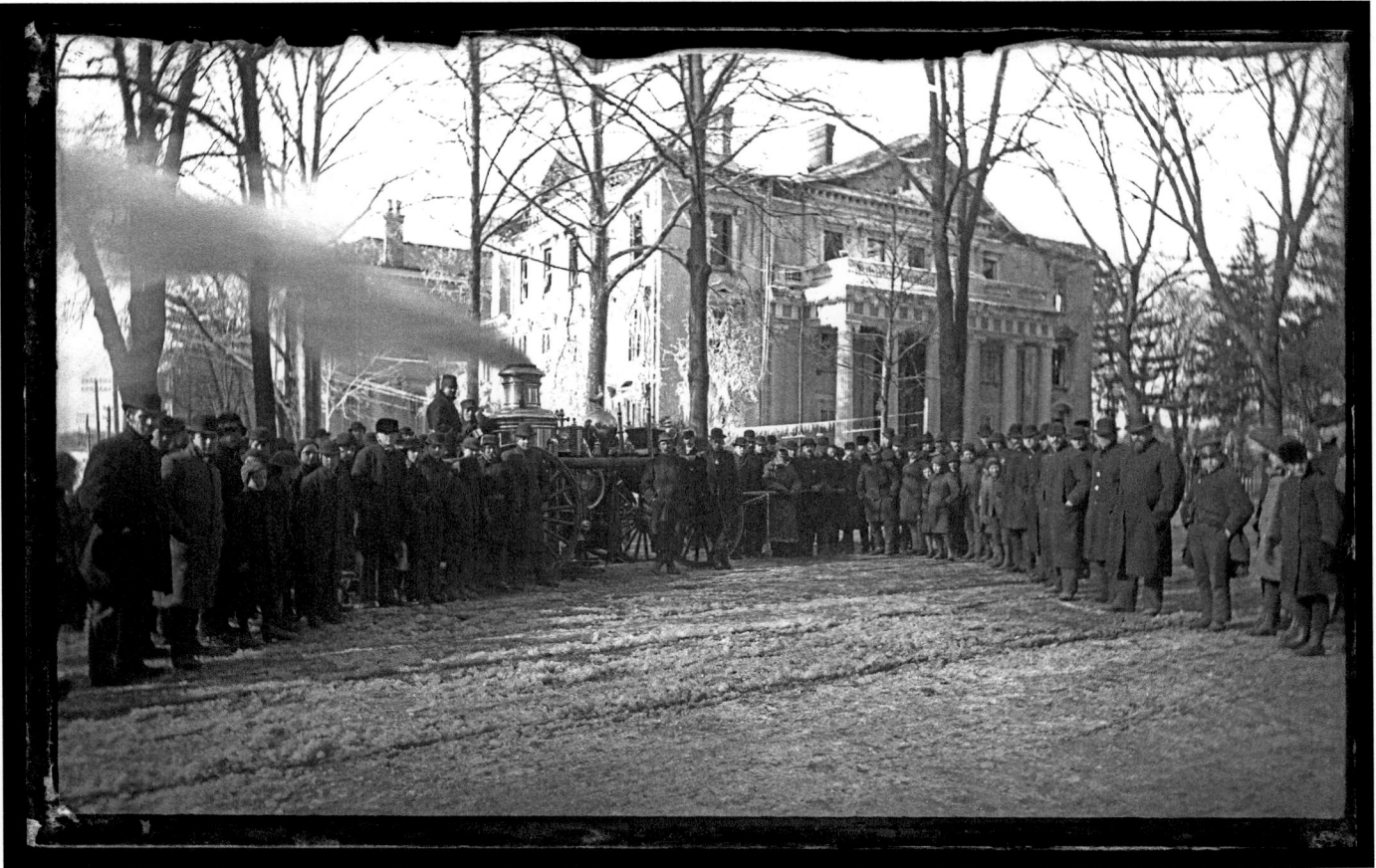

structures were razed in the process of urban renewal and re-placed by parking areas and modern buildings.

Castner probably waited patiently on a busy street corner to get the shot in **plate 32**, triggering the shutter just when a woman, oblivious to the camera, and a streetcar simulta-neously entered the frame. Both human and machine are in motion at the same angle. The former travels in the simplest manner possible, on foot. The other surges forward under the revolutionary power of electricity. Dressed in a fur stole for her neck and muff for her hands, she appears lost in her own thoughts or in a hurry to get out of the cold. People on the crowded sidewalk are concerned with their own business or focused on their companions, suggesting that by this time cameras had become commonplace on the city's streets. Still, a few individuals can be seen casting curious glances toward the photographer. Only one of about twenty men in the photo

Plate 30. Aftermath of New Jer-sey State House fire, Trenton, New Jersey, 1885. Digital positive from 5" x 8" glass plate negative. CH2019.6.505.

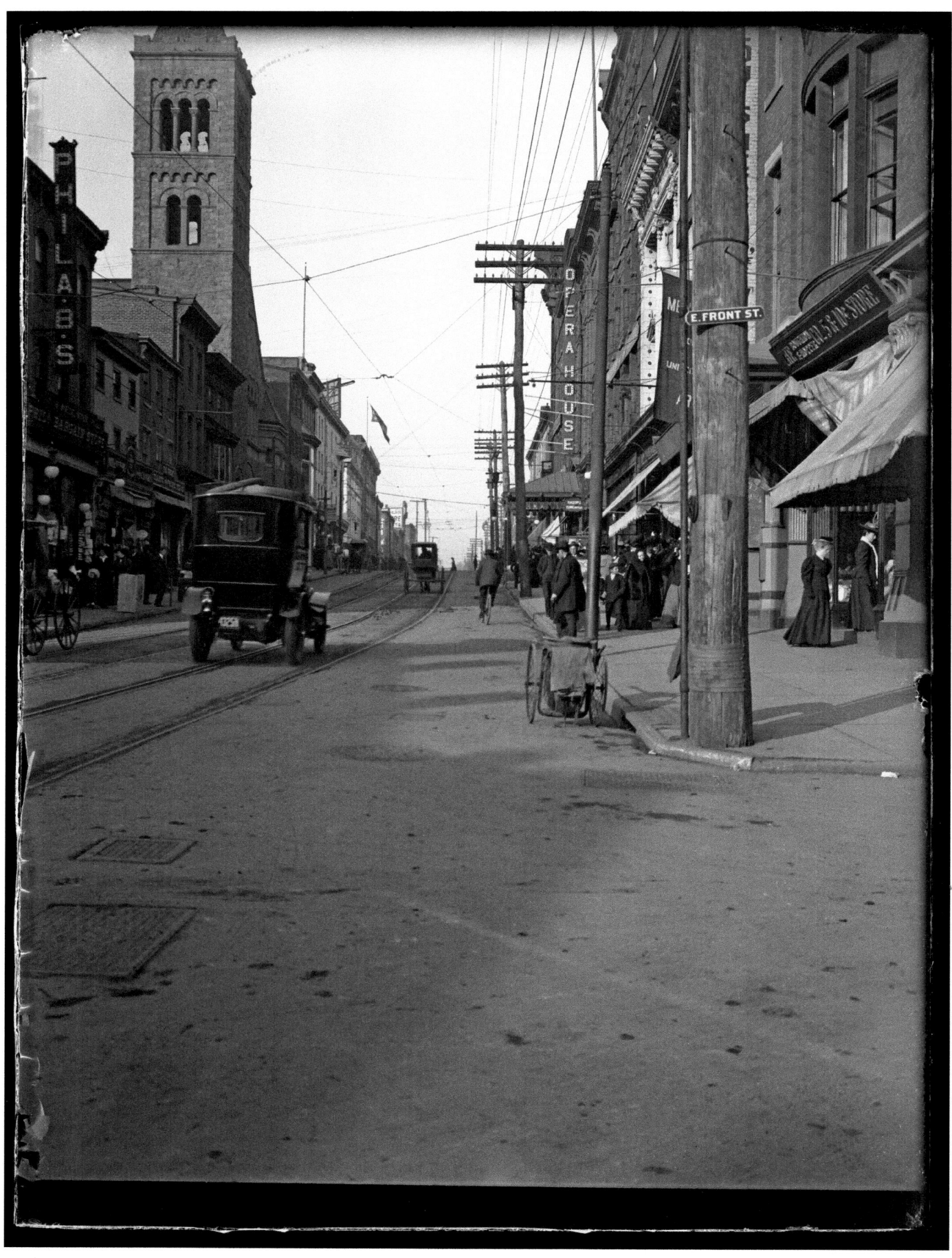

Plate 31. South Broad Street, view to the north from Front Street, Trenton, New Jersey, c. 1910. Digital positive from 3.25" x 4.25" glass plate negative. CH2019.6.531.

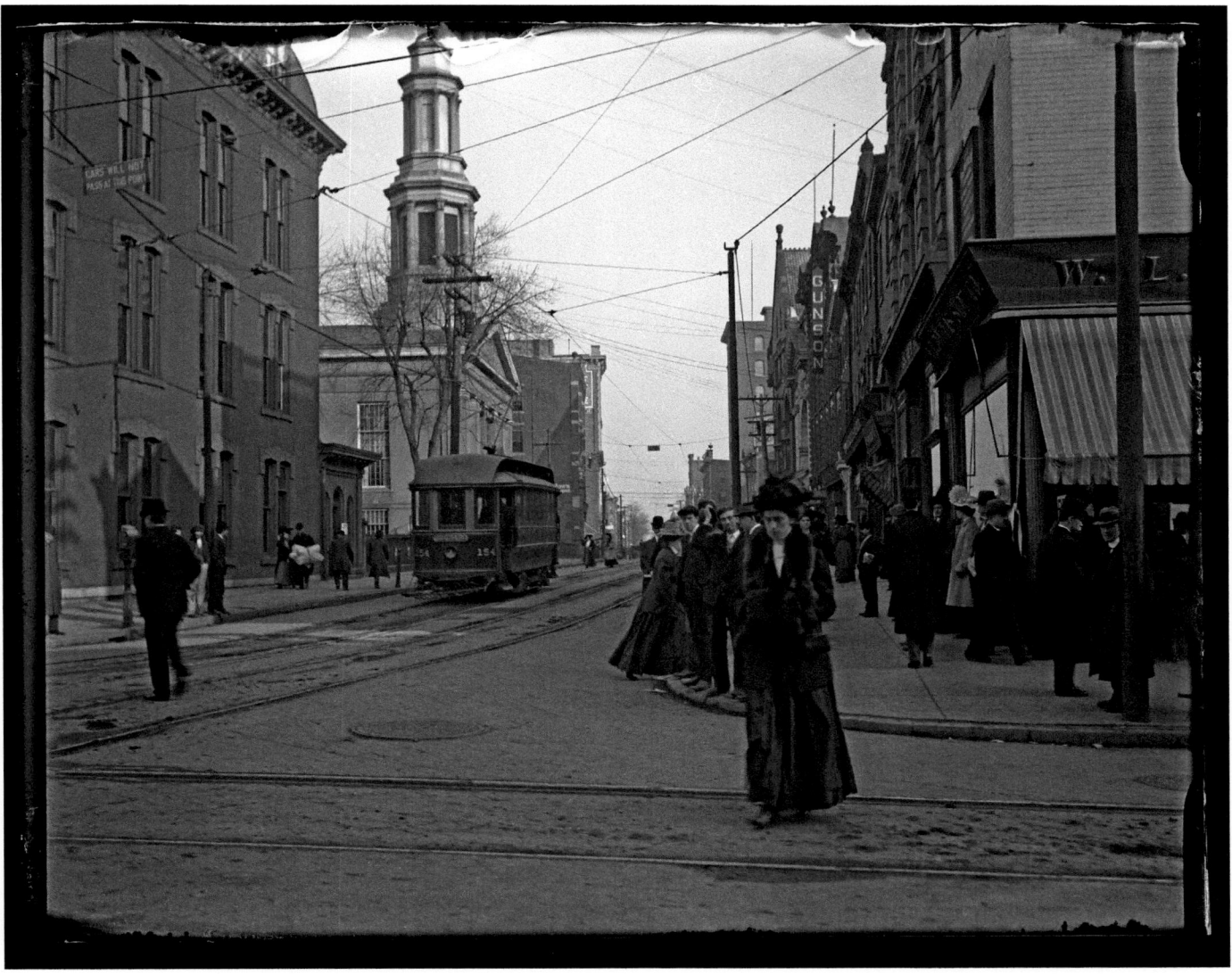

is hatless. East State Street's First Presbyterian Church, now one of the city's oldest religious structures, is at the left.

It was a bleak winter morning when Castner took **plate 33** on South Clinton Avenue near Clinton Street Station, now the Trenton Transit Center. One of several railroad stations in the city at the time, this bustling transportation hub served thousands of New Jerseyans traveling between New York and Philadelphia or more distant destinations on the famed Pennsylvania Railroad. Perhaps poised to pick up rail passengers, a line of horse-drawn carriages flank historic Mercer Cemetery. Those arriving and departing the station could also hop on the streetcar line that ran north from this point and then turned west on State Street and toward the businesses, homes,

Plate 32. East State Street, view to the east from Broad Street, Trenton, New Jersey, c. 1900. Digital positive from 3.25" x 4.25" glass plate negative. CH2019.6.534.

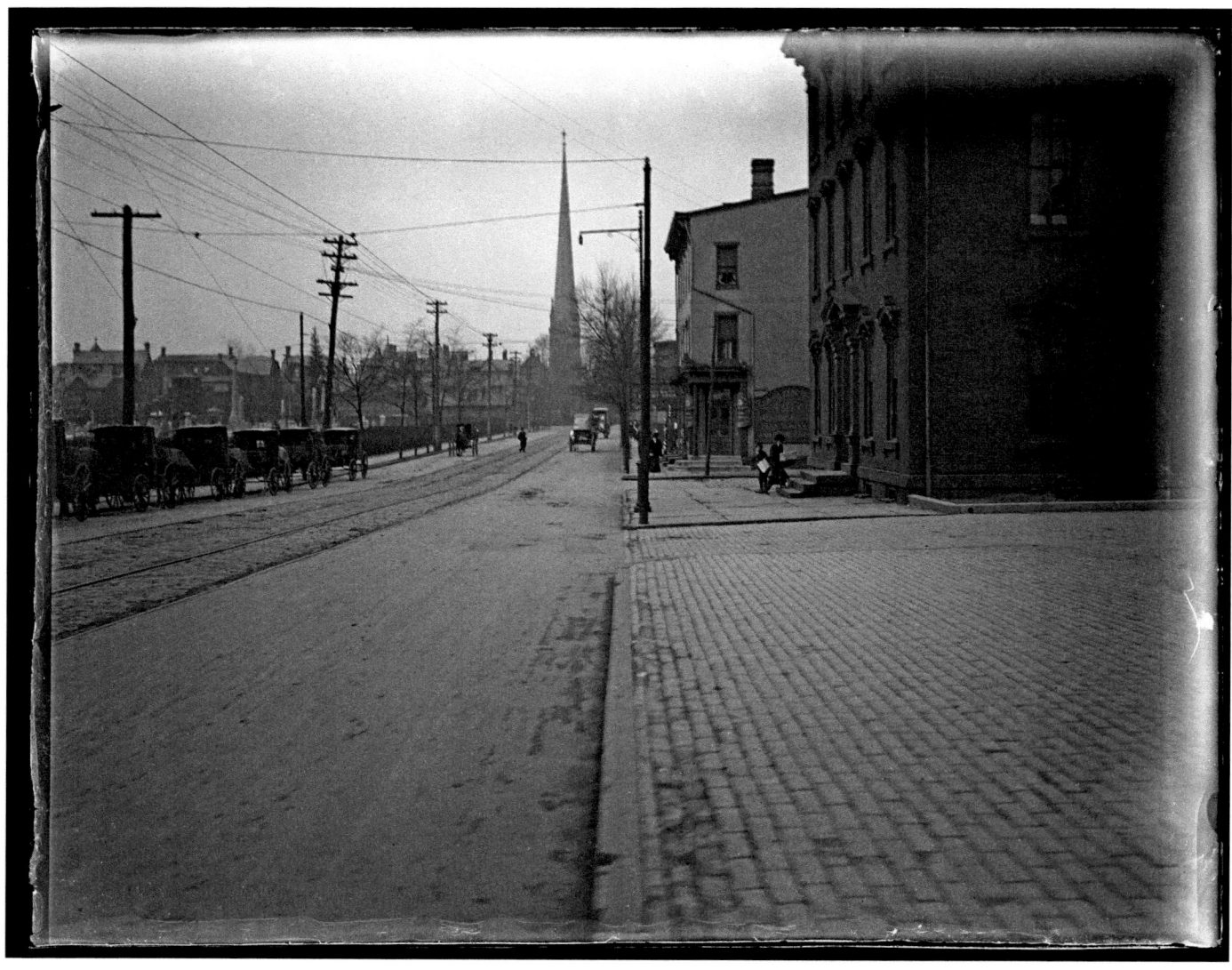

Plate 33. South Clinton Avenue, view to the north from train station, Trenton, New Jersey, c. 1890. Digital positive from 3.25" x 4.25" glass plate negative. CH2019.6.532.

and government buildings that lined this bustling downtown thoroughfare. On the east side of South Clinton Avenue, two newspaper boys are hard at work in front of a building holding offices of the Pennsylvania Railroad. Towering in the distance, just north of the intersection with East State Street, is the spire of Fourth Presbyterian Church. Although the image depicts a point just north of a busy transit hub, the street seems particularly quiet. It may have been taken in the early morning, suggesting that the amateur photographer used these off-peak hours to take pictures before his own workday began.

Grant Castner's self-portrait with a bicycle on a Belgian block-lined street (**plate 34**) suggests one of the ways in which the thirty-one-year-old photographer traveled around the city

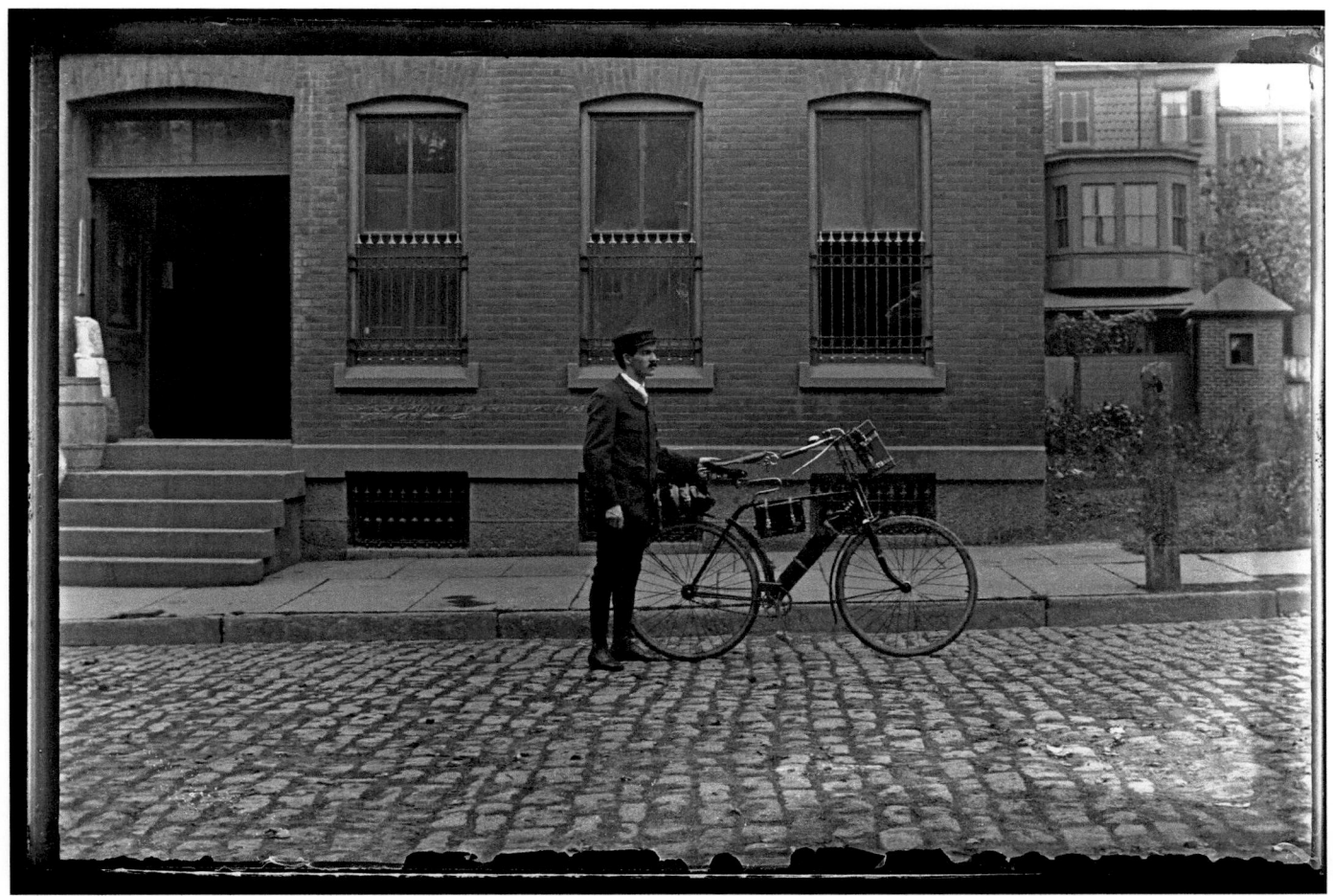

in search of his next photograph. His box camera is securely lashed to the handlebars and leather messenger bags on the rear tire rack likely hold other photographic equipment such as his glass plate negatives. This photo was likely taken by a friend or family member, perhaps his sister Ida. While Castner might have used a time exposure valve that worked with air pressure, such devices were rare before 1900. Photographers taking self-portraits usually used a long thread to trip the shutter, but no thread is visible in this photograph.

In the 1910s, automobiles began to appear more frequently on the streets of Trenton. At the dawn of the automotive era, women had few opportunities to challenge prevailing, gendered notions about their place behind the wheel. But before long, a number of pioneering women undertook highly publicized, long-distance automobile jaunts in order to prove the stereotypes wrong. Two of the first were from

Plate 34. Grant Castner with safety bicycle, Trenton, New Jersey, 1894. Digital positive from 4.25" x 6.5" glass plate negative. CH2019.6.498.

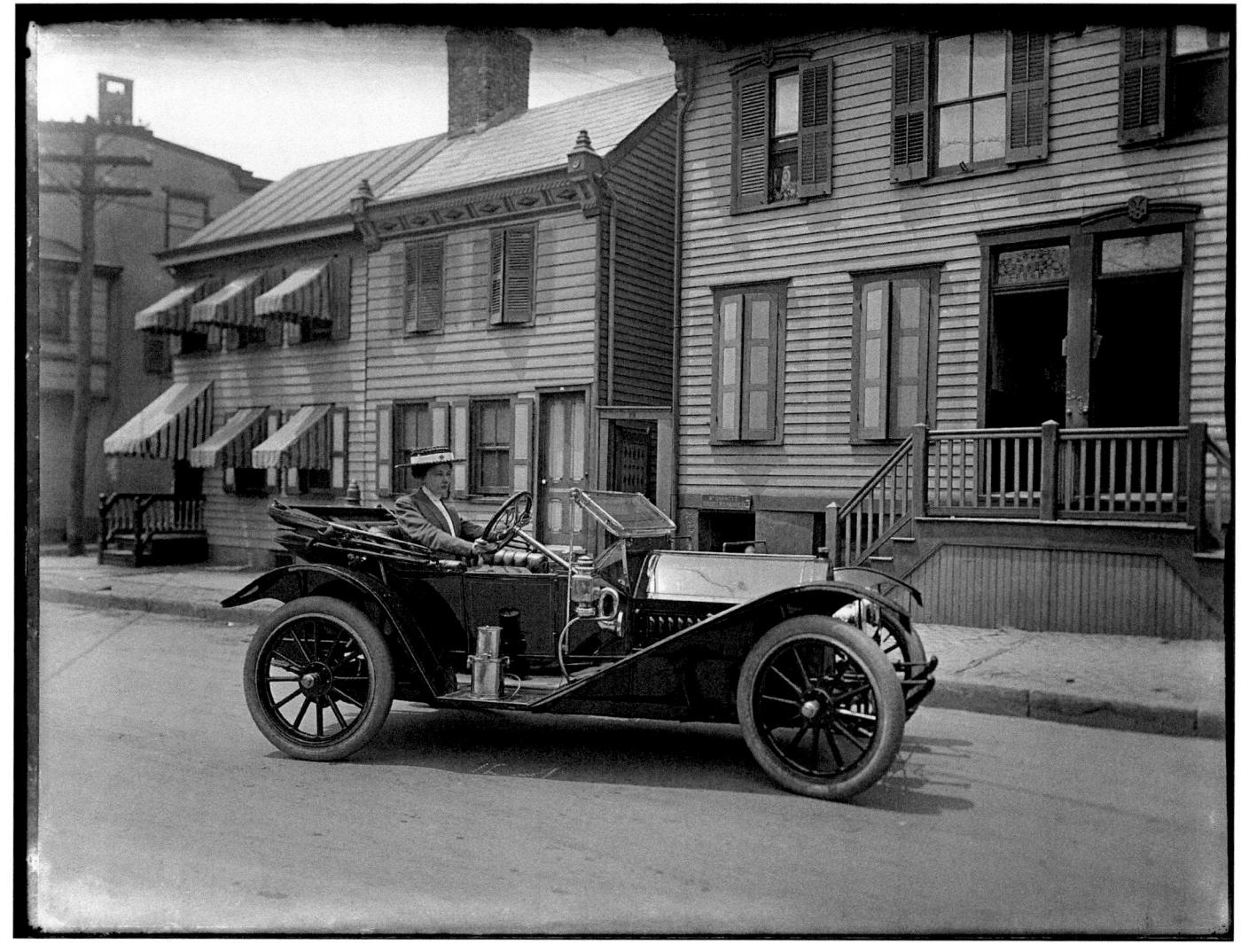

Plate 35. Unidentified woman driving an automobile, Trenton, New Jersey, c. 1912. Digital positive from 6.5" x 8.5" glass plate negative. CH2019.6.942.

New Jersey: Alice Huyler Ramsey, of Hackensack, and Harriet White Fisher, of Trenton. The automobile also became an important tool in the movement toward women's suffrage, with female drivers taking advantage of the utility offered by early automobiles to campaign for the right to vote. The name and identity of the confident female driver photographed by Castner in **plate 35** is unknown. The automobile is either a model 1912 Regal Model N Roadster or a model 1912 Regal Underslung. Based in Detroit, Regal manufactured midsized automobiles for about ten years before declaring bankruptcy.

4

Work

Grant Castner learned the value of work at a young age. At fifteen, he started his own newspaper in Belvidere. A monthly, four-page publication called *The Starry Flag*, its content included humorous anecdotes, local news, and human interest stories. He financed his paper through a monthly subscription fee and the sale of advertising space. It is no surprise that Castner went on to a career in journalism. For many years, he worked as manager of the Union News Company newsstands in central New Jersey. Castner also served as a regional sales agent for publications such as *Ladies' Home Journal* and *The Saturday Evening Post*.

Castner's career in the news industry related to much of his photography. Printed reproductions of photographs, rare before 1890, were coming into widespread use in newspapers and magazines. Many of Castner's images have a similar journalistic quality. His subjects are often immersed in the actions of their day-to-day lives, especially their work. From farmers to firefighters, Castner's glass plate collection is a tribute to the centrality of work in the lives of New Jerseyans.

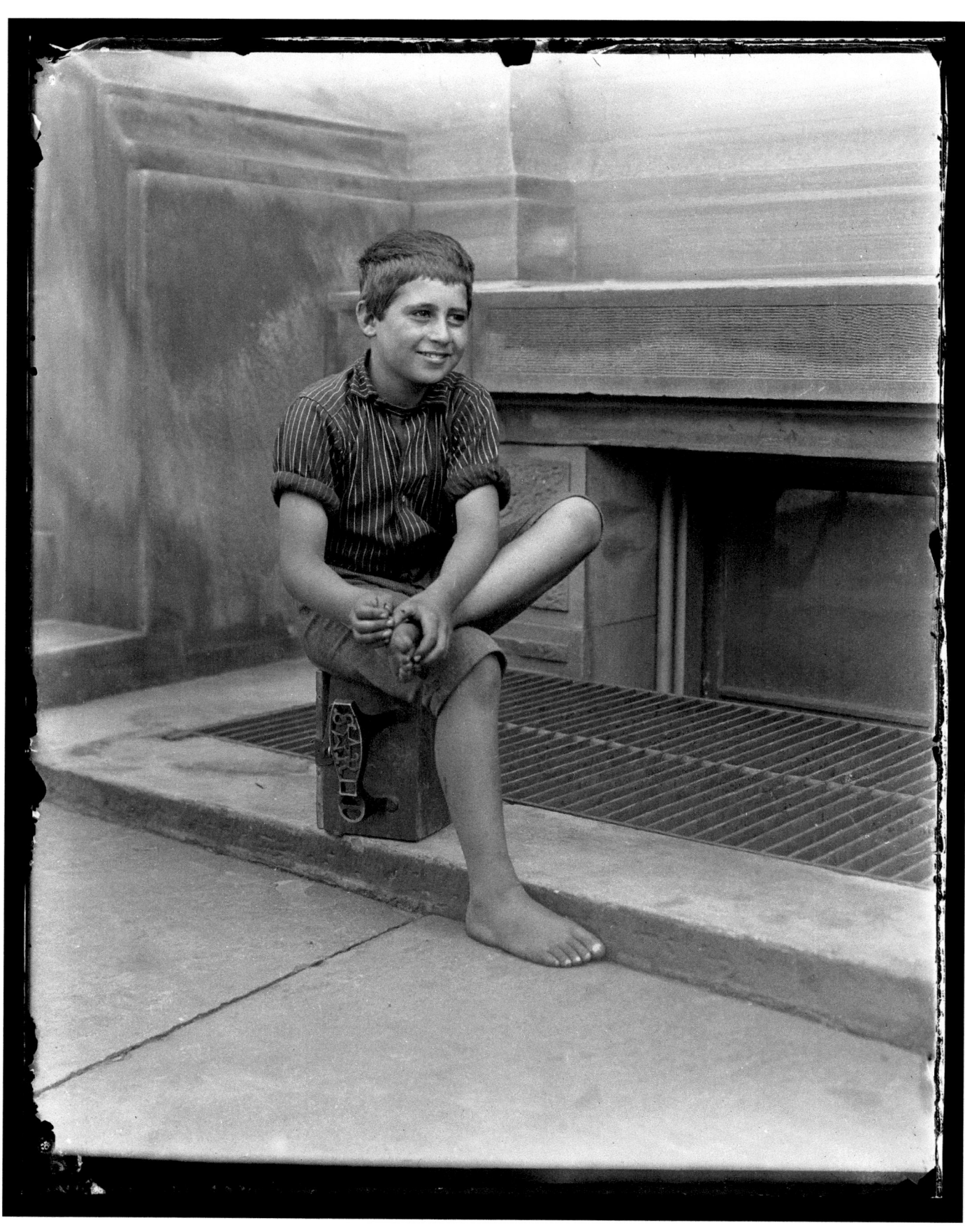

Plate 36. *Happy Again*. Shoe-shine boy, Trenton, New Jersey, 1902. Digital positive from 4" x 5" glass plate negative. CH2019.6.42.

A newspaper distributor by trade and an enthusiastic reader of popular photography magazines, Castner was surely familiar with the work of the great social documentary photographer, Lewis W. Hine (1874–1940). Initially a schoolteacher at the Ethical Culture School in New York, Hine was best known for his photographs of children, who worked in dangerous conditions for long hours and low pay, to spread a political message against the ills of child labor. Castner's close-up image of an Italian shoe-shine boy has the feel of a Lewis Hine portrait, even if minus the political undertones (**plate 36**). While it is unknown whether Castner knew Hine's photographs, he likely was influenced by *Boy with Thorn*, a well-known Greco-Roman bronze sculpture of a boy withdrawing a thorn from the heel of his foot, now in the Palazzo dei Conservatori in Rome. This image is the second of two glass plate negatives that Castner also prepared as lantern slides and shared with the public and camera club members in slideshows using a magic lantern projector. The first negative shows this same individual, head down, with an expression of pain and concern.

Castner's image of the man in **plate 37** at work may be a simple, straightforward portrait of one of his acquaintances, a shoe shiner at one of the railroad stations that the photographer regularly visited. But it may also be Castner's subtle commentary on the social and economic inequality that existed in railroad occupations. In Castner's day, railroad jobs such as engineer, conductor, and ticket agent were usually held by whites. African Americans worked primarily as porters and trackmen and in other service positions, often for the longest hours and lowest pay. The photographer's title for the image describes the work being performed. But the term *shine* also has a negative connotation. In some contexts, "shine" was used as a derogatory slur for African Americans that stemmed from the perceived lower-status jobs that they commonly

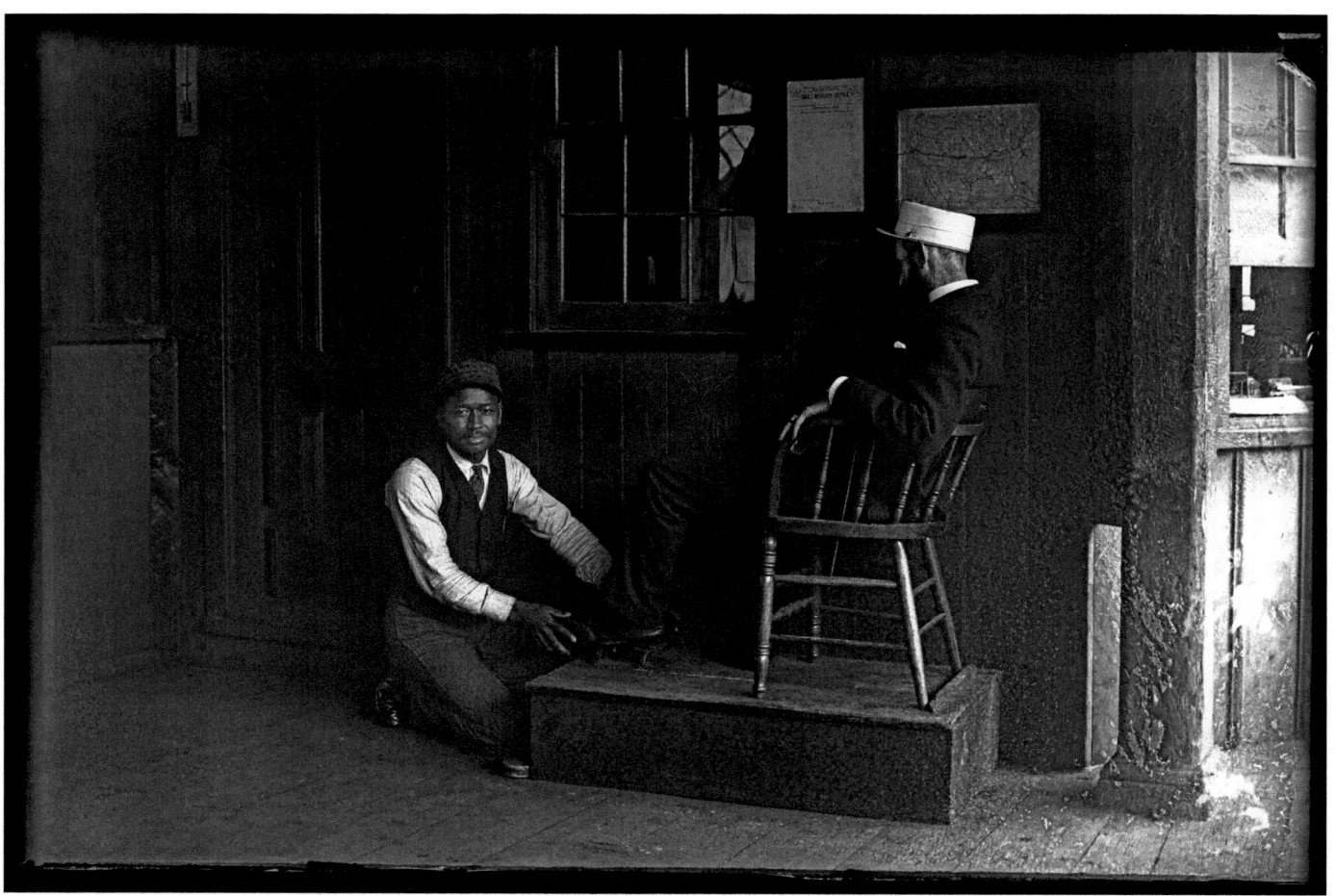

Plate 37. *Shine.* Shoeshine man, unidentified train station, New Jersey, 1890. Digital positive from 4.25" x 6.5" glass plate negative. CH2019.6.454.

held. Castner's image, however, appears to convey a sense of respect and admiration for this man and his work, rather than reducing him to a stereotypical caricature. The white cap worn by the man having his shoes shined closely resembles those worn by sleeping car porters, a common railroading job held by African Americans.

The origins and early history of the city's cracker-making industry are not entirely clear, but it is believed to have started around the time of the Civil War. Two Trentonians, Adam Exton and Ezekiel Pullen, each developed their own cracker recipes and then started to mass produce and sell their products as an accompaniment to oyster stews. By the late nineteenth century, Trenton was home to a number of cracker bakeries. Pictured in **plate 38**, Thorn and Brother was located on the southwest corner of Cooper and Factory Streets. The photo is from a collodion glass plate negative that has suffered

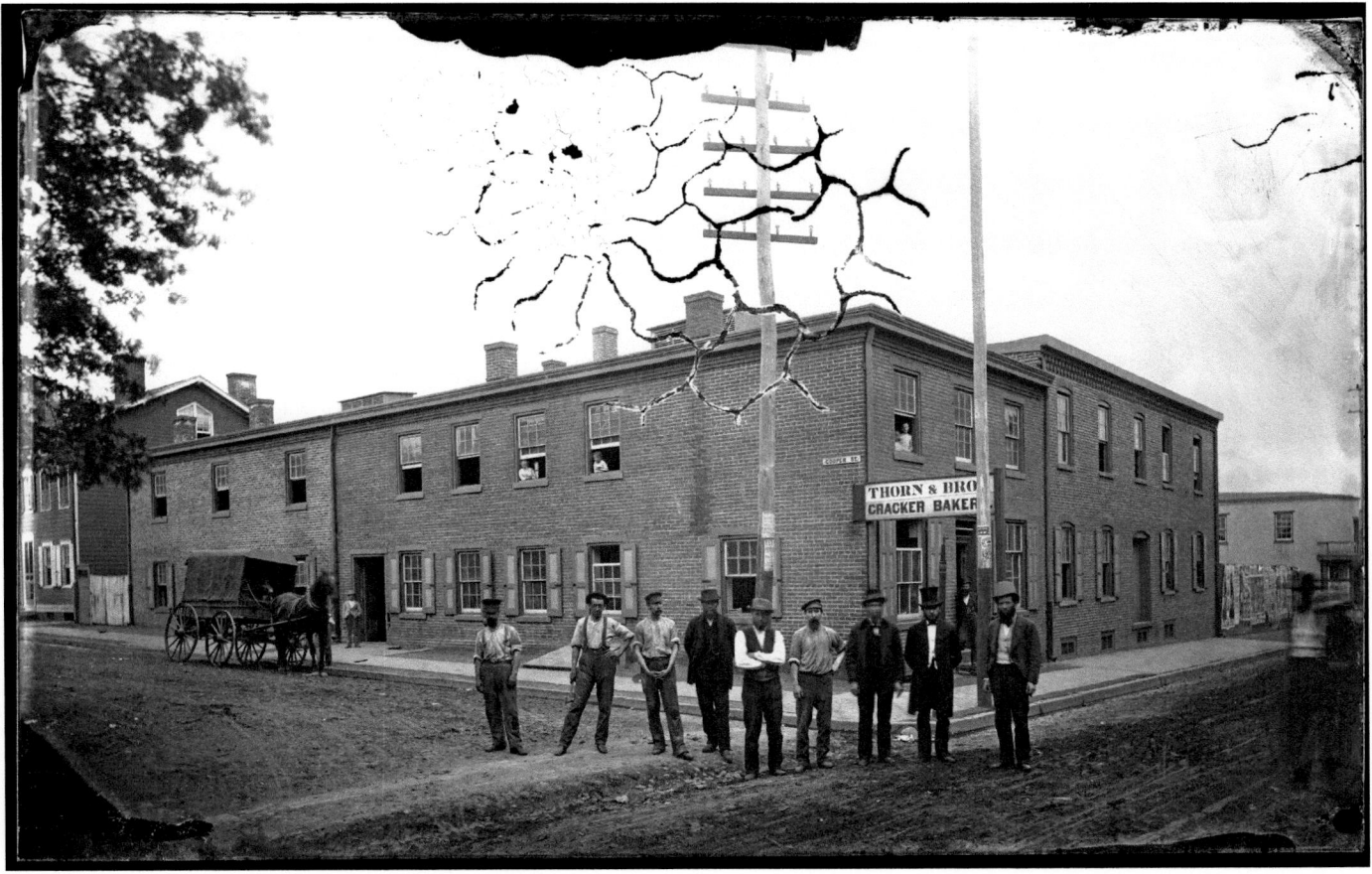

emulsion cracks, probably from exposure to high humidity. Collodion, a sticky clear liquid, was poured on the glass by the photographer and then, in near darkness, placed in a bath with a silver compound to sensitize it to light. Although some photographers used dry collodion plates for outdoor work that did not require short exposures, the vast majority used the more light sensitive wet collodion process in which the photographer had to take the photo and then develop it before the collodion dried. In about 1880, most photographers switched to the more convenient gelatin dry plate negatives, which were manufactured ready to use and could be developed any time after exposure. Because it dates so early in Castner's archive and before he moved to Trenton, it is possible that this view was taken by another photographer.

In **plate 39**, the photographer's eye was probably drawn to the whitewashed facade of the building, which stands in stark contrast to the many red brick structures that surround

Plate 38. Thorn and Brother Cracker Bakery, Trenton, New Jersey, c. 1880. Digital positive from 5" x 8" glass plate negative. CH2019.6.510.

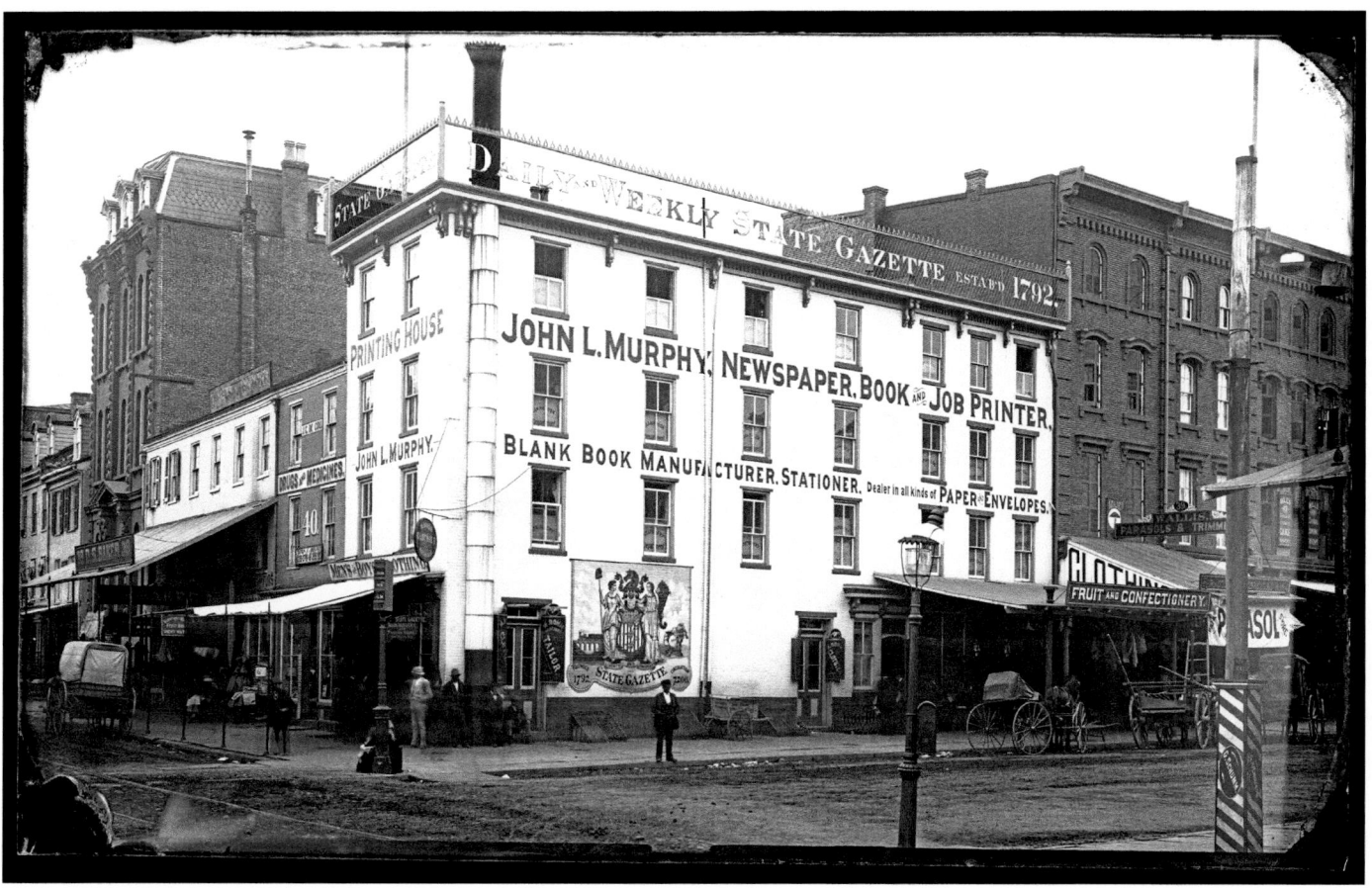

Plate 39. *State Gazette* newspaper building, Trenton, New Jersey, late 1870s. Digital positive from 5" x 8" glass plate negative. CH2019.6.508.

it. The wide-angle view captures the substantial size of the building, which was home to one of the oldest newspapers in New Jersey. The *State Gazette* building at this location on the northwest corner of Broad and State Streets went through numerous architectural changes in the late nineteenth century. The building looked as it does in the photo only from circa 1875 through 1883, when the exterior was significantly altered. Since Castner was still living in Belvidere in 1880, he likely acquired the negative later from another photographer who made it in the late 1870s. The negative is hand-coated collodion, as can be seen by the lack of image layer in the corners of the glass plate. The much more convenient gelatin dry plates adopted by photographers about 1880 were coated edge to edge by the manufacturer.

In the late 1910s, Castner placed a series of want ads in the classified section of the *Trenton Evening Times*. He was looking

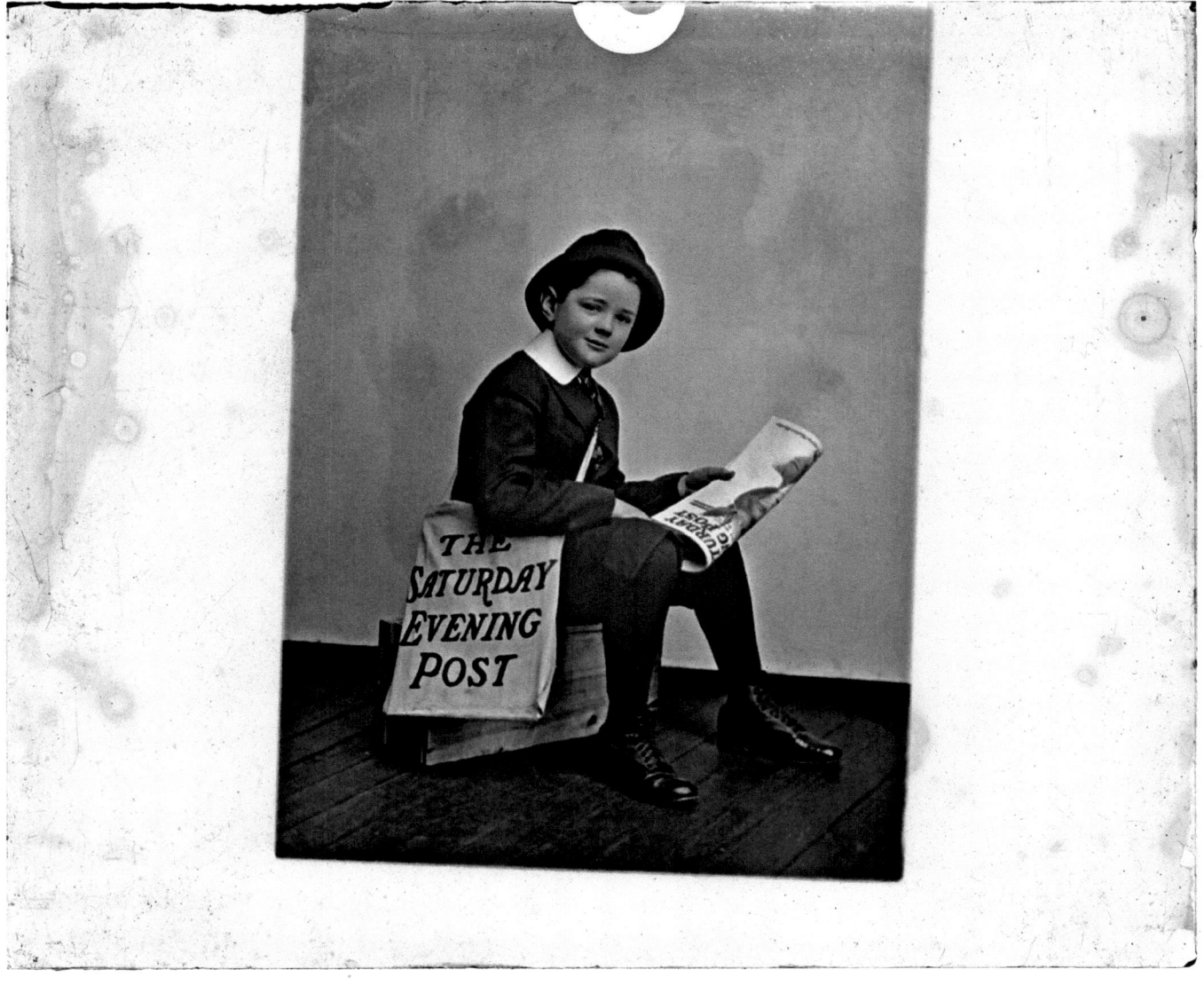

for boys between the ages of nine and fourteen to assist him in his business of distributing three popular periodicals of the day—*Country Gentlemen, Ladies' Home Journal*, and *The Saturday Evening Post*. The photograph in **plate 40** is likely of one of the boys he hired for the job. Unlike most of the items in the Grant Castner archive, this image is not a negative. It is a positive photographic image on glass that Castner probably made to use in a slideshow with a magic lantern projector.

Castner worked as a distribution agent for the Union News Company, the leading supplier of reading material for sale at the newsstands found at railroad stations all across New Jersey. His glass plate archive contains many images of the kiosks

Plate 40. News delivery boy, Trenton, New Jersey, c. 1915. Digital scan from 3.25" x 4" glass lantern slide. CH2019.6.1080.

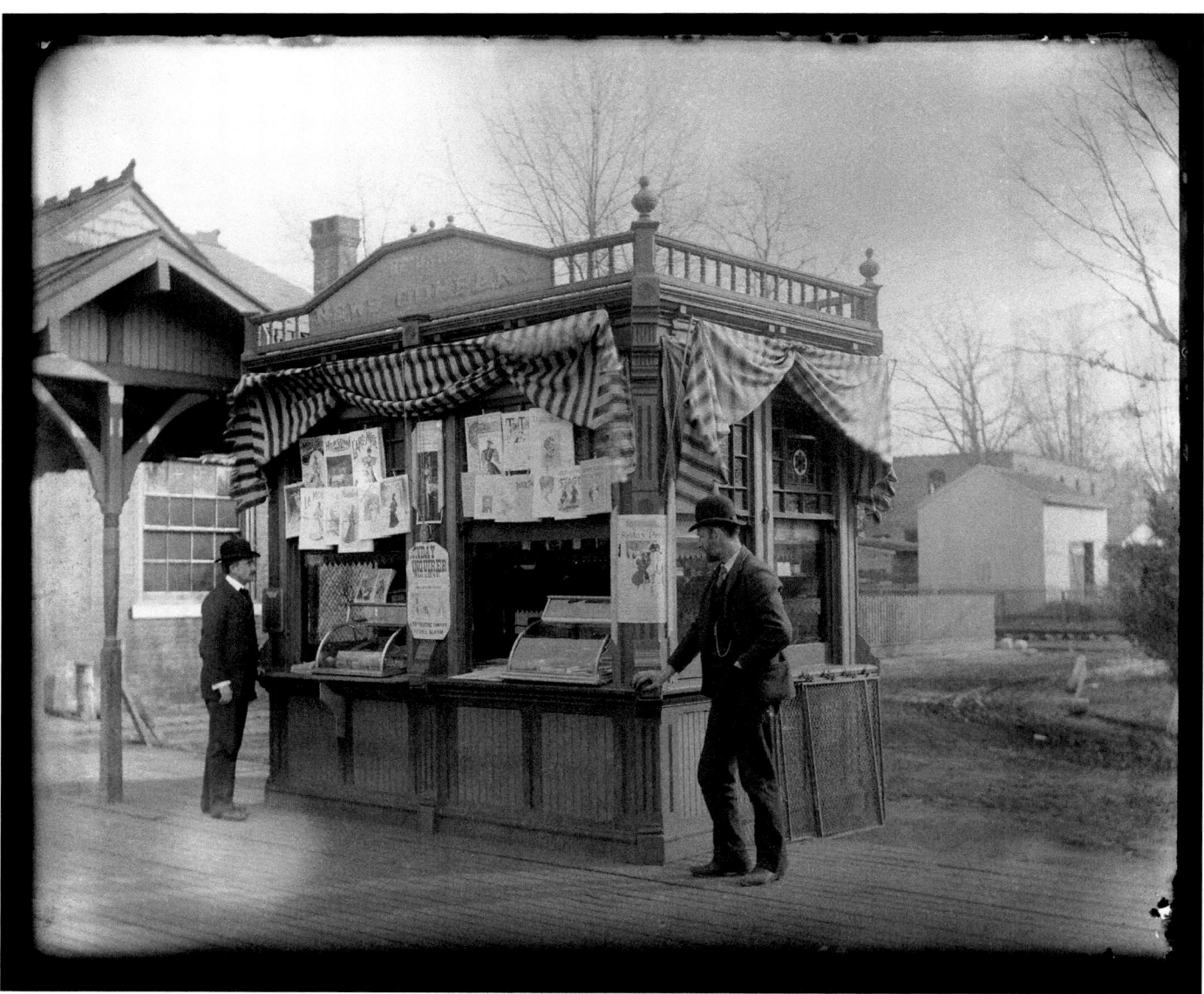

Plate 41. Union News Company newsstand, Merchantville, New Jersey, 1896. Digital positive from 4" x 5" glass plate negative. CH2019.6.97.

that he serviced and the clerks who operated them. **Plate 41** is of the newsstand adjacent to Merchantville Station, a stop on the Camden and Burlington County Railroad that connected Camden and Mount Holly. The famed Camden and Amboy Railroad and the Pennsylvania Railroad later leased the line served by the station, which was built in the 1880s. A wide variety of periodicals are displayed for sale, including *Leslie's Illustrated Weekly, McClure's, Town Topics, Sunday Inquirer Magazine,* and *L'Art de la Mode,* a popular women's fashion publication known for its large color plates featuring the latest styles. Though the news stall in this photograph is gone, the station building, which can be seen in the left of the frame, still stands.

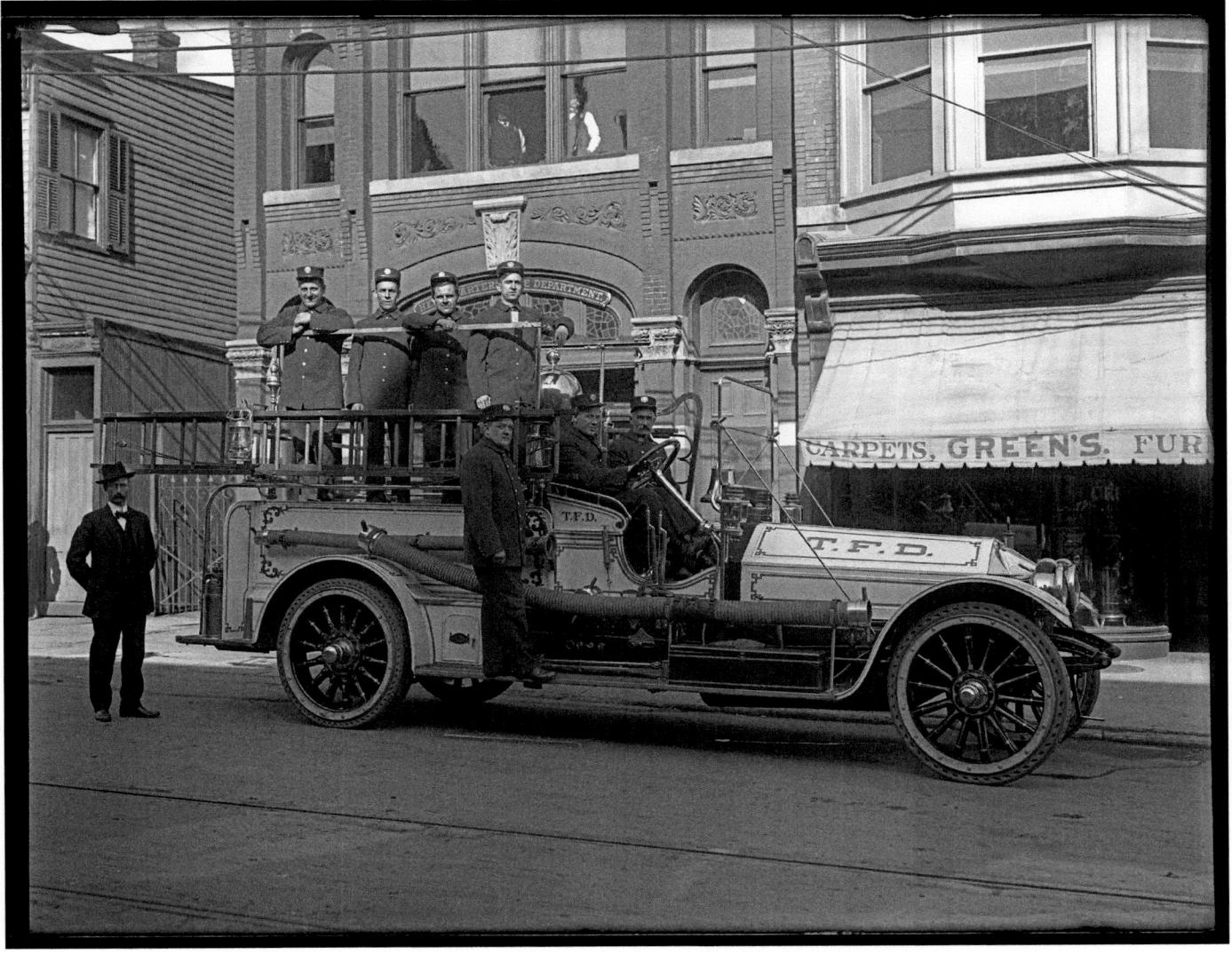

At the dawn of the automobile era, firefighters nationwide began to transition from their outdated steam-driven engines to more modern ones. Acquired by the Trenton Fire Department in 1913, the vehicle in **plate 42** is a state-of-the-art pumper made by the Webb Company of Allentown, Pennsylvania. It was capable of dispersing more than 750 gallons of water per minute. The firefighters posing with their shiny new vehicle look directly at Castner's camera, and their stern faces exude the calmness and determination demanded by their dangerous profession. One, perhaps the good-natured jokester of the bunch, flashes a wry smile. At the time of the photograph, the departmental headquarters building was located on the north side of Perry Street between Warren and Broad Streets.

Plate 42. Firefighters, Trenton Fire Department Headquarters Building, Trenton, New Jersey, 1913. Digital positive from 6.5" x 8.5" glass plate negative. CH2019.6.598.

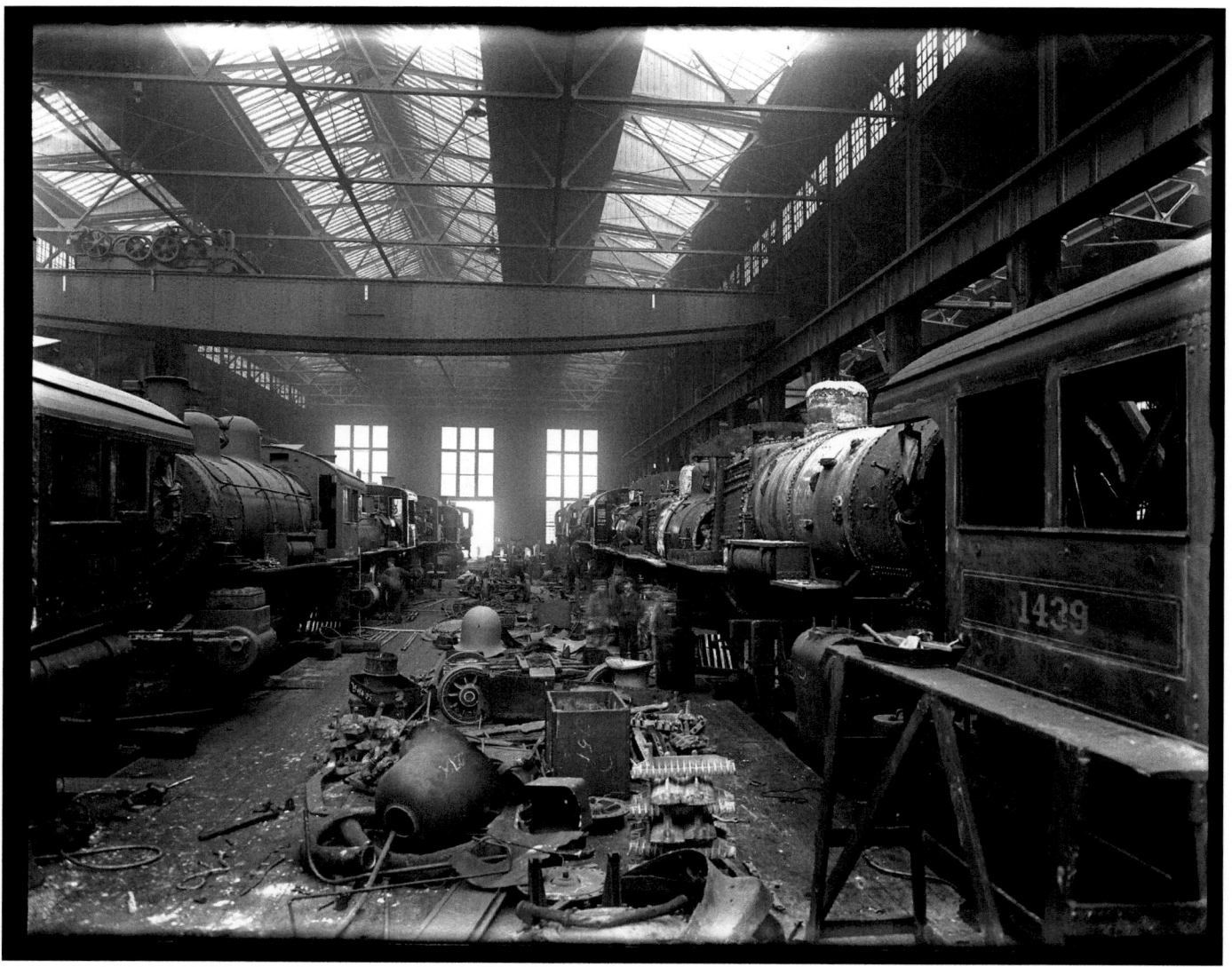

Plate 43. Employees at work, Pennsylvania Railroad Repair Shops, Hamilton Township, New Jersey, c. 1915. Digital positive from 6.5" x 8.5" glass plate negative. CH2019.6.590.

Castner's extant notes do not indicate where he took **plate 43** of workers inside a locomotive repair shop. But it is highly likely that he was visiting the Pennsylvania Railroad engine repair complex located in Hamilton Township, not far from the grounds of the Inter-State Fair that the photographer is known to have visited regularly. Two rows of locomotives angle toward the bright white light of windows in the distance, drawing the viewer's eye into the scene. Tools, equipment, and general detritus litter the scene, a suggestion that train work was messy business. To maximize the superb sharpness of detail from foreground to background on this glass plate, Castner used a small aperture on his lens, which necessitated a longer exposure and resulted in capturing the movement of the workmen.

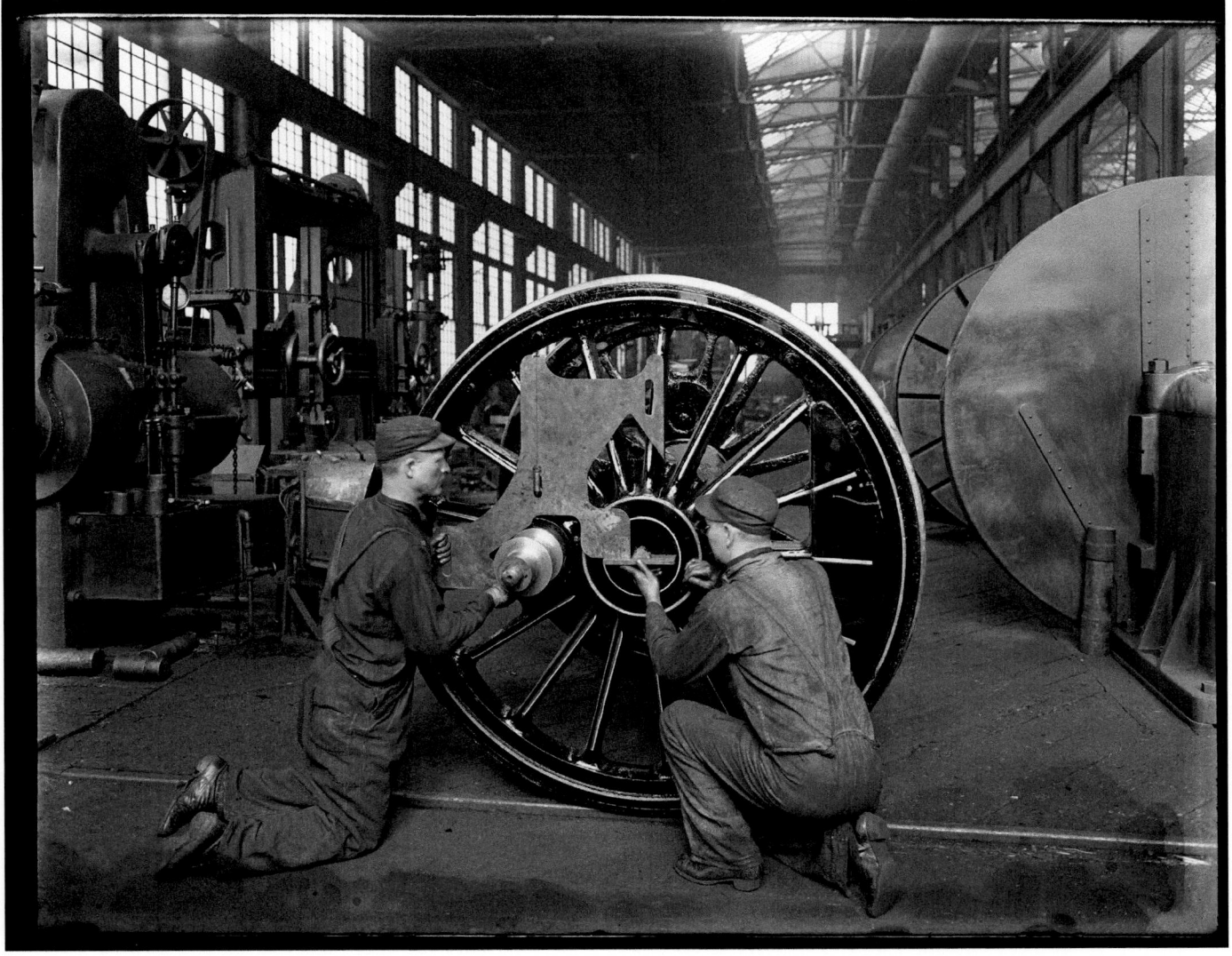

Probably taken at the Pennsylvania Railroad Repair Shops in Hamilton Township, the close-up of two men laboring on a huge locomotive wheel in **plate 44** records the highly specialized work that was required to keep engines on the tracks. The men appear to be using a large template, or jig, complete with plumb bob, to test the wheel and its crankpin. Through capturing the essence and feel of the machine age, Castner's photograph anticipates by a few years photographer Lewis Hine's well-known *Power House Mechanic* (1919), which depicts a profile view of a muscular laborer wielding a wrench, dwarfed by the large, circular-shaped metal machine on which he works. Hine's focus was on the worker turning a nut on a huge wheel, while Castner's composition depicts the full environment in which his two subjects toil.

Plate 44. Workers with engine wheel, Pennsylvania Railroad Repair Shops, Hamilton Township, New Jersey, c. 1915. Digital positive from 6.5" x 8.5" glass plate negative. CH2019.6.737.

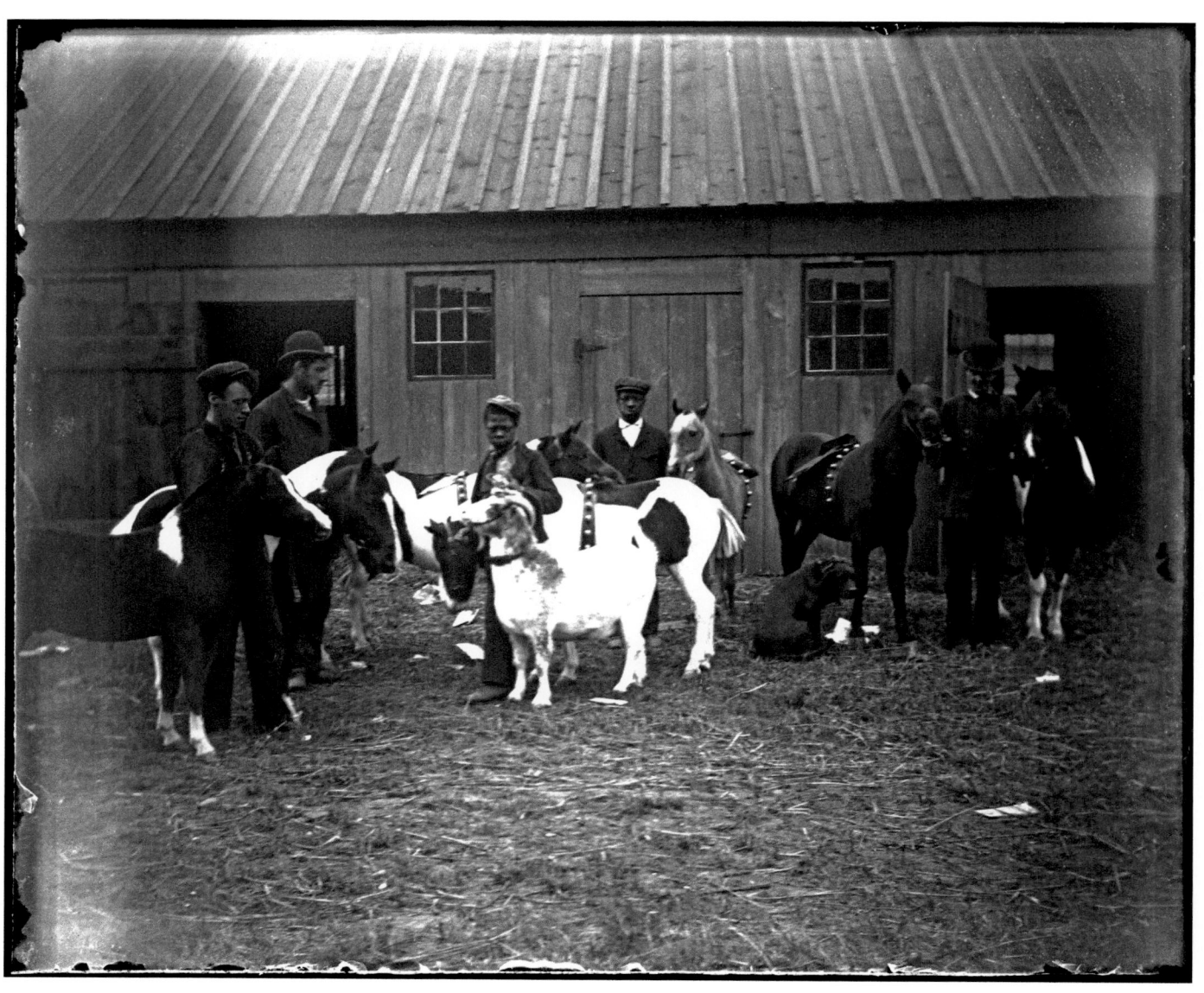

Plate 45. Stable workers, Inter-State Fair, Hamilton Township, New Jersey, 1896. Digital positive from 4" x 5" glass plate negative. CH2019.6.150.

For some, the Trenton Inter-State Fair was a day of frivolity and fun. For others, it was work. Located on the east side of the fairgrounds, a sprawling, L-shaped stable building housed the many animals that helped to make visiting the annual, multiday event a memorable experience. Castner visited the stables in 1896 and captured **plate 45** of its occupants and their handlers. Adorned with jangly sleigh bells, these sprightly ponies are set to perform as part of Morris's Pony Circus, a traveling vaudeville troupe. It is not known if the sheep at the center of the photograph was part of the show or, more likely, one of the many specimen animals exhibited in the fair's popular livestock displays. An unskilled, low-paying job that also required long hours, the work of

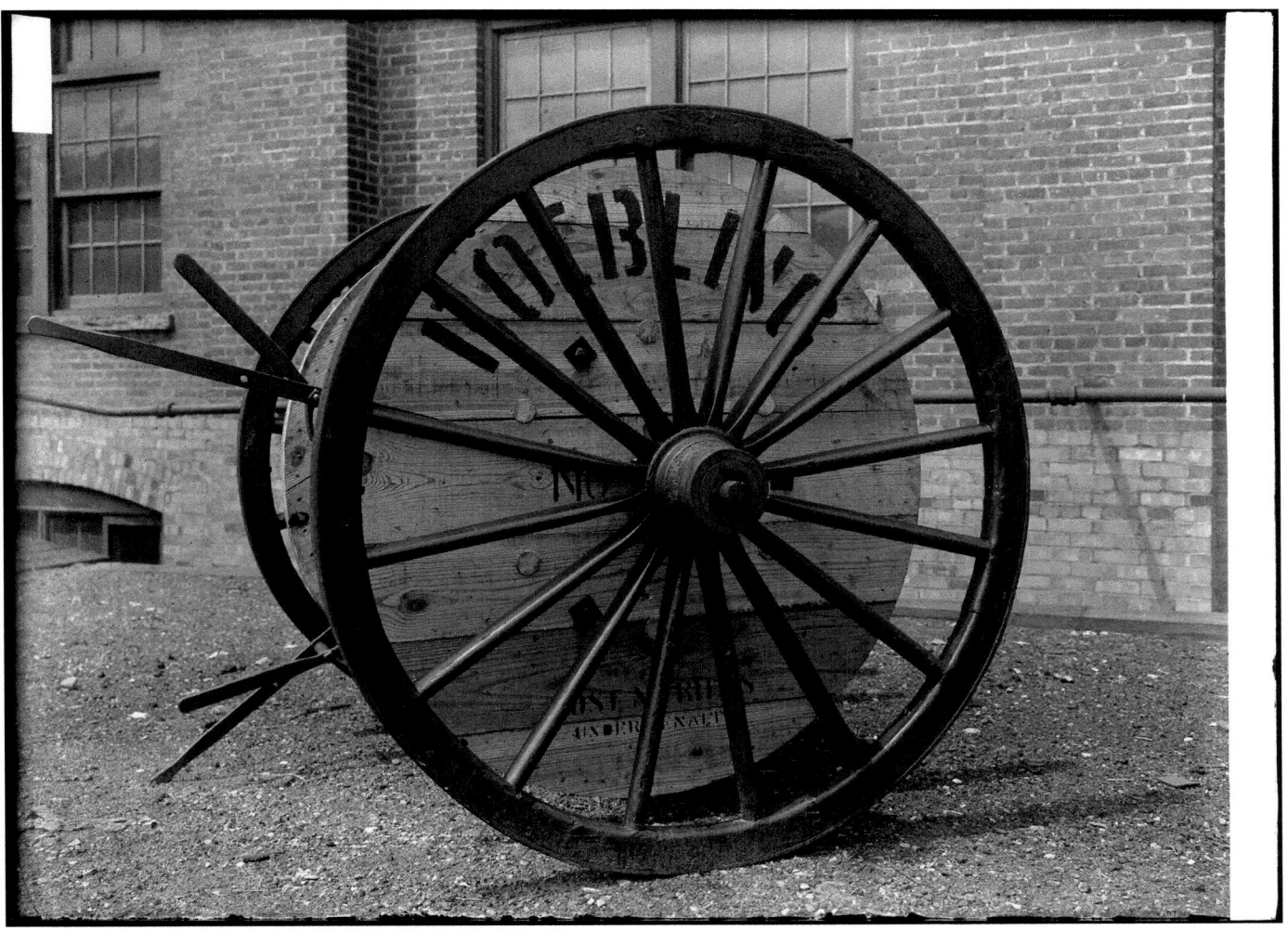

stable hands involved cleaning stalls, feeding and watering animals, and ensuring their safe and timely transit to and from fair activities.

An immigrant from Prussia, John Augustus Roebling (1806–1869) came to the United States in 1831 and soon developed a novel idea: twisting wire to create rope-like cables capable of supporting large suspension bridges. Roebling, who moved to Trenton in 1848, proposed using his wire rope technology to build the Brooklyn Bridge but died from an accident during the planning. The construction, begun in 1870, was completed by his son and daughter-in-law in 1883. Following the family patriarch's death, Roebling's descendants grew the company into a major American manufacturer and important regional employer. Castner visited the Roebling Works in Trenton and captured the rare image of a carriage

Plate 46. Wire rope spool carriage, John A. Roebling's Sons Company, Trenton, New Jersey, c. 1905. Digital positive from 5" x 7" glass plate negative. CH2019.6.767.

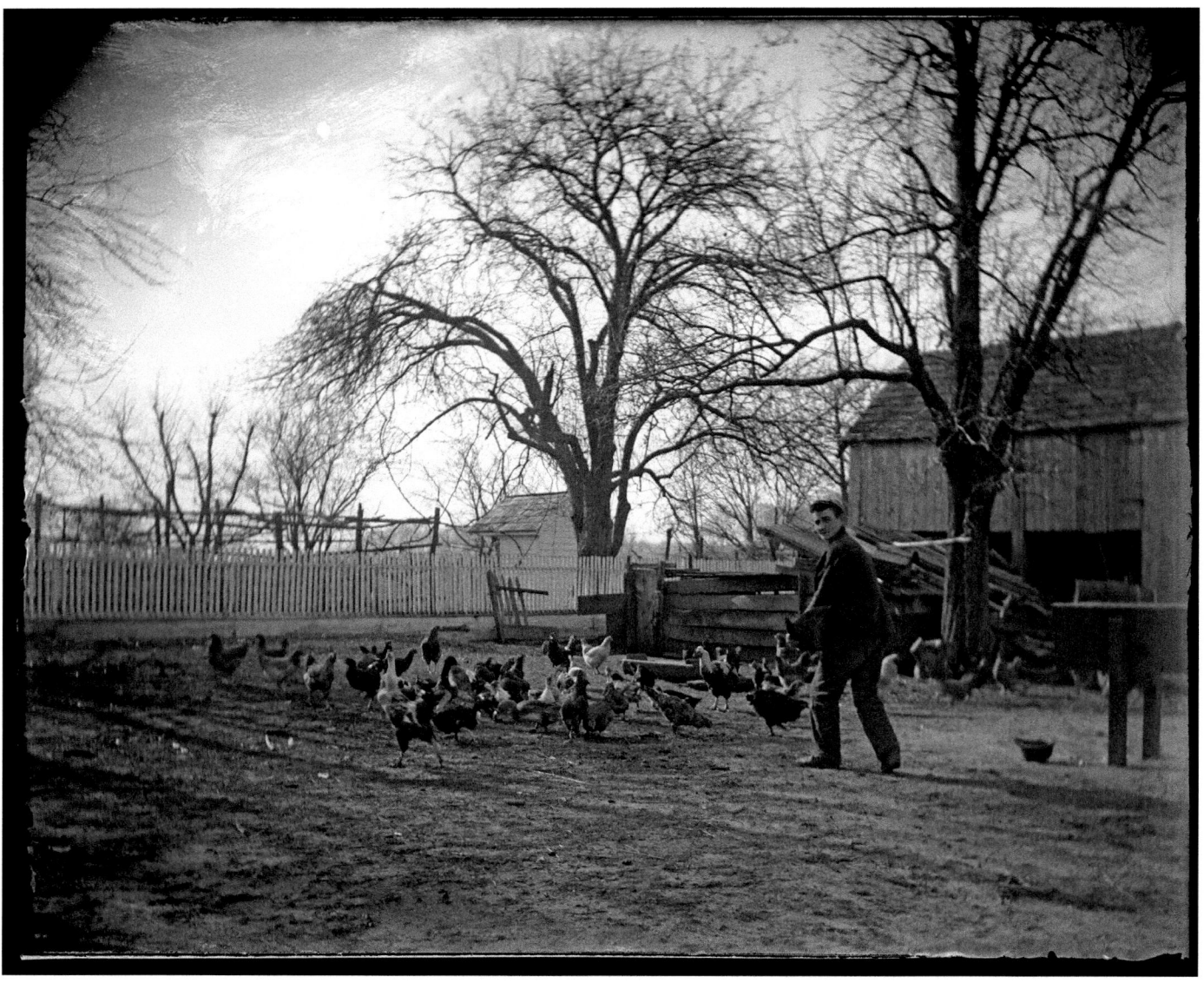

Plate 47. *Scattering Feed.* Farmer at work, New Jersey, 1895. Digital positive from 4" x 5" glass plate negative. CH2019.6.293.

used to move a reel of wire rope around a job site (**plate 46**). The hand bars are brakes that would secure the carriage in a stationary position when unwinding rope from the reel. The lettering at the bottom reads "Post No Bills, Under Penalty" so that the reel could be returned to Roebling for reuse. In photographing this device, Castner made a respectful homage to both the simple beauty of functional, industrial design and the significance of the Roebling name to his city and state. The location is either Roebling's Upper Works on Broad Street or the Lower Works on Jersey Avenue.

A startled look of surprise suggests that the unidentified man in **plate 47** may have been unaware of Castner's presence until the last second, perhaps immersed in his morning's work

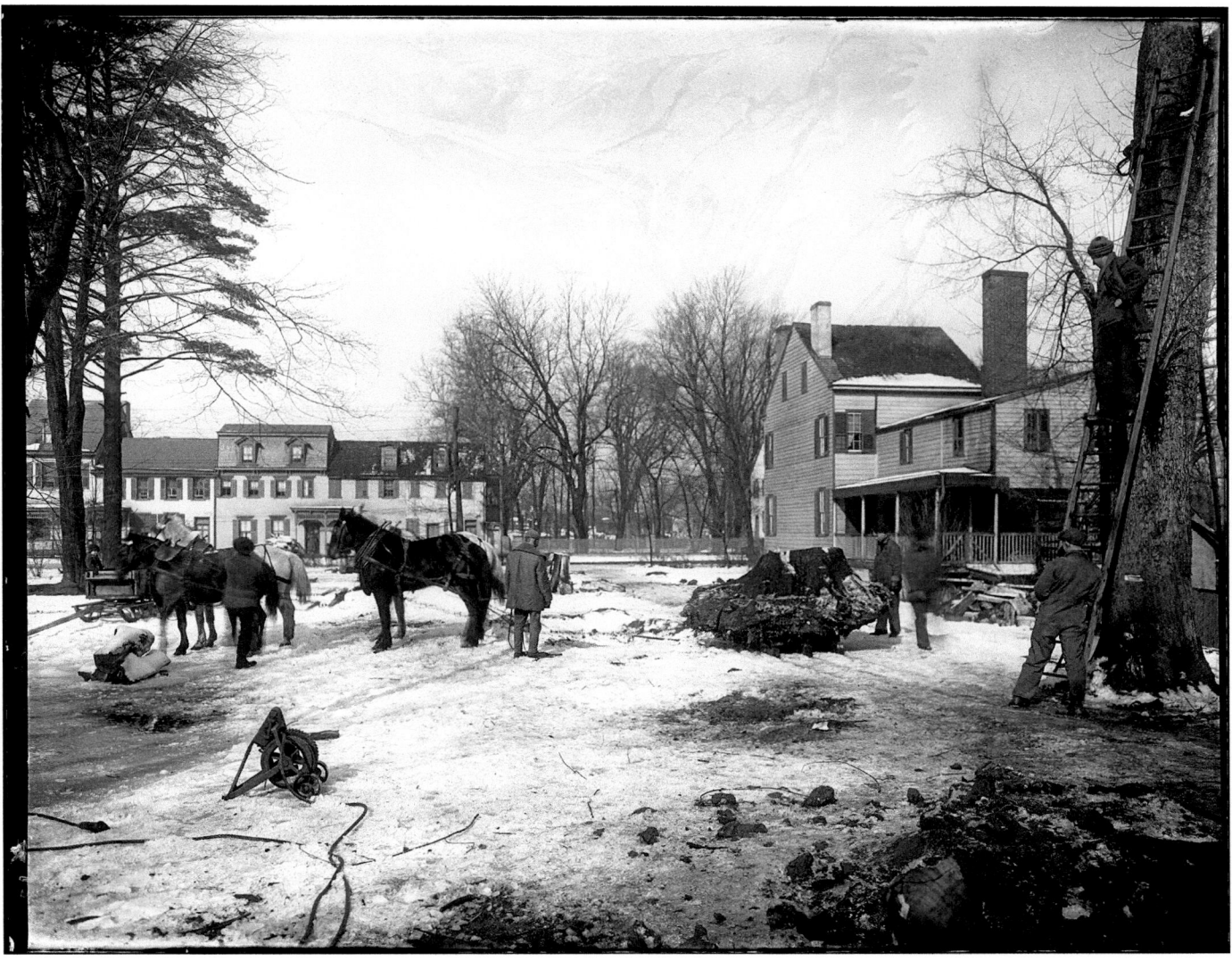

feeding the livestock. The barn, picket fence, and rural back-ground suggest that the location is likely a farm somewhere in central New Jersey. Though nicknamed "Garden State," New Jersey's economy in 1895 was no longer exclusively dominated by agriculture as it had been in earlier generations. However, farming was still an important endeavor. In South Jersey, cranberry bogs and tomato fields were important agribusi-nesses, with the latter supplying the famed Campbell's Soup Company based in Camden. Smaller family farms throughout the state also provided many New Jersey families with their livelihood.

The action-packed image in **plate 48** is a testament to the raw might and historical importance of New Jersey's offi-cial state animal, the horse. At an unknown location, a team

Plate 48. Stump-pulling, New Jersey, c. 1900. Digital positive from 6.5" x 8.5" glass plate negative. CH2019.6.835.

of workhorses prepare to haul away the massive stump of a felled tree. Throughout New Jersey, people relied on the power of horses in all stages of agriculture—from the stump pulling needed to prepare fields for planting to the pulling of the plows that tilled the soil. Horses were equally important in urban areas. They transported citizens to work and pulled fire engines. They hauled garbage and waste. They moved construction materials. They were living machines. This scene depicts the use of horses in tree work. Possibly a tree trimmer, the worker perched high on a ladder seems to marvel at the raw power of his equine coworkers. Today, New Jersey is renowned for its many horse farms, a testament to the continuing significance of horses to the cultural fabric and identity of the Garden State. In 1900, there were more than one hundred thousand horses in New Jersey; less than half that quantity are in the state today.

In 1895, Castner traveled to Monmouth County and took photographs of a quintessential New Jersey industry: the making of apple jack brandy. His series documents a still house (**plate 49**) in Upper Freehold Township operated by George Cross and, later, by Henry Stewart. The term *apple jack* refers to a traditional freeze-distillation method of production in which fermented cider was frozen and the ice removed, resulting in a higher alcohol content. The drink became known as "Jersey Lightning" due to its historical connections to the Garden State, which first produced it in the colonial period. By the time of World War I, apple jack was still so interconnected with New Jersey that the soldiers of the 78th Infantry Regiment, which was organized at Camp Dix in Burlington County, voted "Lightning Division" as their unit's nickname. It is not known if the smiling women caught in the act of siphoning apple jack from a cask are employees or family members. But their enjoyment of the Jersey beverage is forever preserved by Castner's heartwarming image.

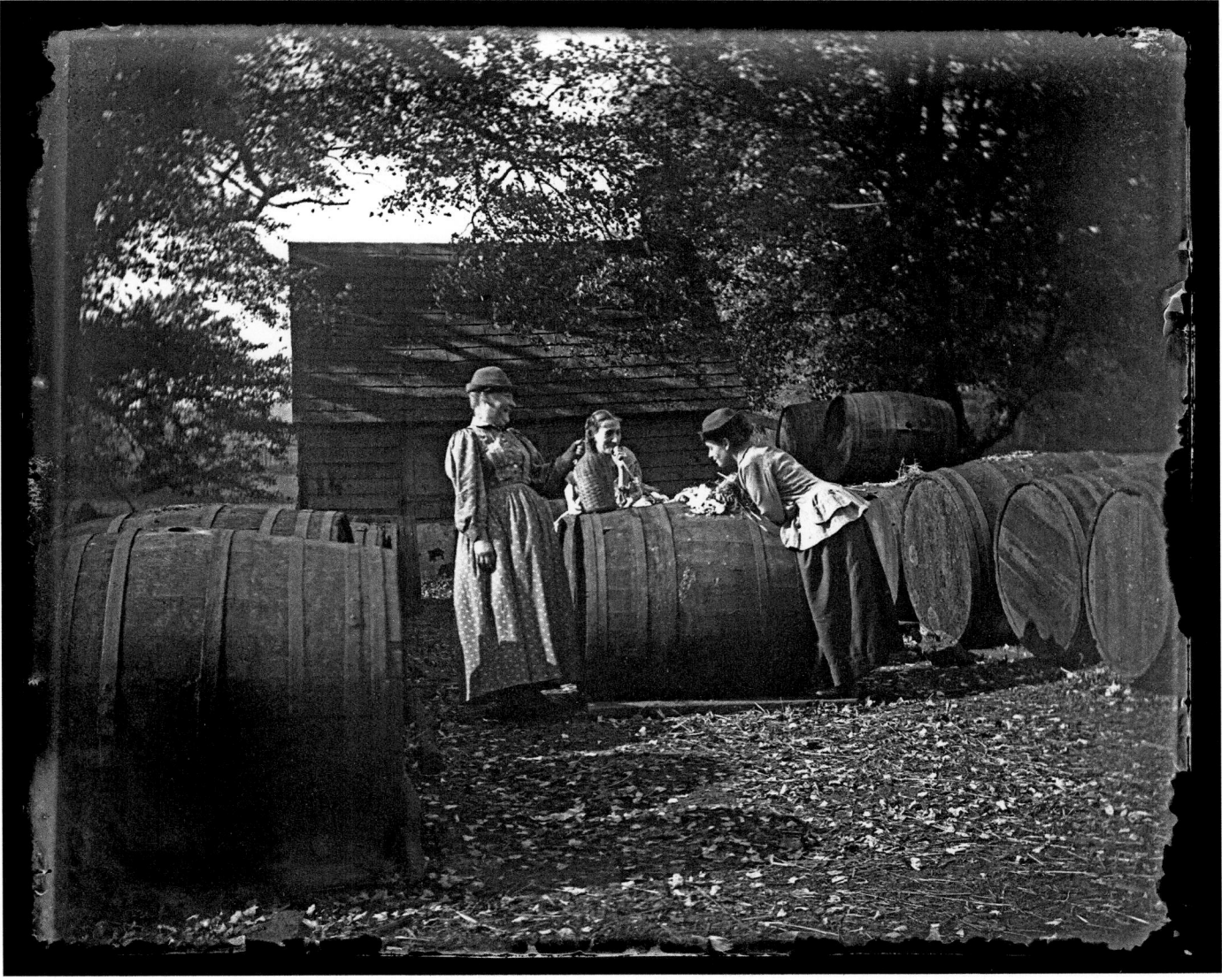

The Grant Castner archive primarily consists of glass plate negatives. However, it also contains some pieces of ephemera and a small number of photographic prints. The silver gelatin print in **plate 50** is one of a series of photographic images depicting the charcoal industry. To make charcoal, industry workers set up temporary camps in the forest to fell trees, collect the wood, and construct charcoal "pits." Charcoal was made by building a large, domed structure of wood and topping it with sections of sod to make it airtight. A fire was set at the base and left to burn slowly for eight to ten days while being monitored by the smoke escaping from a central

Plate 49. *Tapping the Barrel.* Three women with cask at the Cross distillery, Ellisdale, New Jersey, 1895. Digital positive from 4" x 5" glass plate negative. CH2019.6.222.

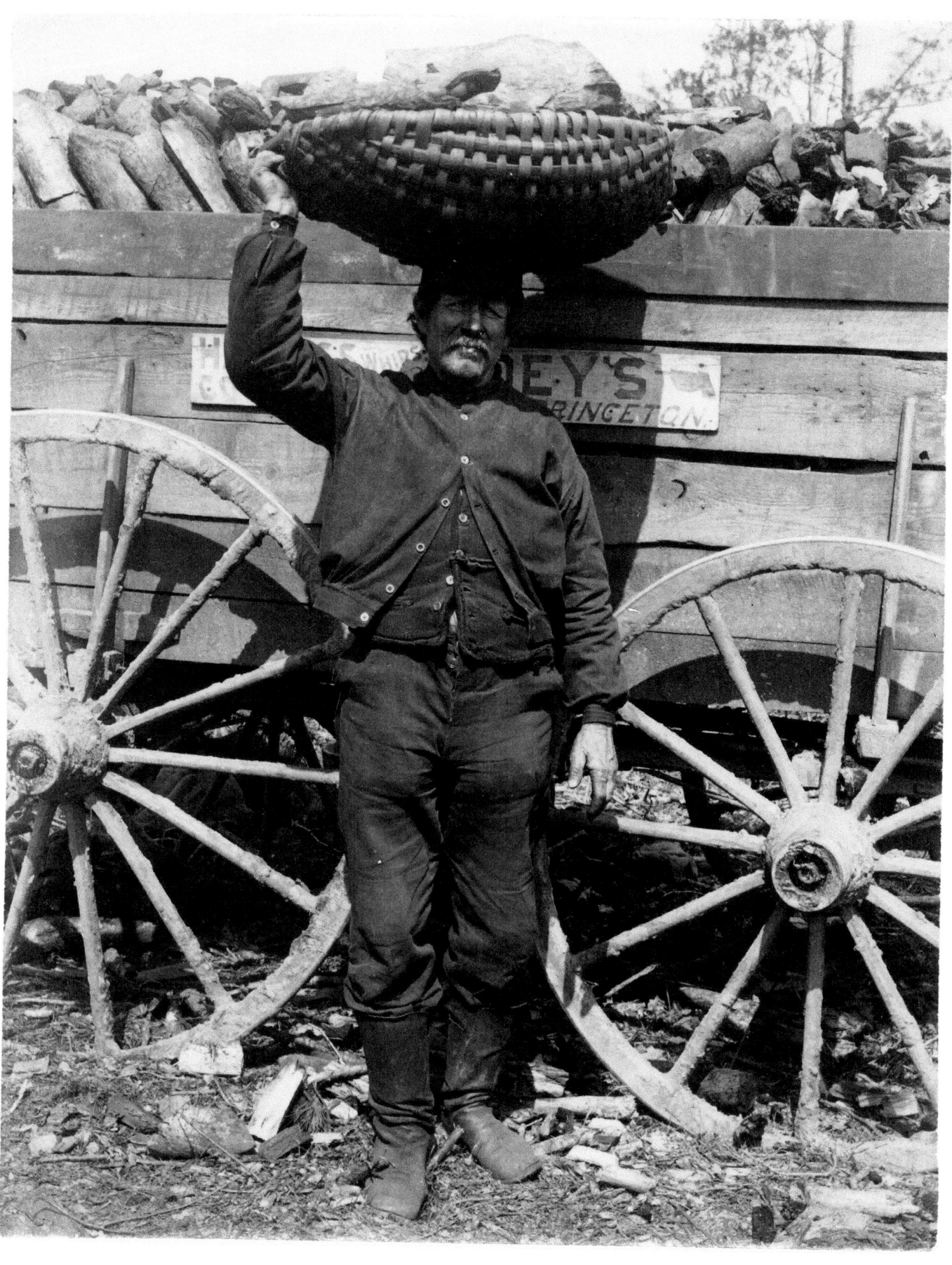

Plate 50. Worker carrying charcoal basket, Ocean County, New Jersey, c. 1900. Digital scan from 3.5" x 4.5" silver gelatin print. CH2019.6.1127.

chimney. When the burn was complete, workers raked the finished charcoal out of the pit and used uniquely shaped charcoal baskets and wagons to transport this important fuel source to regional markets.

5

Youth

Some of Grant Castner's most memorable images are those documenting children and schools. His photographs of the exteriors of urban and rural schoolhouses included the Carroll Robbins School in Trenton and the Columbia and Lanning schools in Ewing Township. He also ventured inside and preserved unusual views of students at their desks—shots that may have been work for hire once the amateur began to self-identify as a professional photographer. Castner also took pictures of children learning the value of hard work at community gardens and lemonade stands. But his best images of New Jersey's youth are of children doing what children do best: play.

Castner's lifetime coincided with a movement toward widespread public education in New Jersey. From 1852 to 1854, Clara Barton taught at the state's first free public school in Bordentown, and some other towns soon followed. In 1875, New Jersey passed a constitutional amendment that called for "thorough and efficient education for children between the ages of five and eighteen." The amendment led to an effort to build more schools, train more teachers, and remove financial barriers to education. Castner's camera documented schoolchildren during this period of educational reform. His work also recorded the racially segregated schools that still dotted the New Jersey scholastic landscape.

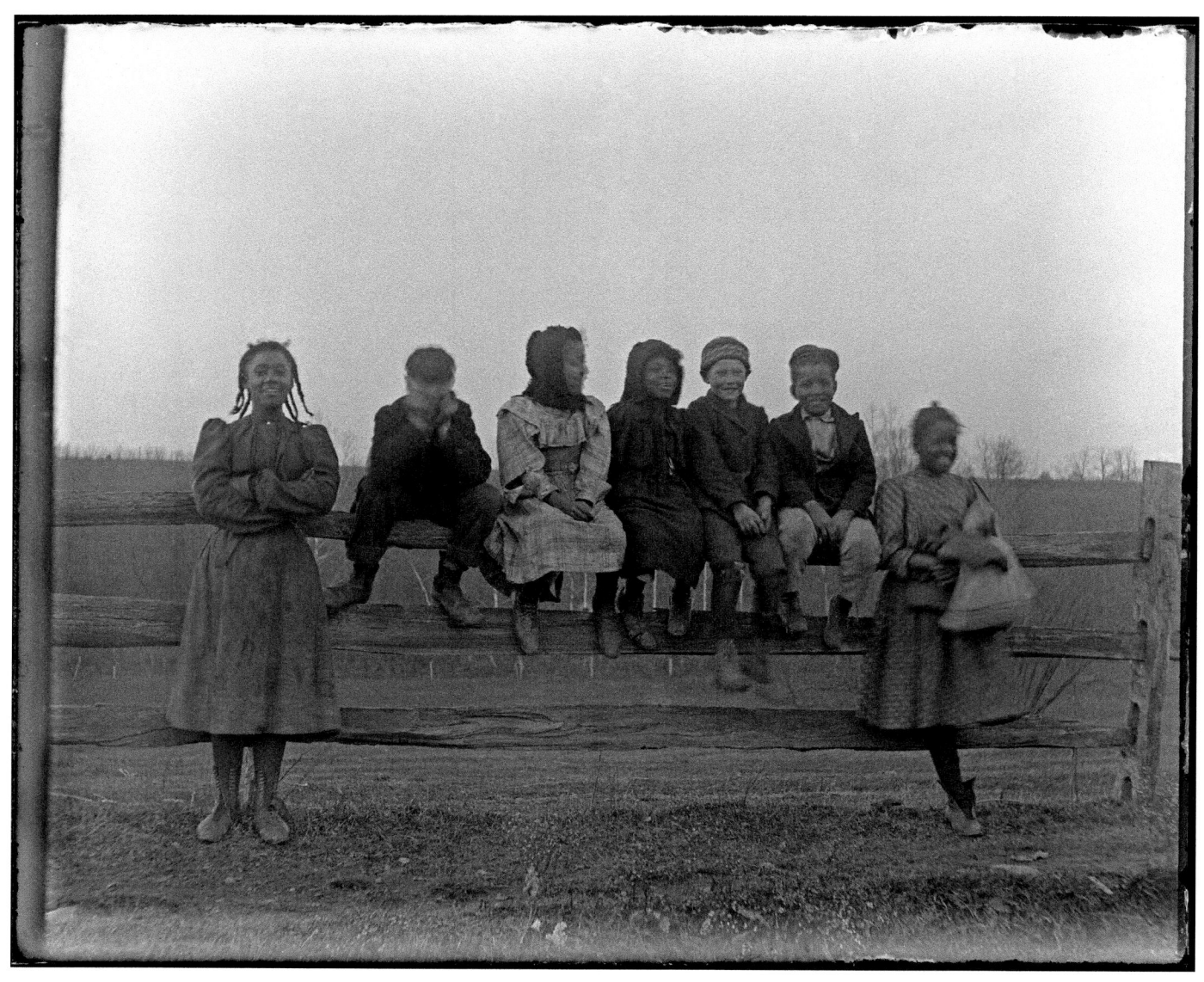

Plate 51. Children on fence, near Jacobs Creek, Ewing Township, New Jersey, 1899. Digital positive from original 4" x 5" glass plate negative. CH2019.6.437.

The joyful pleasures of youth and the bonds of neighborhood friendships are on full view in Castner's uplifting image of children on a fence in their rural New Jersey community (**plate 51**). The photographer carefully posed his subjects with the older girls standing at either end and the younger kids seated in the middle, forming a pleasant, arc-shaped composition. The faces of the children, probably neighbors, suggest the multicultural make up of New Jersey, then as now. Perhaps distracted by their friends, some of the kids shift and squirm on their perch. Unable to sit still for the camera, their movements are captured as blurs in Castner's negative. The raised shoulders and big sleeves worn by the girl on the left were still

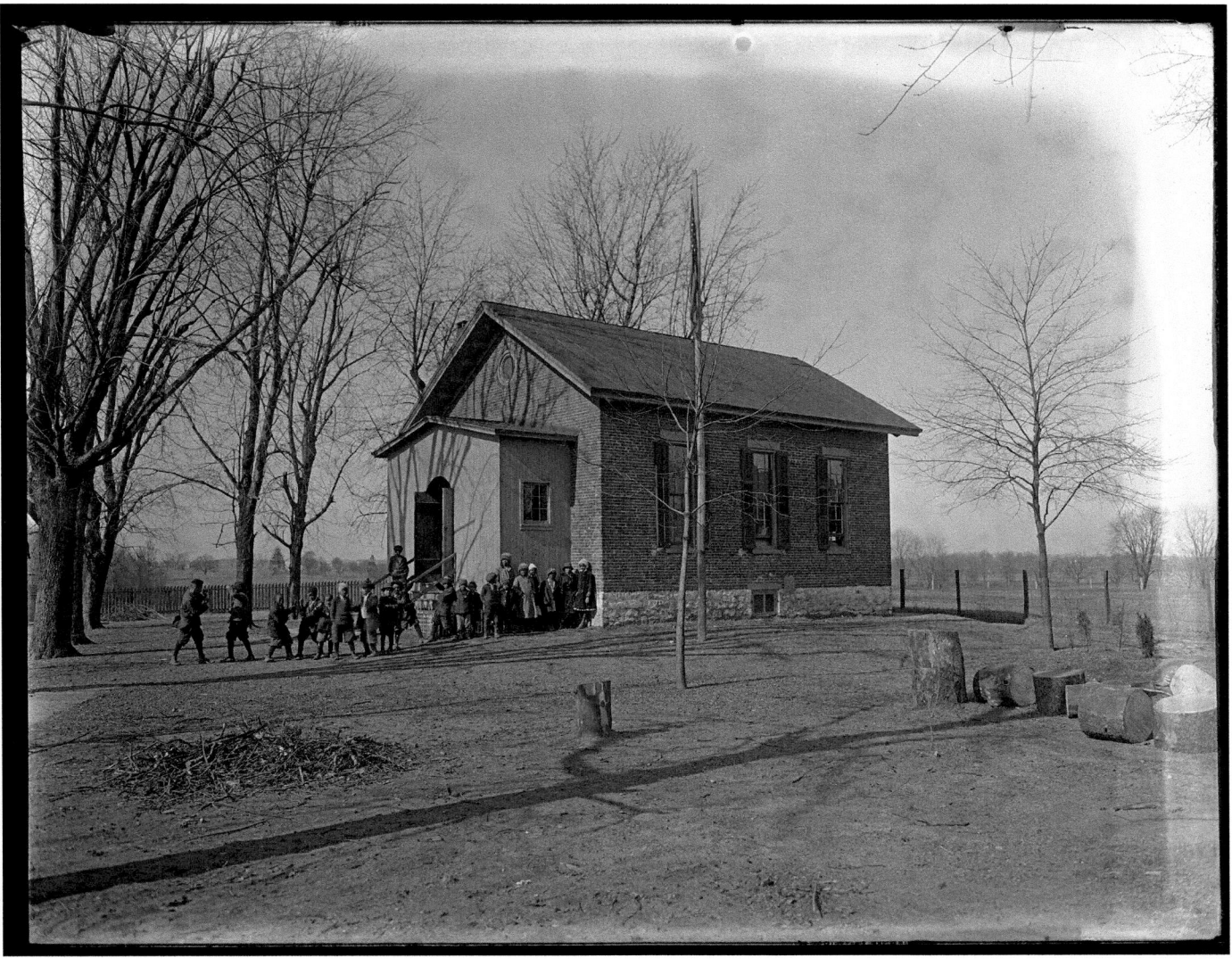

in fashion in the late 1890s, although their sizes had diminished since peaking about 1895.

The Columbia School (**plate 52**) stood on the west side of Pennington Avenue near the modern-day intersection with Parkside Avenue. Castner photographed the school at a time of controversy. As reported in the *Trenton Evening Times*, the newer, modern Lanning School had just opened a few miles north on Pennington Road. While white students living near the Columbia School were transported by wagon to the new Lanning School, African American children living in the same neighborhood were compelled to walk to the old school. Castner captured the faces of these latter students as they congregated in the schoolyard of the Columbia School. The girls, on

Plate 52. Columbia School, Ewing Township, New Jersey, c. 1915. Digital positive from 6.5" x 8.5" glass plate negative. CH2019.6.591.

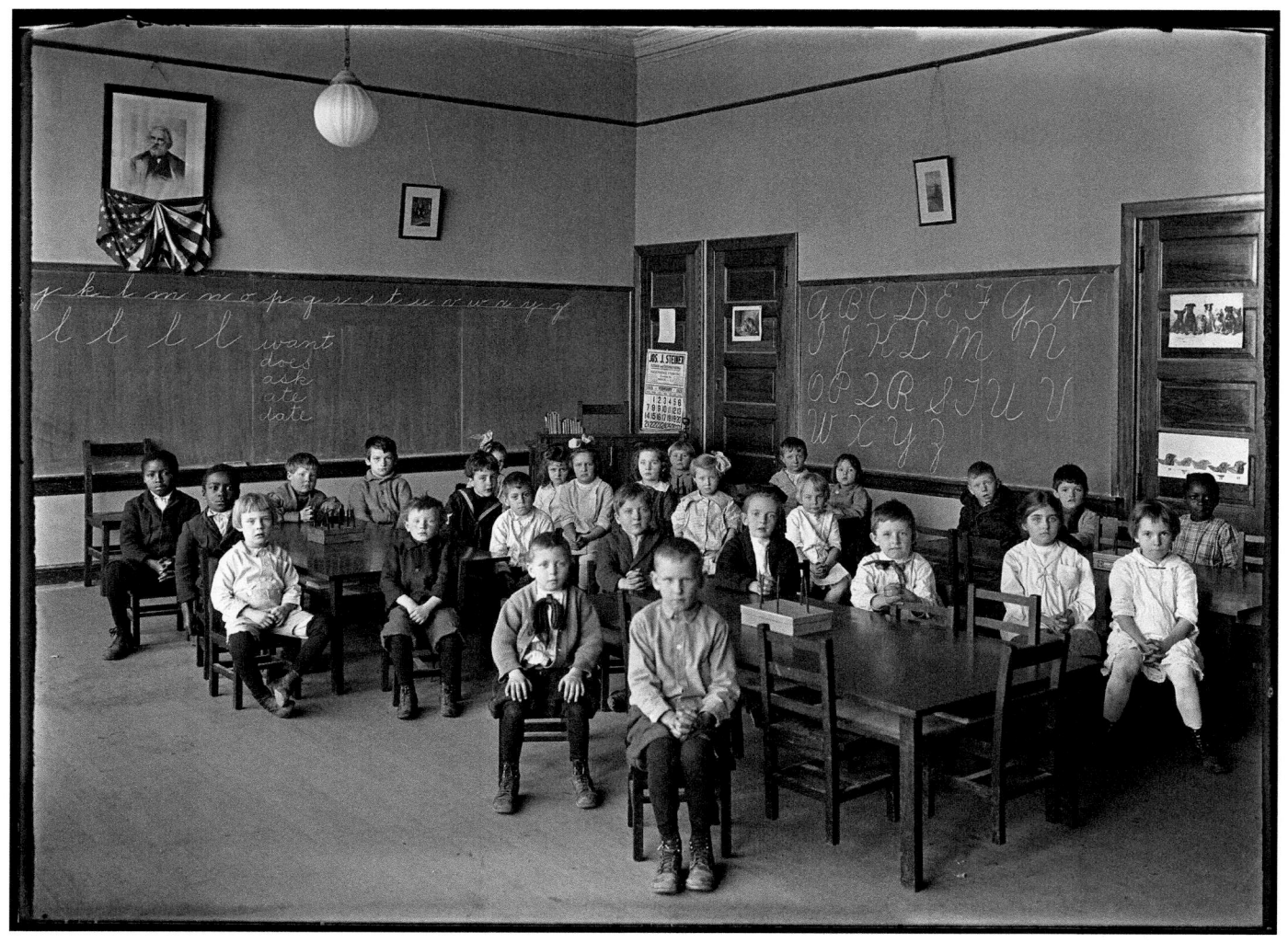

Plate 53. Students at tables, Lanning School, Ewing Township, New Jersey, 1915. Digital positive from 5" x 7" glass plate negative. CH2019.6.759.

the right, stand stoically, while the boys ham it up for the camera by emulating their favorite boxers. The Columbia School eventually closed, and its students attended the Lanning School. Castner may have photographed the school in winter when the lack of leaves enabled a better view of the building. The long shadows of the trees suggest that it was taken in the morning.

It is not certain where Castner took **plate 53**, but it was most likely in a classroom at the recently built Lanning School in Ewing Township. Named for local Judge William Mershon Lanning, this highly anticipated modern school opened in 1914 as part of an effort to replace the outdated schoolhouses of previous years. Castner's crisp, richly detailed photograph is a remarkable time capsule of student life in New Jersey in

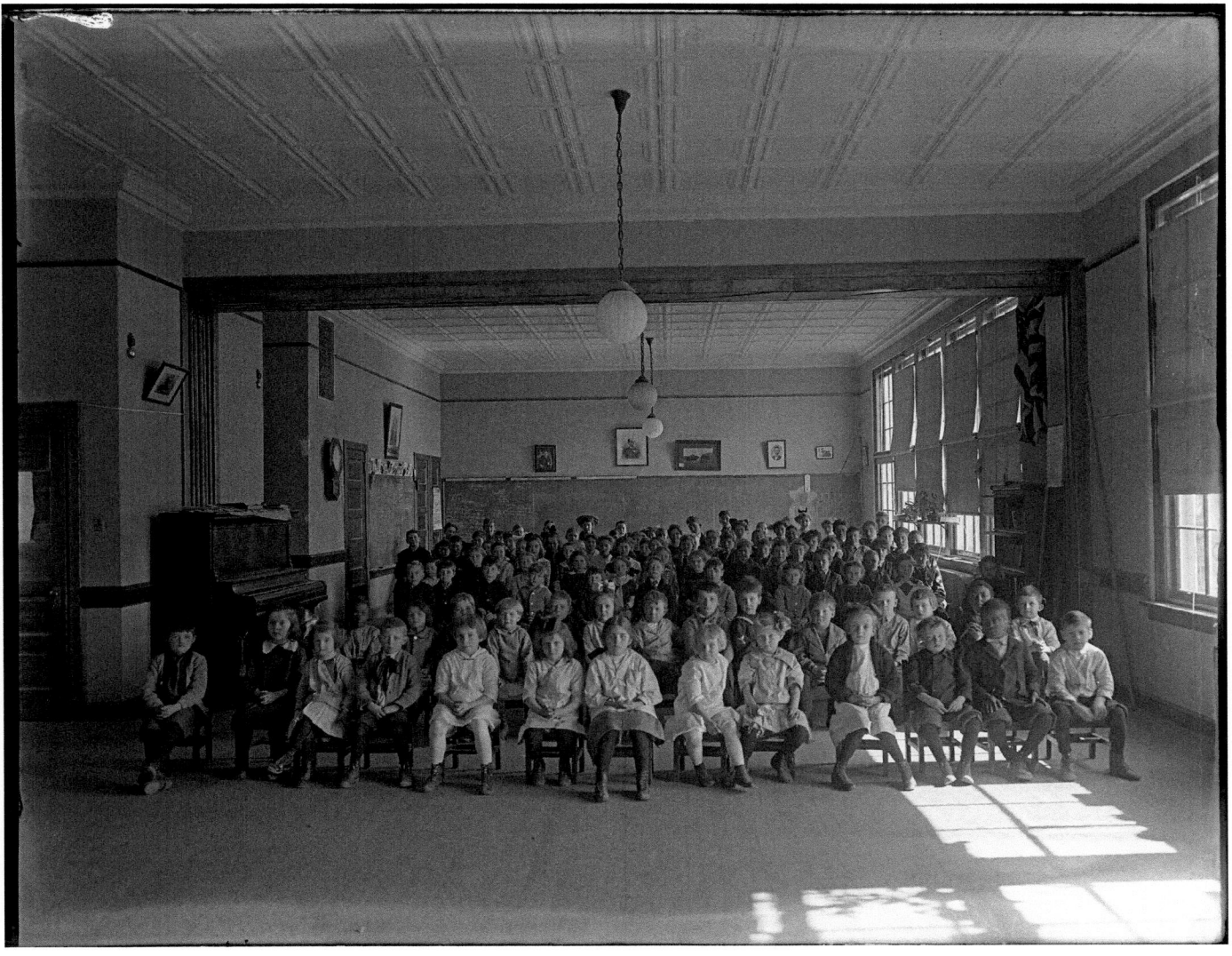

the 1910s. The students sit together at large workstations, their pencils at the ready. The lesson of the day is cursive handwriting. The students pose solemn faced for the camera, suggesting the teacher's control over the classroom and respect for the seriousness of a visit by a photographer. A portrait of celebrated American poet Henry Wadsworth Longfellow hangs on the wall. A calendar provides the date: February 1915. Castner is believed to have visited the Lanning School to document the newsworthy hoopla surrounding its recent opening.

Since it was intended to serve substantially more students than the one-room schoolhouses that it replaced, the Lanning School design called for a large auditorium capable of holding the entire student body (**plate 54**). This room's open,

Plate 54. Children in assembly room, Lanning School, Ewing Township, New Jersey, 1915. Digital positive from 6.5" x 8.5" glass plate negative. CH2019.6.599.

multipurpose floor plan gave school staff the flexibility to easily rearrange the space using movable desks and lightweight seating to suit a wide variety of scholastic activities. A piano suggests its regular use as a performance space while the large, wall-length chalkboard underscores its importance as a classroom for large groups. Castner did well to capture detail in the faces of most of the students in this technically challenging situation. He controlled the sunlight by pulling down most of the shades part way so that he did not overexpose his negative in the area near the windows. Since the room was still fairly dark, his relatively long exposure captured blurred motion in students who fidgeted. Uncredited to Castner, this exact image appeared in *New Jersey's Annual Report of the State Board of Education* (1915) as part of an article about the recent opening of the Lanning School. Castner may have been hired by the state to photograph the school for the purposes of illustrating its annual report. Though primarily an amateur photographer, Castner is known to have advertised his services and did take on some commercial work. This photo was taken during a decade when he described himself as a photographer in Trenton city directories.

In **plate 55**, of a room with empty desks, Castner's mind may have been on the juxtaposition of the janitor's quiet, lonely work when compared to the populated environment that characterized that very same space. This photo could have been taken early in the morning before the kids arrived. Note the strong sunlight coming in the windows. The rapidly growing public school population required the construction of new school buildings and the hiring of new teachers. It also sparked a supplemental need for desks, tables, storage cabinets, and other classroom furnishings. Located in Trenton, the New Jersey School and Church Furniture Company was the East Coast's most important maker. The word *church* was eventually dropped from the company name due to its

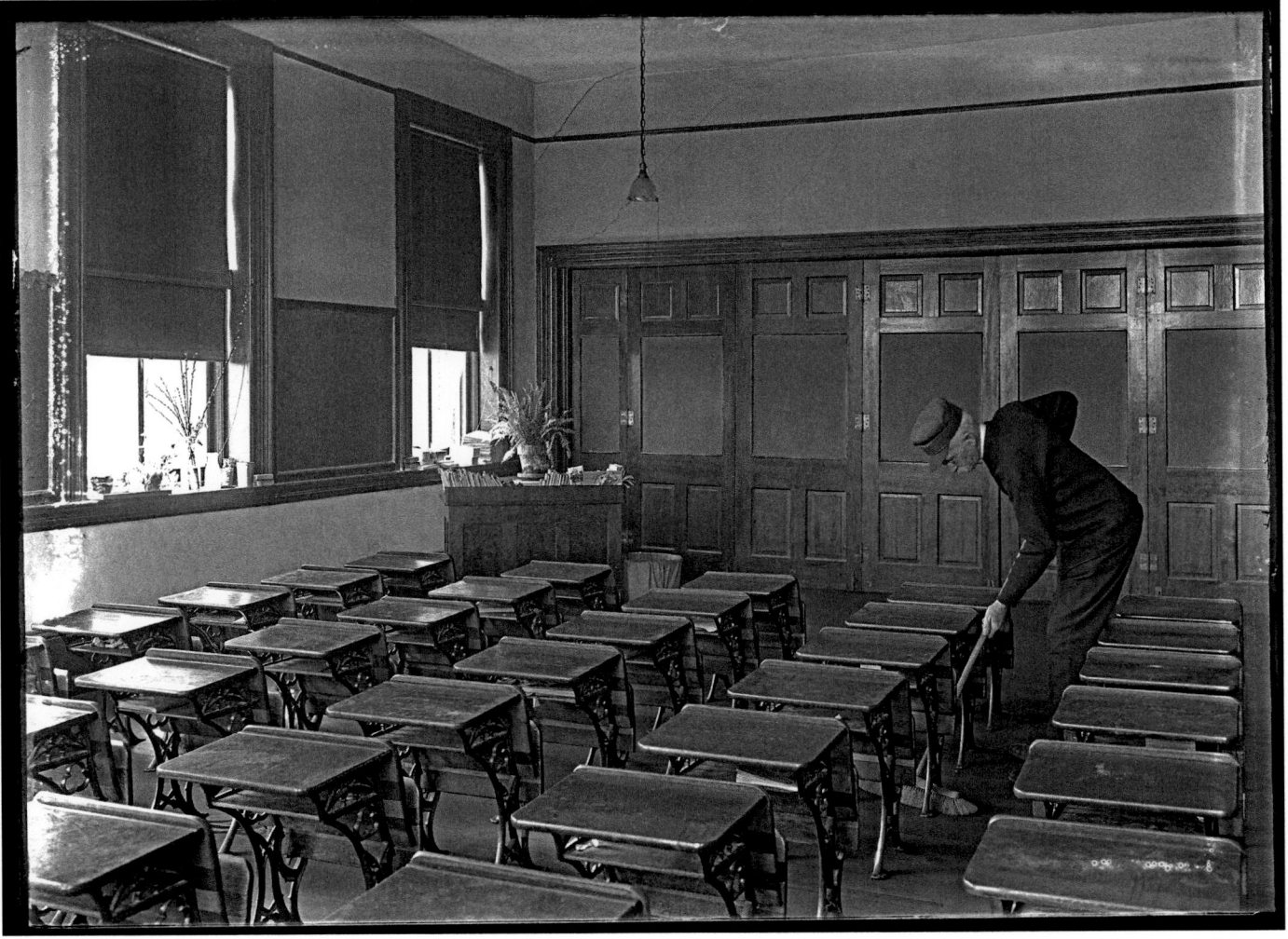

primary focus on supplying furniture to the many new educational institutions opening throughout the region. Easily movable furniture like the desks seen in Castner's photograph enabled the quick and easy transformation of school spaces to suit a variety of functions.

Plate 56 documents the school garden movement that was sweeping the United States in the first decades of the twentieth century. Supplemental lessons included the science of plants, the importance of the natural world, and food production and marketing. In 1915, an article published in *The Country Gentleman* magazine about the national school gardening movement included a glowing review of the program at Trenton's Carroll Robbins School at 283 Tyler Street,

Plate 55. Janitor at Carroll Robbins School, Trenton, New Jersey, 1914. Digital positive from 5" x 7" glass plate negative. CH2019.6.478.

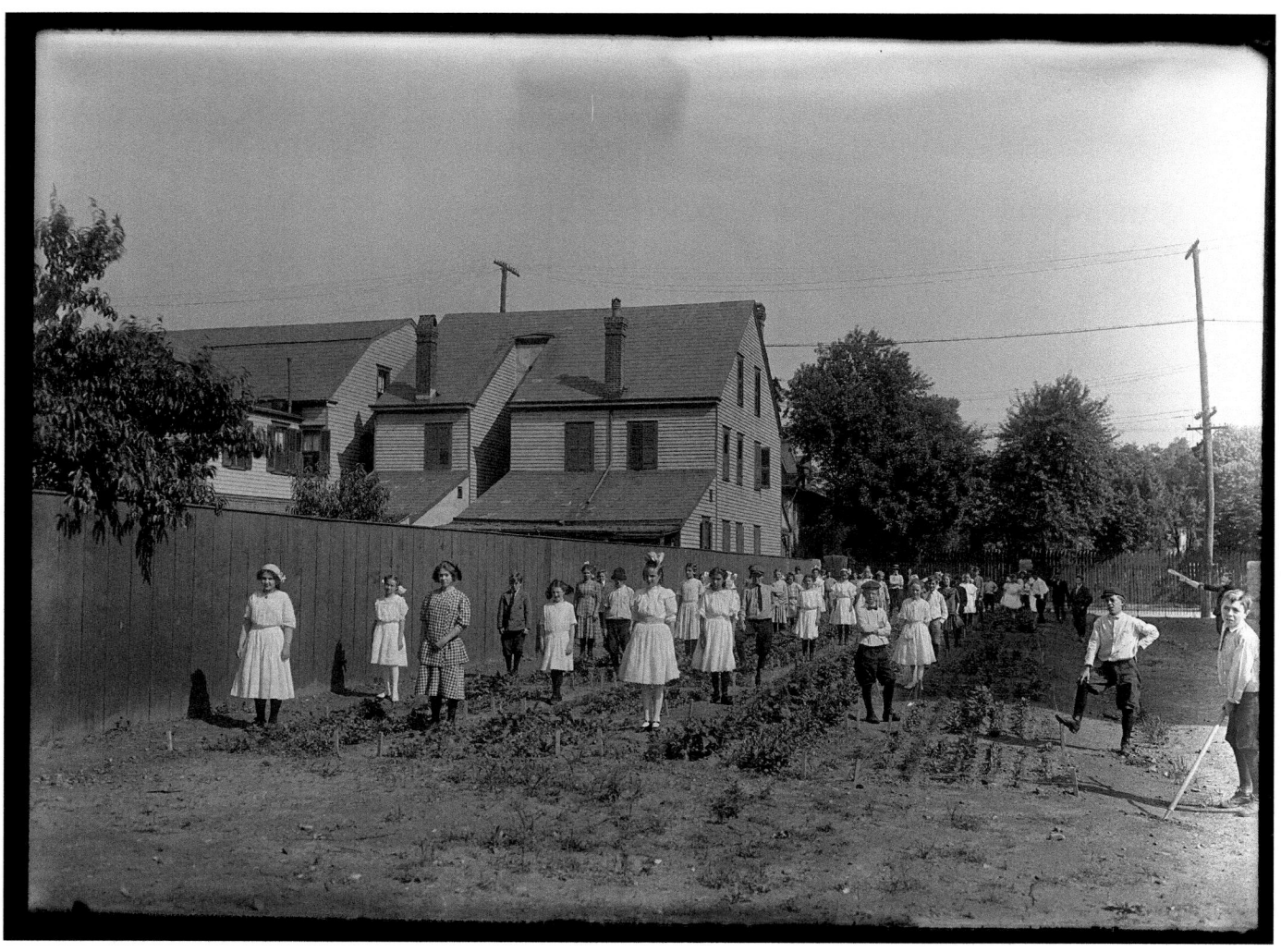

Plate 56. Students tending a garden, Carroll Robbins School, Trenton, New Jersey, c. 1915. Digital positive from 5" x 7" glass plate negative. CH2019.6.63.

near Castner's home. A total of six hundred students tended to the school gardens, with each grade tasked with raising different types of plants. Built in 1908, the Carroll Robbins School was named for a prominent local attorney and member of the Board of Education who died unexpectedly in 1907. Though initiated in 1914, the school garden movement received its greatest boost in 1917 when President Woodrow Wilson encouraged "Victory Gardens" to ward off possible food shortages.

Taken near the point where the Hakihokake Creek empties into the Delaware River, the heartwarming image in **plate 57** captures a quiet moment that reflects both the simple pleasures of youth and the tranquility of nature. Castner's title for the image suggests that the two young boys,

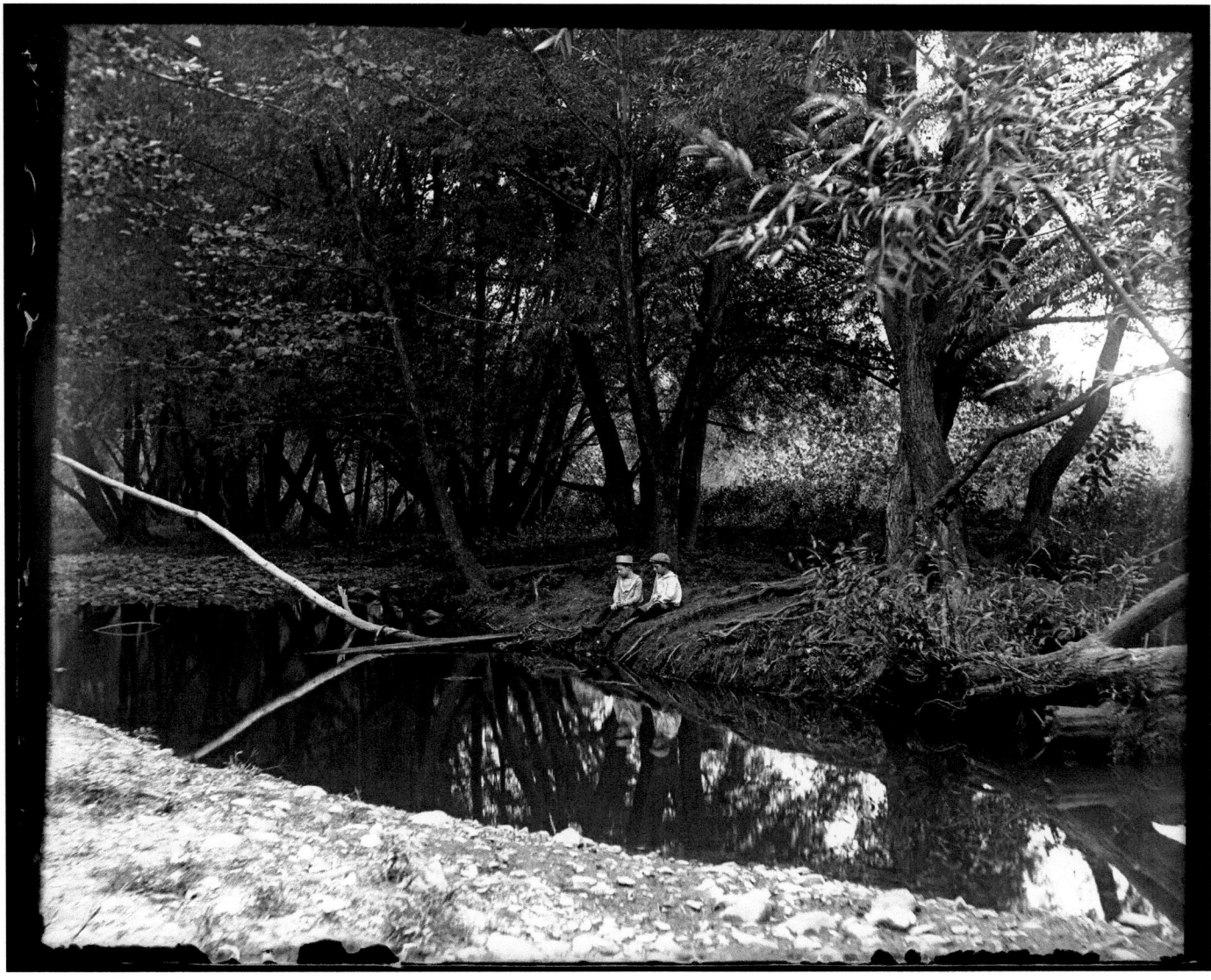

their eyes fixated on the water, are determined to catch sight of fish lurking beneath the surface. The photographer likely happened upon the scene and waited for the right moment to capture the tender moment of friendship. The tiny human figures, dwarfed by tall trees and reflected in the shimmering creek, suggest the omnipresence of nature. Castner elegantly composed this image so that the boys are integrated into the picture space, with a diagonal tree leading to the boys from the left. The photographer may have first observed the natural beauty of this Delaware River tributary on one of his many train rides on the Bel-Del Railroad line connecting Trenton to his hometown of Belvidere. The Bel-Del crossed

Plate 57. *Watching the Fish.* Two boys on the banks of the Haki-hokake Creek, Milford, New Jersey, 1898. Digital positive from 4" x 5" glass plate negative. CH2019.6.178.

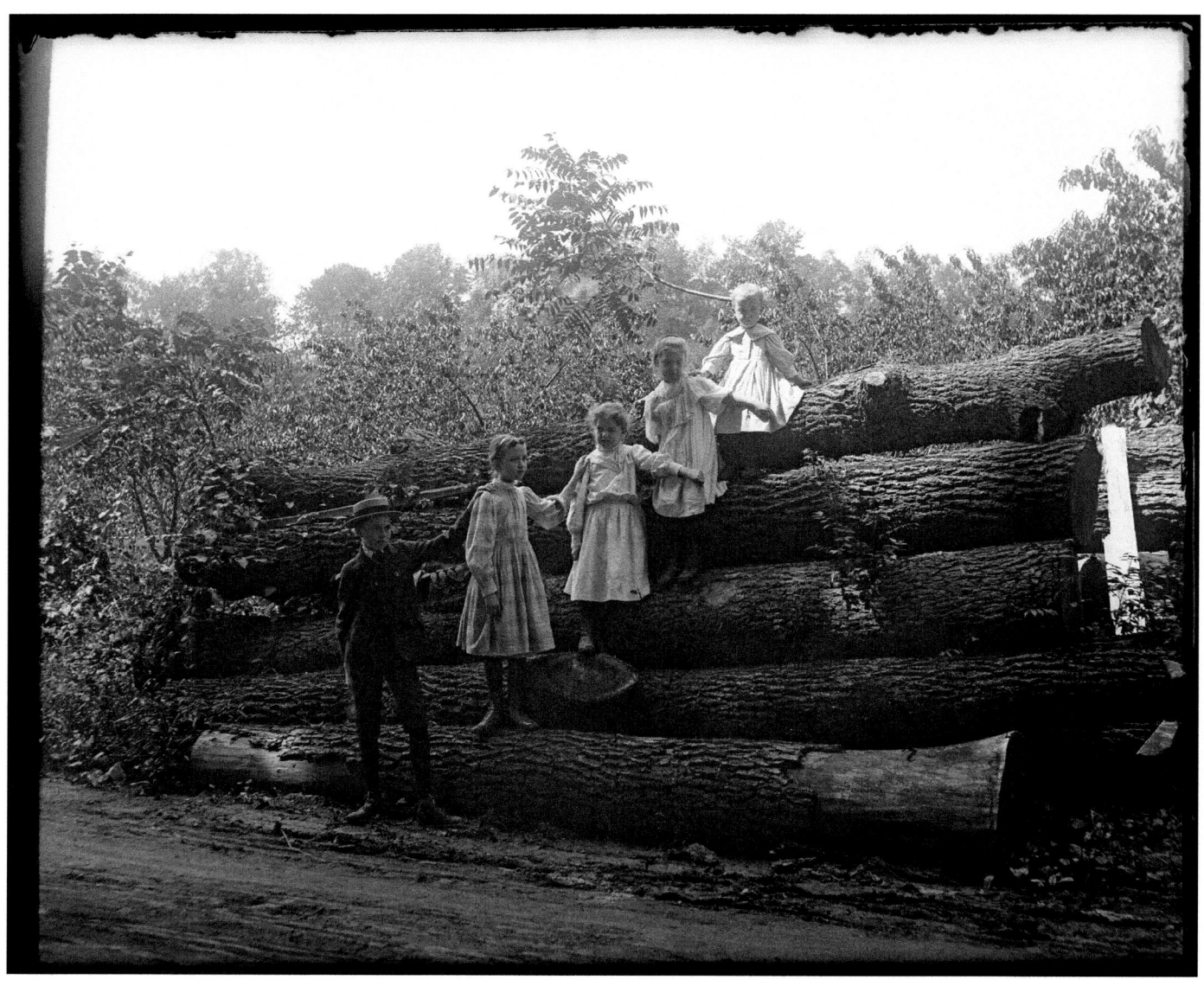

Plate 58. Maxwell Stover and sisters posing on lumbered logs, Erwinna, Pennsylvania, 1897. Digital positive from 4" x 5" glass plate negative. CH2019.6.264.

this wooded section of the Hakihokake Creek on a small railroad bridge in Milford.

Castner's photographic expeditions of the upper Delaware River occasionally took him to points along its western shore. Near Point Pleasant (Bucks County), he came across the small group of children in **plate 58** in the vicinity of a lumbering operation and posed them side-by-side on the trunks of recently felled trees. The association was appropriate. The youths, all siblings, were the five children of Henry C. Stover, a lumber merchant from a multigenerational Bucks County lumbering family. Castner arranged his subjects by their age, oldest to youngest, with thirteen-year-old Isaac Maxwell

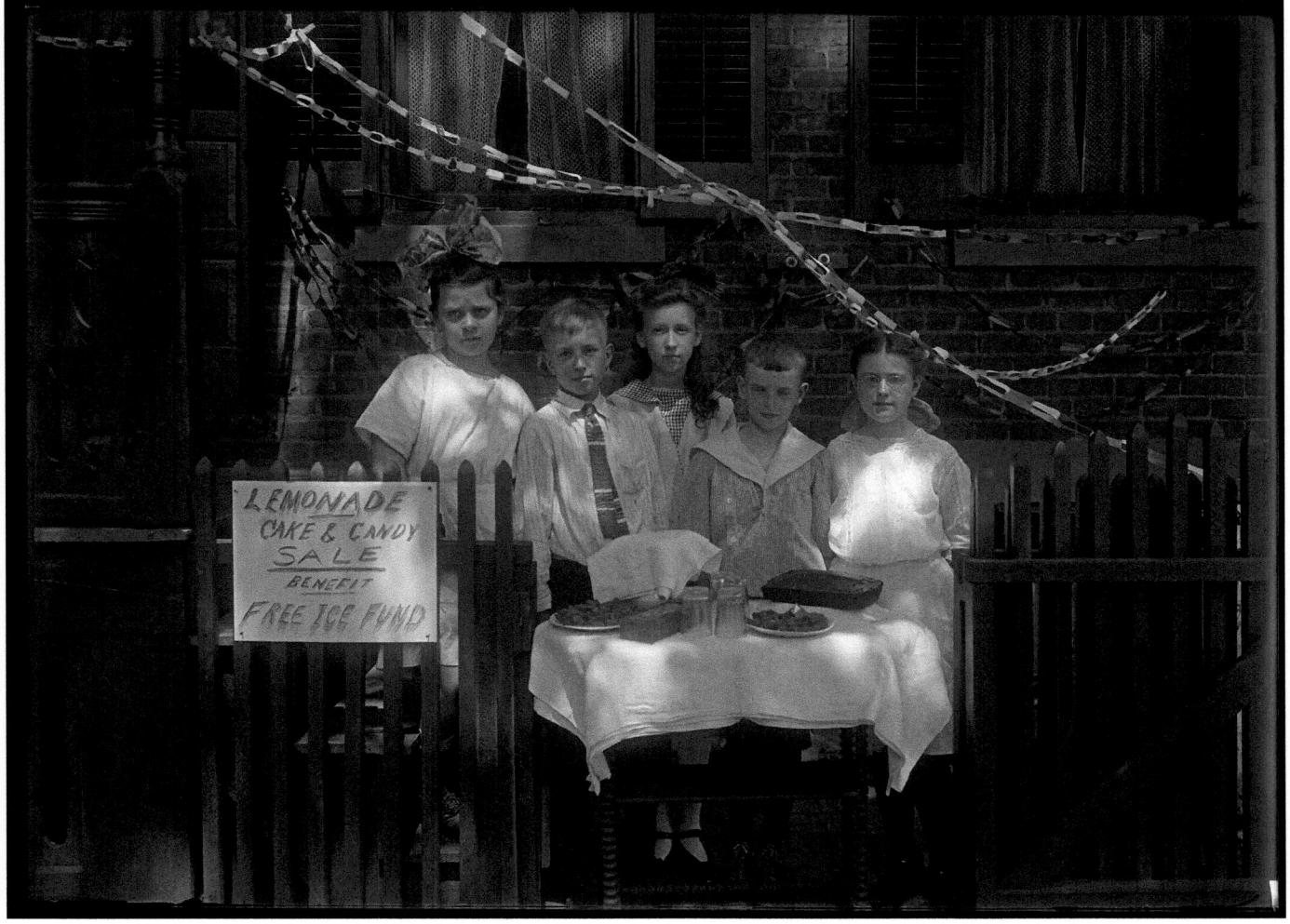

Stover on the far left. At the top is two-year-old Evan Worthington Stover, still young enough to be wearing a dress-like garment, as was custom for small boys in Castner's day. Three sisters—Esther Mercy Stover, Alice Mulford Stover, and Louisa Stover—are at the center. Castner posed these children by size so that the tops of their heads would form more or less a straight diagonal line.

In the 1870s, a ten-year-old Dutch immigrant named Edward Bok created a successful business venture selling lemonade on the streets of New York City. Bok was only one of many people who sold this easy-to-produce beverage. But news of his success as a young entrepreneur eventually traveled far and wide. In time, the humble lemonade stand became a popular venture for American youth—a first life lesson on the value of hard work and entrepreneurship. In **plate 59**, Castner

Plate 59. Theodore Grant Castner (second from right), son of Grant Castner, with friends at lemonade stand, Trenton, New Jersey, 1914. Digital positive from 5" x 7" glass plate negative. CH2019.6.887.

documented his son's lemonade stand on a street in Trenton. In the days before electric refrigerators were first marketed in 1918, the kids were raising money for a city-wide effort to distribute free ice to the poor during the heat of summer for their ice boxes. A cropped version of Castner's photograph was published in the July 24, 1914, issue of the *Trenton Evening Times* to accompany a story about the ice fund.

6

Canal

New Jersey has a long history of innovation in transportation. In the mid-1800s, the state's network of canals was its most impressive transportation system. In north Jersey, the Morris Canal crossed the entire width of the state. In central Jersey, the Delaware & Raritan Canal ran between Bordentown and New Brunswick. Its water-supplying "feeder" canal stretched from Bull's Island in Stockton down to Trenton. On the Pennsylvania shore, the Delaware Canal hugged its namesake river all the way from Easton to Bristol. Mule-drawn boats used the canals to transport anthracite coal, agricultural goods, and other products. The capital city also had another engineered waterway called the Water Power. This long-gone, seven-mile canal from Scudders Falls through downtown provided a power source to the city's early industries.

The heyday for canals was in the 1860s. The arrival of railroads brought about their eventual decline. But the canal infrastructure remained part of the built environment for generations. Castner's collection contains many images documenting this onetime marvel of American transportation. His photographs also record some of the early uses of canal towpaths for leisure.

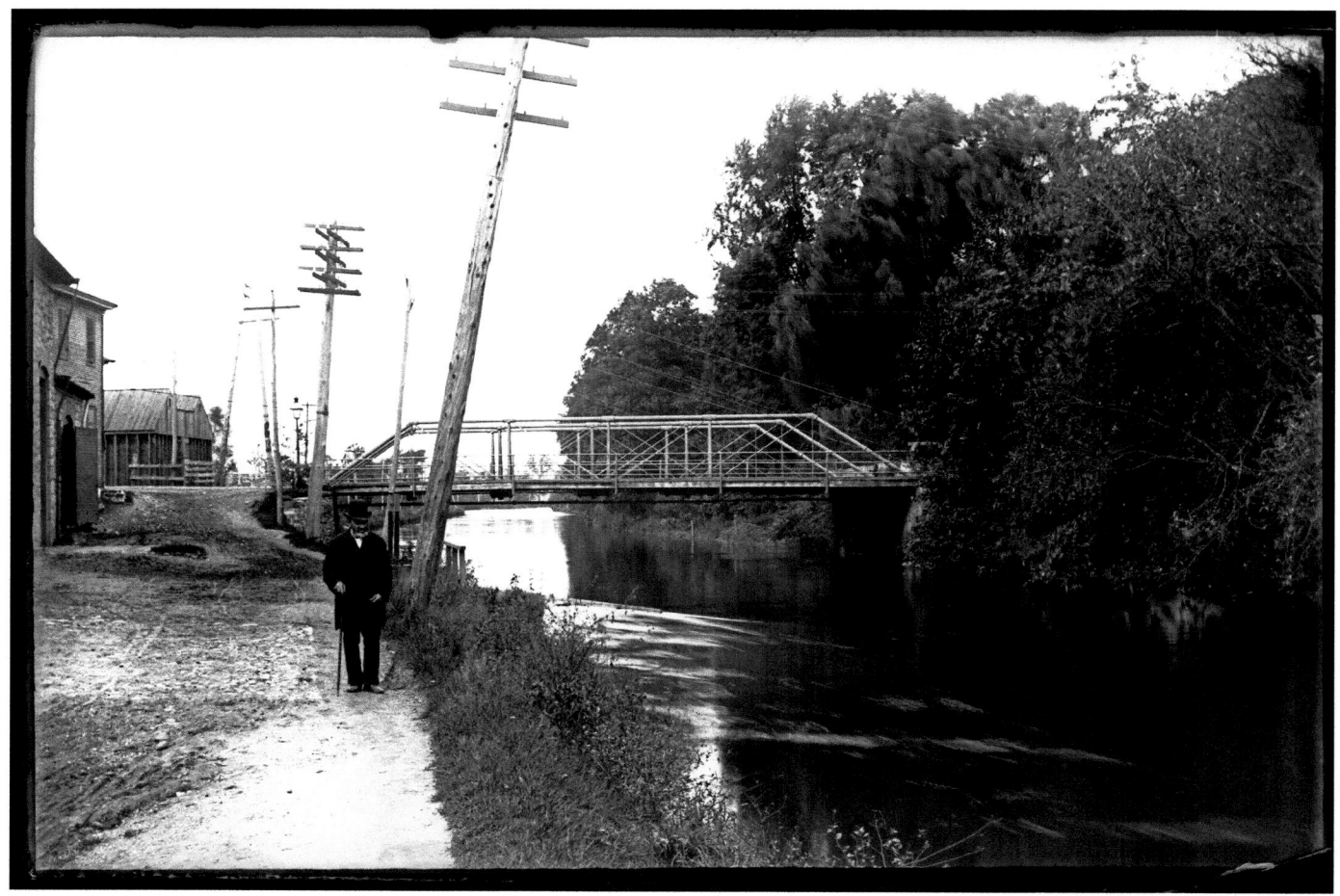

Plate 60. *Old Age.* Unidentified man on the Water Power canal, Trenton, New Jersey, 1890. Digital positive from 4.25" x 6.5" glass plate negative. CH2019.6.163.

Still a young man in his twenties, Castner was probably not thinking of his own advancing years when taking **plate 60** of an elderly man shuffling along the Trenton Water Power path. But as evidenced by the title that he gave to his image, age was certainly on his mind. Perhaps Castner was impressed with the man's ability to explore the city on foot, despite his limitations of mobility. Castner used the "golden section" composition method by dividing his image into a square on the right and a vertical rectangle on the left bordered by the top of the leaning pole. The eye is drawn to the man at the left of the frame, with the flowing canal and the full span of an attractive metal bridge in the background. The buildings are part of the old Trenton Waterworks before it moved to its current location. The bridge, which is no longer there, carried Calhoun Street.

Plate 61 is of Titus and Sons textile mill situated along the Trenton Water Power canal, the last vestiges of which disappeared in the 1950s to make way for Route 29. The

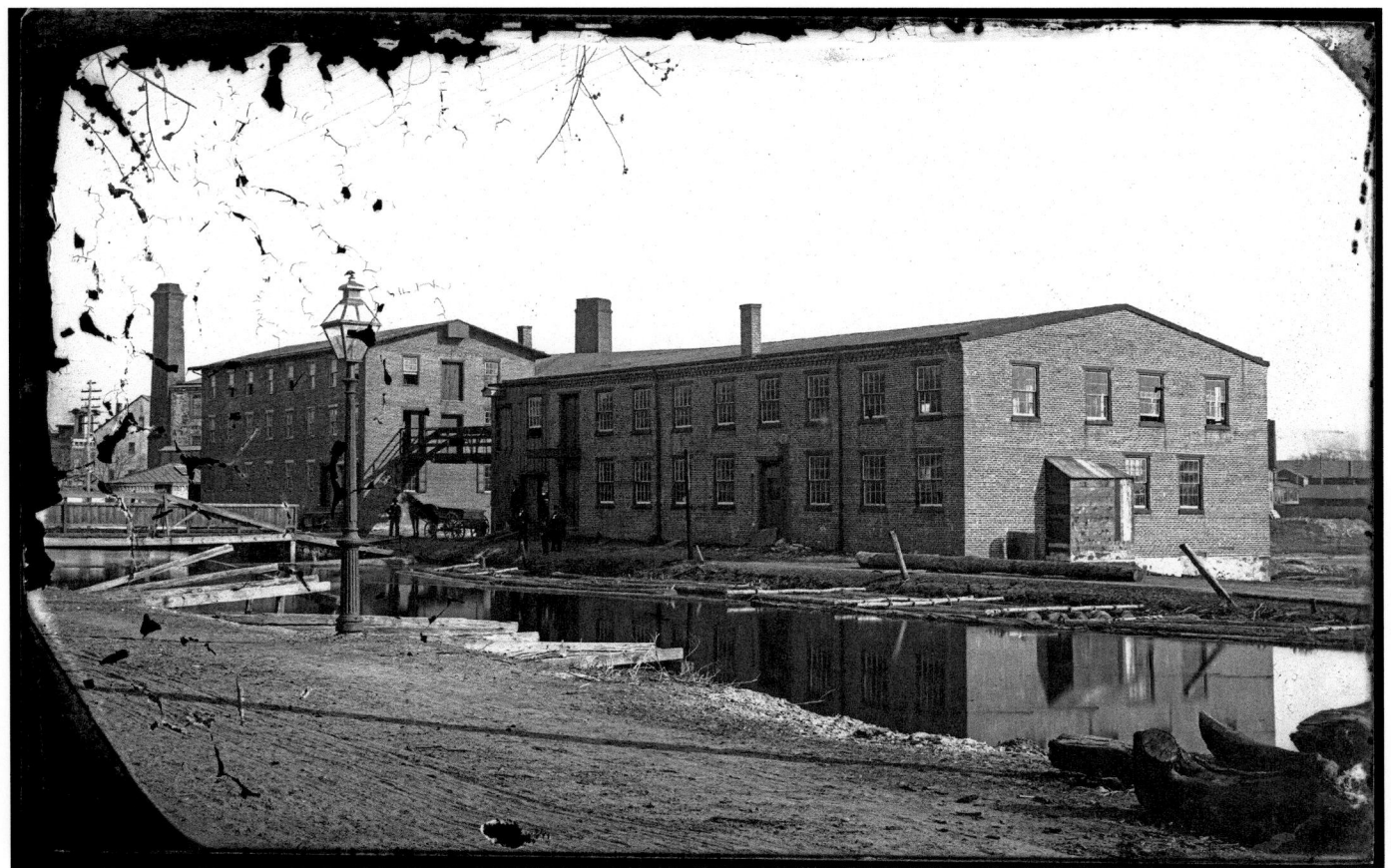

reproduction is from a "wet-plate" collodion glass plate negative, in common use from 1850 to 1880. Collodion is a sticky clear liquid that was poured on the glass by the photographer. One of the telltale signs of a collodion negative is the partial coverage of the emulsion in the corner of the plate where the photographer held it. On this plate, the semicircular shape in the lower left corner is probably a thumb impression. Tests in 1880 by professional photographers showed that the newly available gelatin dry plates were ten times more sensitive than wet-plate collodion and far more sensitive than the dry-plate collodion used by some photographers for landscape photos. They quickly switched to the new technology. Castner may have worked with collodion when first starting out as a photographer, but most if not all of his work up to the 1920s was with gelatin dry plates. It is possible that he acquired this negative from another camera club member.

A point near Bordentown was selected as the southern terminus of the Delaware and Raritan Canal because the

Plate 61. B.W. Titus and Sons Cotton and Woolen Mill, Washington Street (now Lafayette) along the Water Power, Trenton, New Jersey, c. 1880. Digital positive from 5" x 8" glass plate negative. CH2019.6.826.

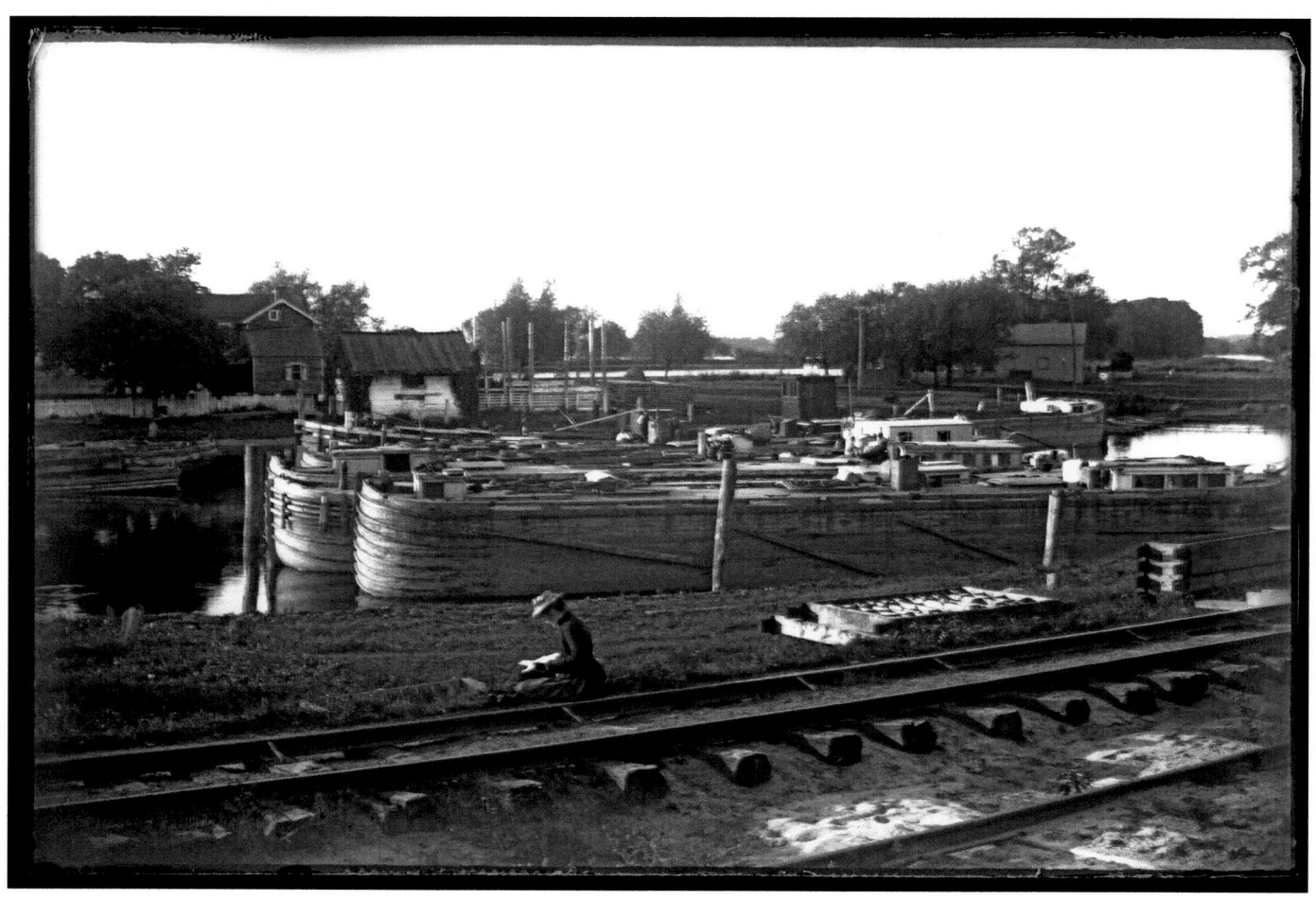

Plate 62. *Canal Boat Village.*
Woman with canal boats, Delaware
and Raritan Canal, Bordentown,
New Jersey, 1890. Digital positive
from 4.25" x 6.5" glass plate negative. CH2019.6.461.

Delaware River to the north tended to freeze over earlier in
the winter months than it did to the south. Choosing this location to start a canal would ensure that the artery could be used
to transport goods between Philadelphia and New York for a
longer period of time throughout the year. Castner's image of
the canal boats at Bordentown documents their long and relatively slender shape (**plate 62**), which allowed them to navigate the narrow waterway. These boats are of the type that also
were commonly used on the Schuylkill Canal in Pennsylvania.
The woman seated in the foreground may be Castner's sister, Ida, who sometimes accompanied the photographer in his
travels around the region.

Castner probably traveled by rail north along the Delaware
River to capture the view of workers at one of several quarries
situated along the feeder of the Delaware and Raritan Canal
in Hopewell Township (**plate 63**). The backbreaking work
involved tearing rock from the hillside, crushing the large

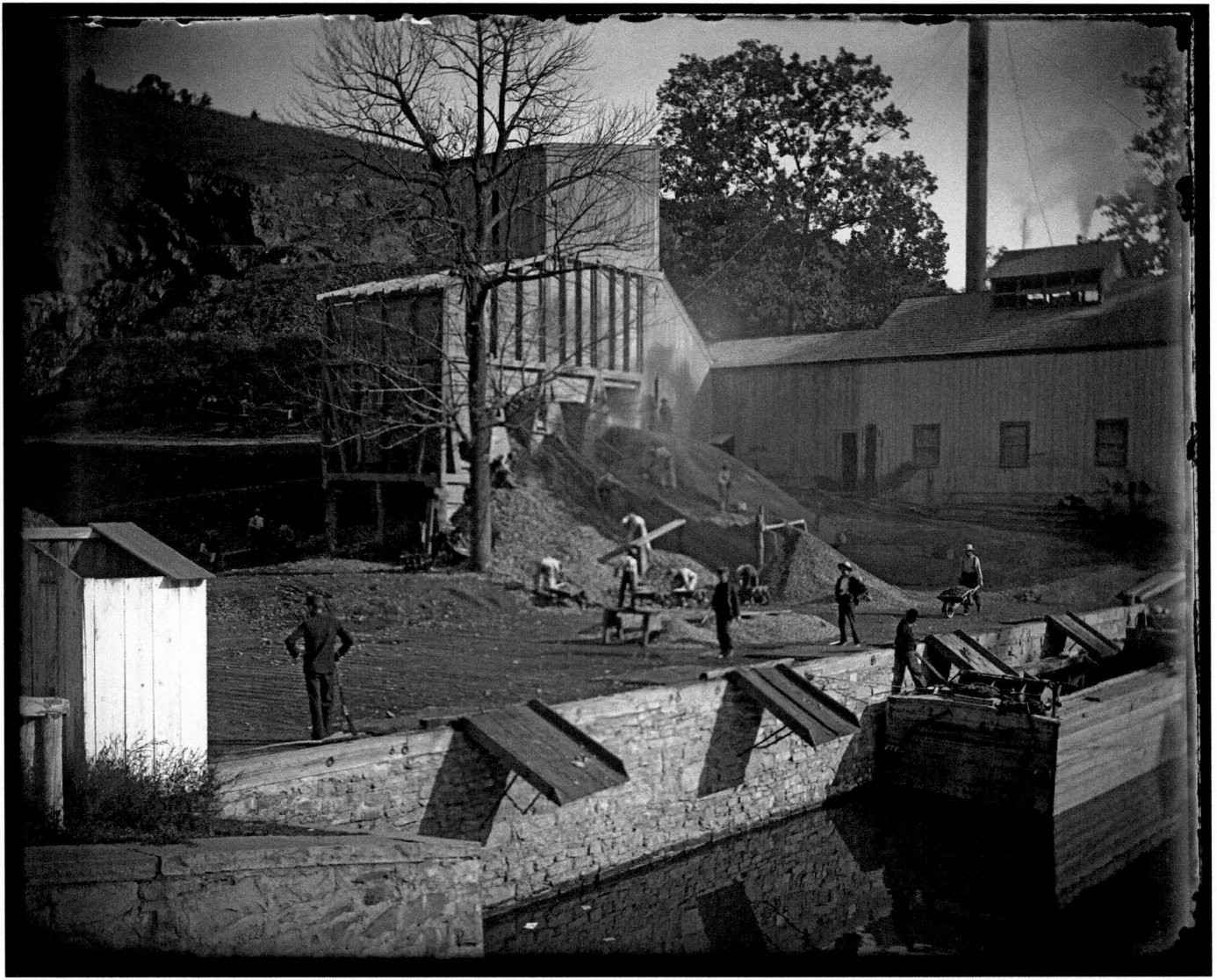

stones into gravel, and moving the crushed stone in wagons and wheelbarrows to canal boats for shipment. On close inspection, the man standing in the left foreground can be seen wearing a uniform and leaning on a rifle. This suggests that these are Mercer County prisoners working the quarry under the supervision of armed guards. Mercer County established the Workhouse Quarry in the 1890s to provide employment to inmates. Their work produced many tons of crushed stone for use on the county's roadways. Today, the remnants of this quarry can be seen on Route 29 near the entrance to the Mercer County Correctional Center. The abandoned crusher that stands on the site today is not the one in Castner's photograph, as it was replaced in the early twentieth century.

Plate 63. *Breaking Stone.* Mercer County Workhouse Quarry, Hopewell Township, New Jersey, 1896. Digital positive from 4" x 5" glass plate negative. CH2019.6.426.

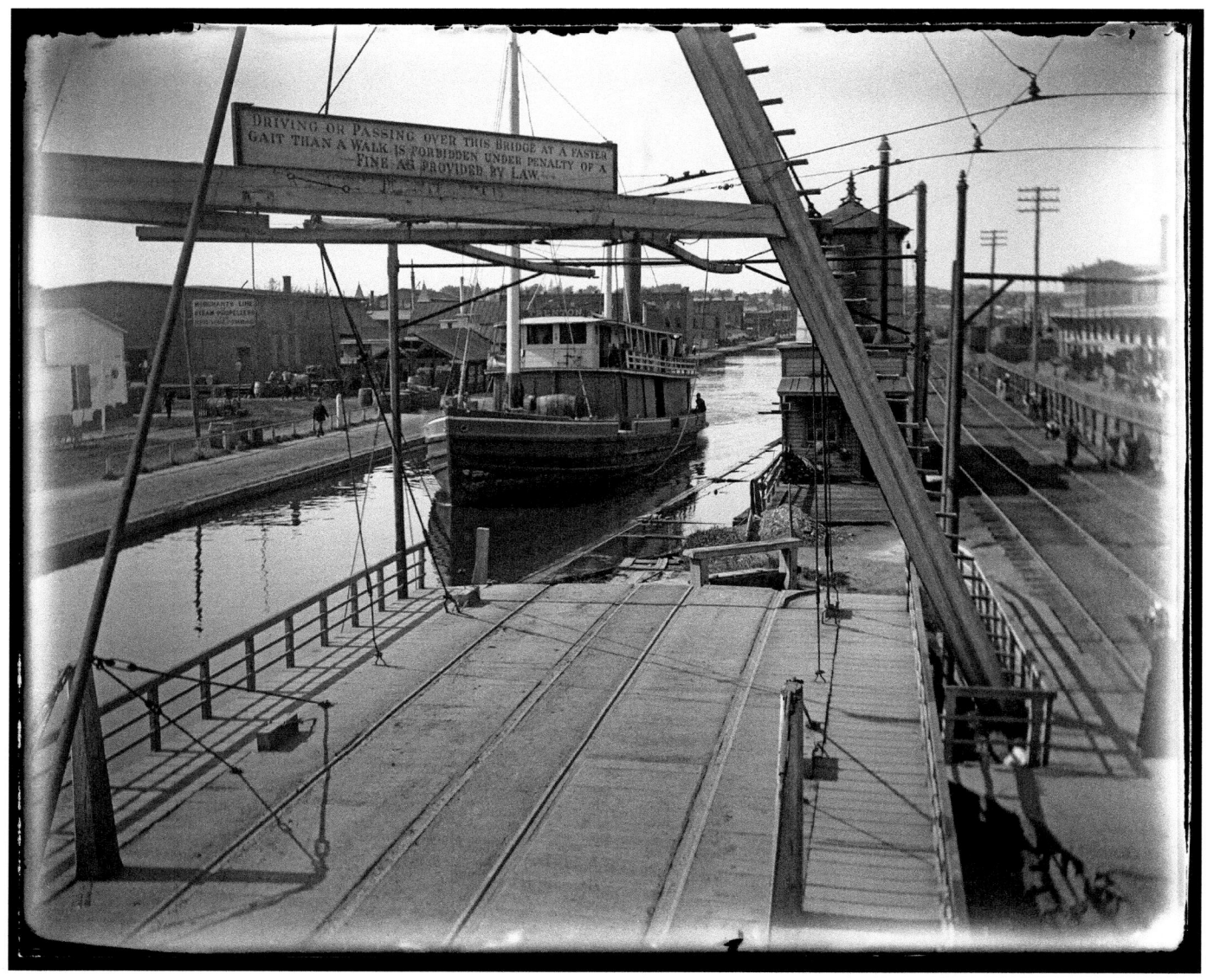

Plate 64. *Snap Shot, State Street.*
East State Street Bridge over the
Delaware and Raritan Canal,
Trenton, New Jersey, 1894. Digital
positive from 4" x 5" glass plate
negative. CH2019.6.427.

Although mule-drawn boats are the vessels most closely
associated with canal transit, a wide variety of watercraft also
navigated New Jersey's Delaware and Raritan Canal. These included sailboats, private yachts, naval vessels, and steam tug-
boats like the one depicted in **plate 64**. The view follows the
canal to the north from the bridge at East State Street, near
one of the many locks that navigated the elevation changes
all along the canal route. The modern-day location is where
East State Street crosses over Route 1, a highway that was constructed on top of the filled-in canal. Castner's title for this
image, *Snap Shot, State Street,* suggests that he was not out to
specifically document the canal but randomly came across the
scene and found the canal boat framed by the large triangle to

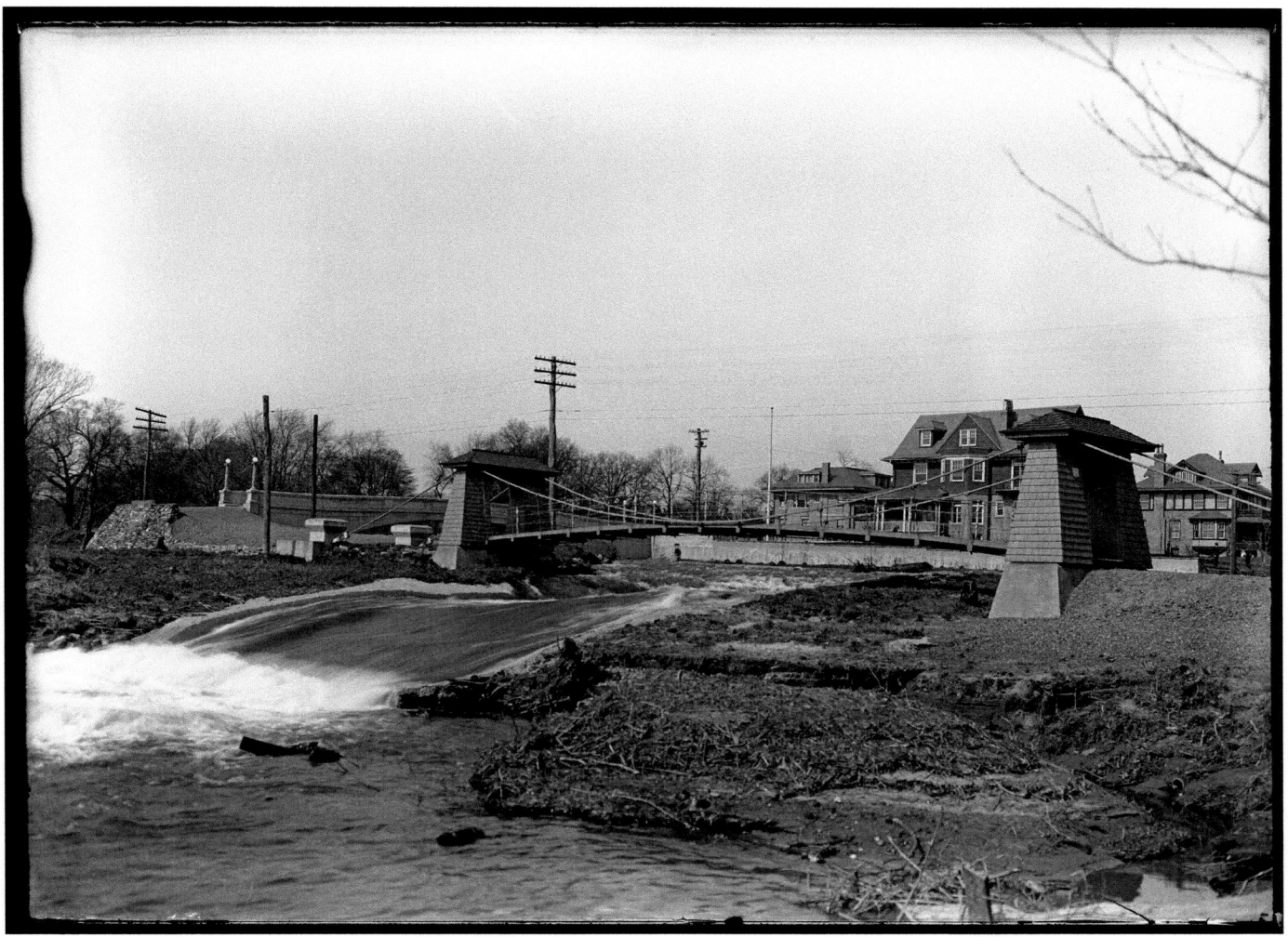

be a compelling composition. Borrowing a hunting term, Sir John Herschel (1792–1871), the English scientist who made notable contributions to photography, coined "snap-shot" in 1860 when, using a hunting term, he predicted that cameras in the future would be able to take pictures in a fraction of a second.

In 1908, the city of Trenton needed a bridge to span the rushing torrent of water that cascaded from the higher ground of the Delaware and Raritan Canal feeder down to the Delaware River via a spillway called the waste weir. Trenton's John A. Roebling's Sons' Company built the bridge, which they designed as a miniature version of their famed 1855 railroad suspension bridge over the Niagara River (**plate 65**). Originally called the "Little Roebling Bridge," the structure eventually became known as the "Shaky Bridge." It still stands today

Plate 65. Roebling "Shaky Bridge," Trenton, New Jersey, 1913. Digital positive from 5" x 7" glass plate negative. CH2019.6.214.

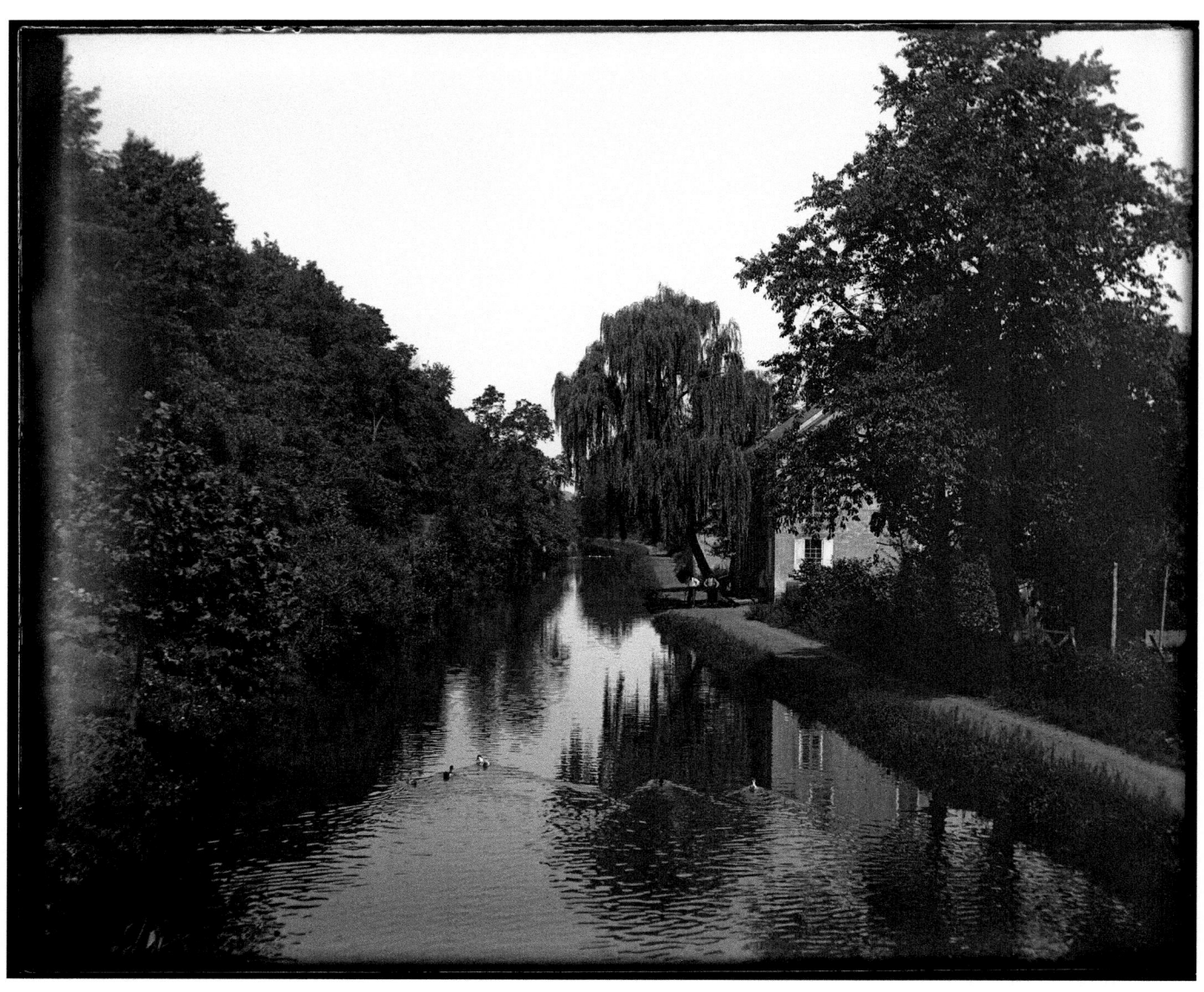

Plate 66. Delaware Canal, south of Erwinna, Pennsylvania, 1897. Digital positive from 4" x 5" glass plate negative. CH2019.6.266.

and is located between Route 29 and the Delaware River near the Trenton Water Works. After repairs, it was rededicated on October 18, 2022, when Trenton Mayor Reed Gusciora cut a blue ribbon to reopen it.

The Delaware Canal, also known as the Delaware Division of the Pennsylvania Canal, stretched sixty miles from Easton to Bristol on the Pennsylvania side of the river. First opened in the 1830s, it was originally intended to transport anthracite coal, building materials, and other goods via mule-drawn canal boats to the larger population centers in and around Philadelphia. In 1897, Castner took the scenic photograph in **plate 66** from atop a carriage road bridge (now River Road) that crossed the Delaware Canal just south of Erwinna.

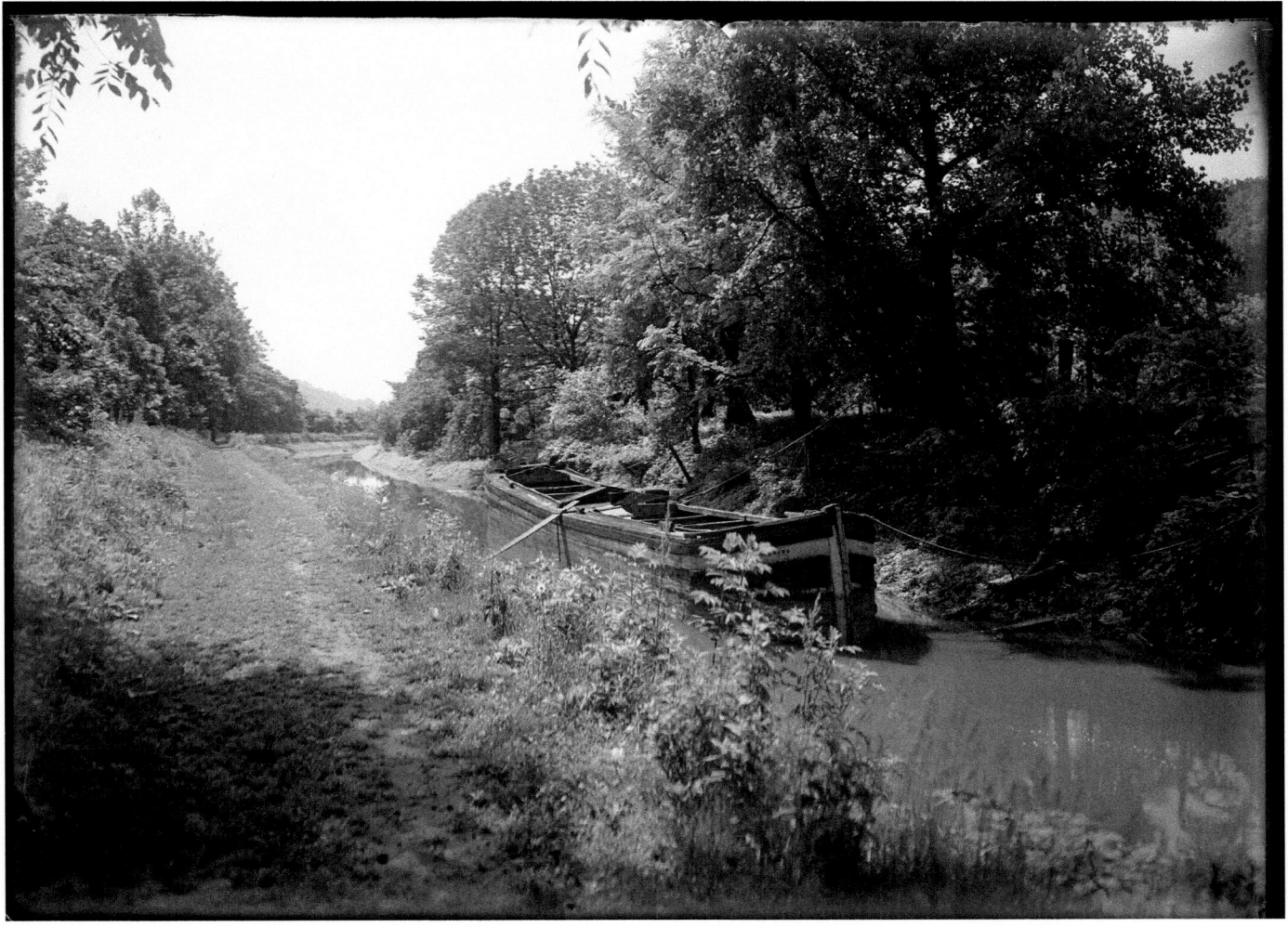

Partially obscured behind the foliage of two towering trees on the right is a long-standing stone structure that served as a tavern and inn. By the time of Castner's visit to the area, the canal was well beyond its heyday, having lost much of its business to the railroads. However, the canal was in the midst of its renaissance as a waterway for pleasure craft. An article in the April 10, 1907, issue of *The Motor Boat* advertised this very same building to its readers as a place where leisure boaters on the canal could find accommodations for the night. The building still stands today and operates as the Golden Pheasant Inn, with upscale restaurant and guest rooms.

While exploring the Delaware Canal towpath in upper Bucks County, Castner happened across the pleasant scene in **plate 67** of an empty canal boat secured by ropes to nearby trees with the graceful, wooded curve of the canal in the

Plate 67. Canal boat on the Delaware Canal, Lumberville, Pennsylvania, 1904. Digital positive from 5" x 7" glass plate negative. CH2019.6.770.

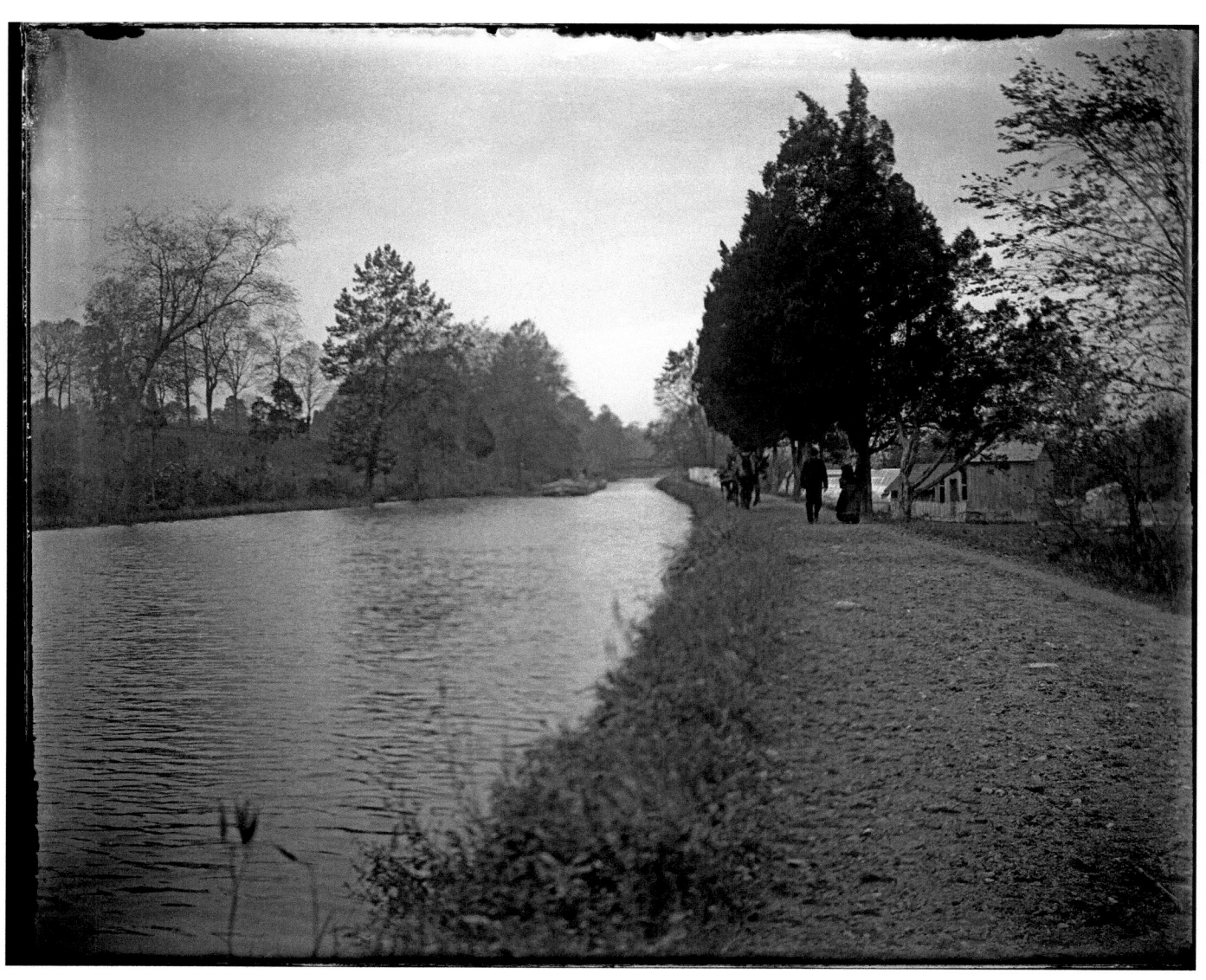

Plate 68. *On the Tow Path*. Delaware Canal towpath, Morrisville, Pennsylvania, 1894. Digital positive from 4" x 5" glass plate negative. CH2019.6.248.

background. Common to eastern Pennsylvania, this type of canal vessel was called a sectional boat or hinge boat. On hinge-style boats, two separate sections were connected by metal fittings and pins. When the pins were removed, the sections could be maneuvered and handled as independent entities. The flexibility of the hinge construction made this type of boat particularly important on canals with tight, narrow bends. It also allowed the boat to be turned around almost anywhere along the length of a canal; one-piece boats needed an extra-wide section in the canal or a designated "boat basin" to do so. Castner took this photograph in the vicinity of Lumberville, a Bucks County village just across the Delaware River from Raven Rock, New Jersey.

Embracing the art of perspective, Castner's pleasant view of a gently winding, tree-lined waterway with a lone wooden bridge in the distance captures the serenity of the Delaware Canal in Morrisville. He took **plate 68** in 1894, nearly thirty years past the heyday of the canal era. However, a team of mules can be seen on the towpath with long ropes pulling a canal boat. Though not as prevalent as in the early years, animal-driven canal boats continued to be used on the region's canals even after self-propelled canal boats came into use and the railroads had largely supplanted canals as the main means of moving goods. In front of the mule team, a man and woman walk along the towpath toward the camera. Their use of the canal for leisure foreshadows its later transformation into a popular, state-owned park in the twentieth century.

7

Rails

Grant Castner loved trains. He took many pictures of conductors, locomotives, cabooses, and engine repair shops. No other subject is better represented in his glass plate collection. His fascination with railroads stemmed from his life in Trenton. Then, as now, the city was an important regional rail hub. From his home just a few blocks from the Clinton Street railroad depot, Castner had a front row seat to the incredible, society-changing power of the Iron Horse.

Railroads played a seminal role in the transformation of New Jersey. Trains facilitated the movement of people, reducing travel time to a fraction of what it had been. Efficient at transporting goods, trains eventually caused the demise of canals. Since trains needed to depart and arrive at consistent times across large geographic areas, rail travel also led to standardized time. In addition to main-line, longer-distance trains, New Jersey was home to shorter passenger railways known as inter-urbans. Within cities, streetcar lines provided convenient service to downtown shopping areas. These types of trains applied the revolutionary power of electricity to public transit.

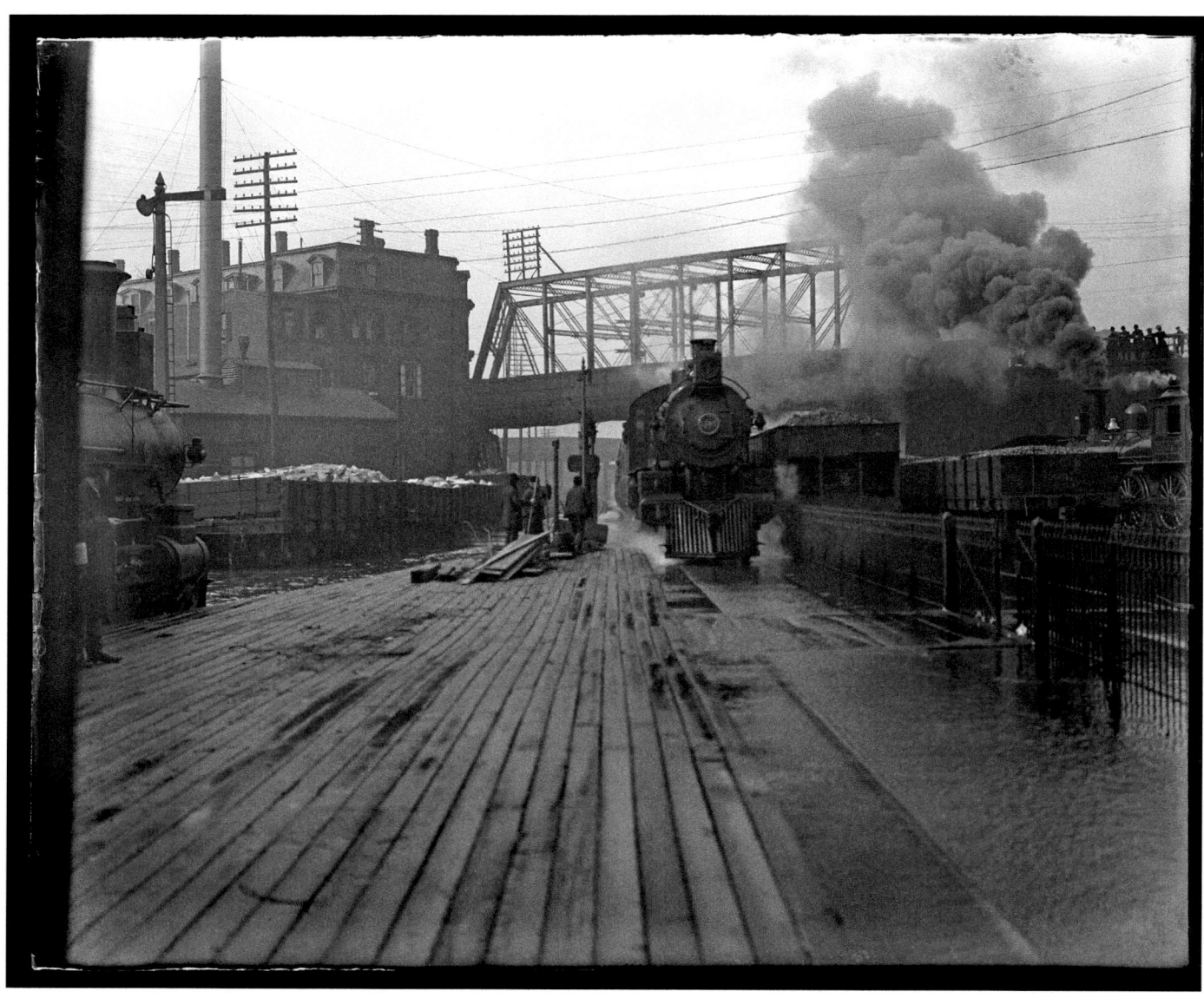

Plate 69. Locomotive entering depot, Clinton Street Station, Trenton, New Jersey, 1902. Digital positive from 4" x 5" glass plate negative. CH2019.6.387.

Plate 69, one of Castner's finest, underscores how photographs can be both documentary artifacts and aesthetically pleasing works of art. As an avid reader of photography journals, Castner was surely aware of the work of the great American photographer Alfred Stieglitz (1864–1946), whose gritty urban photographs demonstrated that art photography need not be limited to such genres as bucolic landscapes and flower arrangements. One of Stieglitz's best known photographs, *The Hand of Man*, taken of a train yard in 1902, features a locomotive in the same position in the frame as Castner's. In his version, Castner carefully chose a spot at the Clinton Street Station, set up his camera, and patiently

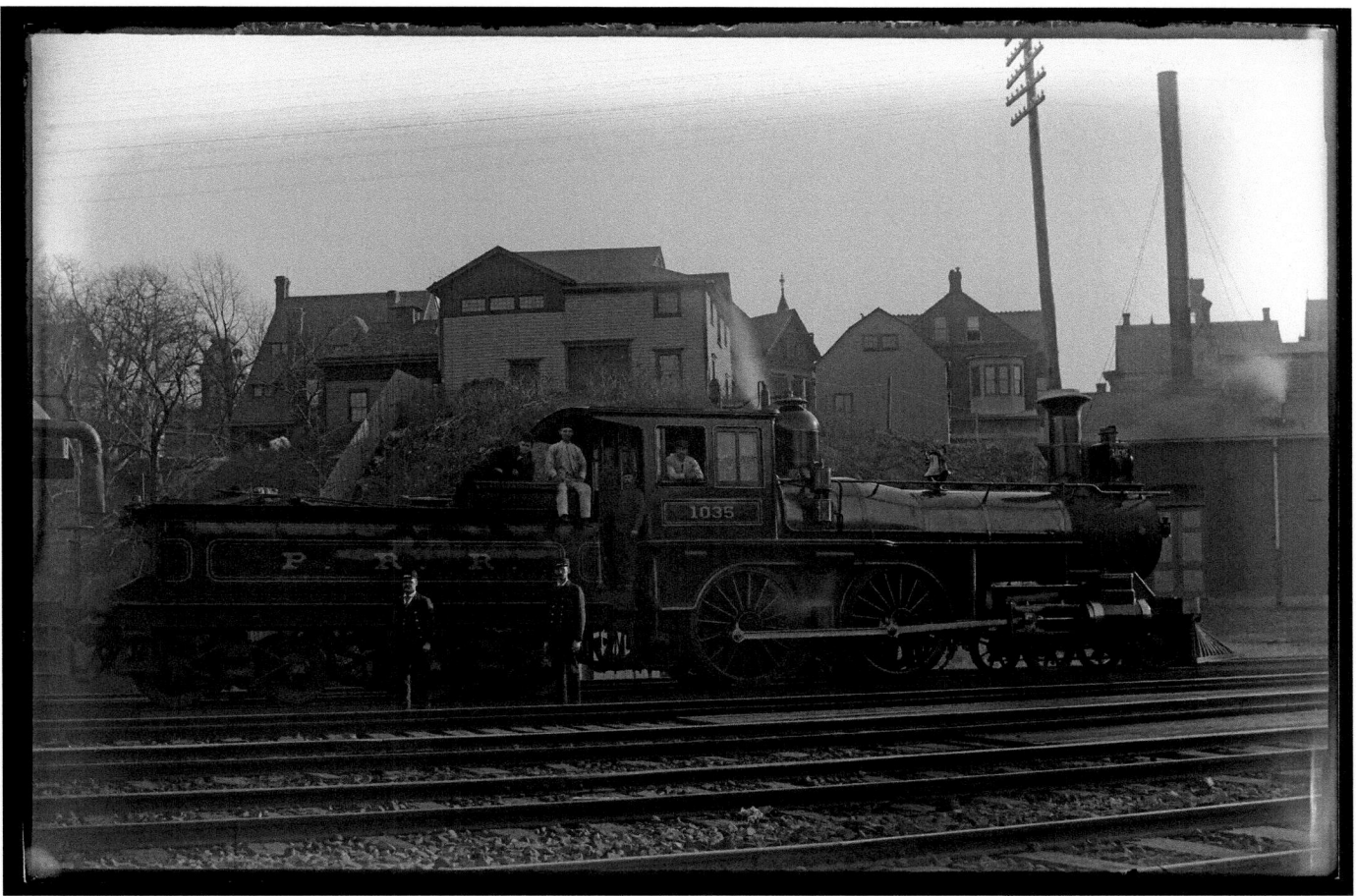

waited, as long as was necessary, for the perfect moment to unfold—just as Stieglitz would have done.

Castner took a number of photographs of locomotives and the railroaders who worked on them. **Plate 70** depicts a Class D7 steam locomotive of the Pennsylvania Railroad with a 4-4-0 wheel arrangement. As seen in the photograph, the 4-4-0 refers to the fact that this common type of American engine had four smaller leading wheels, four larger driving wheels, and no trailing wheels. The engine was built at the Pennsylvania Railroad works in Altoona, Pennsylvania. Conveniently located near the center of the Keystone State, the Altoona Works for building and repairing locomotives and railroad cars began operating in 1850 and continued to expand until 1925. By the 1920s, the huge site featured 125 buildings and was one of the largest facilities of its kind in the world.

Plate 70. Pennsylvania Railroad locomotive #1035 and tender, New Jersey, 1892. Digital positive from 4.25" x 6.5" glass plate negative. CH2019.6.443.

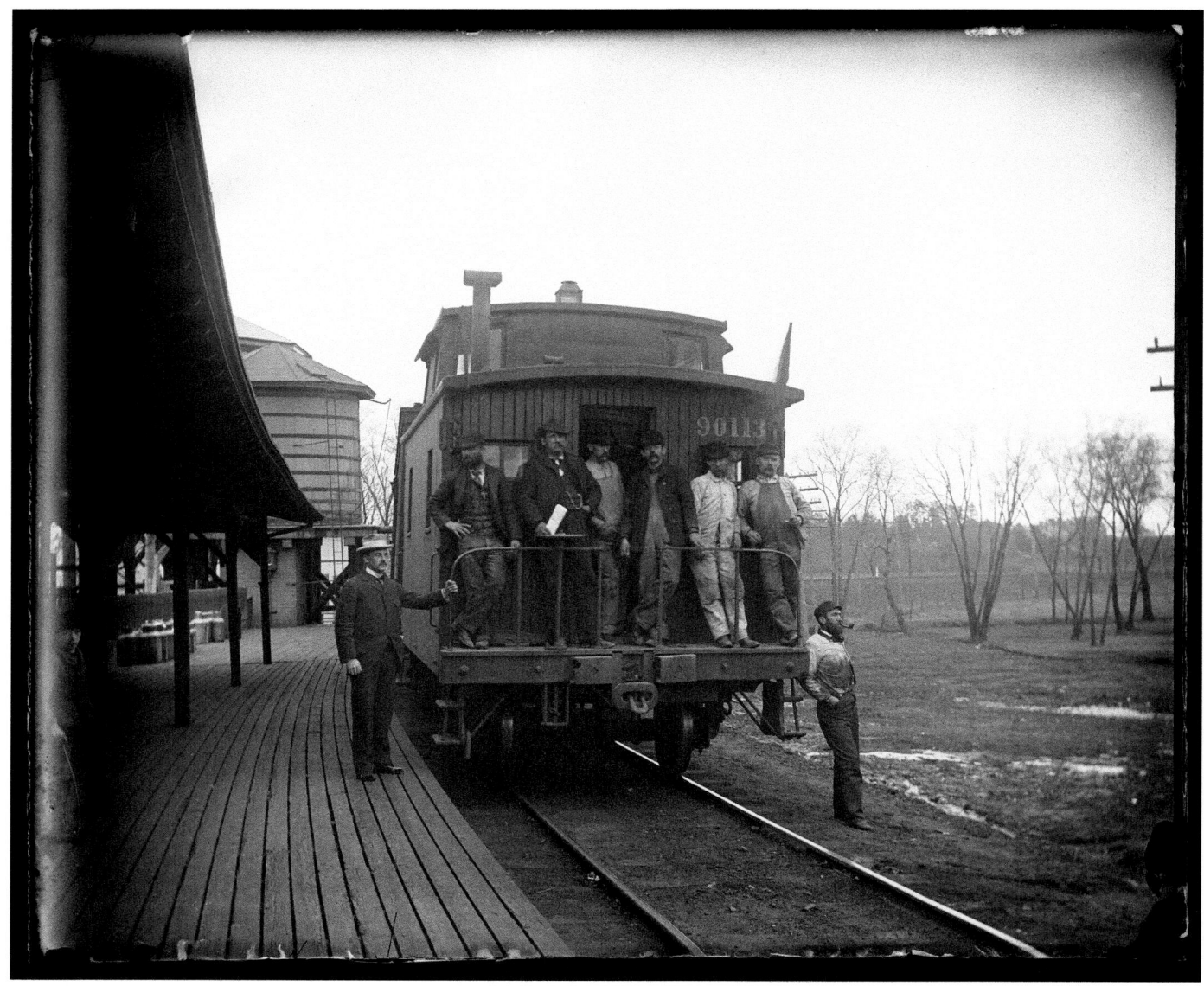

Plate 71. Train crew on cabin car (caboose), Bordentown, New Jersey, c. 1900. Digital positive from 4" x 5" glass plate negative. CH2019.6.156.

Castner embraced the photogenic potential of locomotives. He was naturally drawn to the churning, steaming machines that made passenger rail travel and freight transit possible. But his image of the humble caboose in **plate 71** is equally iconic. Known in the Pennsylvania Railroad network as a cabin car, the caboose marked the back of the train and provided a location where crew members stored tools, took breaks, ate meals, and socialized when not working on their designated tasks. It also served as a veritable mobile office for the piles of paperwork that railroad work required. Castner's image wonderfully captures the grit and spirit of a New Jersey train crew posing in their rolling workplace. According to the photographer's notes on the glassplate sleeve, Castner made

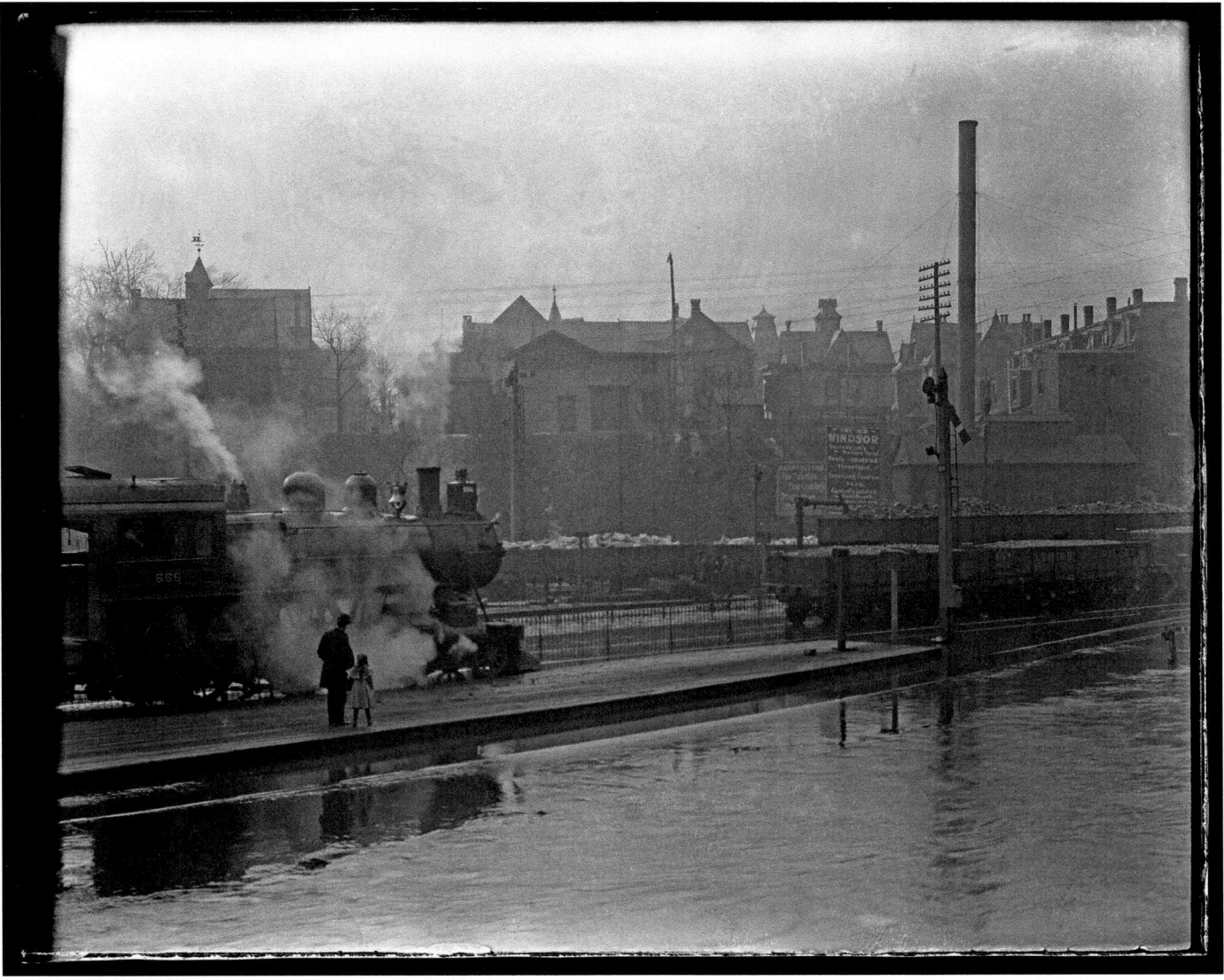

five prints of this image, which were likely distributed to some of the men in the photo.

Bringing young children to see trains was a common occurrence in Castner's time, just as it is today. On a rainy winter day at Trenton's main train station, the photographer captured the heartwarming image in **plate 72** of a man and his daughter getting an up-close view of Locomotive No. 556. The massive, steaming engine towers over the figures, a suggestion of how machines could dwarf humanity. The child was no doubt awestruck by the close presence of the monstrous and noisy locomotive, and the father, sensing its raw power, protectively grips the child's hand. Castner also records elements of the booming city for which this train station was an

Plate 72. *High Water*. Unidentified man and child with locomotive, Clinton Street Station, Trenton, New Jersey, 1902. Digital positive from 4" x 5" glass plate negative. CH2019.6.521.

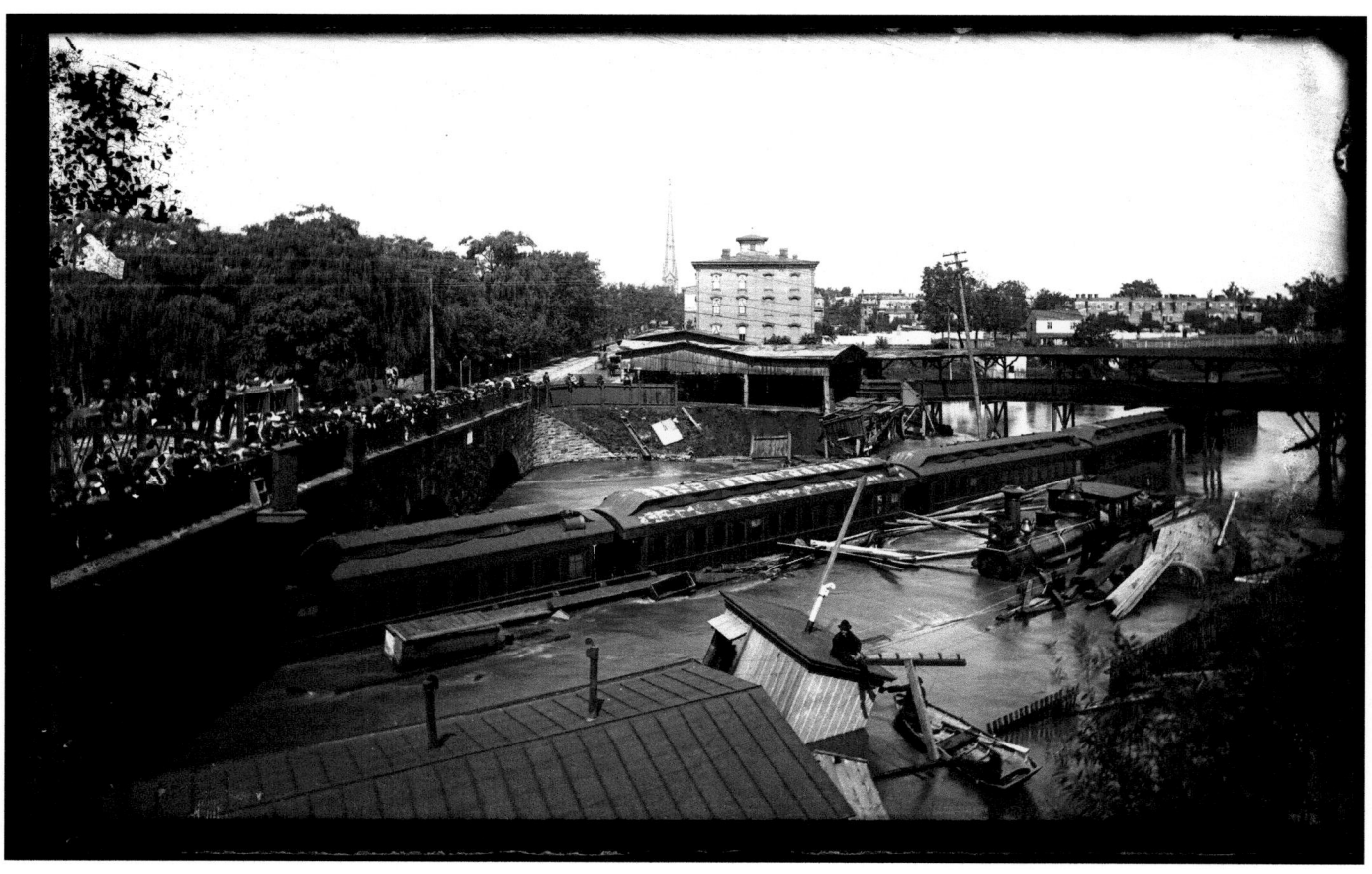

Plate 73. Crowds observing flood damage, Clinton Street Station, Trenton, New Jersey, 1882. Digital positive from 5" x 8" glass plate negative. CH2019.6.742.

important center. Coal cars hold the fuel that made the city's transportation and industry possible. Row houses, the homes for city workers, trace the skyline. Hand-lettered billboard advertisements, one promoting a hotel, suggest Trenton's status as an important East Coast travel stop and commercial hub.

Trenton's station on Clinton Street, still a central hub for trains, is depicted in **plate 73**. This image from a collodion or "wet-plate" negative is probably dated too early to have been made by Castner, who moved to Trenton around 1885 and was only 19 years old in 1882. He probably obtained it from another photographer and kept it as part of his personal collection. The scene depicts the aftermath of flooding at the main Trenton railroad station on Clinton Street (now South Clinton Avenue). Toppled structures and debris litter the scene. A locomotive and several Pullman cars remain submerged from the high water of the nearby Assunpink Creek. Throngs of people have gathered to observe the chaos from the safety of a bridge. Perhaps inspired by this earlier image, Castner would go on to

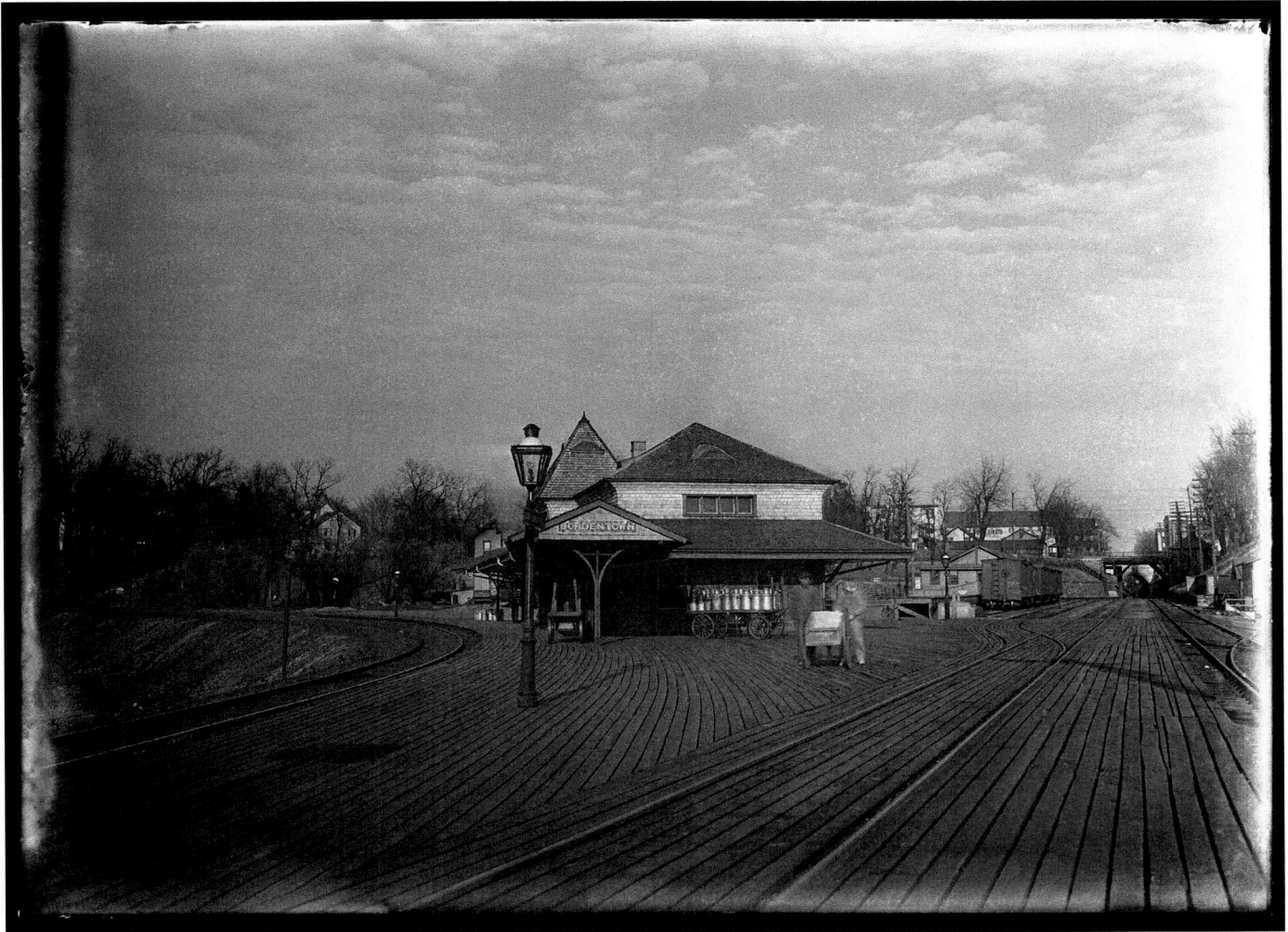

regularly document the flood waters that frequently troubled the station.

Castner's love of trains mandated a visit to Bordentown, a municipality in northern Burlington County with an important connection to New Jersey transportation history. The famed Camden and Amboy Railroad, the first passenger rail service to connect two American cities, passed through Bordentown. In 1832, the very first section of this historical railroad opened between Bordentown and Hightstown. Taken many years later from a point where Black's Creek enters the Delaware River near the mouth of Crosswicks Creek, **plate 74** captures a full view of the shake-shingled Bordentown Depot. The graceful curve of the rails on the left complements the straightaway on the right. The long triangle created by these converging lines perfectly frames the depot at the center, drawing the eye to the

Plate 74. Bordentown Train Depot, Bordentown, New Jersey, c. 1901. Digital positive from 5" x 7" glass plate negative. CH2019.6.78.

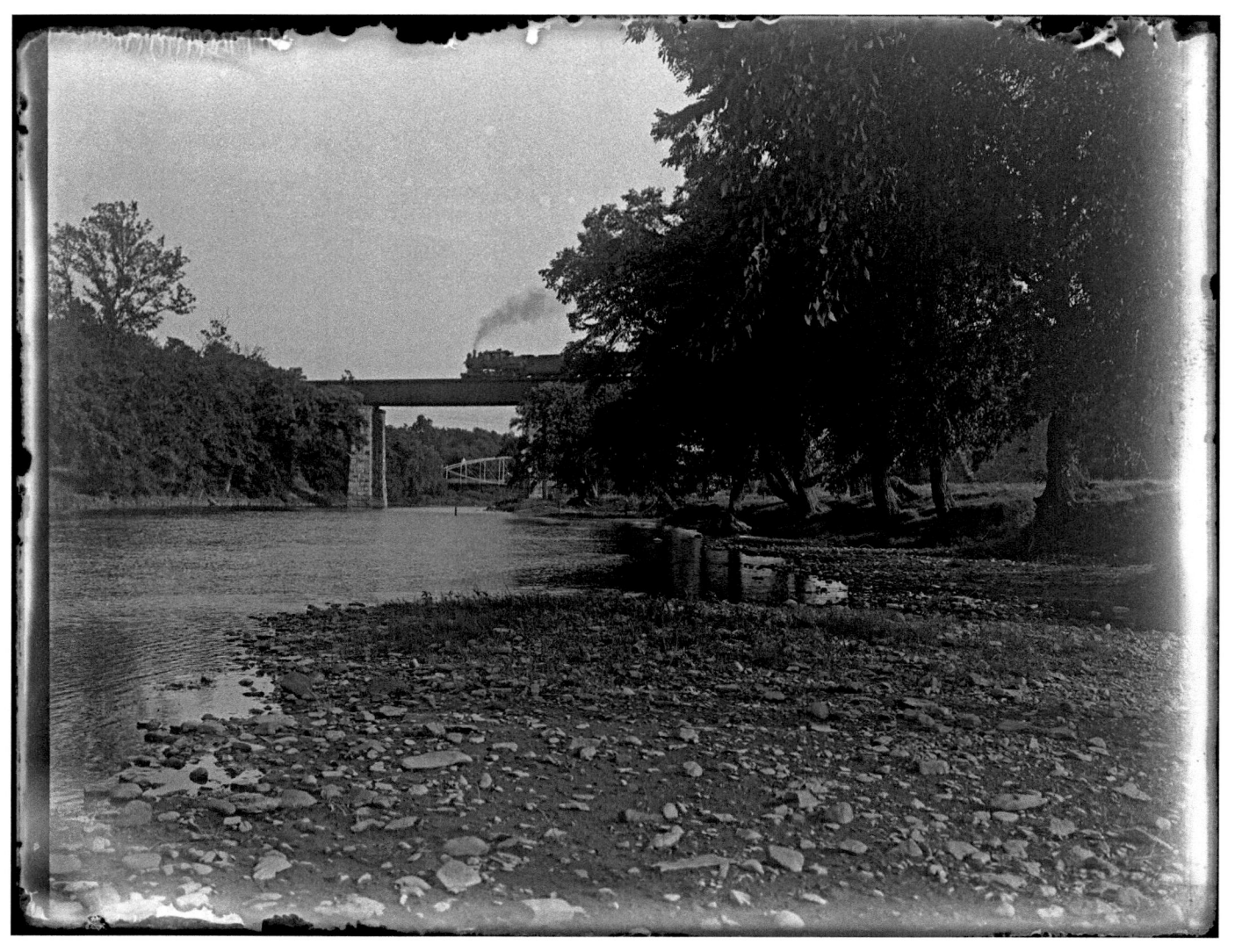

Plate 75. Train crossing the south branch of the Raritan River on the Lehigh Valley Railroad Bridge, with the Neshanic Station Bridge (Elm Street Bridge) in the background, Neshanic Station, New Jersey, 1909. Digital positive from 3.25" x 4.25" glass plate negative. CH2019.6.58.

structure itself and the two ghostly figures in front of it. Just visible at the far end of the frame is the graceful stone arched tunnel and the bridge carrying Farnsworth Street, lasting artifacts from the early days of the Camden and Amboy.

Timing was everything in this nicely composed shot (**plate 75**) of a steaming locomotive chugging its way across the south branch of the Raritan River on the Lehigh Valley Railroad Bridge in Neshanic Station (Hunterdon County). Taking advantage of the low water level, Castner set up his camera and tripod on river rocks just downstream from the bridge and waited for the perfect moment to capture a moment of action. The essence of this "decisive moment" photograph is the contrast between the serene, peaceful waterway flowing quietly by the tree-lined banks and the powerful, noisy steam engine bellowing smoke.

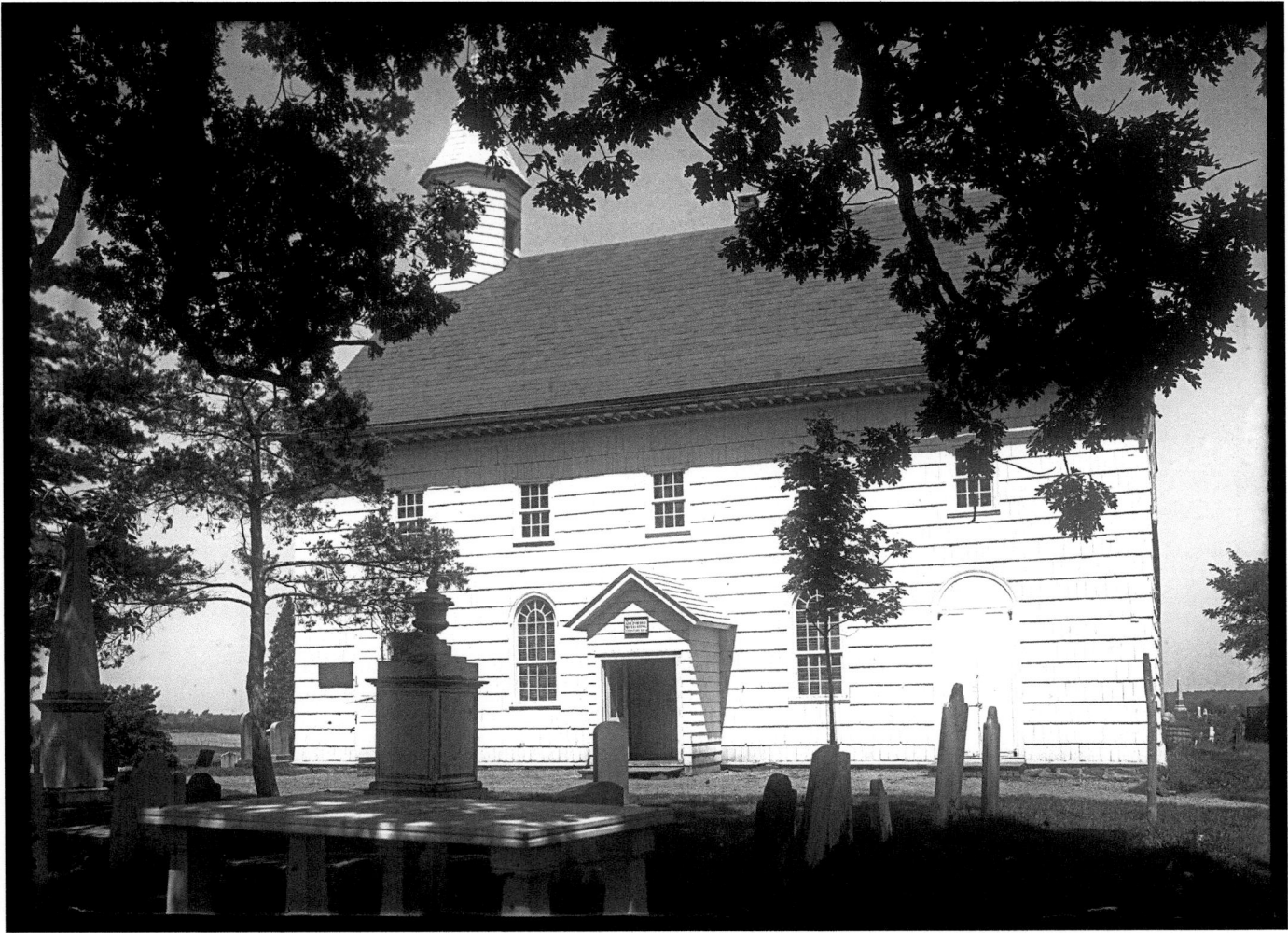

When Castner took the photograph, the train still represented the success and power of the United States by carrying freight and passengers to faraway destinations over land in days instead of weeks and months using horse- or oxen-drawn vehicles. The Lehigh Valley Railroad was originally built for the purpose of hauling anthracite coal from northeastern Pennsylvania to markets in New York City and other large population centers. Visible between the stone supports of the railroad bridge is the iron Neshanic Station Bridge, also known as the Elm Street Bridge. This historically important, lenticular truss bridge was built in 1896 by the Berlin Iron Bridge Company. It still stands and is on the National Register of Historic Places.

In 1904, Castner traveled by rail across central New Jersey to photograph the Old Tennent Presbyterian Church and burying ground (**plate 76**). It may have been a pilgrimage of

Plate 76. Old Tennent Presbyterian Church, Tennent, Manalapan Township, New Jersey, 1904. Digital positive from 5" x 7" glass plate negative. CH2019.6.7.

sorts for the young Presbyterian, who was an active parishioner of Bethany Presbyterian Church in the Chambersburg section of Trenton. His interest in history may have attracted him to the church, which was built in 1751 and traced its roots to Scottish immigrants who formed the congregation in 1692. During the Battle of Monmouth on June 28, 1778, the church served as a field hospital for the Patriots. In Castner's photo, the midsummer sunlight reflects on the wooden shingles, making the structure glow with a spiritual warmth. Castner took the shot from beneath a nearby oak tree, its dangling limbs framing the façade of the structure and adding a sense of solemnity and pastoral peace that, in Castner's mind, befit this revered religious institution. Castner included a photo of this church in the annual exhibit of the Trenton Photographic Society in February of 1907.

Castner had a friend take the picture of him in **plate 77** on the grounds of the Old Tennent Presbyterian Church. The cameraman was John S. Neary, a fellow amateur photographer who lived and worked in Trenton from the 1890s through 1920s—the same time frame as Castner. While it is not known how they met, they both were members of the Trenton Camera Club, also called the Trenton Photographic Society, organized in January 1898. Castner posed with the tools of his trade, a camera case serving as a makeshift seat and a camera mounted on a tripod behind him functioning as a hat stand for his fedora.

Plate 78 documents tiny Tennent Station, a stop on the short-line Freehold and Jamesburg Agricultural Railroad that crossed Monmouth and Middlesex Counties in central New Jersey. Although passenger rail travel to Tennent ended long ago, the line is still used occasionally for freight and is now called the Freehold Industrial Track. The raking light on the peaceful railroad stop provides complementary shadows that enhance the three-dimensionality of the photograph. To the right of Castner is John S. Neary, his fellow amateur

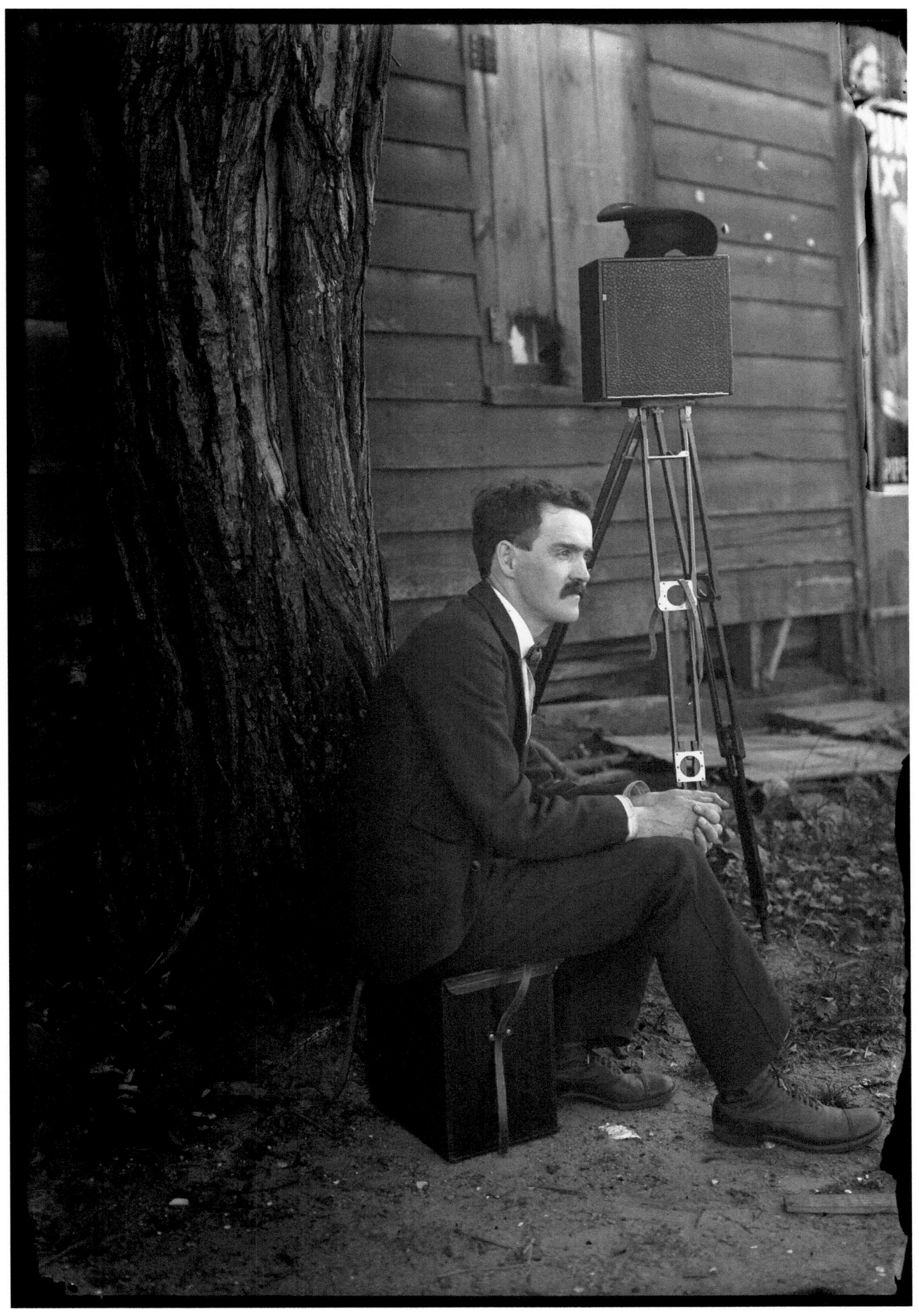

Plate 77. Grant Castner on the grounds of Old Tennent Presbyterian Church, Tennent, Manalapan Township, New Jersey, 1904. Digital positive from 5" x 7" glass plate negative. CH2019.6.908.

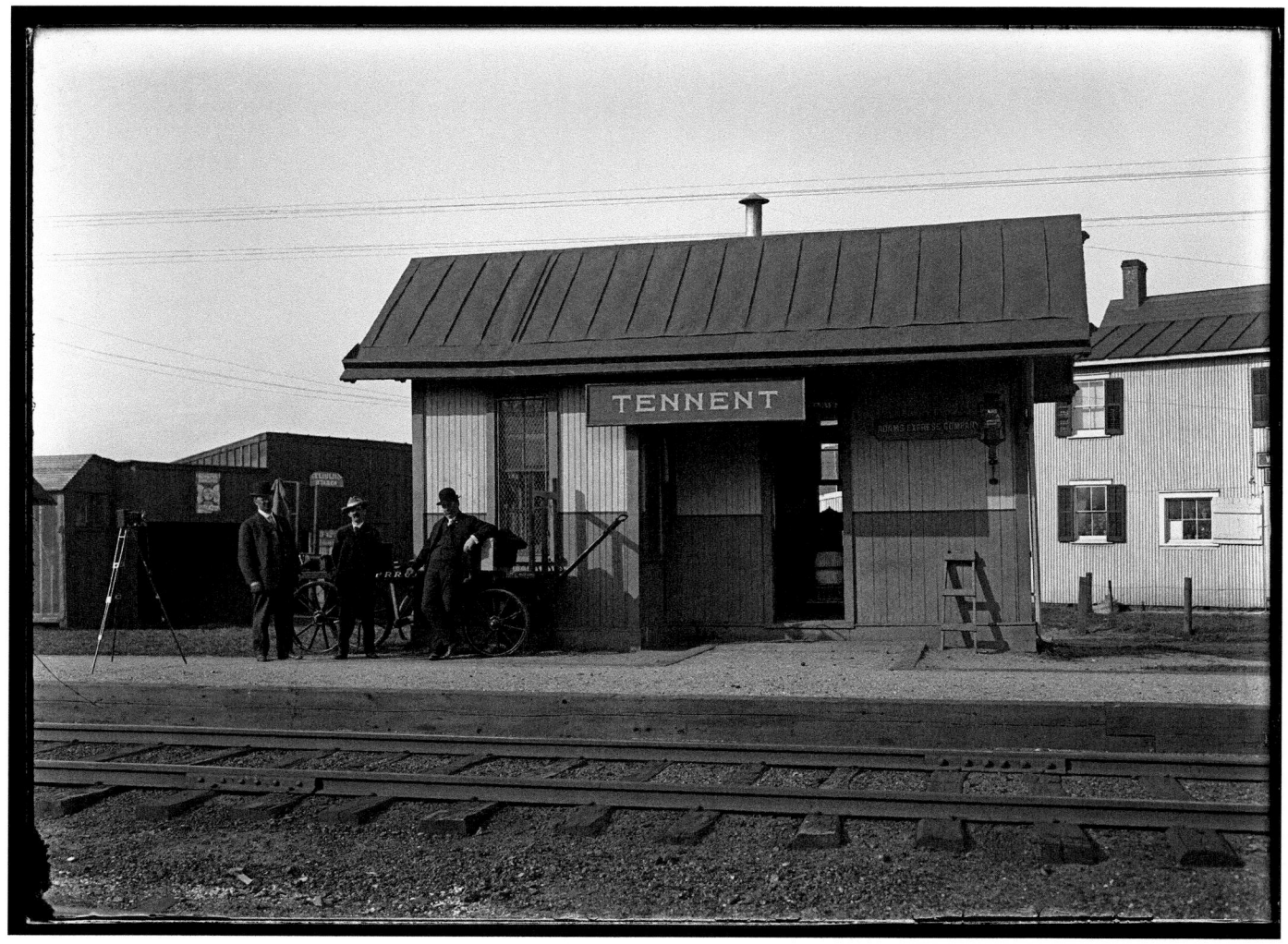

Plate 78. Grant Castner (center) at Tennent Rail Station, Tennent, Manalapan Township, Monmouth County, New Jersey, 1904. Digital positive from 5" x 7" glass plate negative. CH2019.6.140.

photographer from Trenton. The second camera on a tripod at the far left of the frame was deliberately included in the shot—a symbol of the friends' passion for the medium of photography. Castner and Neary are interred near each other in Greenwood Cemetery, Hamilton Township, New Jersey.

Incorporated on December 22, 1894, the Burlington and Mount Holly Traction Railroad Company operated an electrified, shorter-distance transit line that shuttled passengers between Burlington, the county's largest city, and the county seat. Three combination baggage and passenger cars, including Car 2 pictured in **plate 79**, were built at the Jackson and Sharp Company shops in Wilmington, Delaware. In his image, Castner was careful to include the hardware and cables that supplied power to the vehicle from above, highlighting the novelty of applying the power of electricity to public transit.

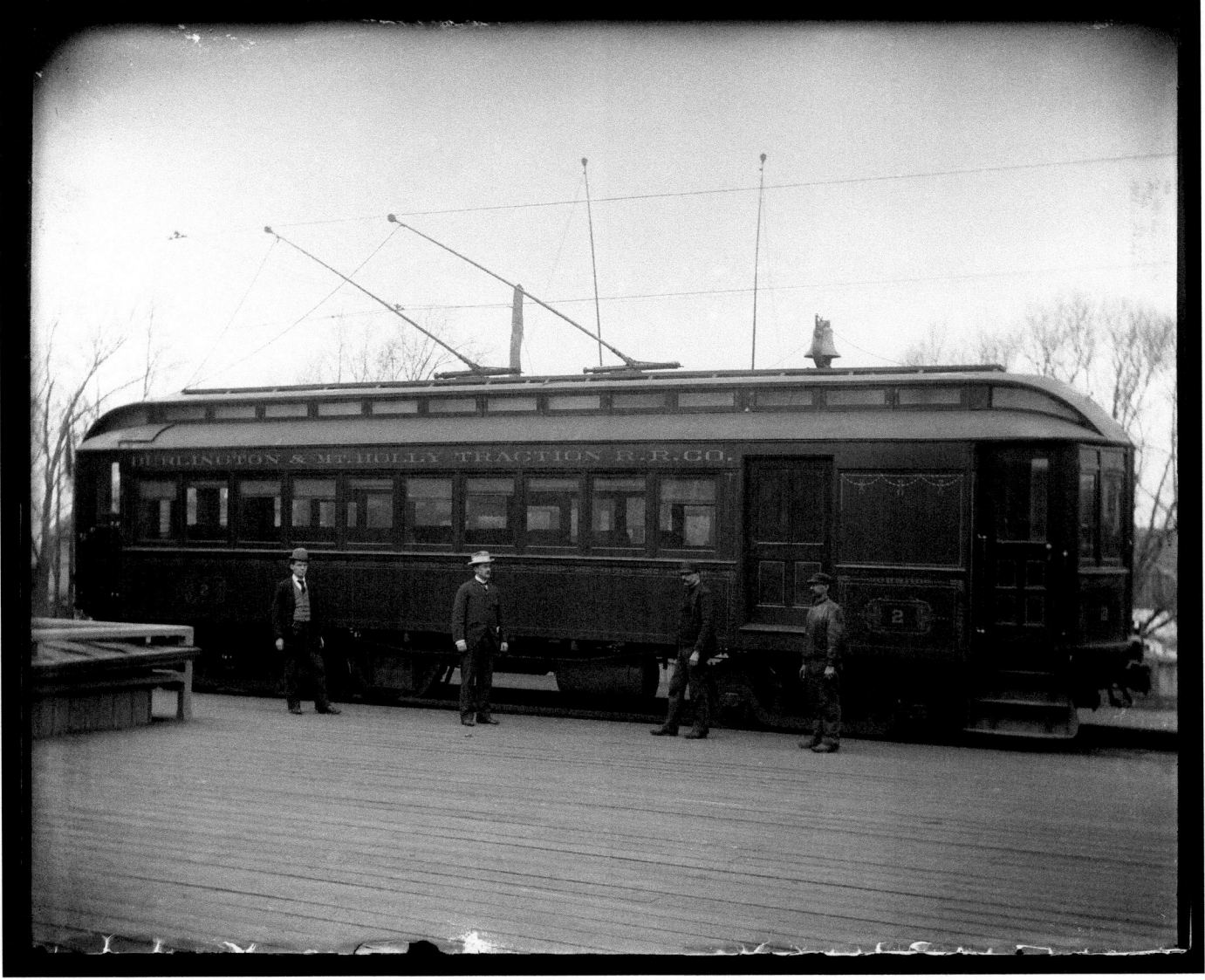

Castner's notes indicate that the man at the center is H.A. Hasson. He may have been a fellow Trenton resident named Harry Hasson, a career railroader who worked his way up from flagman to brakeman to conductor in the first decade of the twentieth century. Since Hasson appears in other Castner photographs, he may have been a friend of the photographer who accompanied him on some of his travels by rail.

Though unrelated to New Jersey politically, the borough of Morrisville and other parts of Bucks County, Pennsylvania, have had an indelible cultural and economic connection to the Garden State, particularly the city of Trenton. Many Trenton industries employed Pennsylvania residents who commuted to work by crossing the river. Nearby Pennsylvanians relied

Plate 79. Burlington and Mount Holly Traction Railroad Company, Burlington County, New Jersey, 1896. Digital positive from 4" x 5" glass plate negative. CH2019.6.157.

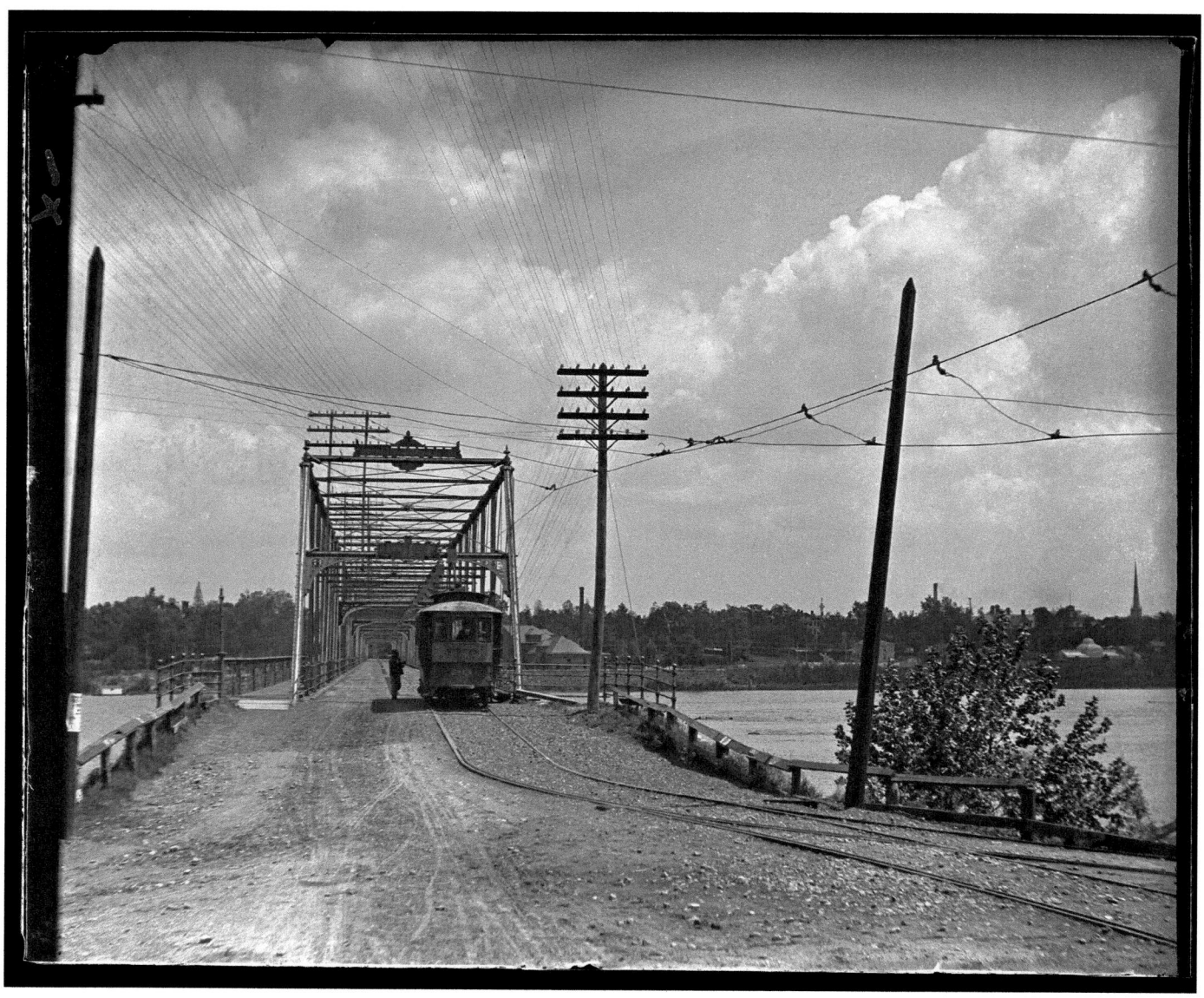

Plate 80. Streetcar, Calhoun Street Bridge, Morrisville, Pennsylvania, 1902. Digital positive from 4" x 5" glass plate negative. CH2019.6.438.

on Trenton, a booming, regional hub with a large commercial district, for business and recreation. **Plate 80** depicts the electric streetcar line that crossed the Delaware River at Calhoun Street to transport people back and forth from Bucks County to downtown Trenton. Castner set up his camera on the Pennsylvania side of the river. His photograph looks east across the Calhoun Street Bridge, preserving a view of Trolley 20 as it stops to pick up a passenger. Just shy of twenty years old when Castner took the image, the Calhoun Street Bridge was renovated and rededicated in 2009–2010 for its 125th anniversary. It still connects the two states today.

8

River

Grant Castner, a native of the riverside town of Belvidere, New Jersey, grew up with a strong affection for the Delaware River. By the late 1800s, the Delaware had become an important economic force. Industries lined its banks. Communities drank its water. Large watercraft transported goods to the Delaware Bay, Philadelphia, and Trenton. Ferries and bridges provided inter-state transit avenues from shore to shore. Fishermen and duck hunters harvested its wildlife. But the river was about more than work. It was also a place for leisure. The waterway was a perfect respite for people hoping to escape crowded, smoky cities for the great outdoors.

The Delaware River is a recurring subject in Castner's glass plate collection. The photographer often spent his free time exploring and photographing along the waterway. To the south of Trenton, he found a wide, tidal river that showed many signs of the industrialization and urbanization characteristic of the day. To the north, he documented a picturesque, forest-lined river coveted for recreation.

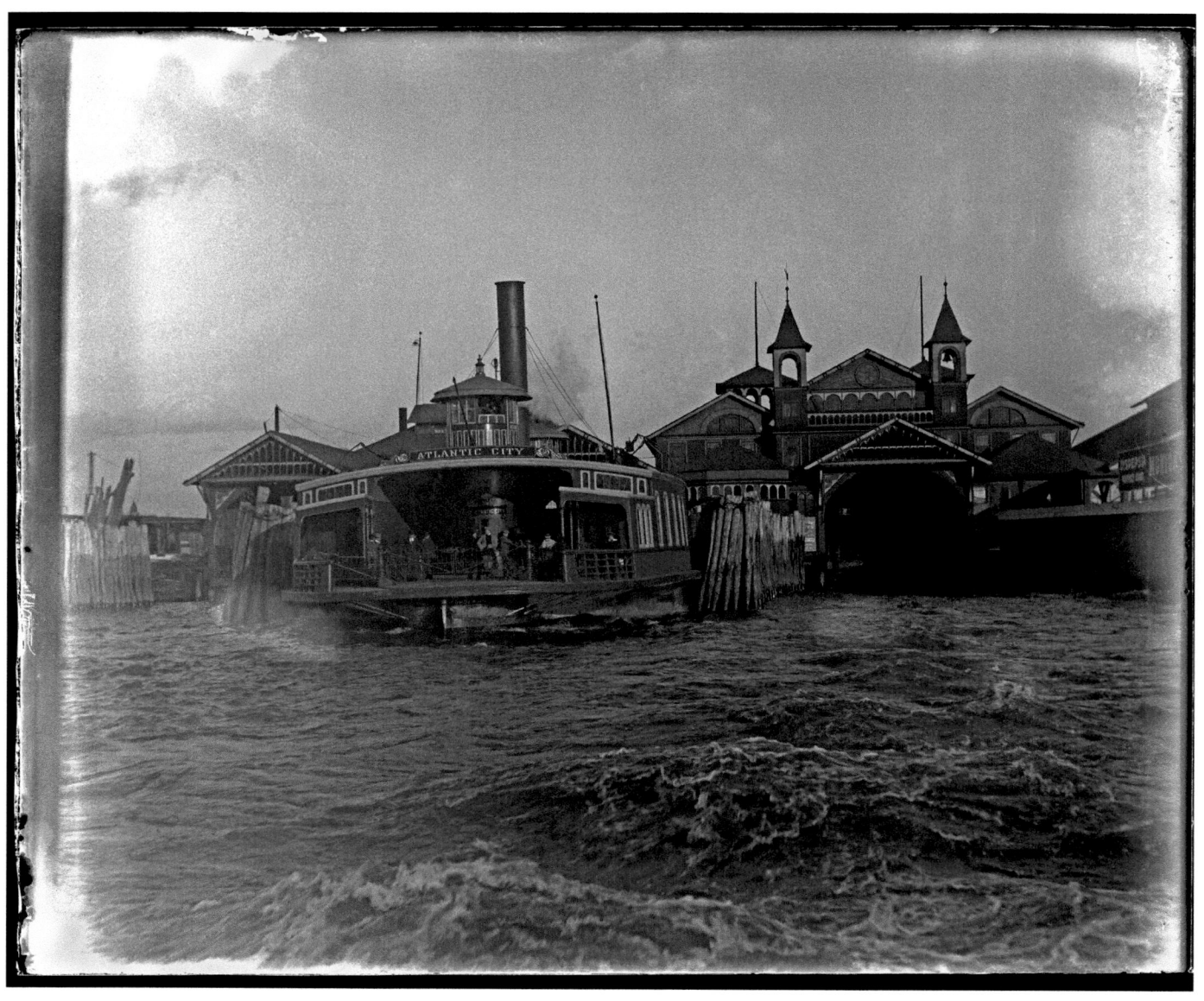

Plate 81. Kaighn's Point Ferry House, Camden, New Jersey, 1896. Digital positive from 4" x 5" glass plate negative. CH2019.6.216.

Castner visited Camden thirty years before the building of the first of the massive suspension bridges that now connect the city with neighboring Philadelphia. At the time, a primary means of crossing the river was by ferry. The photographer captured the view in **plate 81** of a ferry after it had left the terminal building at Kaighn's Point in Camden. The foreboding sky and white-capped waves in the foreground convey a sense of frenetic energy, even angst—the big city in action. A sign in view reads "Atlantic City" because the Philadelphia and Atlantic City Railroad (part of the Reading Railroad system) routed its trains into Kaighn's

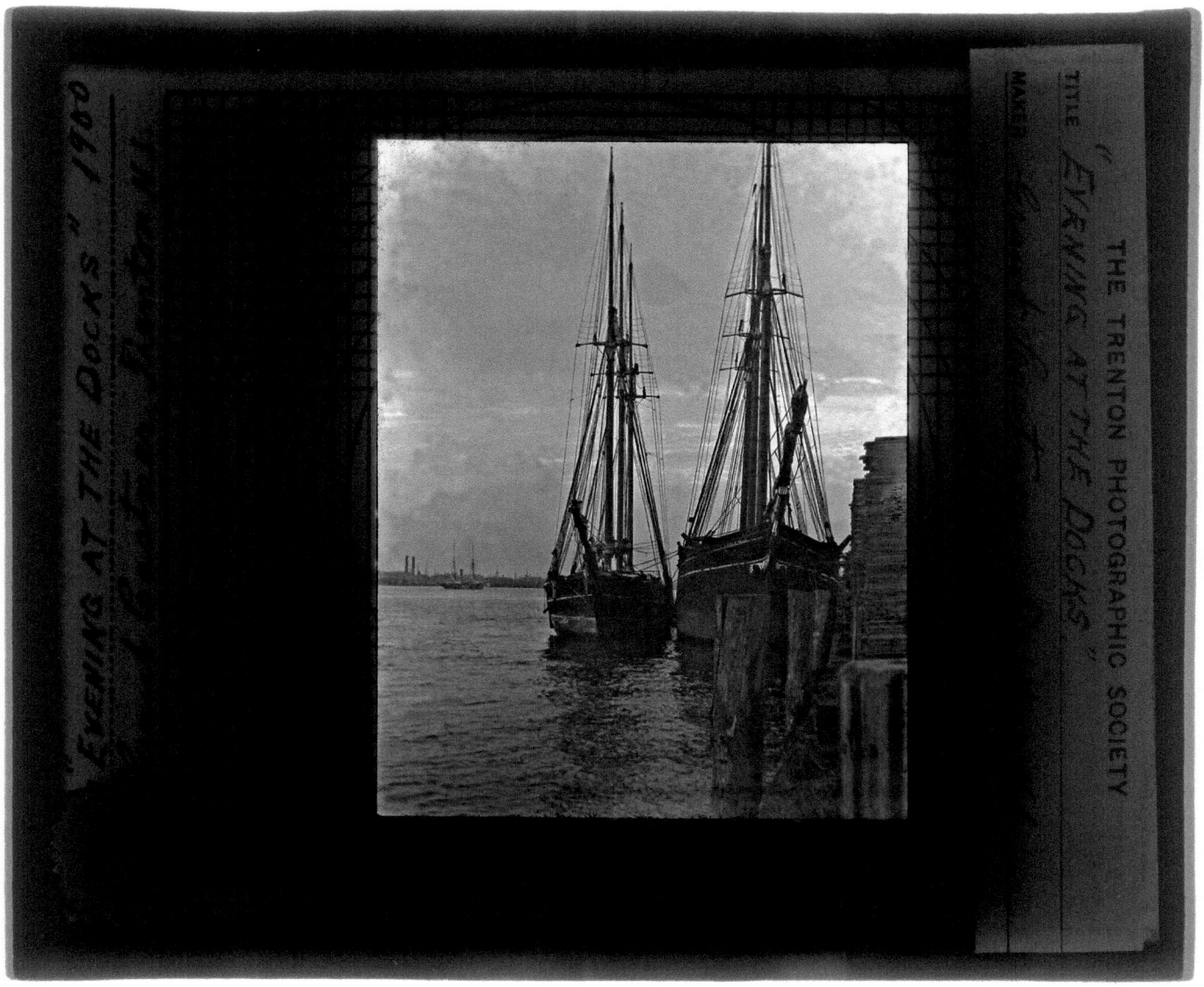

Plate 82. *Evening at the Docks.* Delaware River tall ships, Cooper's Point, Camden, New Jersey, 1900. Digital scan from 3.25" x 4" glass lantern slide. CH2019.6.1088.

Point. Many Philadelphians en route to the attractions of the Jersey Shore passed through this very station. In 1888, the ferry was reorganized as the Delaware River Ferry Company of New Jersey and operated through 1938. Ferry travel declined after the opening of the Delair Bridge (a railroad bridge) in 1896 and the Delaware Bridge, now called the Ben Franklin Bridge, in 1926. The Walt Whitman Bridge opened in 1957.

Castner's juxtaposition of the towering masts of tall sailing ships against the evening sky at dusk in **plate 82** earned high praise and accolades among his peers, for whom

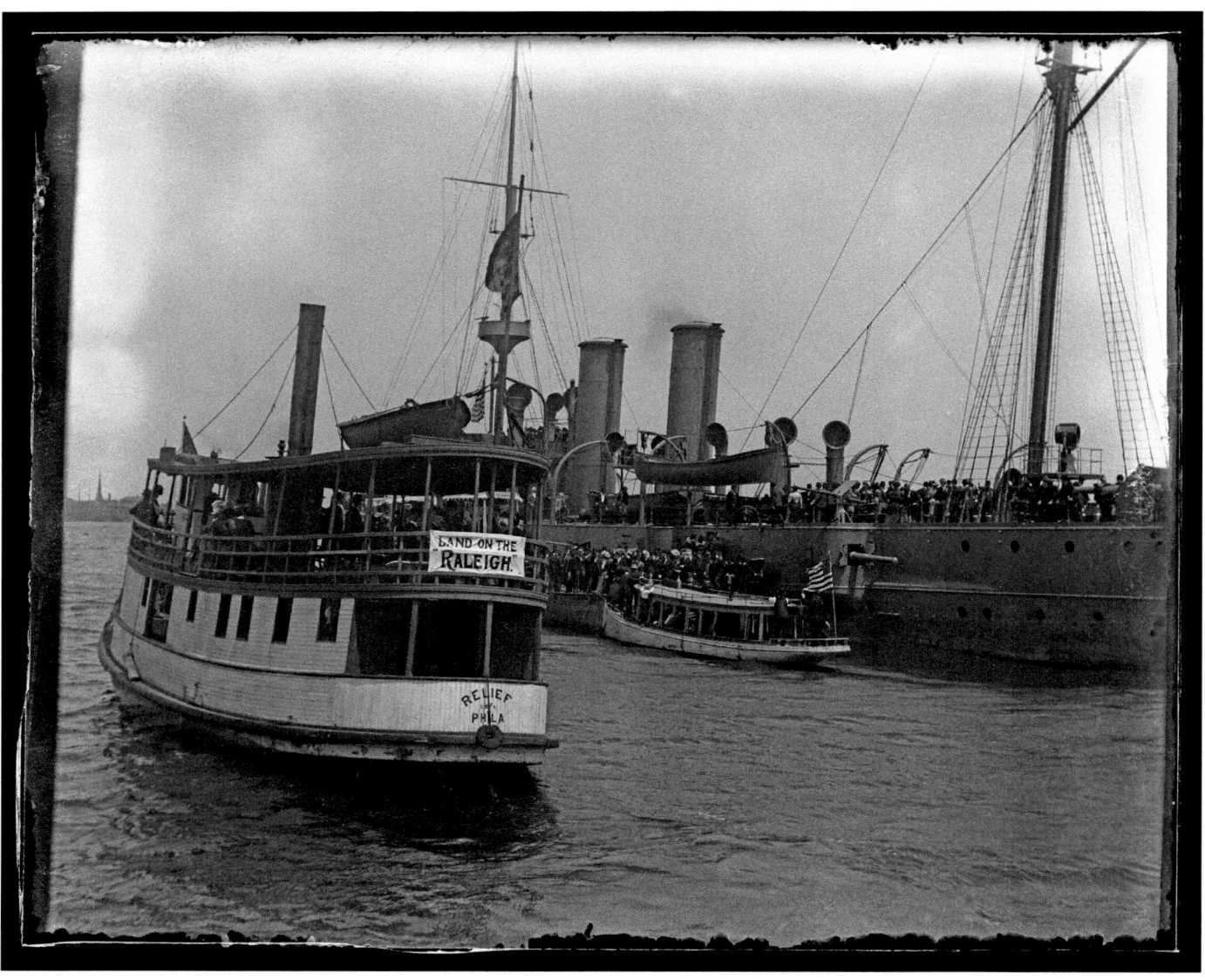

Plate 83. *U.S.S. Raleigh*, Delaware River, near Camden, New Jersey and Philadelphia, Pennsylvania, c. 1898–1899. Digital positive from 4" x 5" glass plate negative. CH2019.6.240.

maritime views constituted a popular photographic genre. Perhaps a historical nod to the colonial era when huge seagoing ships were the first European vessels to navigate the deep, tidal waters of the lower Delaware River, it was taken at Cooper's Point, Camden, with the sprawling skyline of Philadelphia in the distance. In March of 1903, Castner exhibited a framed print of this image at Trenton Photographic Society's fourth annual exhibition held at the School of Industrial Arts. The photograph was so admired that it was one of ten submissions chosen to hang permanently inside the school. Unfortunately, the print's current whereabouts, if it still exists, is unknown. The reproduction here is from a glass lantern slide, a positive transparency that Castner made for magic lantern slideshows that he prepared for camera club members and the general public.

In 1898–1899, a flotilla of naval ships that saw service in the recent Spanish-American War gathered in the Delaware River between Camden and Philadelphia. One, the *U.S.S. Raleigh*, was marketed as a tourist attraction since it had played a key role in the May 1, 1898, Battle of Manila Bay. Castner was on the scene to document the patriotic event, snapping **plate 83** of crowds of visitors arriving at the *Raleigh* aboard smaller watercraft. Part of the squadron led by famed Admiral George Dewey, the *Raleigh* is credited with firing the first shot in the important battle—an engagement that marked a resounding defeat for the Spanish navy. It was sold for scrap in 1921, but the *U.S.S. Olympia*, Dewey's flagship at the Battle of Manila, had a better fate; it is now a museum attraction at Penn's Landing in Philadelphia.

Plate 84 earned Castner a write-up in the *Trenton Evening Times* on September 20, 1899. The newspaper admired how the photographer took the image through the bore of a monstrous, 14-foot cannon aboard the *U.S.S. Raleigh*: "Mr. Castner placed his camera close to the muzzle of the gun, while the one whose picture was taken looked in at the breech. In a quarter of a second, the photograph was taken, and it is surprising to note how plain the man's features can be seen. The interior of the gun, too, is plainly visible in the picture and the twist of the grooves can be distinguished." Castner was also quite pleased with the composition as this was one of the images that he prepared as a lantern slide.

In 1895, Castner captured the rare image in **plate 85** of a barge using the power of wind to sail up the wide expanse of the Delaware River with the Philadelphia skyline on the horizon. The cargo may have been intended as feed for horses—strong,

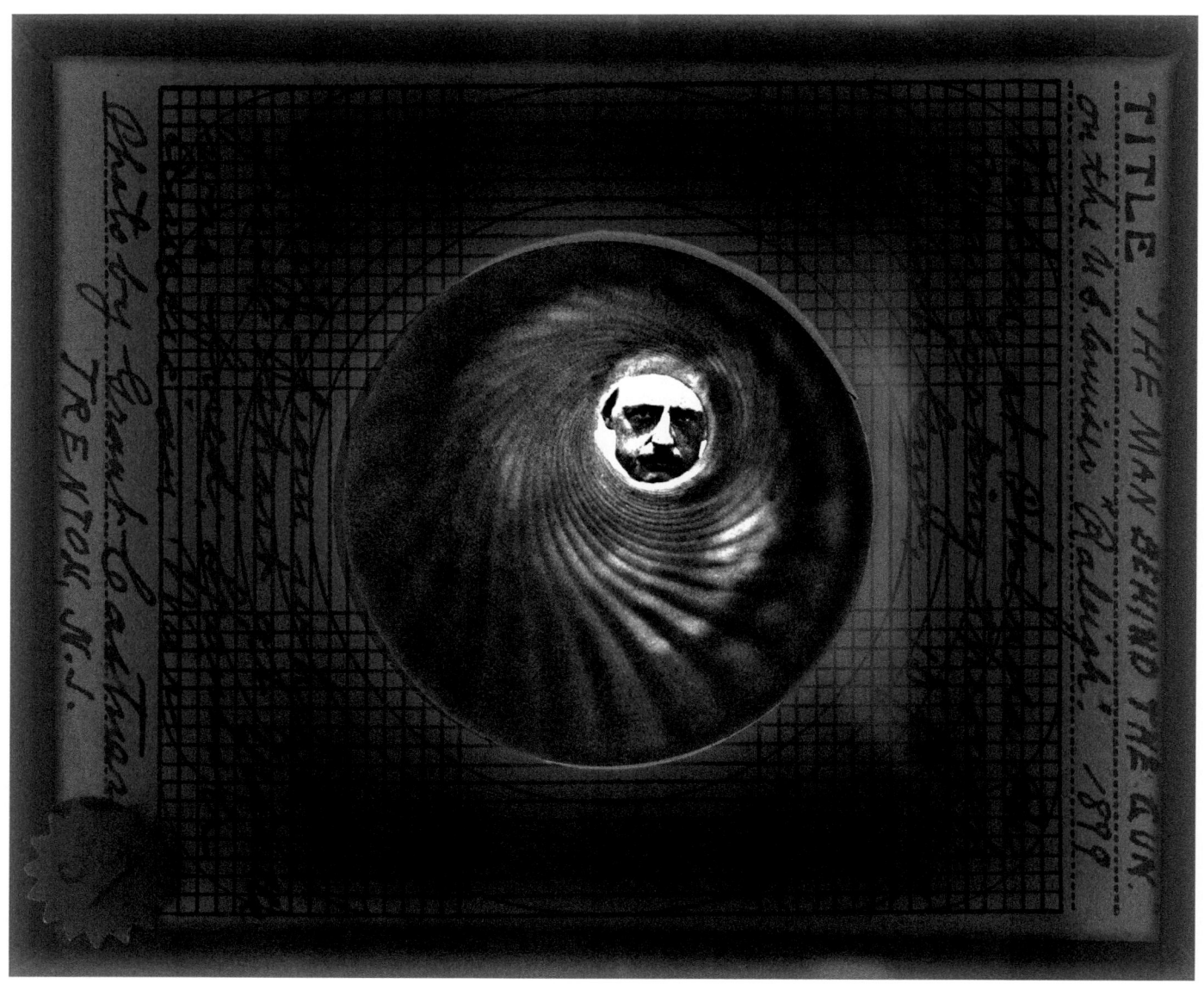

Plate 84. *The Man Behind the Gun.* Unidentified man aboard the *U.S.S. Raleigh*, Delaware River, near Camden, New Jersey and Philadelphia, Pennsylvania, c. 1898–1899. Digital scan from 3.25" x 4" glass lantern slide. CH2019.6.821.

reliable animals that continued to serve important functions in American cities at the turn of the twentieth century. But it is more likely that the barge carried salt hay, an essential but often-overlooked product in New Jersey history. Harvested from the salt marshes of South Jersey, the term *salt hay* encompasses multiple types of seedless grasses that are impervious to rot. Builders used salt hay to insulate concrete and masonry work to prevent freezing. Farmers used it to protect their harvest from frost. Transportation workers placed it on roads to help with traction. Perhaps most importantly, salt hay served as packing material for the delicate ceramics and glass

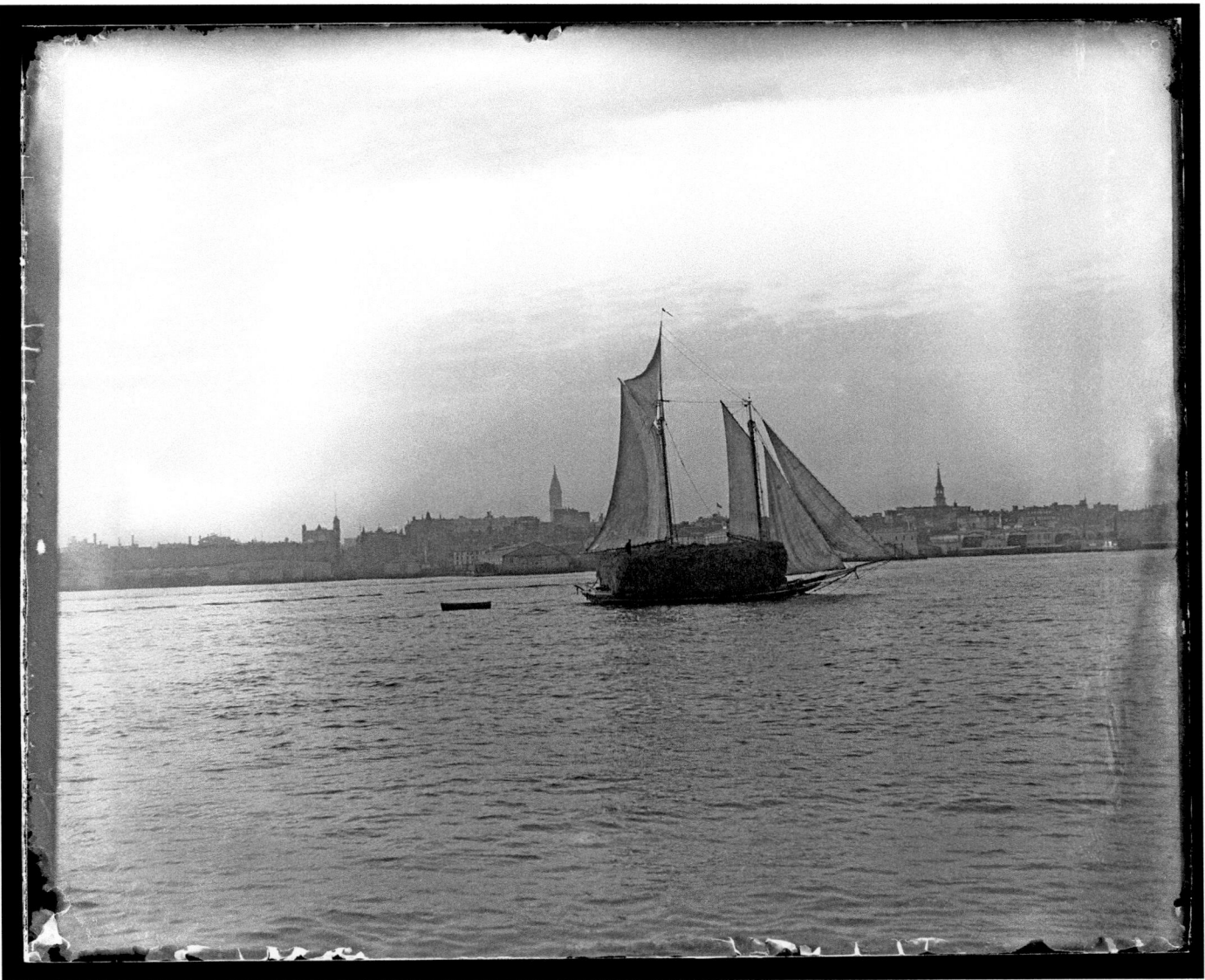

manufactured by local companies to protect the goods during shipment.

Titled *Ship Construction* by Castner, **plate 86** depicts two men hard at work on the hull of an unidentified wooden watercraft. Since Bordentown was one of the termini of the Delaware and Raritan Canal, the craft under construction most likely was some sort of canal boat. However, steamboats were also very important vessels on the Delaware River between Philadelphia and Trenton in the nineteenth century, and the labor depicted might be on the hull of a steamboat. Alternatively, since the deep river was also popular for pleasure craft,

Plate 85. Hay barge, Delaware River, near Camden, New Jersey, and Philadelphia, Pennsylvania, 1895. Digital positive from 4" x 5" glass plate negative. CH2019.6.298.

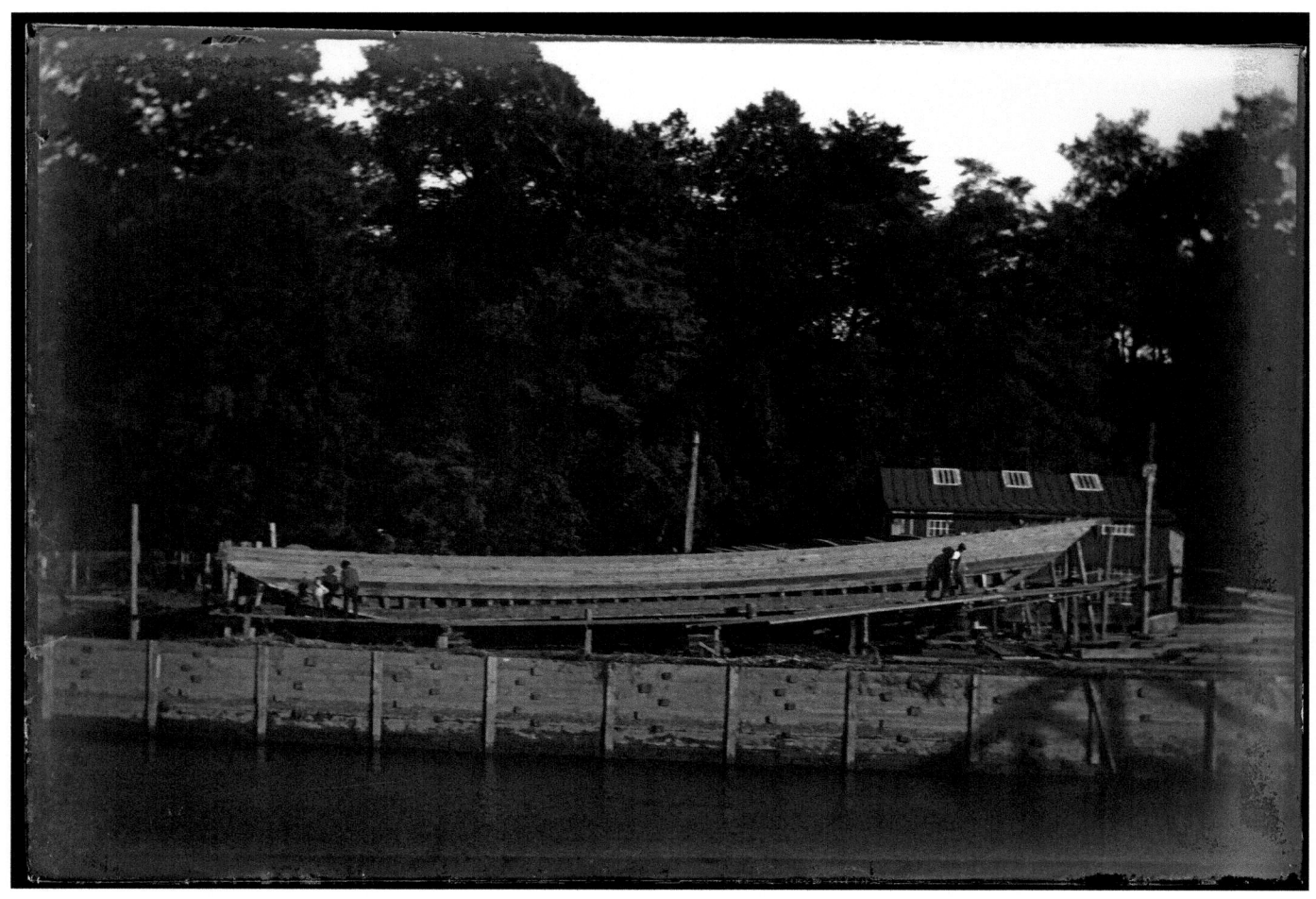

Plate 86. *Ship Construction.* Workers building a wooden vessel, Bordentown, New Jersey, 1890. Digital positive from 4.25" x 6.5" glass plate negative. CH2019.6.462.

the hull might also be that of a large, seaworthy sailing vessel. The location of the photograph is likely the long wooden wharf that was located down a steep embankment at the north end of Prince Street, close to the point where Crosswicks Creek empties into the Delaware River.

The counterbalanced angles of the two boats, human reflections in the water and long tree line dividing river from open sky beautify **plate 87** of shad fishermen at work. Then as now, the shad spend a few years at sea and then swim hundreds of miles up the Delaware River to spawn in the spring months. Lacey's Shad Fishery is believed to have operated at a place near Trenton called Hog Hole, at Morris Island (sometimes called Lacey's Island), on the Pennsylvania side of the Delaware River among the three, more well-known islands:

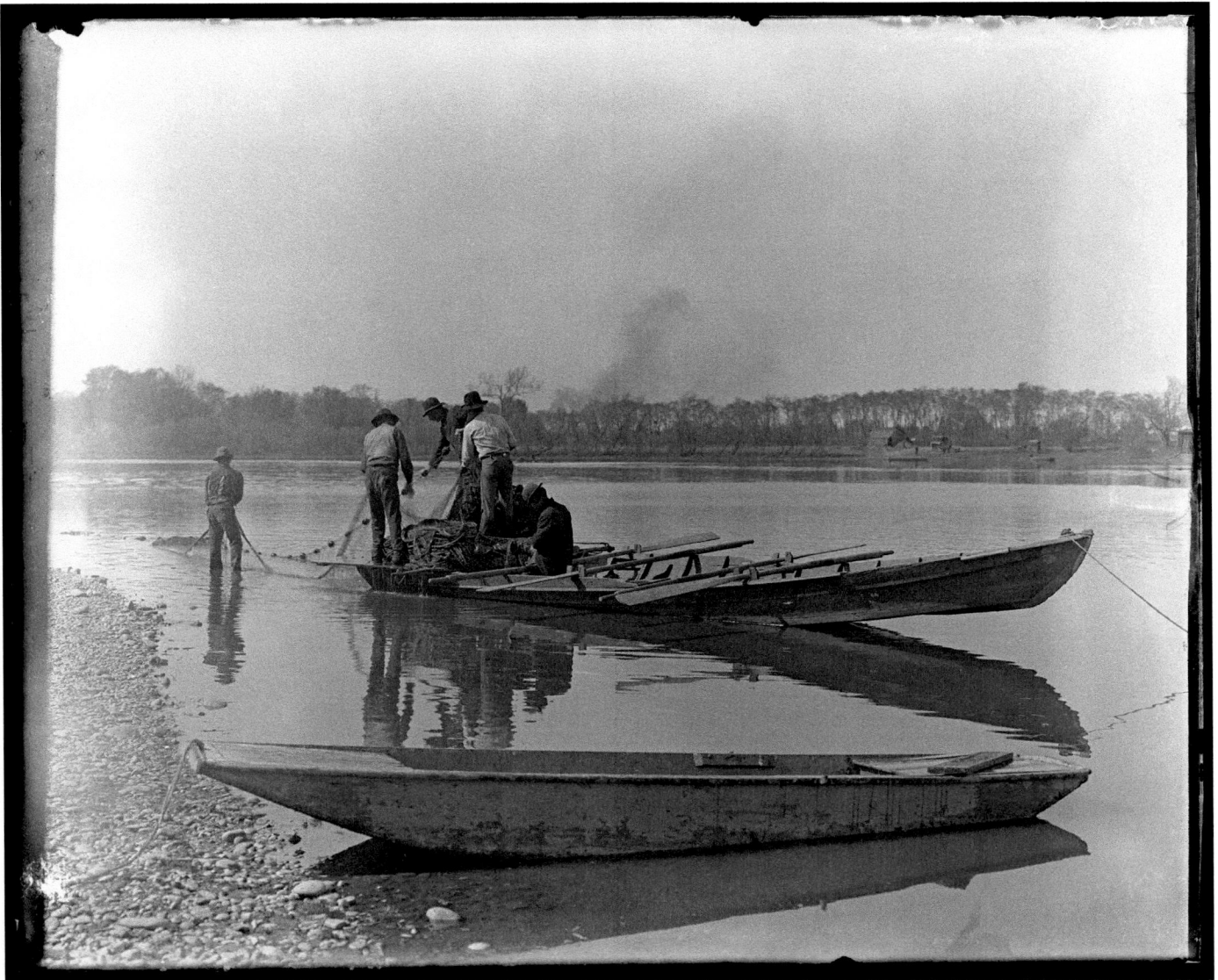

Moon Island, Biles Island, and Duck Island. Castner took the photograph on the Pennsylvania side of the river, and the view is toward New Jersey on the far shore.

For the most unfortunate of reasons, Castner received a write-up in a local newspaper for **plate 88** of three boys as they emerged from skinny dipping in the waters of the Delaware River in Morrisville. He came across the youths while walking along west side of the river on a late September day in 1900. The location is believed to be along Mill Street, now Delmorr Avenue. At the time, Mill Street ran alongside a channel of the Delaware that separated mainland Morrisville

Plate 87. *Leading the Nets.* Lacey's Shad Fishery, Delaware River near Trenton, New Jersey, 1901. Digital positive from 4" x 5" glass plate negative. CH2019.6.422.

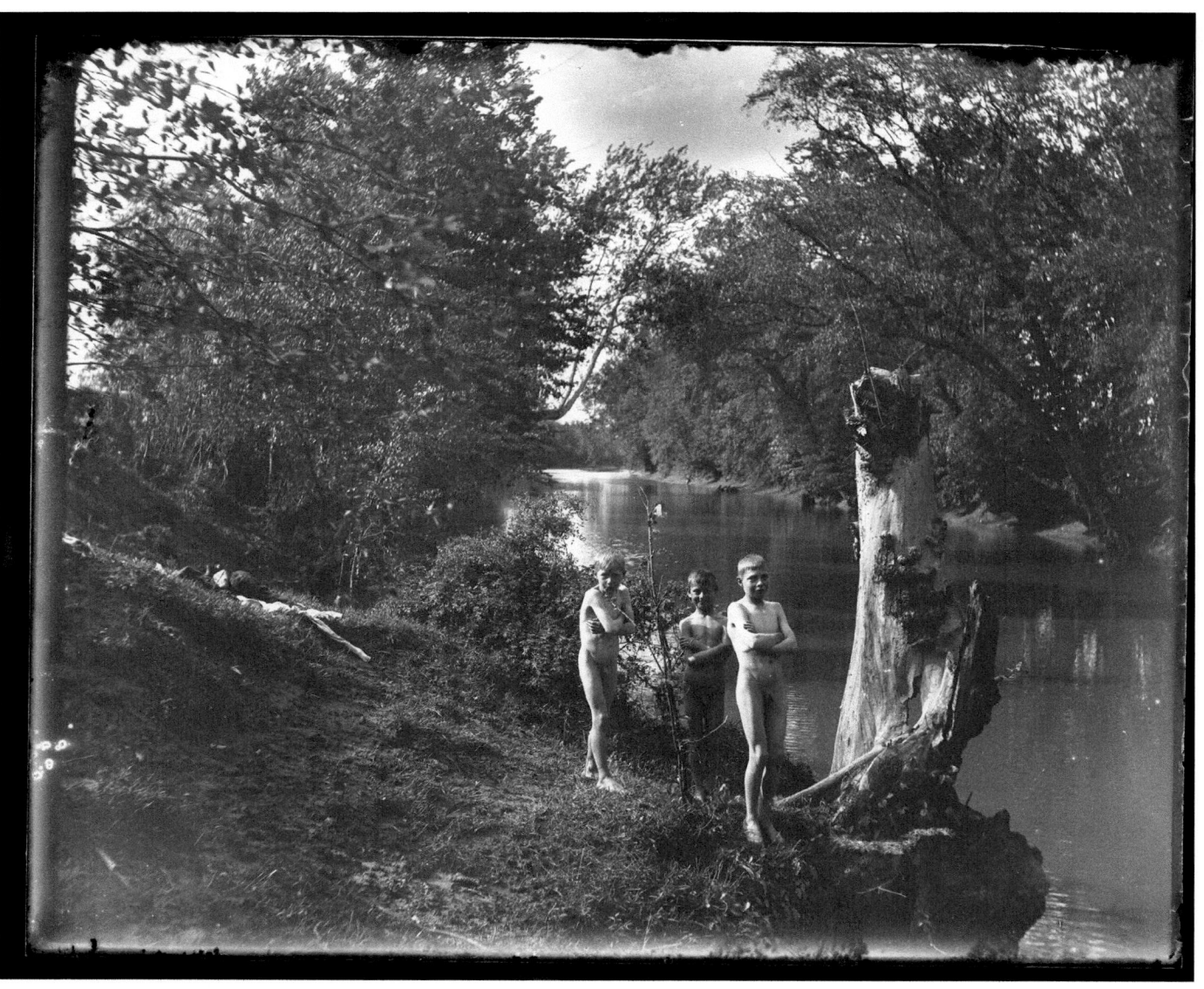

Plate 88. John Holderman and friends, Delaware River, Morrisville, New Jersey, 1900. Digital positive from 4" x 5" glass plate negative. CH2019.6.210.

from a partially wooded area called "The Island." On September 18, 1900, the *Trenton Evening Times* reported that one of the swimmers, John Holderman, had been struck in the head by a horse's kick and died at St. Francis Hospital in Trenton. The article was entitled, "Has Dead Boys Picture." There is no hint of Holderman's imminent fate in this bucolic scene, reminiscent of Thomas Eakins's photographs and paintings of young male swimmers in the 1880s.

Plate 89 documents a long-gone aspect of the architectural history of the upper Delaware River: the covered bridges that once connected New Jersey with neighboring Pennsylvania.

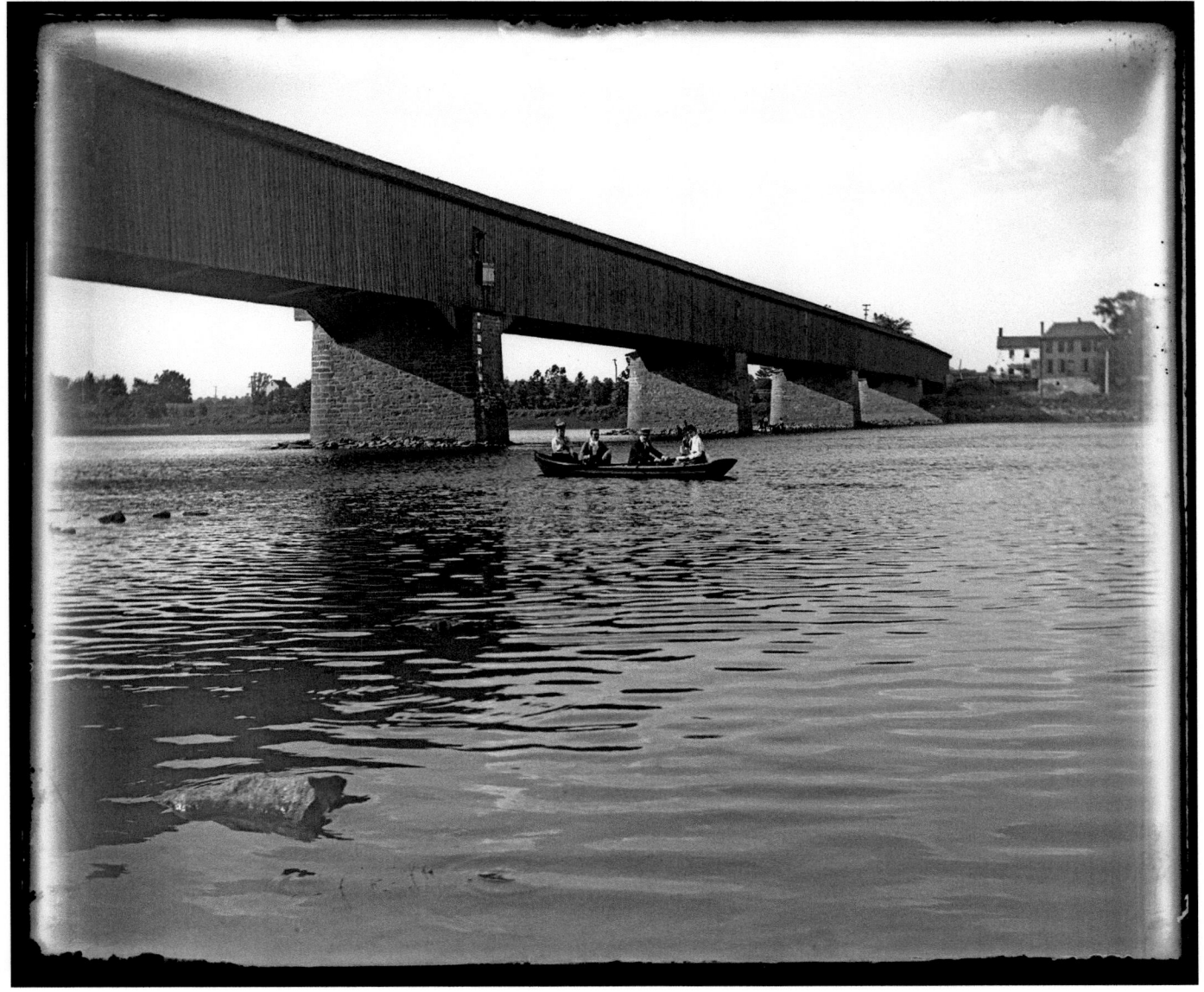

At one time, there were ten such bridges crossing into Bucks County alone. Castner used the wide diagonal line of the Yardley-Wilburtha Bridge as the key visual element in this photograph of boaters enjoying an outing on the Delaware River. The view is from the Pennsylvania side of the bridge looking east toward Wilburtha, a part of Ewing Township earlier known as Greensburg. This iconic bridge and several others were destroyed by The Great Pumpkin Flood in October 1903, when after twenty inches of rain numerous pumpkins ripped from adjacent fields floated downriver.

Plate 89. *Boating Party*. Delaware River at Yardley-Wilburtha Bridge, between Yardley, Pennsylvania, and Wilburtha (Ewing Township), New Jersey, 1894. Digital positive from 4" x 5" glass plate negative. CH2019.6.393.

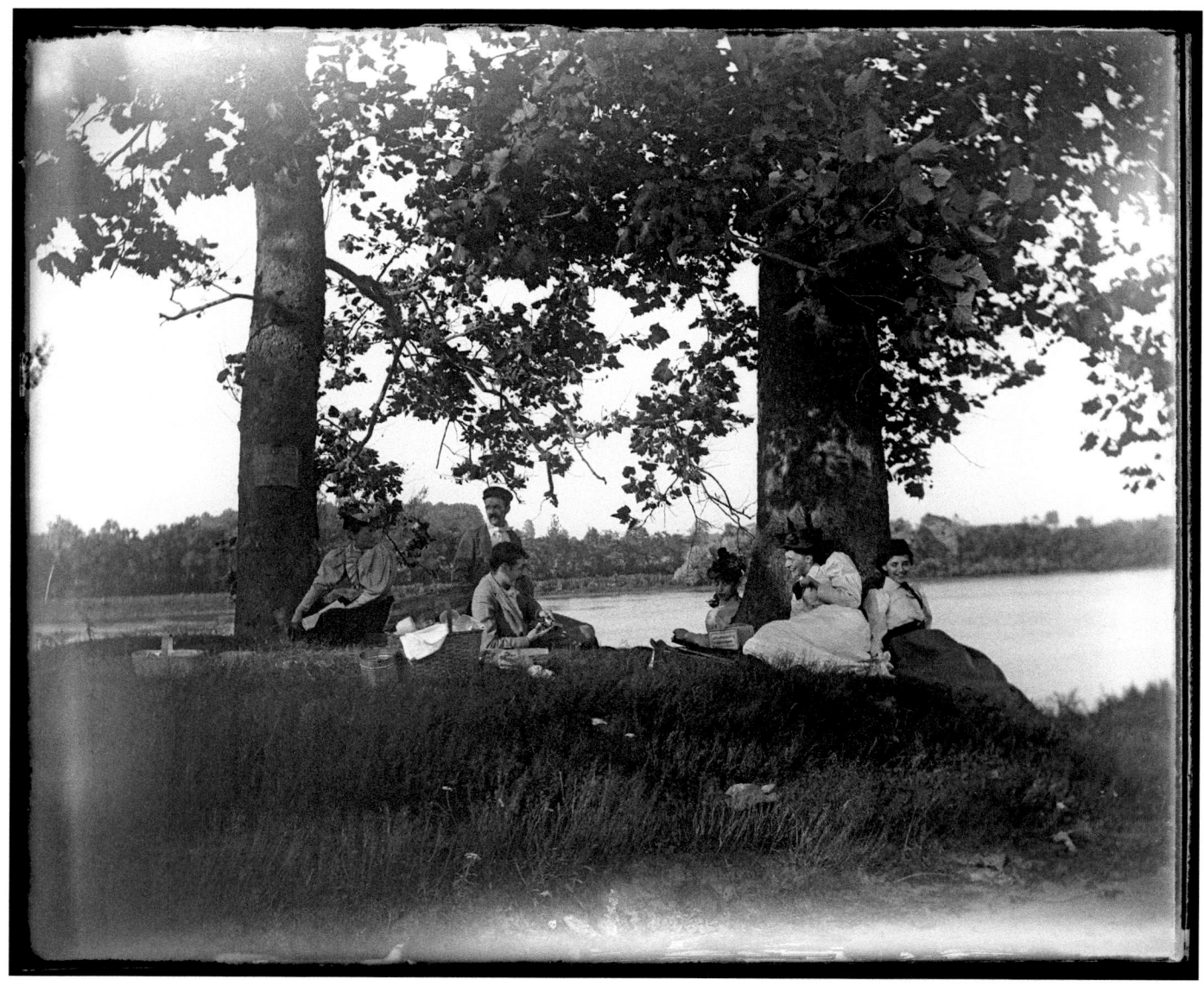

Plate 90. Grant Castner (center rear) and friends, Delaware River, near Yardley, Pennsylvania, 1894. Digital positive from 4" x 5" glass plate negative. CH2019.6.380.

The period clothing, smiling faces, and furtive glances of young friends picnicking on the picturesque Delaware River make **plate 90** a nostalgic historical document of late nineteenth-century courtship rituals. The image exudes a carefree feeling of joy and youth. On close inspection, the frivolity of the scene may have a darker side as the seated man brandishes a shiny revolver. However, the true reason for the pistol can be found in Castner's notes that date the photograph to an exact month, day and year: July 4, 1894. The firearm was probably a means to celebrate America's birthday with a bang at an Independence Day holiday picnic.

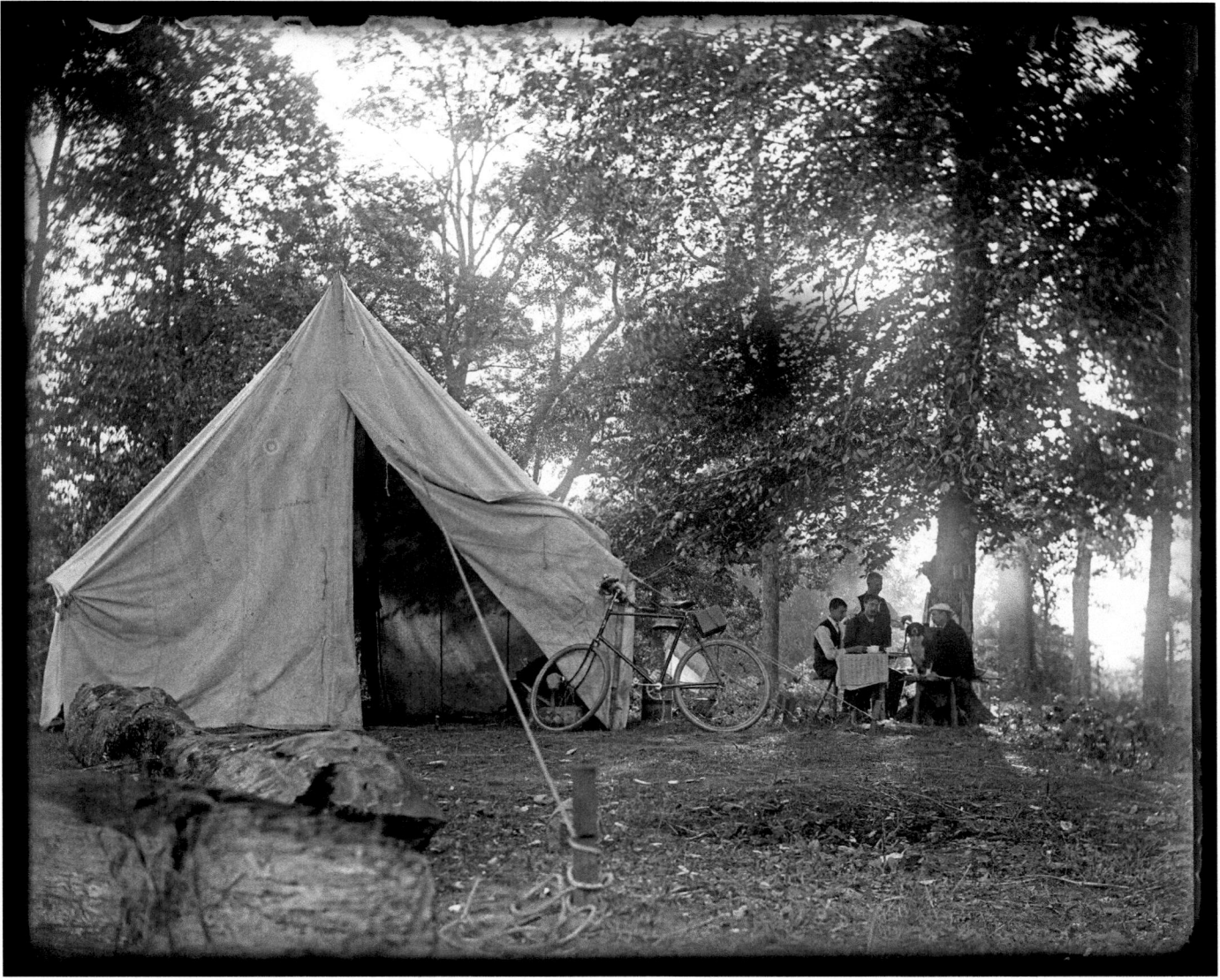

The joy of taking a four-legged friend on a camping trip is on full view in the humorous, wonderfully composed view of a group of men enjoying outdoor tea next to their canvas tent in **plate 91**. The dappled sunlight cascading through the towering deciduous trees is an ethereal highlight, adding a pleasant aura to the scene. The pet dog sits at the table, humanlike, gazing straight into the camera lens. The bicycle has a camera box mounted on its rear carrier showing how the photographer traveled to reach the camp site. The location is on or near Eagle Island, a small island in the Delaware River near Stockton in Hunterdon County.

Plate 91. *In Camp*. Unidentified campers, Eagle Island, Delaware River, near Stockton, New Jersey, 1896. Digital positive from 4" x 5" glass plate negative. CH2019.6.230.

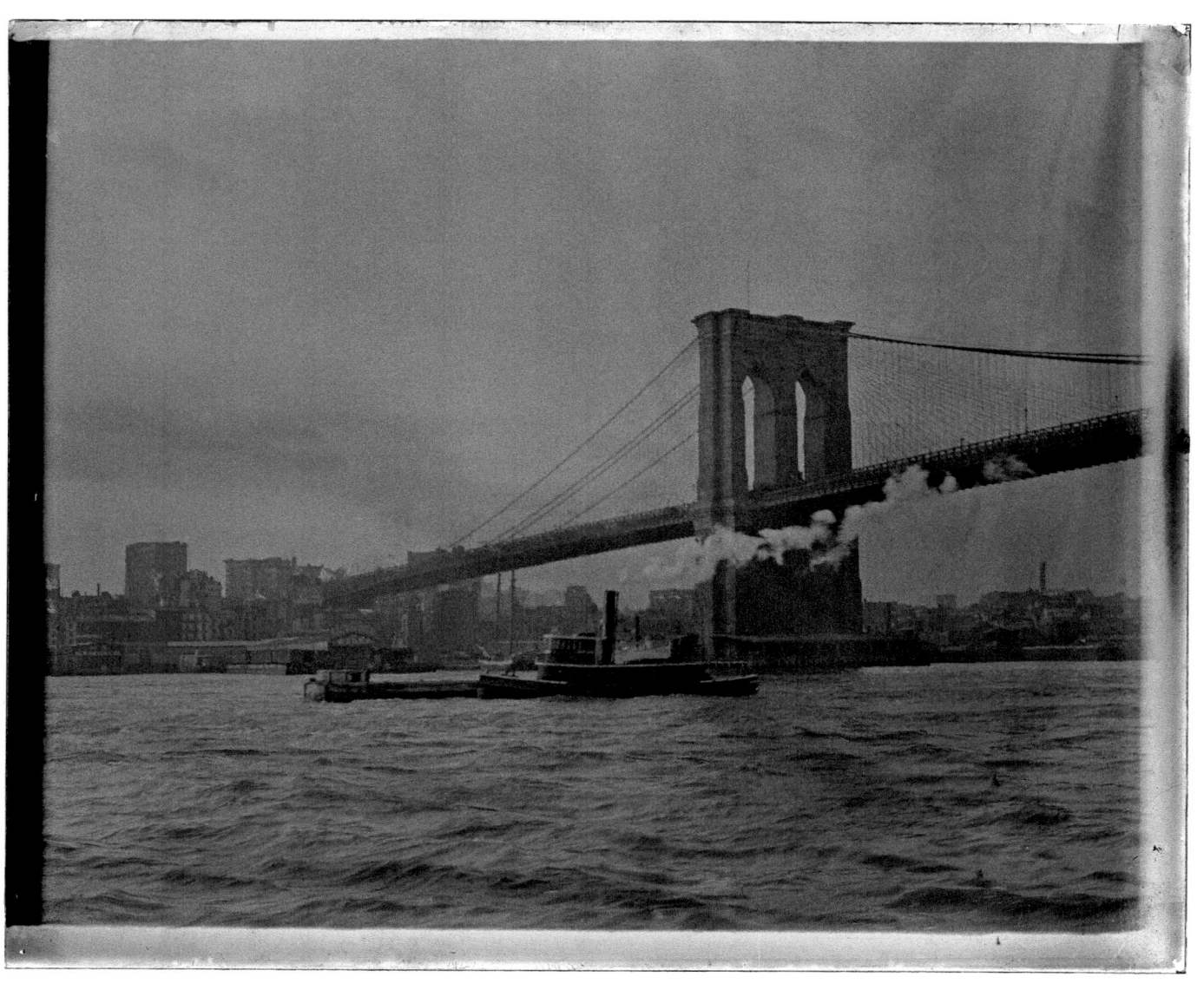

Plate 92. *New York Harbor.* East River tugboat and Brooklyn Bridge, New York, New York, c. 1897. Digital scan from 4" x 5" glass lantern slide. CH2019.6.45.

Built by the Roebling family of Trenton using cutting-edge wire rope technology, the Brooklyn Bridge (**plate 92**) was the longest suspension bridge in the world at the time of its opening in 1883. Its towers were among the largest structures in the Western Hemisphere and immediately became an irresistible subject for photographers. In one of his few extant photographs taken in New York State, Castner recorded the gigantic scale of this marvel of modern engineering during a foray to the Upper Bay, Hudson River, and East River in New York. The view is toward the Manhattan shoreline and the many railroad piers that lined it in the vicinity of the Brooklyn Bridge. In the foreground, a tugboat steams its way toward the harbor through the choppy waters. The delicacy of its trailing white smoke creates a visual counterpoint to the tenebrous, massive bridge tower. Castner was clearly fond of this image. He placed a framed print of it on display in the living room of his home on Tyler Street in Trenton. It can be seen hanging on the wall behind the family Christmas tree in another photograph (**plate 5**) that Castner took of his wife and young son on December 25, 1905.

9

Shore

Waves crashing on the beach. Parasols on the sand. Sailboats in the bay. Crowds along the boardwalk. Grant Castner documented these quintessential sights of the great Jersey Shore. The photographer and his family spent their summer vacations in Cape May Point. Castner also visited other towns on the Atlantic. These included Ocean Grove, Toms River, Point Pleasant, and, of course, Atlantic City. He always had his camera with him.

Indigenous people were the first to explore and utilize the resources of New Jersey's 130-mile-long coastline. Early European settlers used the shore for whaling, fishing, shellfish harvesting and salt making. Like the Delaware River, the Shore has always been a place for both work and play. Railroads catapulted the Jersey Shore into the forefront as a vacation destination. The populations of large East Coast cities now had easy access to the ocean beaches. Opulent hotels and fine restaurants followed, especially in Atlantic City. During Castner's lifetime, Atlantic City earned a well-deserved national reputation for its beaches, piers, hotels, and boardwalk—the first in the country.

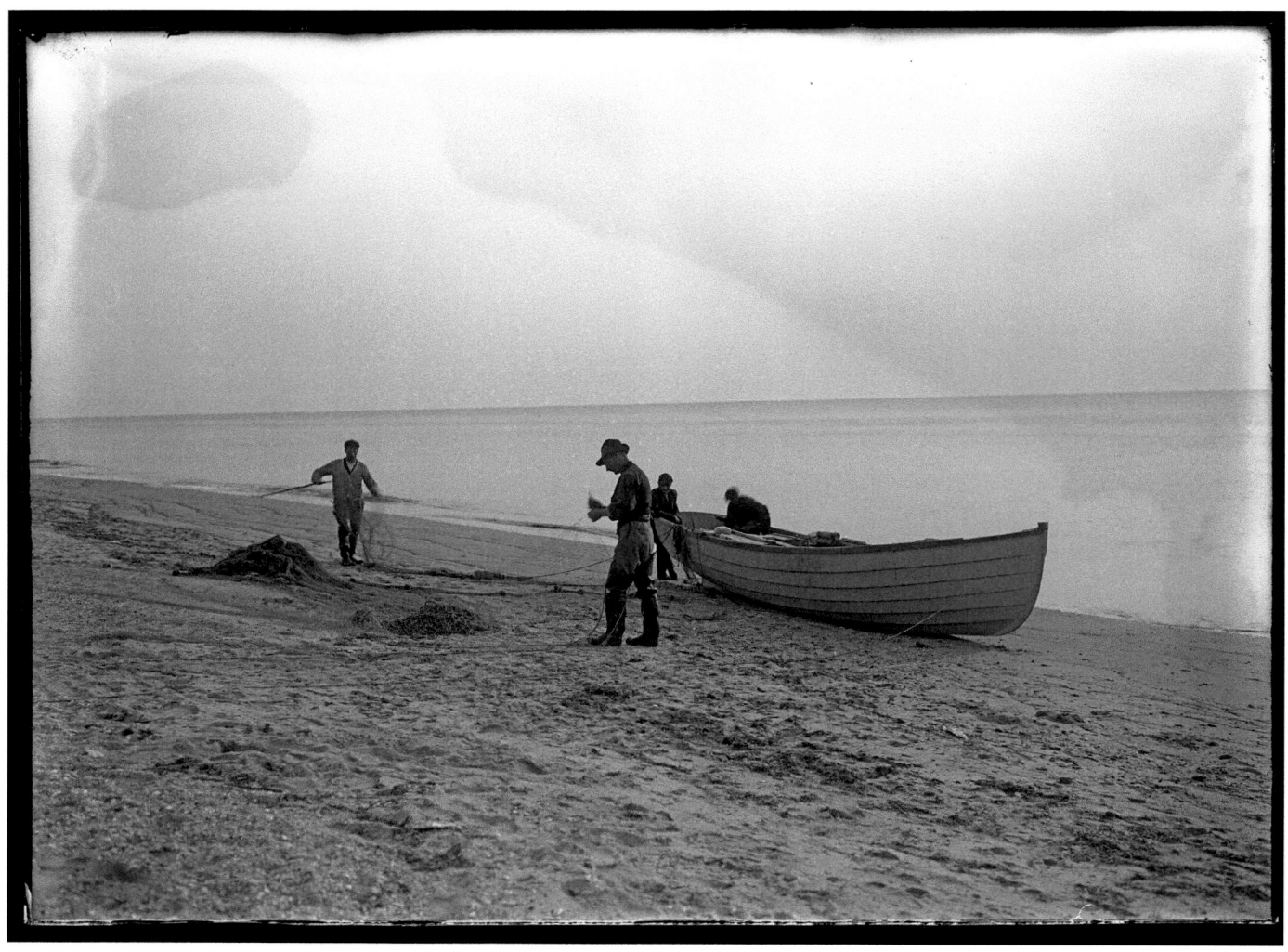

Plate 93. Fishermen, Cape May Point, New Jersey, 1910. Digital positive from 5" x 7" glass plate negative. CH2019.6.16.

Castner's photograph of fishermen at Cape May Point illustrates how the Jersey Shore was a place for work as well as play. Shore work often involved gathering food for market. So-called market gunners hunted wild waterfowl for the city restaurants, fostering a New Jersey decoy-carving tradition that continues today. Perhaps even more important was the fishing industry, which ranged from the harvesting of oysters, clams, and other shellfish to pound fishing, a common Jersey Shore practice using poles and nets to trap fish. In **plate 93**, the beach seems particularly quiet and lonely, suggesting that Castner came upon the scene of fisherman in the early morning. Two of the men are engaged in the tedious task of mending and preparing the nets. A second pair of men tend to their

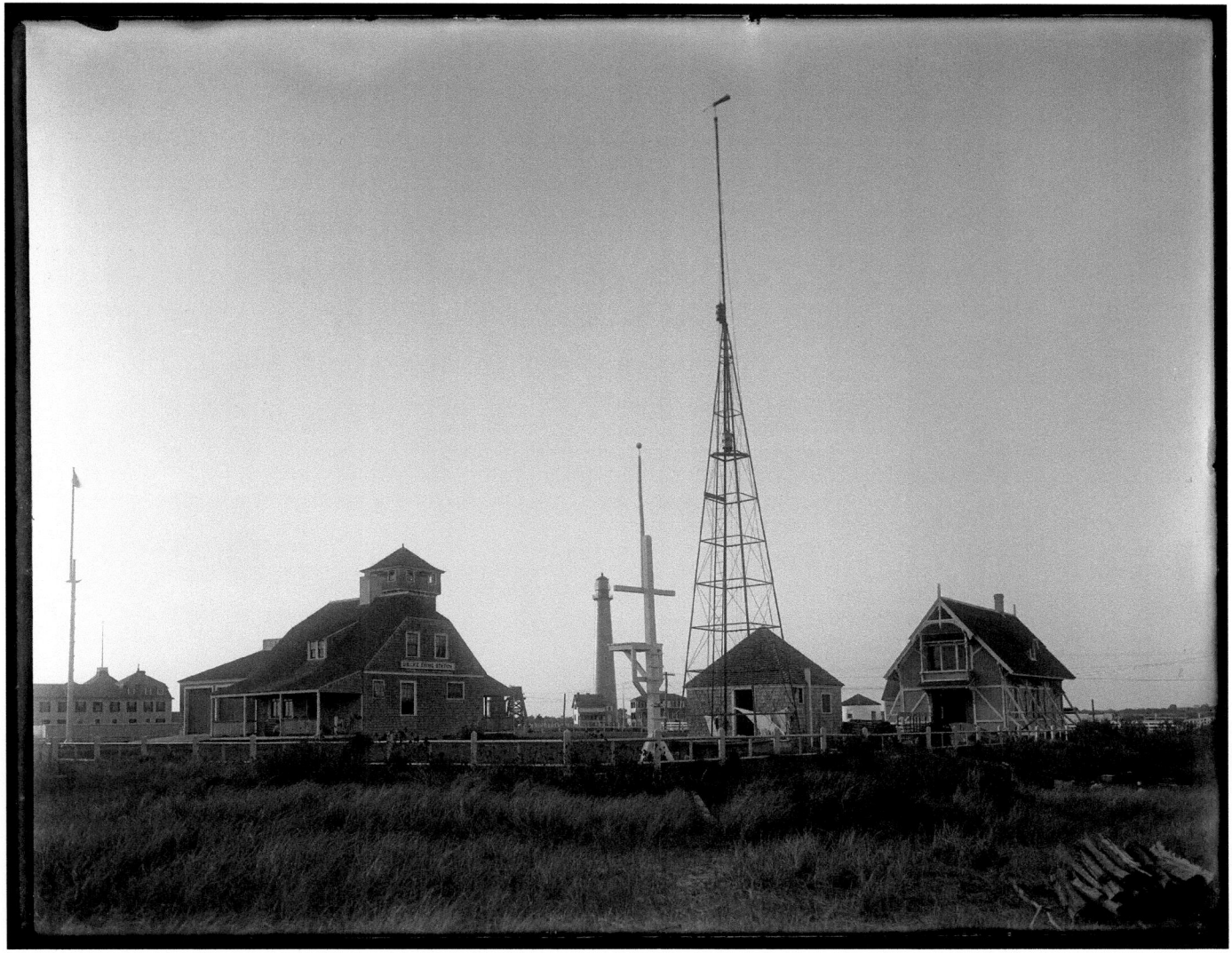

wooden vessel, a classic New Jersey fishing boat called the *Sea Bright Skiff*.

In the mid-nineteenth century, an alarmingly high number of shipwrecks along New Jersey's coastline led to the state's involvement in the creation of an extensive national network of rescue stations (**plate 94**). Each station in the network, formalized as the United States Life-Saving Service, contained rescue boats and other specialized equipment designed to save shipwreck victims. The first responders, known as "surfmen," were also instrumental in saving the lives of beachgoers. Classified as District 4, New Jersey had forty evenly spaced stations stretching from Sandy Hook to

Plate 94. Life-Saving Station, Cape May Point, New Jersey, 1910. Digital positive from 6.5" x 8.5" glass plate negative. CH2019.6.22.

Cape May. The importance of the Life-Saving Service is encapsulated in a letter from a grateful Camden mother to Surfman George Bohm, published in the Service's 1910 annual report: "With feelings of deep gratitude I take this opportunity to express my thanks and appreciation of your rescue of my daughter Bessie from what might have been a watery grave in the ocean at Cape May Point on August 30. It would give me pleasure to have you call at my home and allow me to shake hands with you and express orally my gratitude for what you did on that memorable day."

Tousled hair and the flittering strings of a bonnet suggest that it was a breezy day on the Jersey Shore when Castner took an endearing image of his two children (**plate 95**). Six-year-old Theodore Grant and younger sister Eleanor hold hands during a midsummer visit to the beach, with sand at their feet and waves crashing in the distance. Not looking toward the camera, the children may have been paying attention to their mother standing to the left of Castner behind the lens. Eleanor holds a sand pail with a lithographic decoration of dancing bears, a sign of how tinplate toy manufacturers saw great potential in increased beach travel as a market for their goods. One New Jersey manufacturer, J. Chein and Company, developed a full line of vibrantly decorated tinplate pails, watering cans, and sand mills beginning in the late 1910s.

Gathered on the front porch of this beachfront house in Cape May Point are Grant Castner, wife Sarah Frances, son Theodore Grant, daughter Eleanor, and Grant Castner's sister, Anna Kampen (**plate 96**). The two-story wooden frame house with clapboard and shingle siding and a large front porch with ornamental fretwork embodies the architectural style for which Cape May is renowned. The Castner family either owned or rented the house, which was their regular vacation destination in the summers. It was located on Beach Avenue (now Harvard Avenue), a few blocks from the Cape

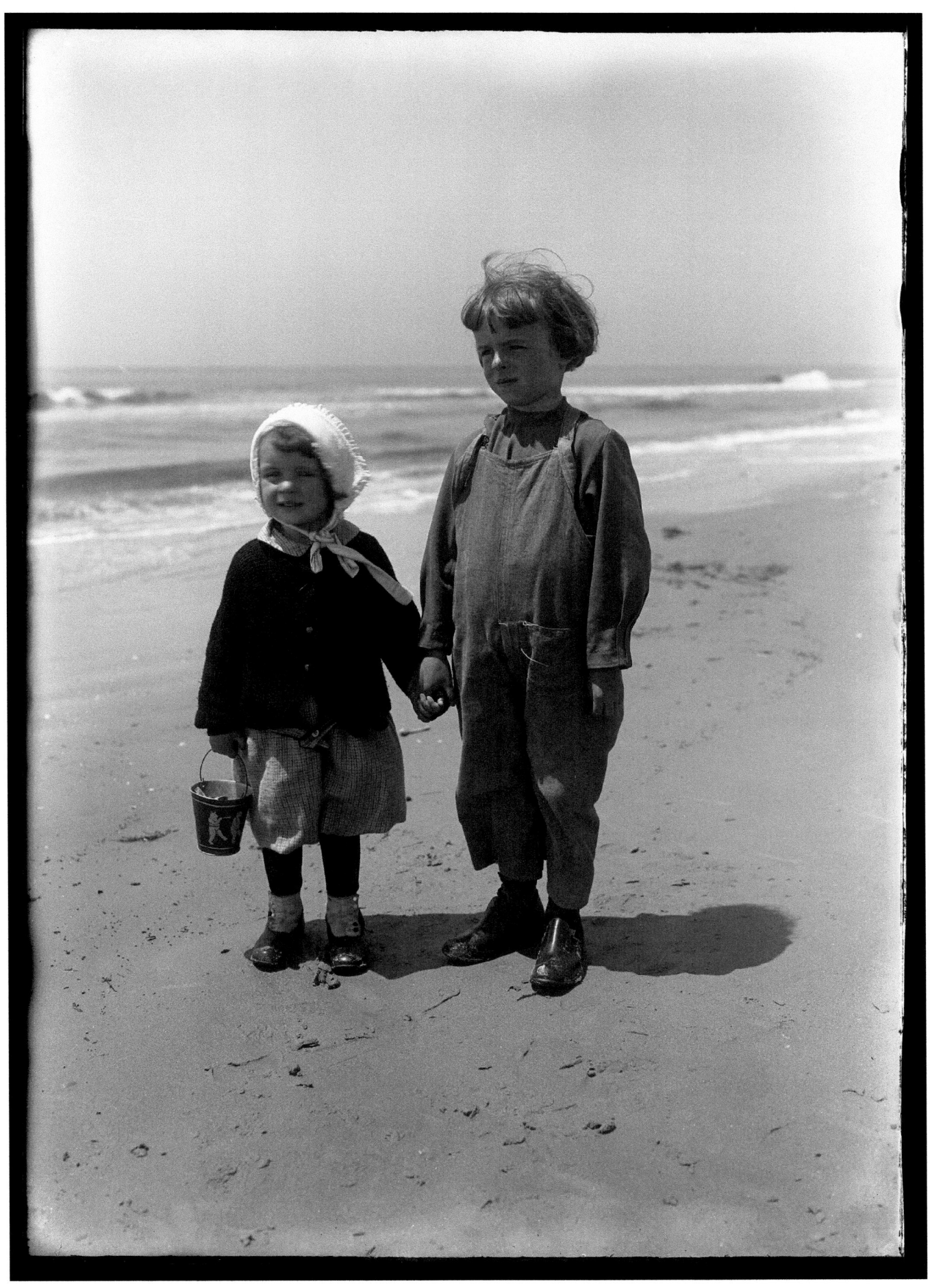

Plate 95. Castner children, Cape May Point, New Jersey, 1910. Digital positive from 5" x 7" glass plate negative. CH2019.6.18.

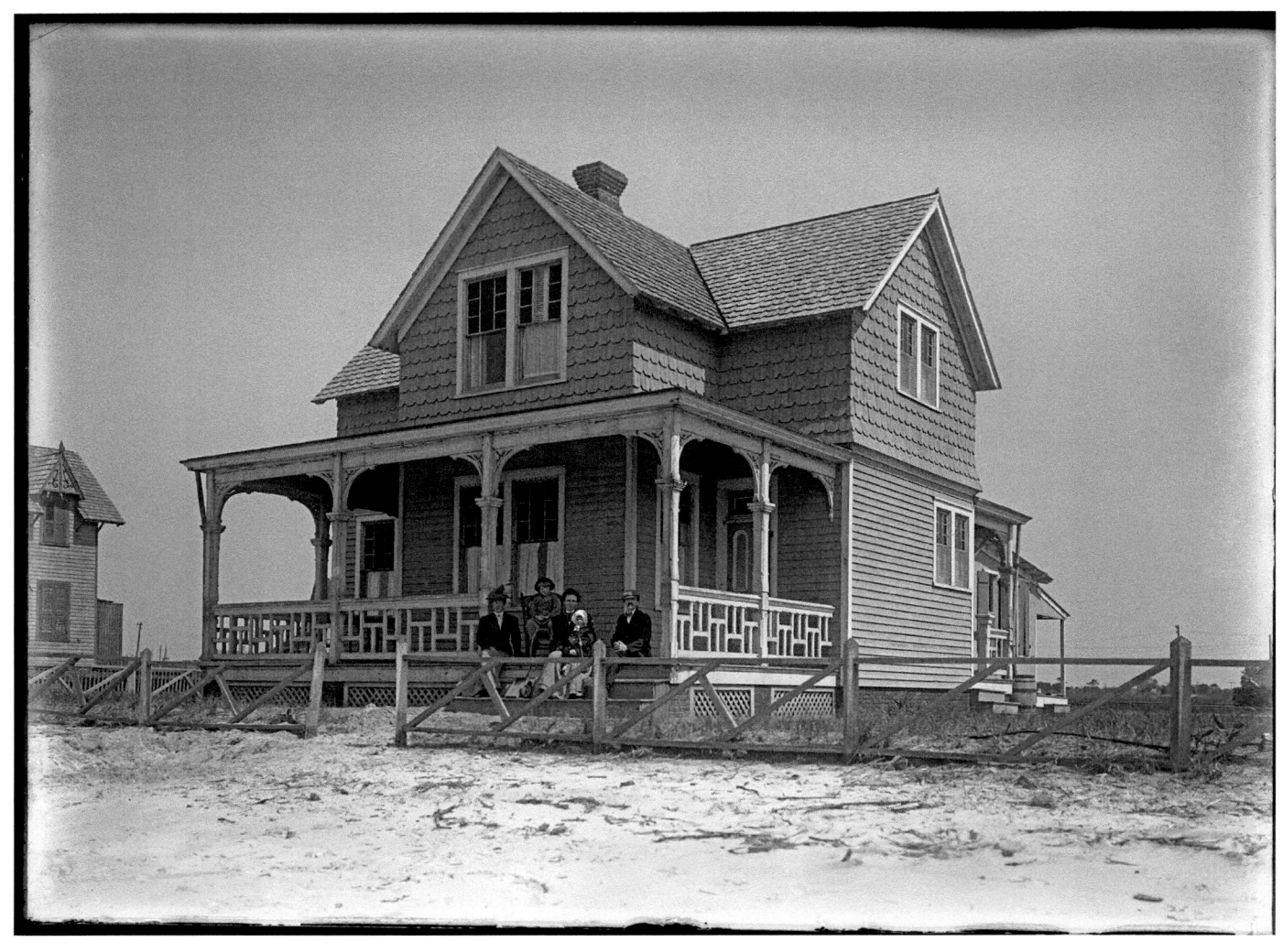

Plate 96. Castner beach house,
Cape May Point, New Jersey, 1910.
Digital positive from 5" x 7" glass
plate negative. CH2019.6.19.

May Lighthouse. Since Grant is among the group posing on the porch, he may have recruited his sister Ida to take the picture after setting up his camera and framing the scene.

In **plate 97**, Castner's visit to Toms River depicted the marine-oriented environment of the Ocean County community situated on a river estuary off Barnegat Bay. Castner used a fairly long exposure that smoothed out the waves, creating a more peaceful impression, although it did result in blurring the lines attached to the mast in the foreground. The larger boat in the background, with the two masts, is a type of schooner. Its stern bears the name *Outing*, which suggests a pleasure craft. The vessels on the left are likely

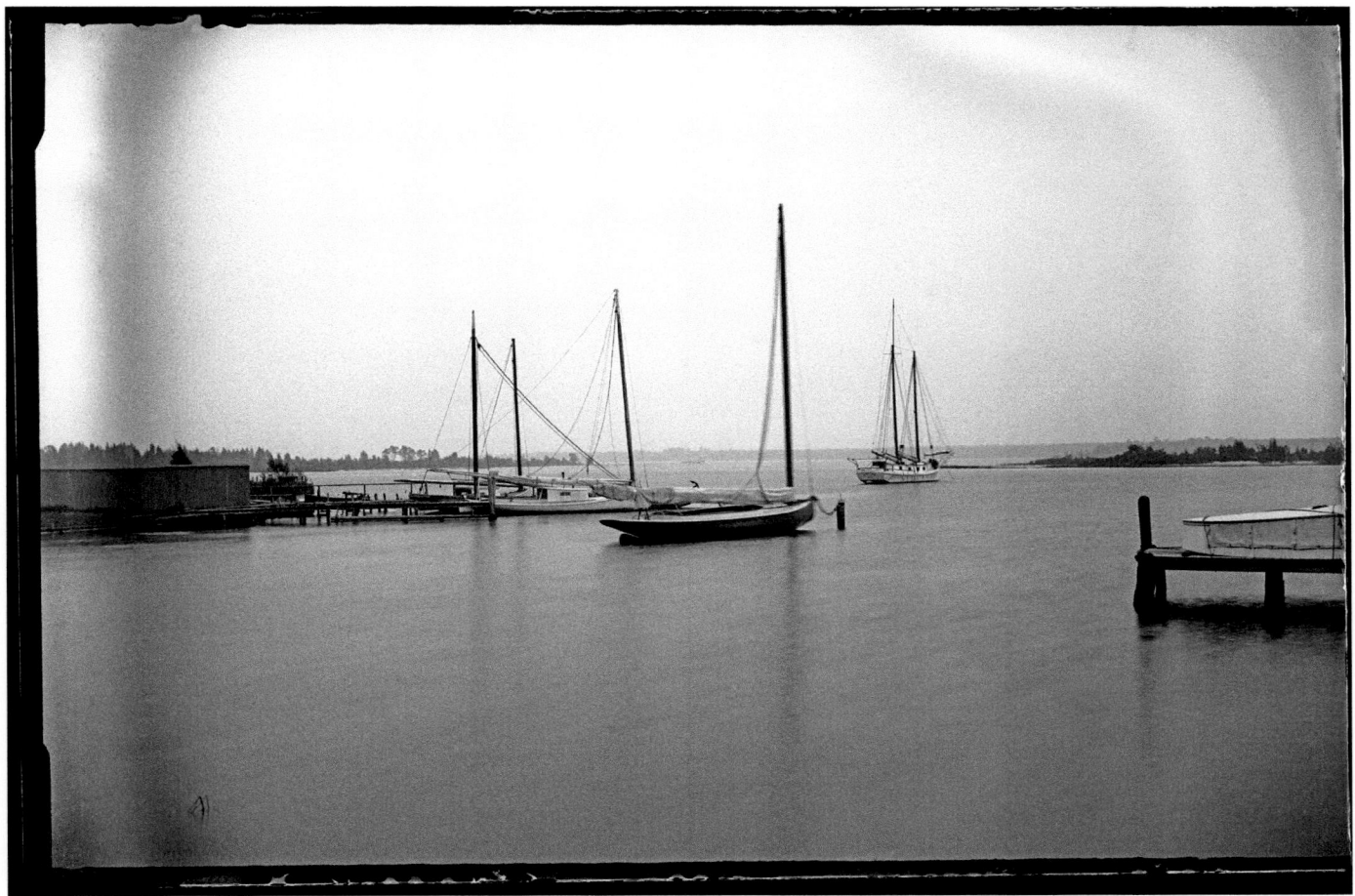

workboats used for oyster gathering. The boat with its mast set far forward in the bow is a cat boat, a staple of Barnegat Bay watercraft since the nineteenth century. With retractable keels, cat boats can operate in shallow water and in Castner's day were used to transport visitors from the mainland to the barrier island.

With a veritable forest of masts stretching into the sky, **plate 98** of a busy marina in Point Pleasant underscores the ubiquitous presence of sailing vessels at the Jersey Shore. The heavy clouds above the boats provided Castner with effective pictorial contrast to the thin verticals of the masts and provided balance to the dark tone of the water. The widespread use of such boats went hand in hand with the emergence of sail making as an important cottage industry. With specialized

Plate 97. Sailboats, Toms River, New Jersey, 1894. Digital positive from 4.25" x 6.5" glass plate negative. CH2019.6.31.

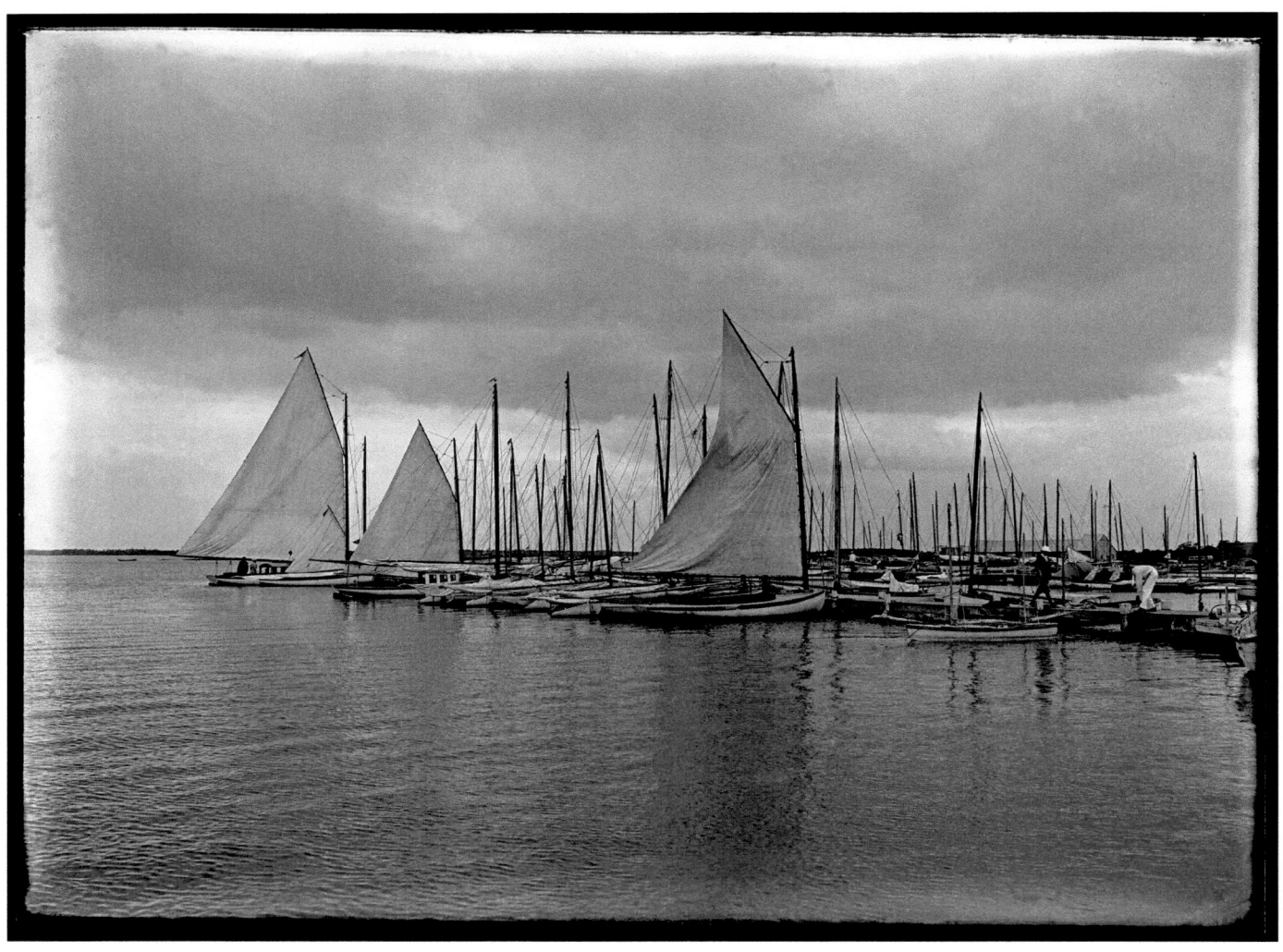

Plate 98. Sailboats, Point Pleasant, New Jersey, 1909. Digital positive from 5" x 7" glass plate negative. CH2019.6.633.

tools like *fids*, which were used to open sections of rope and cloth, and *palms*, which protected the hands when sewing, sailmakers found steady employment making and repairing sails for both fishing vessels and pleasure craft. A uniquely shaped device called a sailmaker's bench provided a long flat plane on which the artisan could attach a sail to work on it, with a secondary section of the device keeping his tools within easy reach.

Ocean Grove was quite busy on the summer day when Castner took **plate 99**. It was so busy, in fact, that he seems to have captured not only the two intended subjects, but also two unintended ones. The seated women smile politely for the camera from underneath the parasols that shield them from

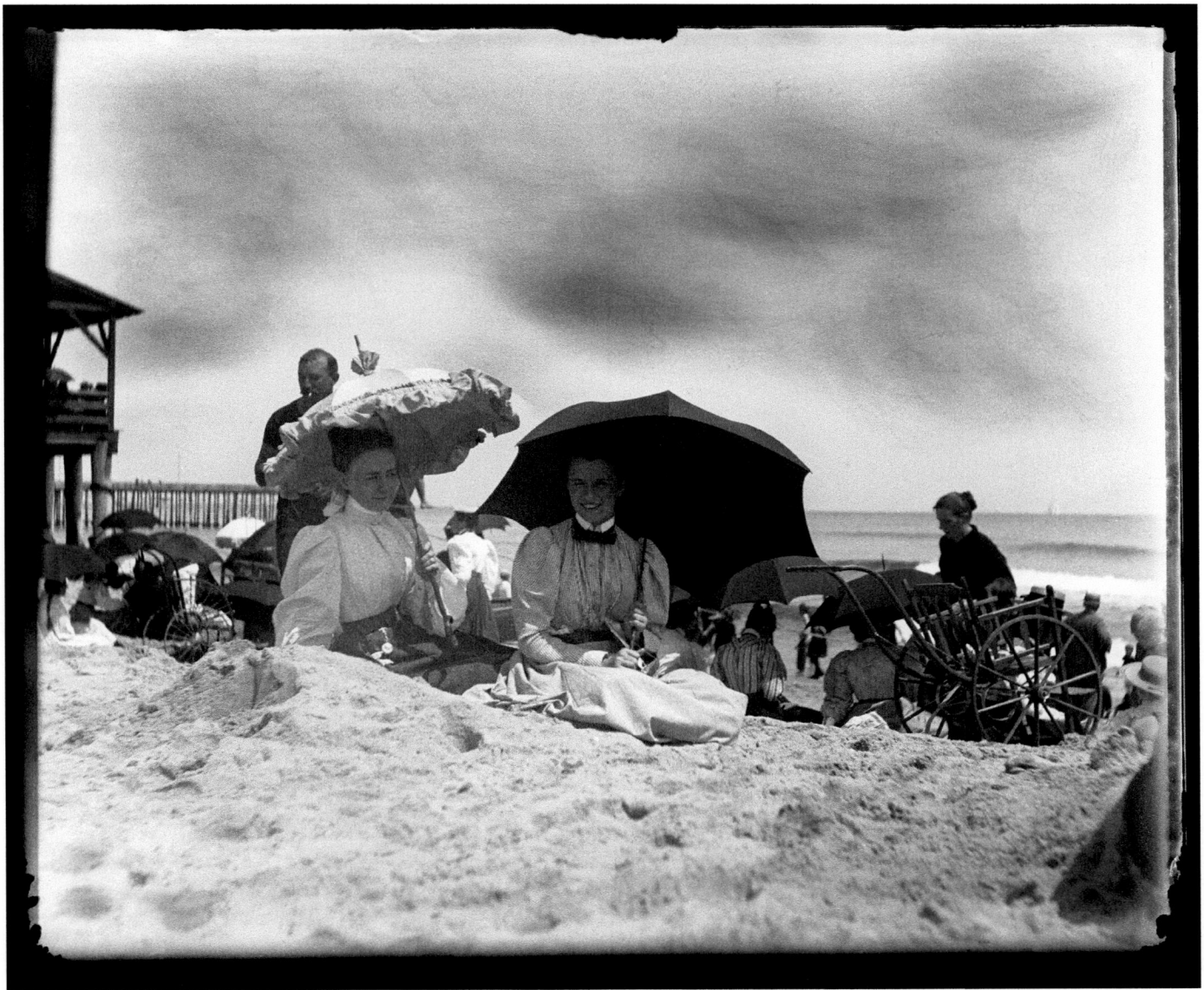

the hot summer sun. The long skirts and tight collars of their clothing, uncomfortable and out of place by today's beachwear standards, imply the gendered mores that defined the era. Two other figures stand out in the photograph: a woman in black, head down, and a man, cigar clenched between his teeth, who inadvertently pops into the shot at the last second. A mound of sand in the foreground, wooden pier in the distance, and the edge of a boardwalk pavilion at the left add further beachy details to this pleasant image of a famous locale on the New Jersey Shore.

Plate 99. *On the Sands.* Unidentified women on the beach, Ocean Grove, New Jersey, 1894. Digital positive from 4" x 5" glass plate negative. CH2019.6.182.

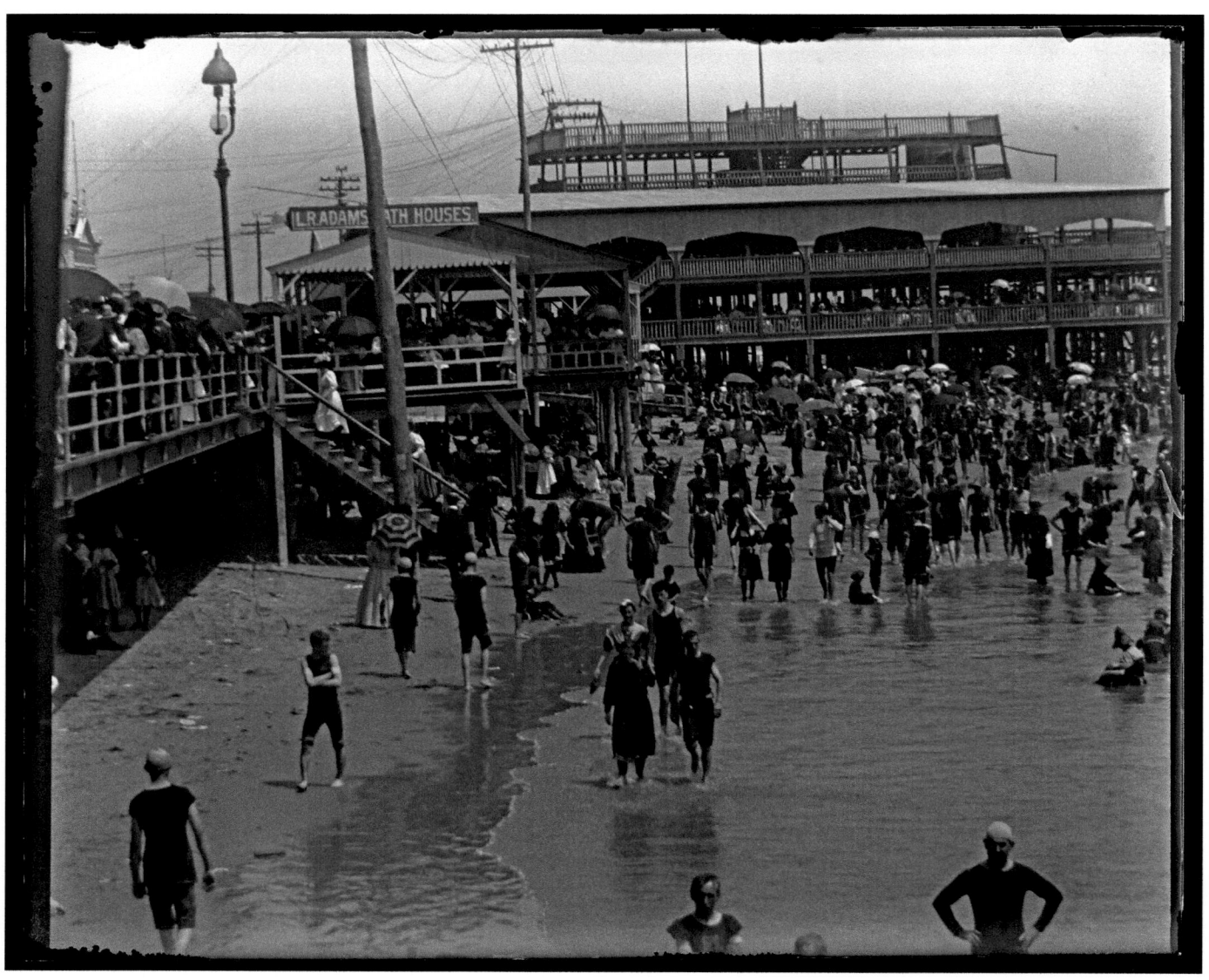

Plate 100. Boardwalk near Young's Ocean Pier and L.R. Adams Bath Houses, Atlantic City, New Jersey, 1897. Digital positive from 4" x 5" glass plate negative. CH2019.6.321.

It is no surprise that the section of the Atlantic City boardwalk in **plate 100** was packed with excited crowds on this summer day in 1897. In the background is Young's Ocean Pier, also known as Young's Million Dollar Pier, one of the most popular attractions on the entire boardwalk. First opened as Applegate's Pier in 1884 by the highly successful Philadelphia and Atlantic City photographer James R. Applegate, it was purchased in 1891 by John Lake Young and Steward McShea. The new owners expanded its length to two thousand feet and added a host of new attractions, including rides, midway games, a theater, and even an aquarium. Castner took the photograph looking north from a point near New York Avenue and the Lewis R. Adams Bath Houses that appear on the left.

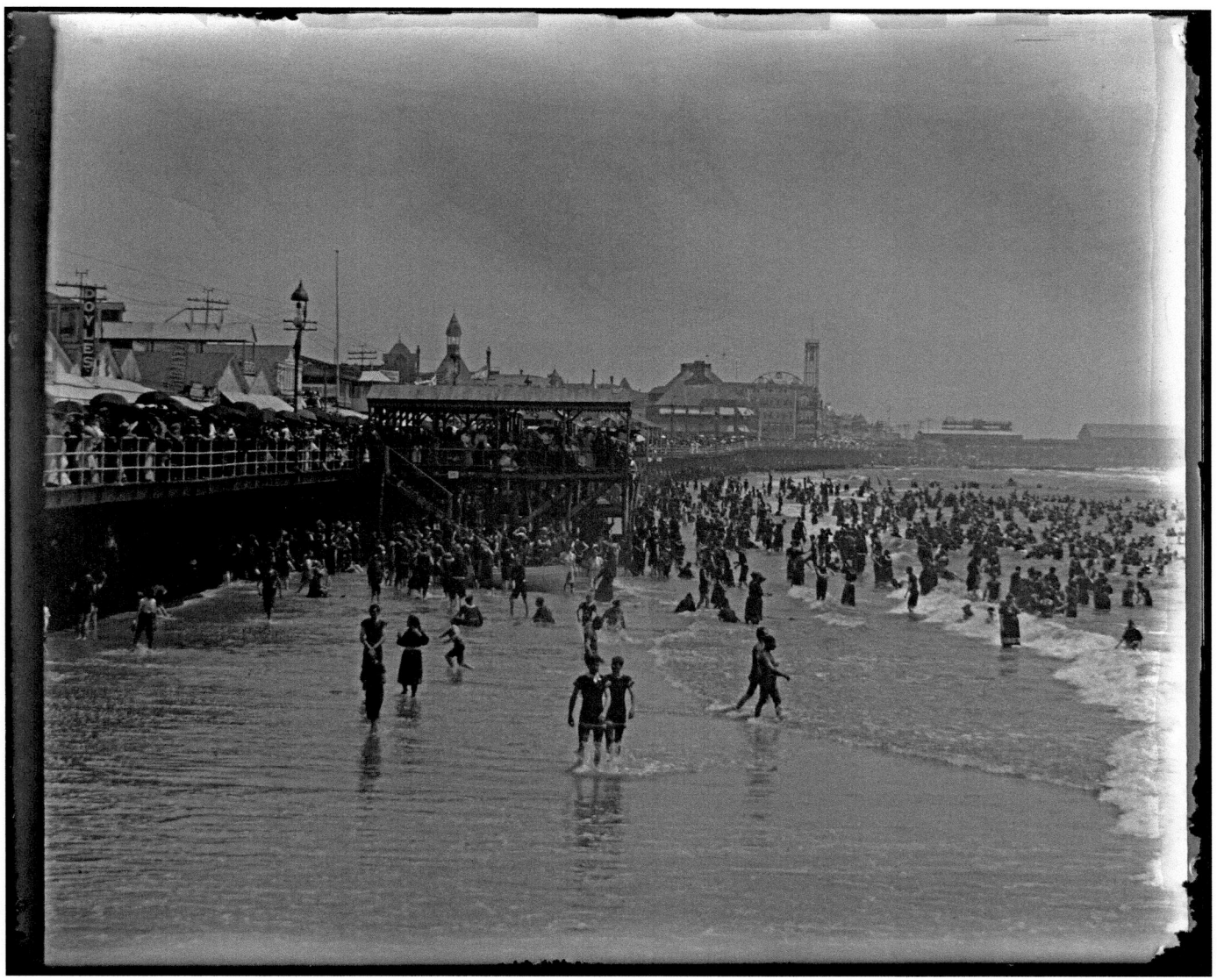

Plate 101. *On the Beach*. Board-walk, Atlantic City, New Jersey, 1897. Digital positive from 4" x 5" glass plate negative. CH2019.6.670.

His image also preserves the common attire of male beachgo-ers at the time—two-piece wool bathing suits and caps. Those not so prepared for the heat and humidity of the South Jersey summer sought shade under the boardwalk.

Plate 101 captures the immense popularity of the Jersey Shore as a tourist destination. Throngs of bathers cool off in the surf, ankle deep and elbow to elbow. The nearby board-walk is equally packed. The crowds are oblivious to the cam-era's presence, except perhaps for the two young men in the foreground who seem to splash forward with some deliber-ate intent. A full half-mile of hotels, pavilions, and other at-tractions fill the scene. Peeking out from behind a building on the horizon is the top of a Ferris wheel. These familiar amusement park attractions were invented by New Jerseyan William Somers, who installed wooden "observation roundabouts" on the Atlantic City boardwalk in the 1890s. Pittsburgh engineer George Ferris admitted that a ride on one of these roundabouts inspired him to build a larger wheel out of iron and steel for the 1893 Chicago World's Fair. The "Ferris wheel" became that fair's quintessential icon, and its builder's name was forever immortalized.

10

Fair

New Jersey, the Garden State, has a long history of agricultural fairs. In the colonial period, these glorified market days brought farmers together for business and pleasure. Rural populations used the events to sell goods and compare farming techniques in a festive setting. After a period of decline, agricultural fairs made a strong resurgence in the mid- to late nineteenth century. New county-level societies helped to fuel this resurgence. These societies organized annual fairs for their residents. County fairs featured displays of farm products and competitions involving farm machinery.

Grant Castner documented New Jersey's greatest fair – the Trenton Inter-State Fair. First held in 1888, the Inter-State Fair took place on the same grounds used by an earlier Mercer County agricultural fair (now the Grounds for Sculpture in Hamilton Township). It had roots in the farming fairs of the past. Yet it was more akin to a World's Fair exposition. Horse races, exhibits, concession stands, and vaudeville acts drew throngs of visitors. In its first five years alone, more than five hundred thousand visitors entered its gates.

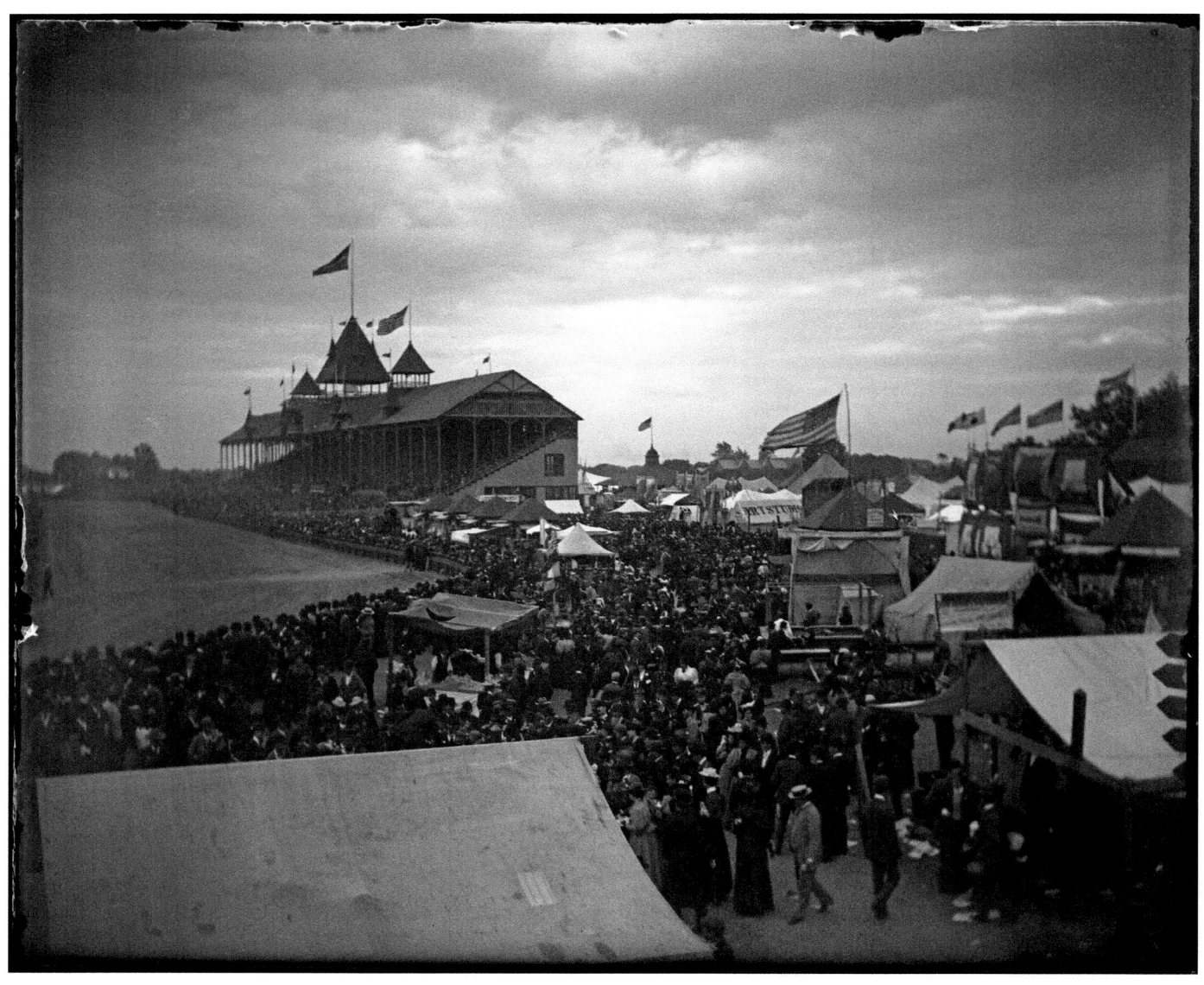

Plate 102. View to the grandstand, Inter-State Fair, Hamilton Township, New Jersey, 1896. Digital positive from 4" x 5" glass plate negative. CH2019.6.149.

The immense popularity of the Trenton Inter-State Fair is on full view in **plate 102** of throngs of fairgoers snaking their way through the maze of concession stands and exhibition booths in the shadow of a towering grandstand. It too is packed shoulder to shoulder with visitors, a sign that the horse and harness races must have been underway. Extensive advertising was responsible, in part, for the humongous crowds. One ad from the September 24, 1896, issue of the *Trenton Evening Times* called the fair "an exposition of all that pertains to farm, garden and household, great as a race meet, great in the way it treats its patrons, great as a livestock show, great as a progressive industrial exposition,

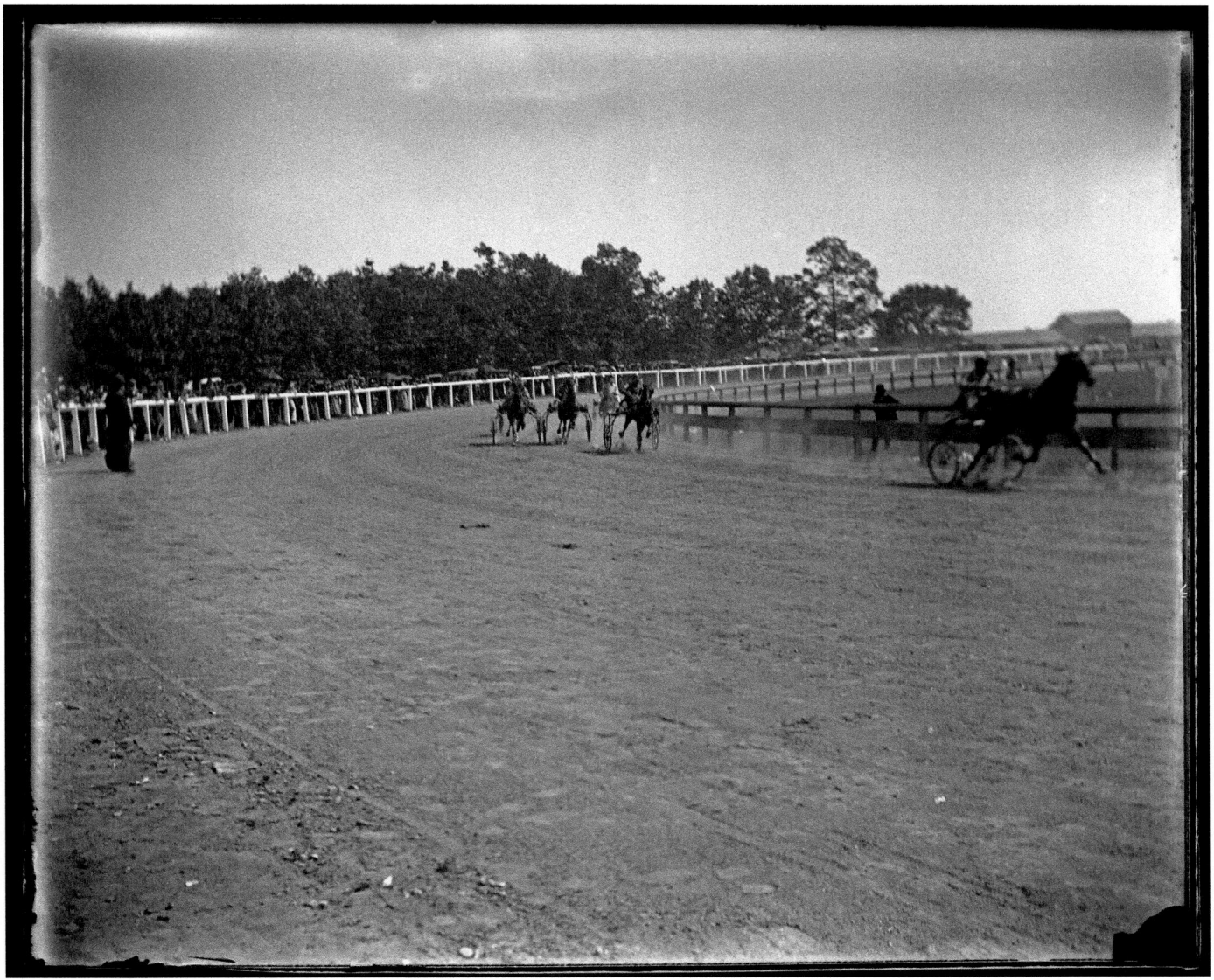

great as a vaudeville show . . . great in ambition, great in achievement."

Each day, hundreds of spectators packed the Inter-State Fair's grandstand to watch—and gamble on—the extensive itinerary of races that took place on the adjacent half-mile track. The fair's popular harness races involved horses competing at different gaits—trotting and pacing—while pulling two-wheeled sulkies. Castner set up his camera trackside to capture the action-packed shot (**plate 103**) of harness racers as they speedily rounded a curve. Photographer Ernest Marx of Plainfield, New Jersey, became well known for instantaneous "photo finish" photography to determine the winner

Plate 103. *Speeding*. Harness racers, Inter-State Fair, Hamilton Township, New Jersey, 1893. Digital positive from 4" x 5" glass plate negative. CH2019.6.328.

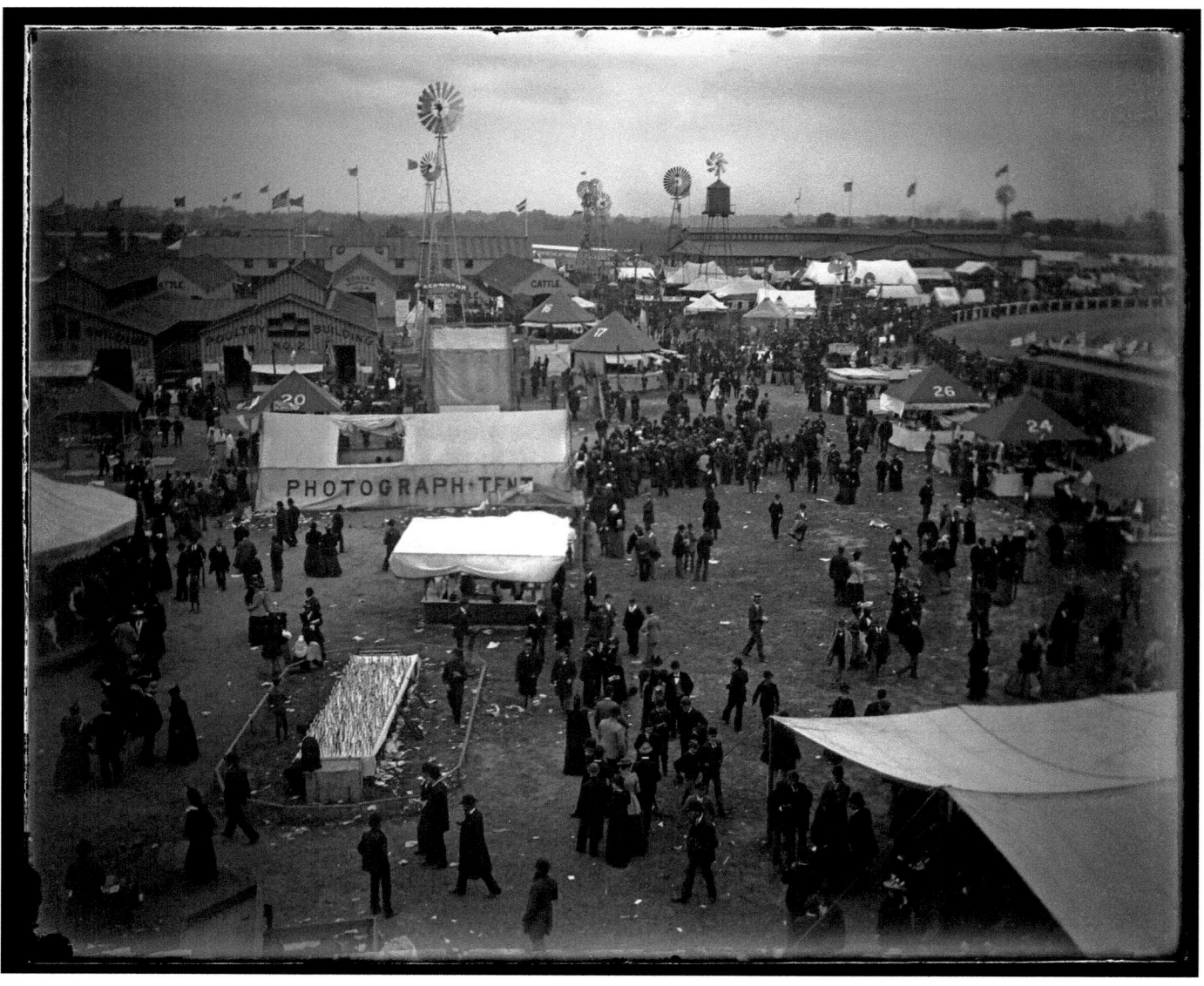

Plate 104. View from the grand-stand, Inter-State Fair, Hamilton Township, New Jersey, 1894. Digital positive from 4" x 5" glass plate negative. CH2019.6.336.

of horse races in 1889. Castner's purpose here, however, was just to enjoy and document the action.

Castner carried his camera and equipment to the top of the racetrack grandstand to capture the bird's eye perspective in **plate 104** looking north into the heart of the fairgrounds. As evidenced by the tent so marked, a photographer was on site at the fairgrounds to take pictures of fairgoers for a modest fee. It is likely that they offered tintypes since they could be processed and delivered in fifteen minutes or less. The tent features a skylight that could be closed in inclement weather. Beyond the photographer's tent are the livestock pavilions, a reminder that the fair still maintained a strong connection to its agricultural roots. Windmills dot the skyline. Since they

GRANT CASTNER

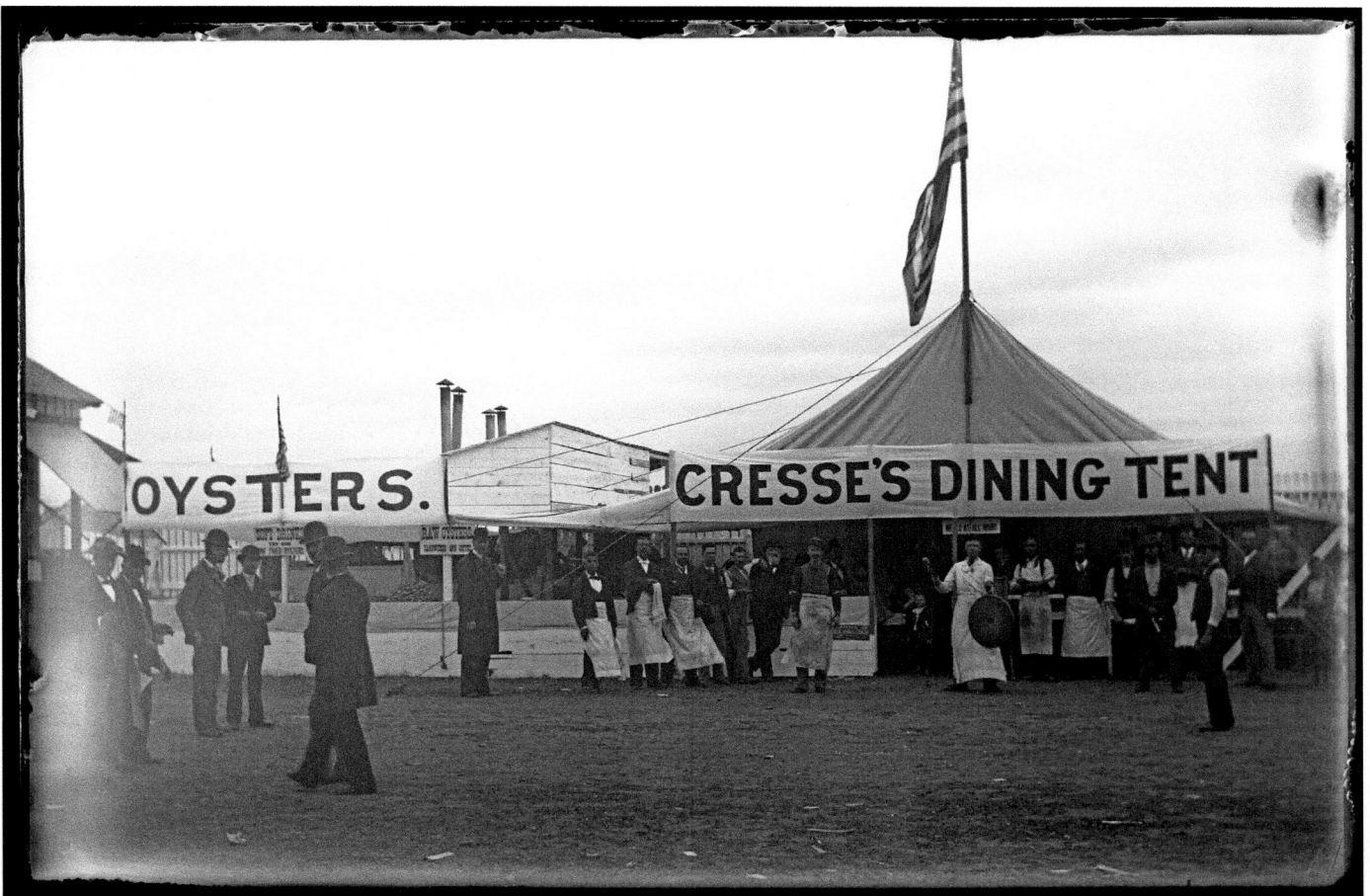

continued to be valued features of many farms in the late nineteenth century, various national windmill makers promoted their latest and greatest mills to those fairgoers who continued to use the Inter-State Fair as a place of agricultural business.

It is no surprise that raw oysters were on the menu at the Inter-State Fair. Harvested extensively along the Jersey Shore for thousands of years, oysters continued to be a popular food in Castner's day. By the late nineteenth century, train transit meant that even inland restaurants could have fresh raw oysters on the table within hours. Whereas raw oysters are now a luxury, around 1900 they were so cheap that people in the New York metropolitan area ate as many as six hundred per year. At Cresse's, a dining tent near the grandstand, a man can be seen at the center of **plate 105** sounding a gong. He is surrounded by the white-aproned kitchen staffers and oyster shuckers who worked long hours to feed hungry fairgoers. The sounding of the dinner bell was not an infrequent

Plate 105. Cresse's dining tent, Inter-State Fair, Hamilton Township, New Jersey, 1894. Digital positive from 4.125" x 6.5" glass plate negative. CH2019.6.282.

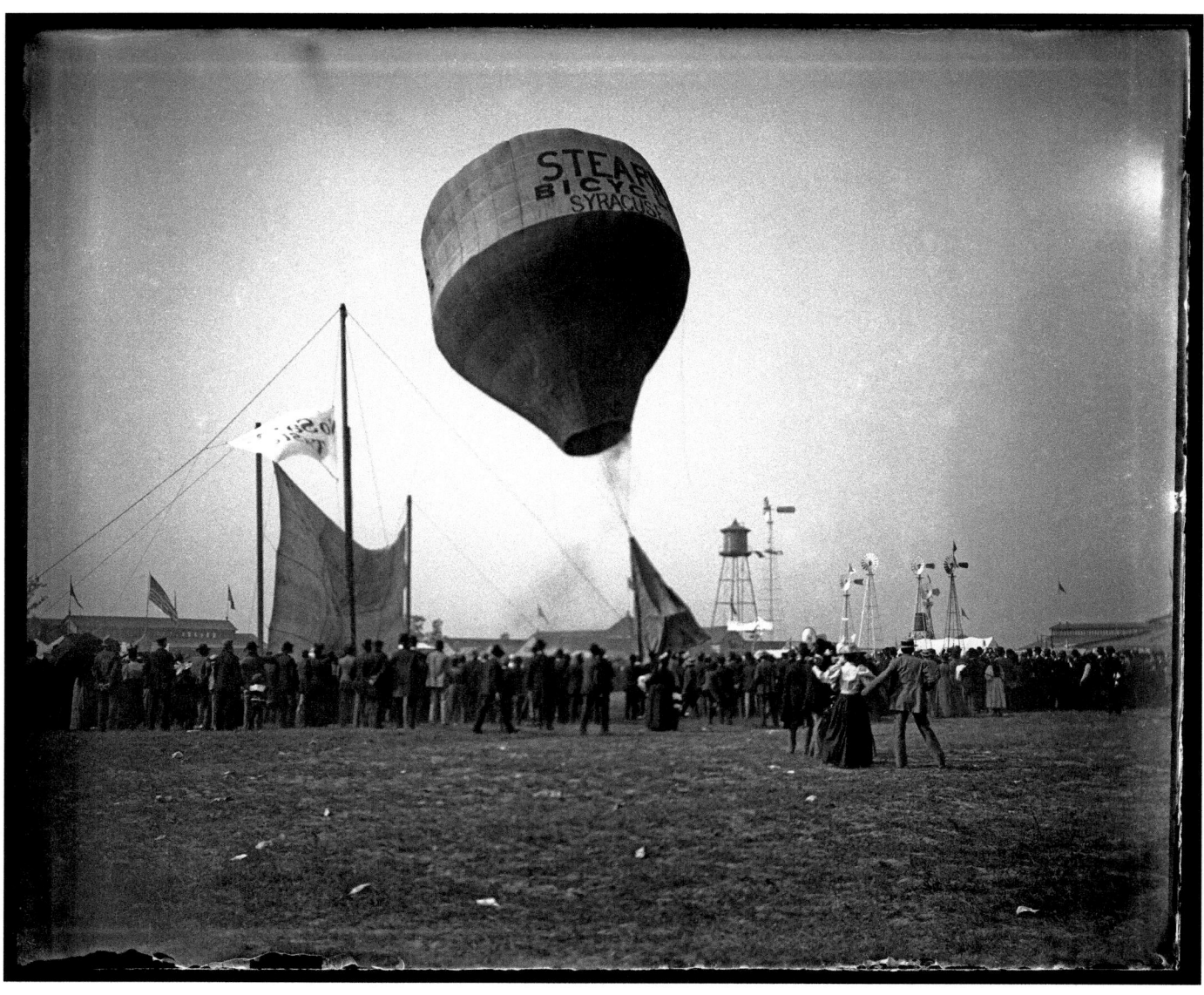

Plate 106. *Balloon Ascension.* Hot air balloon, Inter-State Fair, Hamilton Township, New Jersey, 1895. Digital positive from 4" x 5" glass plate negative. CH2019.6.324.

occurrence. A sign proclaims that Cresse's served meals at all hours of the day.

The large crowd gathered on the scene suggests that **plate 106** is more than just some ordinary hot air balloon. A team of "aeronauts" who promoted themselves as the Jewell Brothers entertained fair crowds by rapidly ascending in a balloon and then leaping from the sky, relying on primitive parachutes to bring them safely back to earth to thunderous applause. Their act was so popular that it was held twice a day on the fair's busiest days. The balloon advertises the Syracuse, New York, bicycle maker E.C. Stearns and Company, which was possibly a sponsor for the aeronauts. The company made a wise choice choosing the Inter-State Fair to promote its products. Late

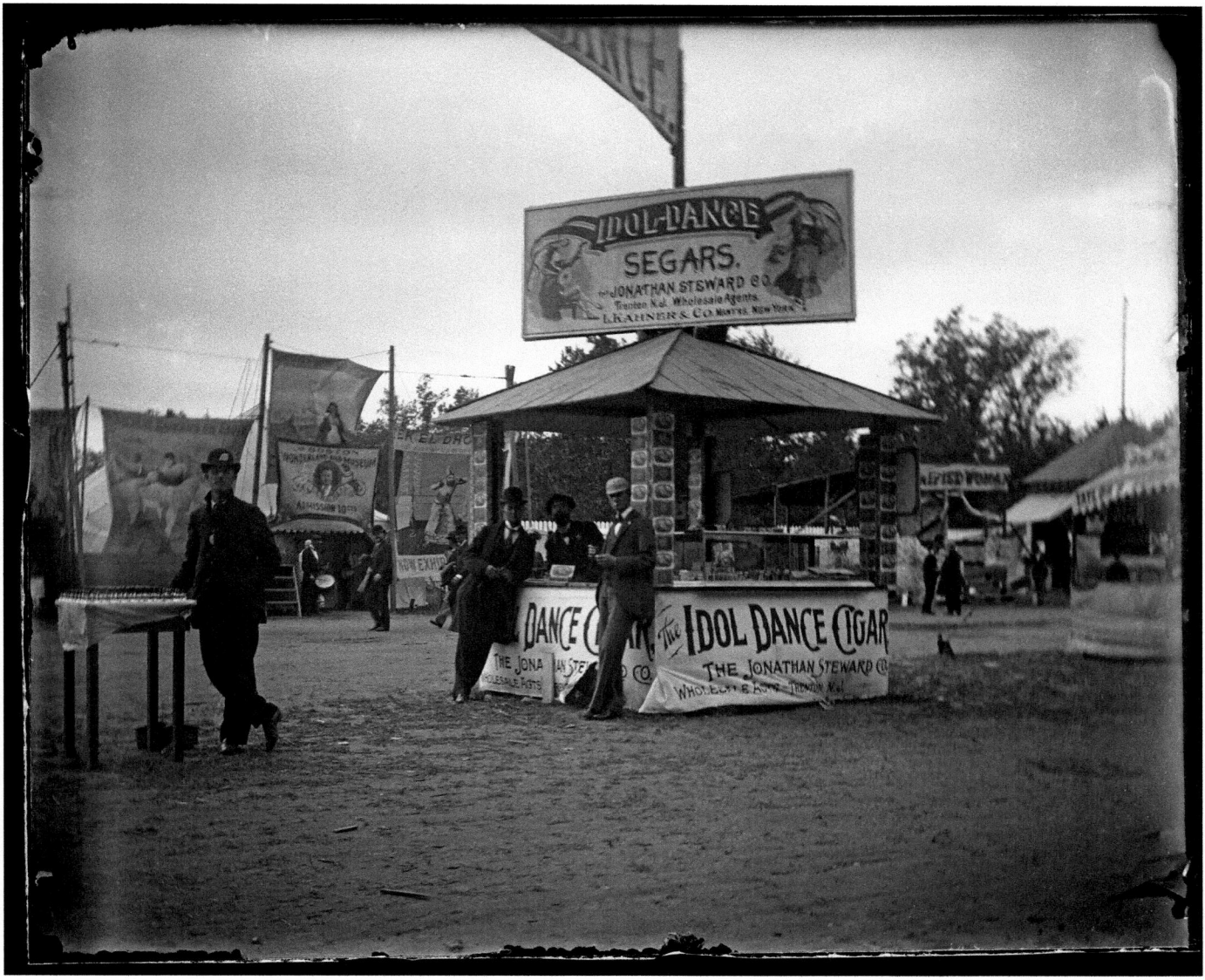

September provided the perfect weather for area bicycle clubs to sponsor large group rides to the fair, which sometimes even offered special "Wheelmen's Days." These bicycle clubs gained in popularity in the 1890s with the advent of the safety bicycle featuring two wheels the same size.

Capitalism was on full view at the Inter-State Fair. Retailers and wholesalers from around the state regularly hawked new or novel products to the tens of thousands who visited the event each year. Castner found the booth in **plate 107** promoting the locally produced "Idol Dance" brand cigars to be worthy of a photograph. Perhaps it was the elaborate, vibrantly decorated signage—which was surely also very colorful—that drew his eye. Or perhaps the photographer found the men having a moment

Plate 107. Jonathan Steward Company tobacco booth, Inter-State Fair, Hamilton Township, New Jersey, 1894. Digital positive from 4" x 5" glass plate negative. CH2019.6.326.

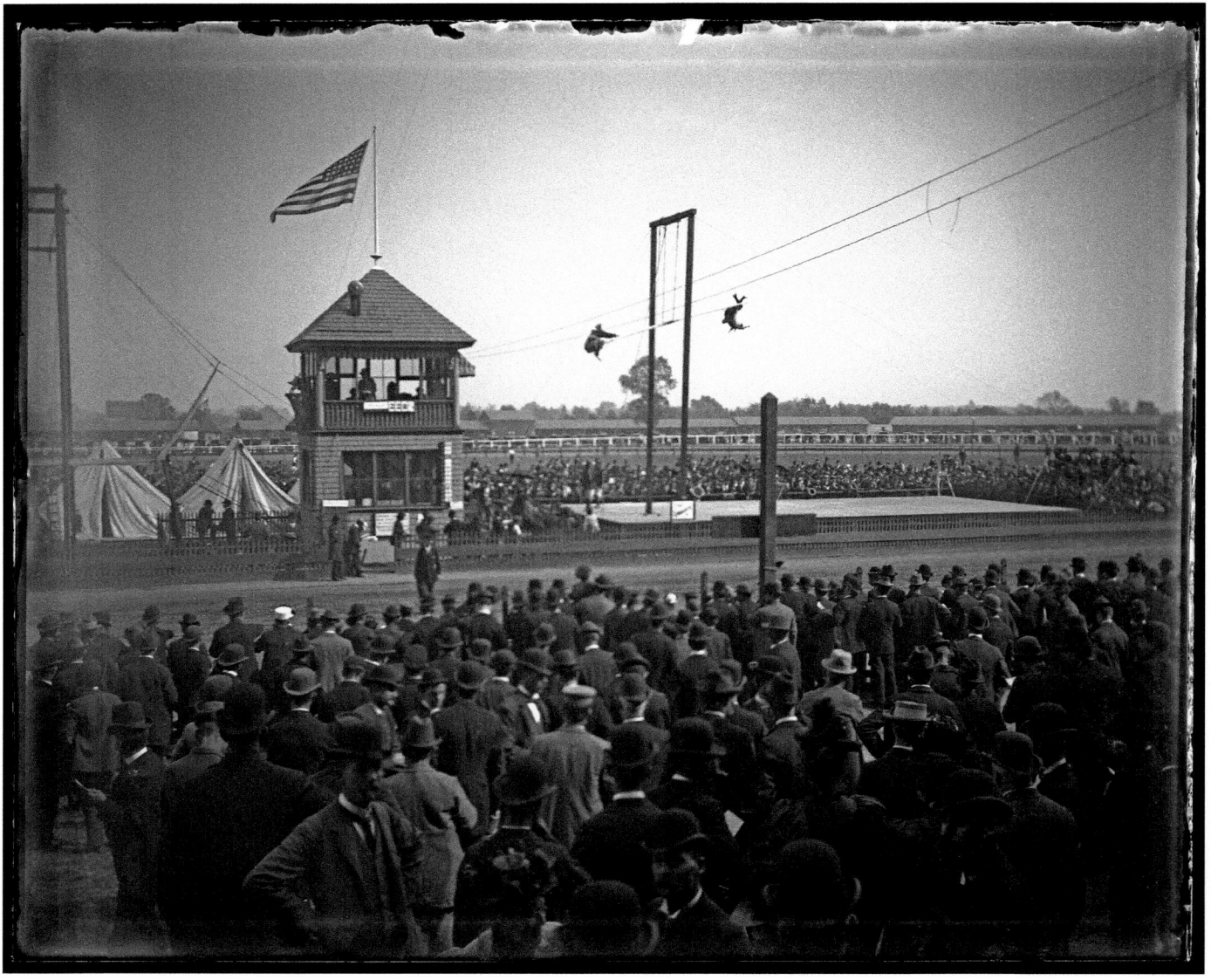

Plate 108. Andrée and Golden diving act, Inter-State Fair, Hamilton Township, New Jersey, 1895. Digital positive from 4" x 5" glass plate negative. CH2019.6.352.

of peace amid the hustle and bustle of the fair to be interesting characters. In the background is the entrance to Walker's Boston Wonderland and Museum, a carnival sideshow with many entertainments considered offensive by today's standards. It featured "heavyweight" ballet dancers, a blackface comedian, Punch and Judy shows, and a natural wonder named Columbus, described as being "the largest snake ever captured" with an astonishing length of twenty-six feet.

Like his fellow fairgoers, Castner was particularly drawn to the many high-flying circus acts at the Inter-State Fair. In 1895, Andrée and Golden, a traveling duo, brought their two-part high diving act to New Jersey (**plate 108**). The first involved climbing to the top of an 85-foot-tall tower, leaping from the

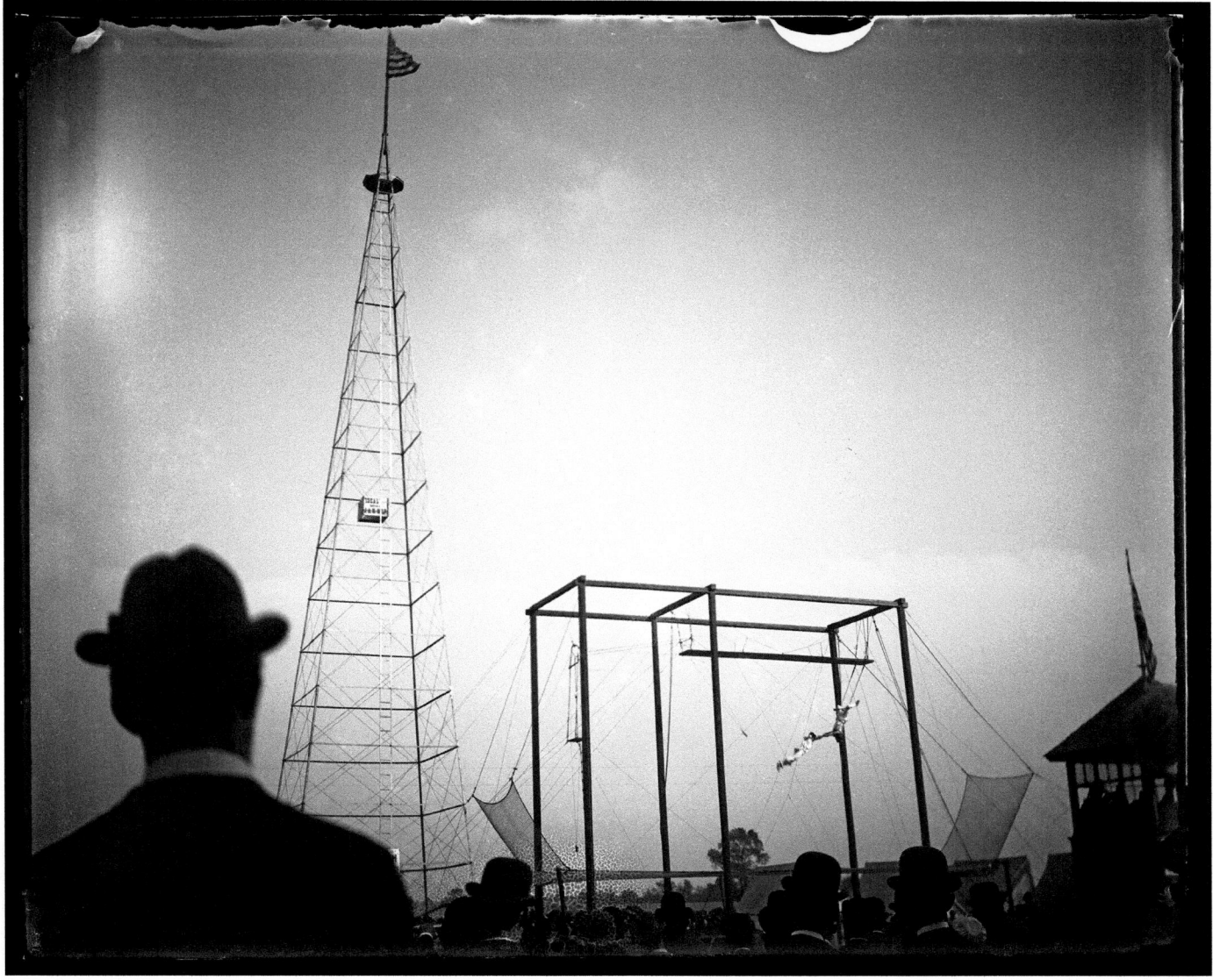

great height and landing in a small tank of water only a mere five feet deep. This image shows the second part of their act, which involved performing exciting aerial acrobatics on a flying trapeze and concluding with dramatic, somersaulting dives into a makeshift pool of water below. The duo performed regularly at fairs in the Midwest and Northeast during the 1890s.

The 1895 Inter-State Fair featured flying trapeze action by a traveling troupe of aerialists known as the Austin Sisters. The hat-capped figure in the foreground makes **plate 109** even more compelling. It conveys the familiar feel of a crowded audience jostling with each other to catch a view of the action. It also gives a sense of scale to the towering apparatuses constructed by the Inter-State Fair organizers purely for

Plate 109. Austin Sisters flying trapeze act, Inter-State Fair, Hamilton Township, New Jersey, 1895. Digital positive from 4" x 5" glass plate negative. CH2019.6.344.

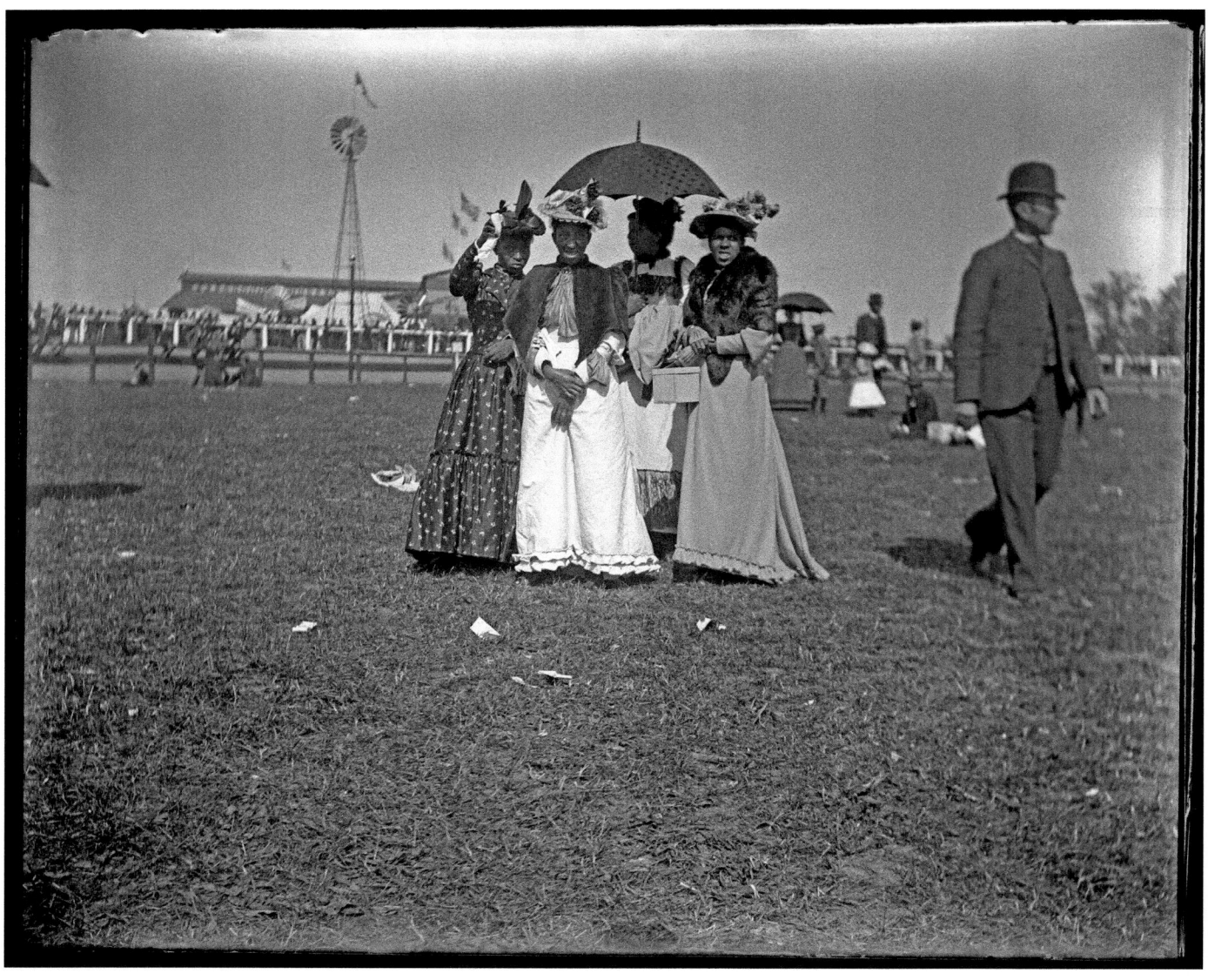

Plate 110. Johnson family at the Inter-State Fair, Hamilton Township, New Jersey, 1894. Digital positive from 4" x 5" glass plate negative. CH2019.6.424.

the entertainment of its visitors. Counterbalanced by the dark tower at the right, the figure in the foreground helps frame the photograph, directing attention to the sensational action at the center. The Austin Sisters can be seen swinging through midair on the right. On the left is the high dive tower used by one of the fair's other featured acts.

Very little is known about the four well-dressed ladies in **plate 110** whom Castner photographed at the Inter-State Fairgrounds in 1894. In the bright sunshine, they huddle tightly together under a single shared parasol, suggesting that they are close relatives, maybe even sisters. The photographer either knew them or asked for their name when he took the photograph. His notes suggest that they are members of a family named Johnson. Their attire—patterned dresses, flowered hats, shawls and furs—suggests that the fair was a place where one should look one's best. The picture was taken on a sunny day in the large grassy field on the east side of the fairgrounds. In the far distance is the harness racing track and grandstand.

11

Nature

He called his photographic forays his "rambles." Camera in hand, Castner loved to escape the busy city to explore New Jersey's natural areas. He traveled by foot, bicycle, automobile, and train. Sometimes he went to places just outside the Trenton city limits. Other times he ventured deep into the countryside. His rambles yielded many images of pastoral landscapes. They capture the peace and tranquility afforded by New Jersey meadows and forests. Castner also experimented with still-life photography, celebrating nature's bounty.

Much of Castner's glass plate collection consists of images of people and events. His known nature photographs are smaller in number. But they were very well received by his contemporaries, including Pictorialist photographers. Castner earned accolades and awards for some of his nature photographs and had others published in notable amateur photography journals.

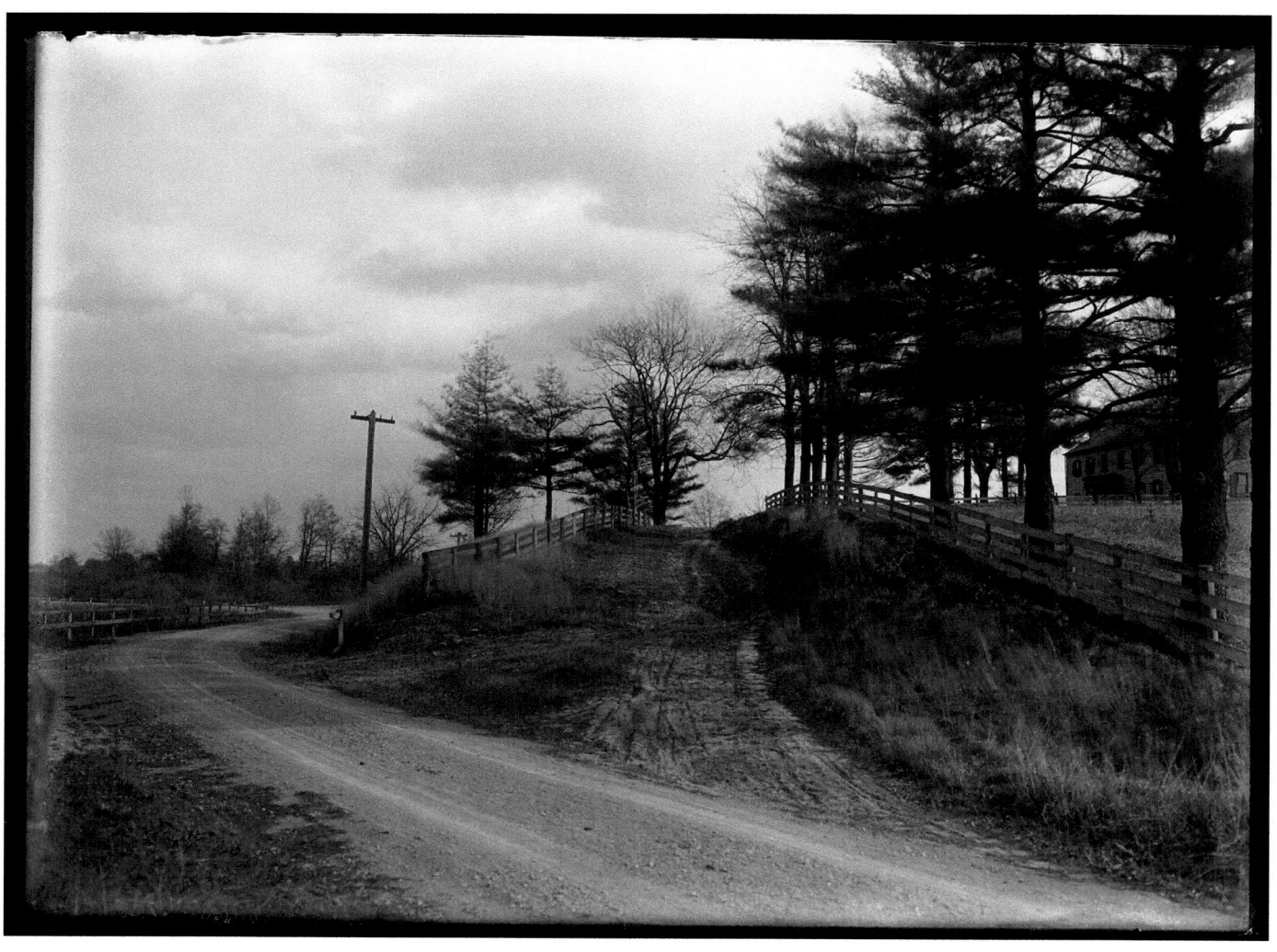

Plate 111. *The Old Homestead.*
White Horse Road, Hamilton
Township, New Jersey, c. 1900.
Digital positive from 5" x 7" glass
plate negative. CH2019.6.89.

Castner was influenced by Pictorialism, a movement in photography that insisted that the medium could do more than just strictly document reality; it could produce works of aesthetic value that used composition and tone to evoke a mood and feeling. In **plate 111**, Castner conveys a sense of pastoral peace and tranquility in a lonely, rural landscape. The home was the summer residence of the Thropps, a Trenton industrial family who operated a multigenerational machinery firm. Some Pictorialists such as Robert Demachy (1859–1936) used textured printing papers or specialized printing processes such as gum bichromate and bromoil prints to make their nature and landscape photographs look more like etchings, woodcuts, or other art processes. Castner's archive consists mainly of glass plate negatives, not prints. From the

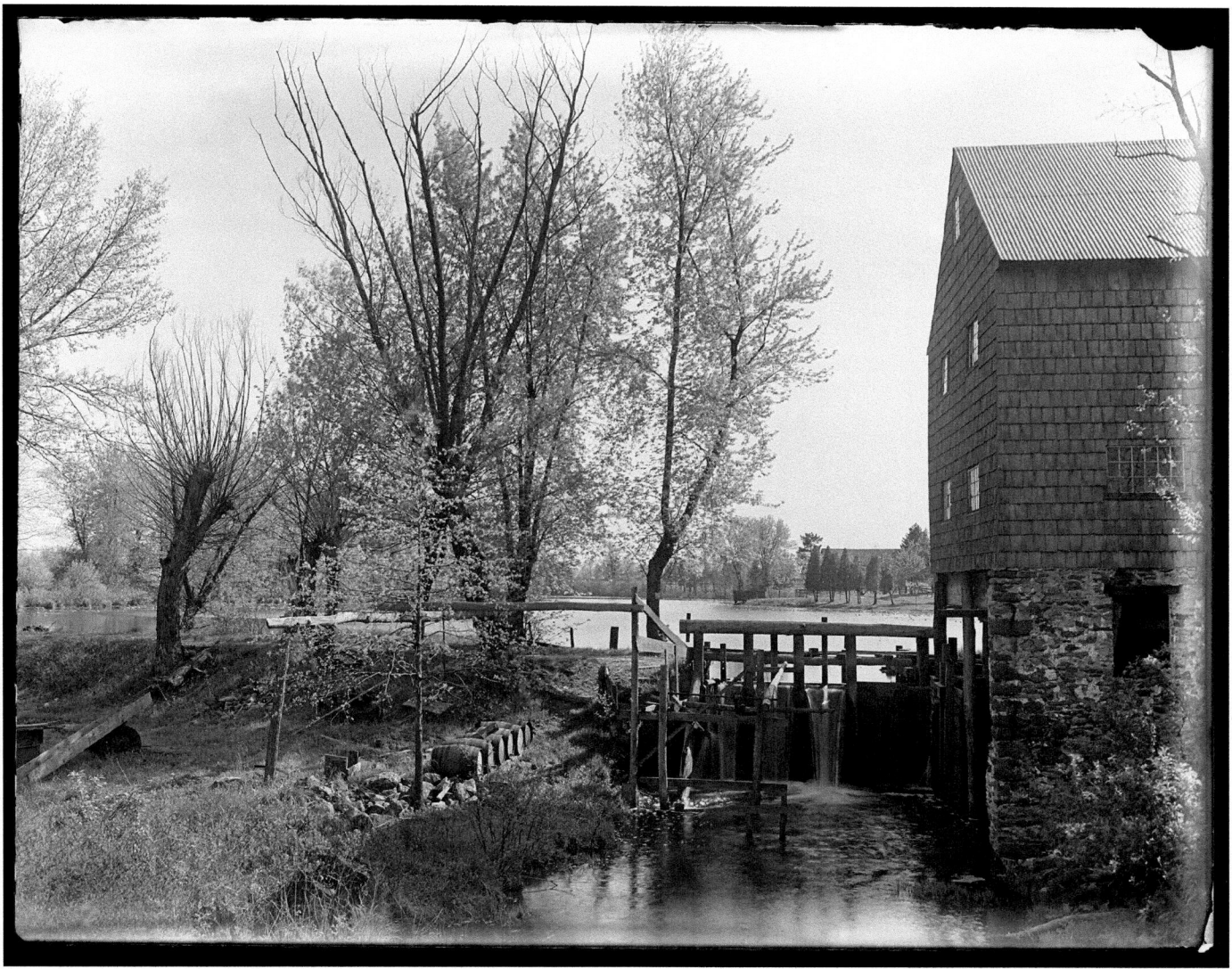

small number of prints that have survived, it does appear that Castner experimented with different printing techniques but primarily made more conventional ones typical of his era.

In Castner's day, the townships outside of Trenton were distinctly rural areas made up of working farms, pastures, and wooded areas often visited by people wishing to escape the congestion of the city. **Plate 112** captures the pastoral beauty of the Garden State as it existed before the major transformations of the landscape in later twentieth century. Known by locals as the "Old Mill," the structure in Castner's photograph was located at Evergreen Farm on Meadow Lakes in Hightstown, East Windsor Township. The mill was originally built in the late 1700s and later repurposed for woolen textile

Plate 112. Old mill and raceway, Hightstown/East Windsor Township, New Jersey, 1909. Digital positive from 5" x 7" glass plate negative. CH2019.6.109.

manufacturing. Once the mill ceased to operate, the area developed a local reputation for its natural beauty and wildlife diversity, which is likely why Castner made it a destination for one of his rambles. The mill is no longer there, and the lake on which it stood is now the center of a retirement community complex.

Though a documentary approach to the medium best defines his body of work, Castner also liked to experiment with still life. By choosing items from the natural world and arranging them in and around readily available manufactured items from the home, Castner could explore composition, form, lighting, and focus. In **plate 113**, he photographed a lovely bouquet of an ornamental flower called Cosmos. He was probably attracted to its delicate, wiry stems, and cheerful, daisy-like flowers, which his camera captured in incredible detail. The curved sides of the ceramic vase and trapezoidal form of the table add strong, simple lines, a contrast to the wild chaos of the many flowers. The embroidery on the tablecloth suggests the form of leaves or flower petals, complementing the contents of the vase that sits upon it. Castner used a sheet for a backdrop to eliminate distracting detail. Through such still life studies, Castner followed in the footsteps of Adolphe Braun (1812–1877), who made celebrated photographs of flowers in the 1850s and inspired many other photographers.

The title that Grant Castner ascribed to the negative in **plate 114** suggests how the photographer was indeed interested in using still-life composition to take his art in new directions. In *Study in Grapes and Quinces*, the photographer has carefully chosen the fruits based on their complementary, rounded shapes—a tribute to the circular form. An avid reader of the many magazines being published at the turn of the twentieth century geared to amateur photographers, Castner may have been inspired by the November 1897 issue of *The Photo-American*. In it, author William McLaughlin explored both practical and theoretical approaches to applying

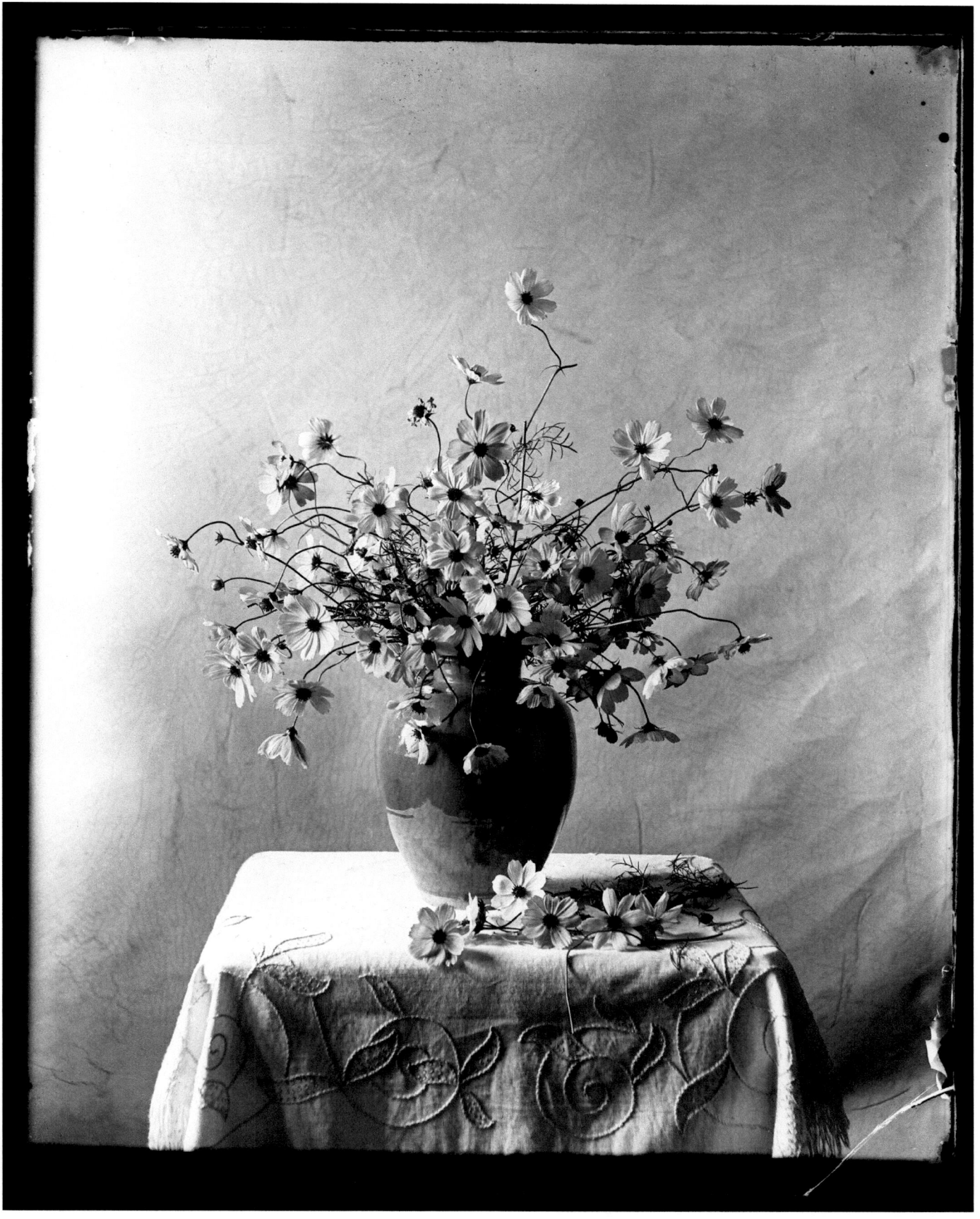

Plate 113. Still life with flowers, Trenton, New Jersey, 1898. Digital positive from 4" x 5" glass plate negative. CH2019.6.268.

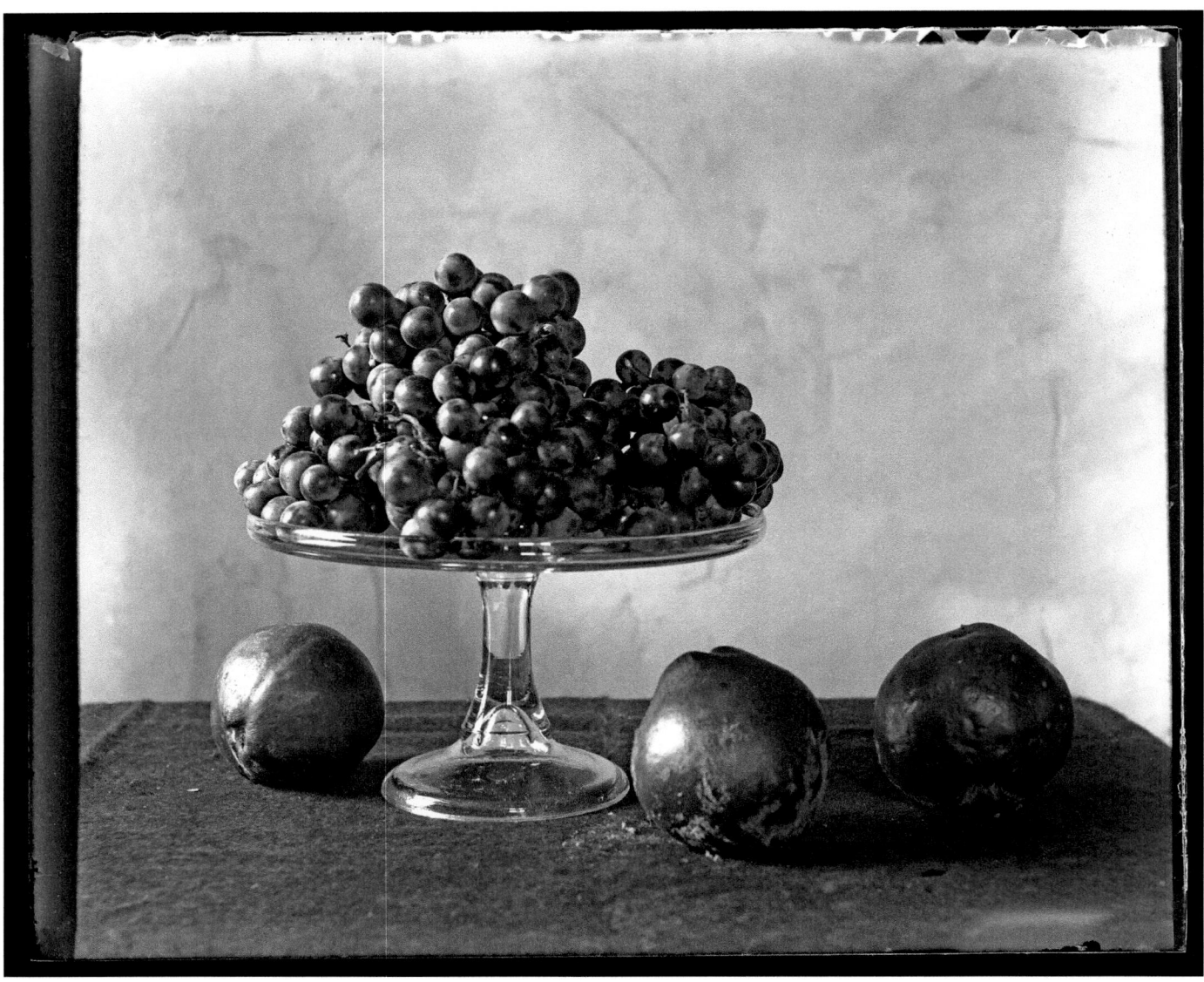

Plate 114. *Study in Grapes and Quinces.* Still life, Trenton, New Jersey, 1898. Digital positive from 4" x 5" glass plate negative. CH2019.6.646.

photography to still-life composition. Alternatively, Castner might have seen a reproduction of Cezanne's *Still Life with Fruit Dish* (1879–1880), which has a strikingly similar content and arrangement.

As part of his adventures in the New Jersey outdoors, Castner enjoyed visiting the many small islands situated in the upper Delaware River in Hunterdon County. Just east of Bulls Island, he came across the historic houses in **plate 115** located at the base of the towering cliffs that mark the southwestern corner of Hunterdon's central plateau. Dwarfed by the cliffs above and partially obscured by the trees of this heavily wooded part of New Jersey, the houses were built in the early nineteenth century when the small hamlet of Raven Rock developed from the

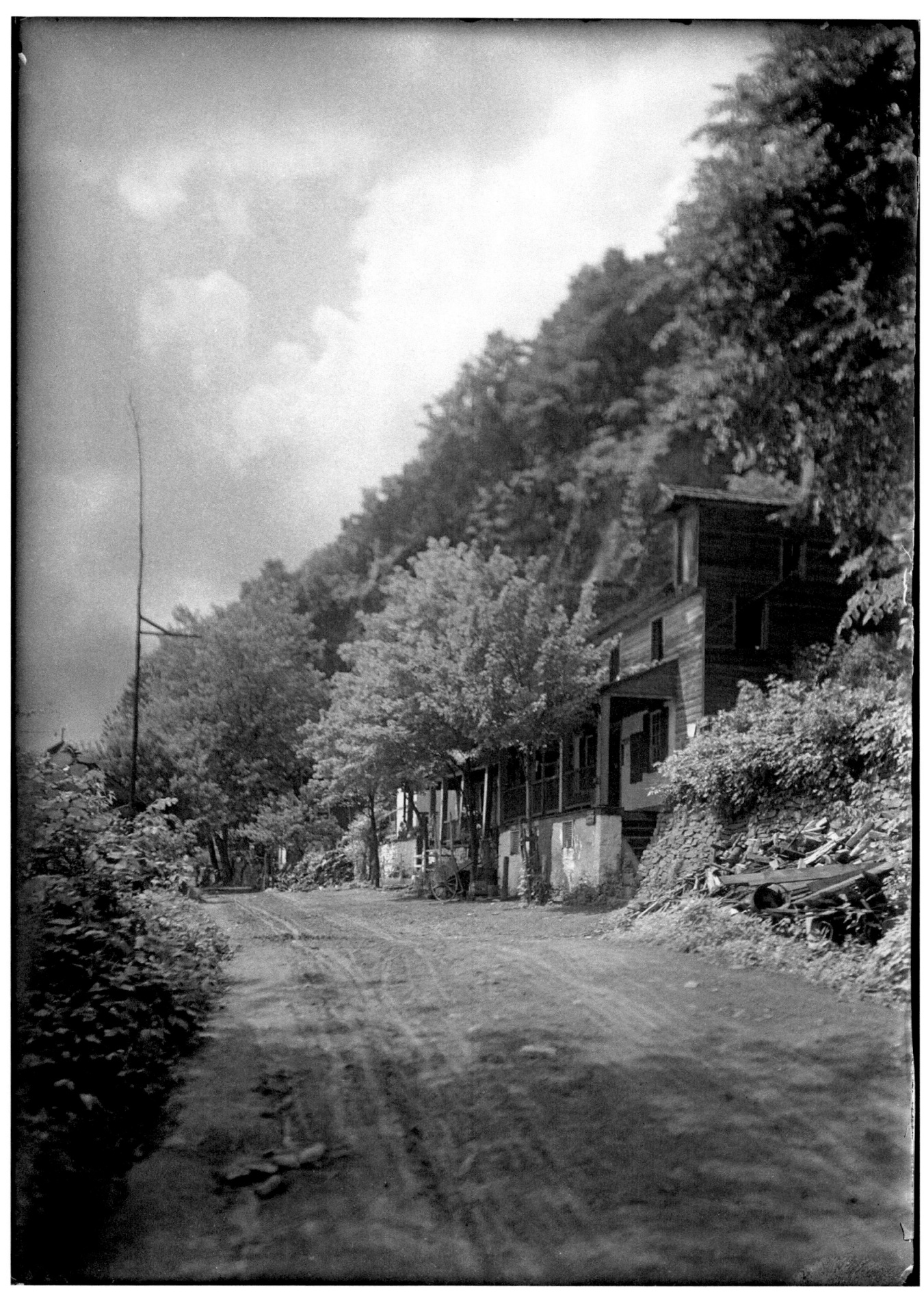

Plate 115. Cliffside houses, Raven Rock, near Stockton, New Jersey, 1904. Digital scan from 5" x 7" glass lantern slide. CH2019.6.756.

nearby northern terminus of the Delaware and Raritan Feeder Canal. Signs of human habitation are minimal, and the structures appear to be almost swallowed up by the natural world that surrounds them. Castner's judicious choice of a vertical composition emphasizes the steepness of the cliff. The houses are still standing to this day and can be observed on Route 29 just north of the entrance to Bulls Island Recreation Area.

When he came across the trees in **plate 116**, Castner may have viewed them not as natural objects, but as figures. The smaller tree in the foreground gently leans into its larger neighbor, with two distinct branches forming the "arms" with which it offers a loving embrace. Along the riverbank, additional pairs of trees also appear to interact with one another as if they too are courting couples out for a leisurely, riverbank stroll. Dappled sunlight cascading through the leaves and bouncing off the water give the composition a warm, pleasant glow, underscoring a message of happiness and love.

In a photograph of his young son, Castner explored the relationships between people and the natural world (**plate 117**). The quiet, bucolic scene conveys a harmonious relationship between people and nature. The tree that rises high above the child sends a message of nature's immense power and humankind's insignificance over the eons-long arc of time. It also suggests a protective relationship with the little boy, like father and son. The tree is pitch pine, a ubiquitous species found throughout central and south New Jersey and often associated with the Pinelands. The pitch pine, which has an open form, flattish top, and gnarled limbs, has long been admired as being particularly photogenic because it tends to takes on interesting forms as it grows into older age.

Castner enjoyed venturing out into nature with his camera in the winter months, especially when there was snow on the ground. He found that photography was perhaps the perfect medium to capture the light, textures, and tones of the natural environment that he encountered in wintertime.

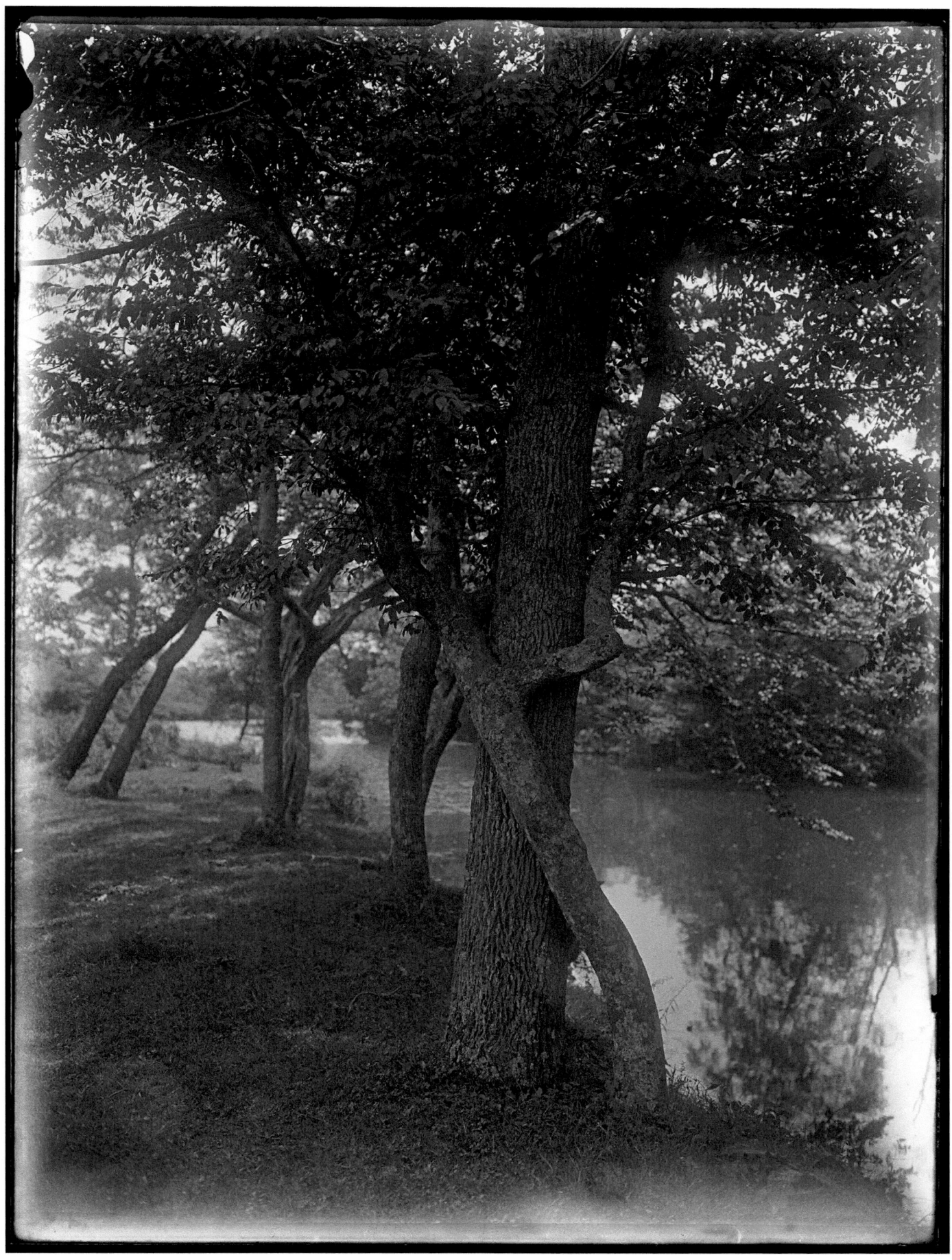

Plate 116. Hugging trees, likely the Manasquan River, Monmouth County, New Jersey, 1913. Digital positive from 6.5" x 8.5" glass plate negative. CH2019.6.712.

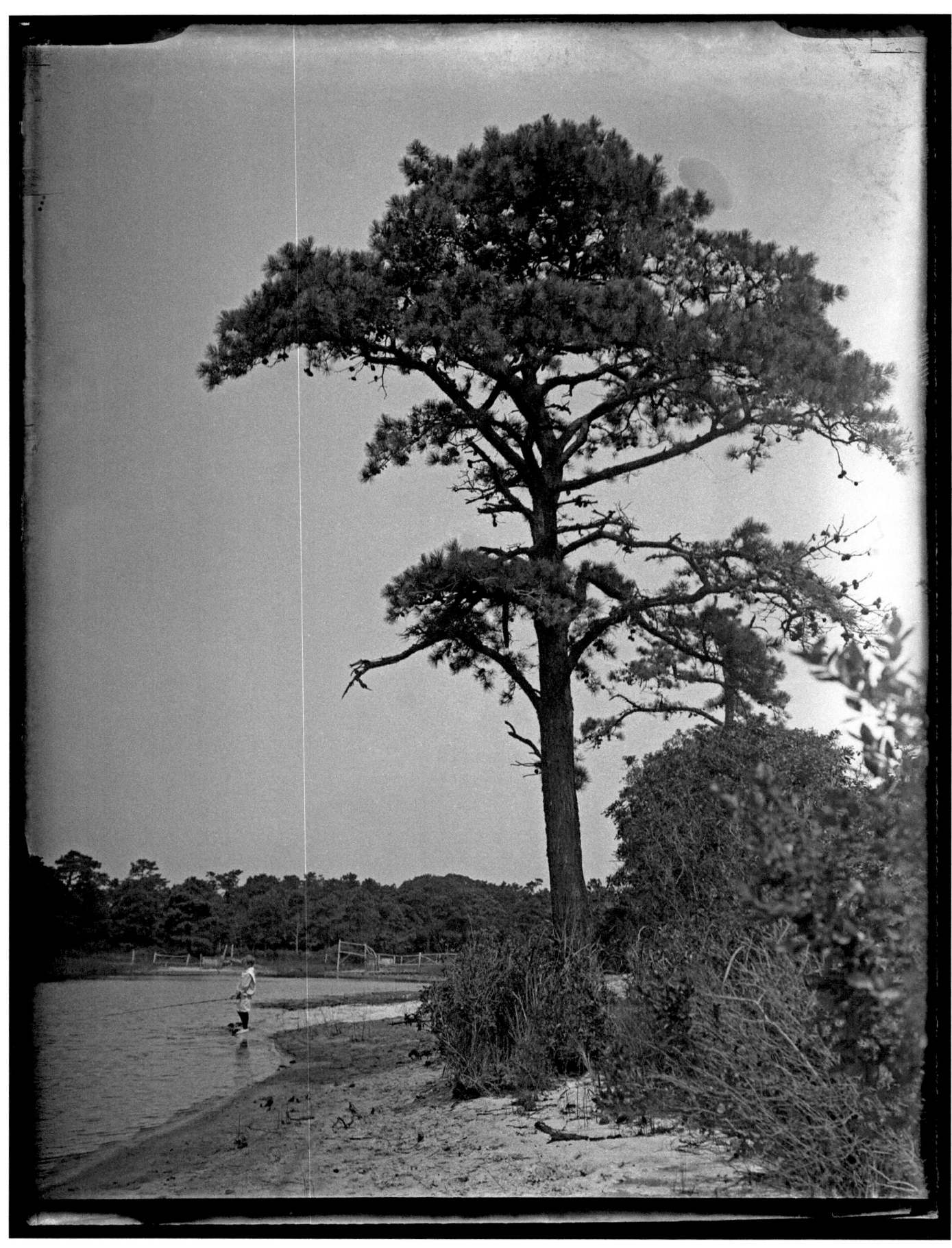

Plate 117. Theodore Grant Castner and pine tree, location unknown, possibly Point Pleasant, New Jersey, c. 1913. Digital positive from 3.25" x 4.25" glass plate negative. CH2019.6.810.

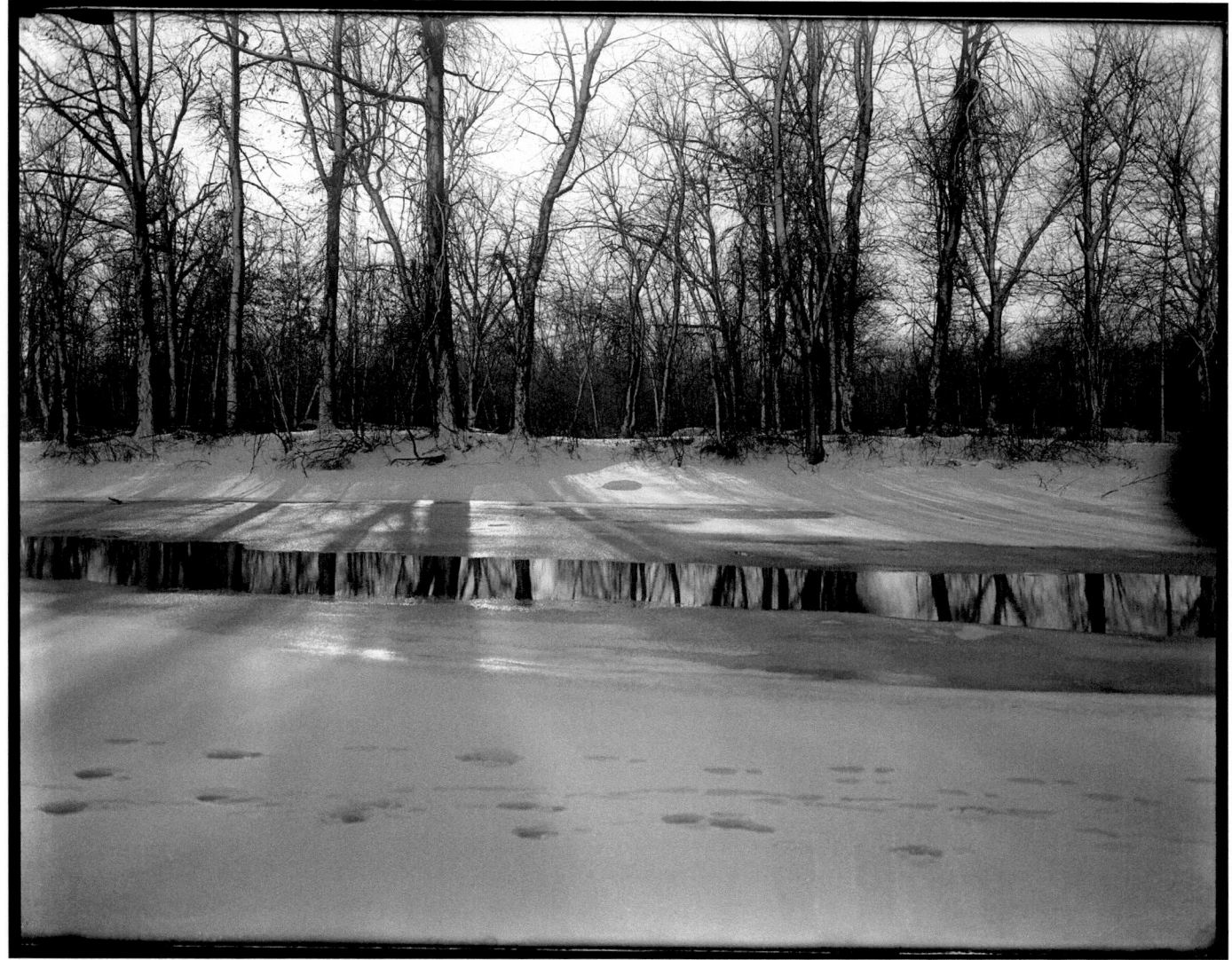

In **plate 118**, one of Castner's finest, the leafless trees in the background form a dynamic tangle of visual interest. They stretch on and on into the far distance, implying nature's vast bounty. In the low winter sun, the trees cast long shadows across a partially ice-covered waterway, possibly Crosswicks Creek. Their shadows magically transform into reflections in the unfrozen part of the creek, then quickly revert back into shadows on the other side. Footprints in the snow suggest that his image is not just about nature, but constitutes a message about the enjoyment of the beauty that could be found therein. The photograph earned Castner warm praise from his peers. It was published in the December 1916 issue of *Photo Era*, a national magazine for amateur photographers.

Plate 118. *Reflections and Shadows.* Trees along an ice-covered creek, location unknown, possibly Crosswicks Creek, Hamilton or Bordentown Township, New Jersey, c. 1910. Digital positive from 6.5" x 8.5" glass plate negative. CH2019.6.934.

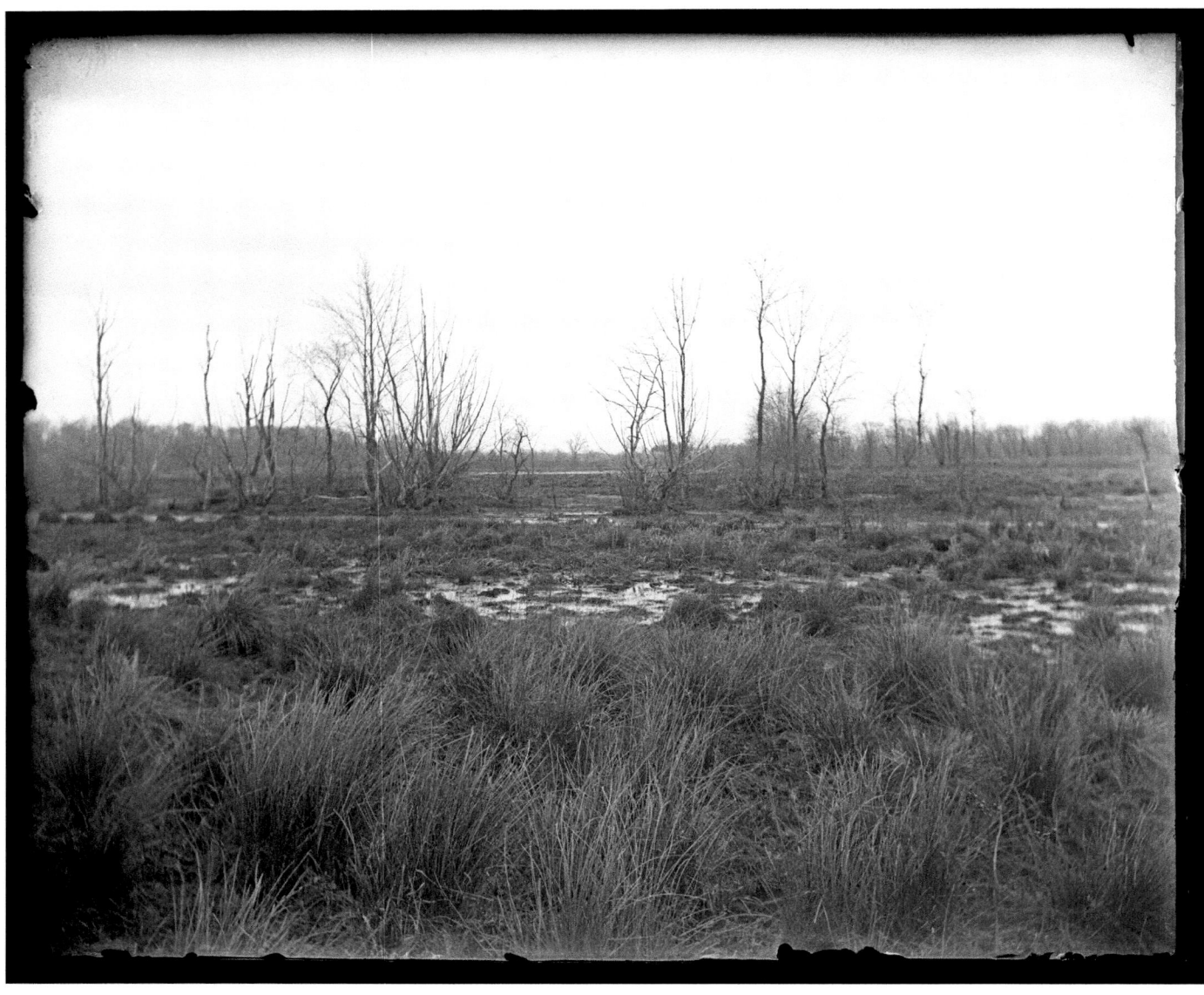

Plate 119. *In Decou's Meadows:*
Where the Frogs like to Croak.
Hamilton Township, New Jersey,
1897. Digital scan from 4" x 5" glass
lantern slide. CH2019.6.647.

More than twenty of Castner's nature images were taken in a place that he referred to as "Decou's Meadows." The Decou and Abbot families owned large tracts of land on the east side of Trenton and in Hamilton Township. In 1889, Isaac DeCou sold a 250-acre farm that was later developed into a residential area known as Broad Street Park. Castner likely took **plate 119** in the general vicinity along the low-lying, marshy areas adjacent to Crosswicks Creek. The craggy limbs of waterlogged trees stretch into a stark April sky amid a landscape of swampland and marsh grasses. While the bleak landscape seems devoid of life, Castner's image title suggests that he photographed the spot on a day when the habitat's large amphibian population was pleasantly announcing the arrival of

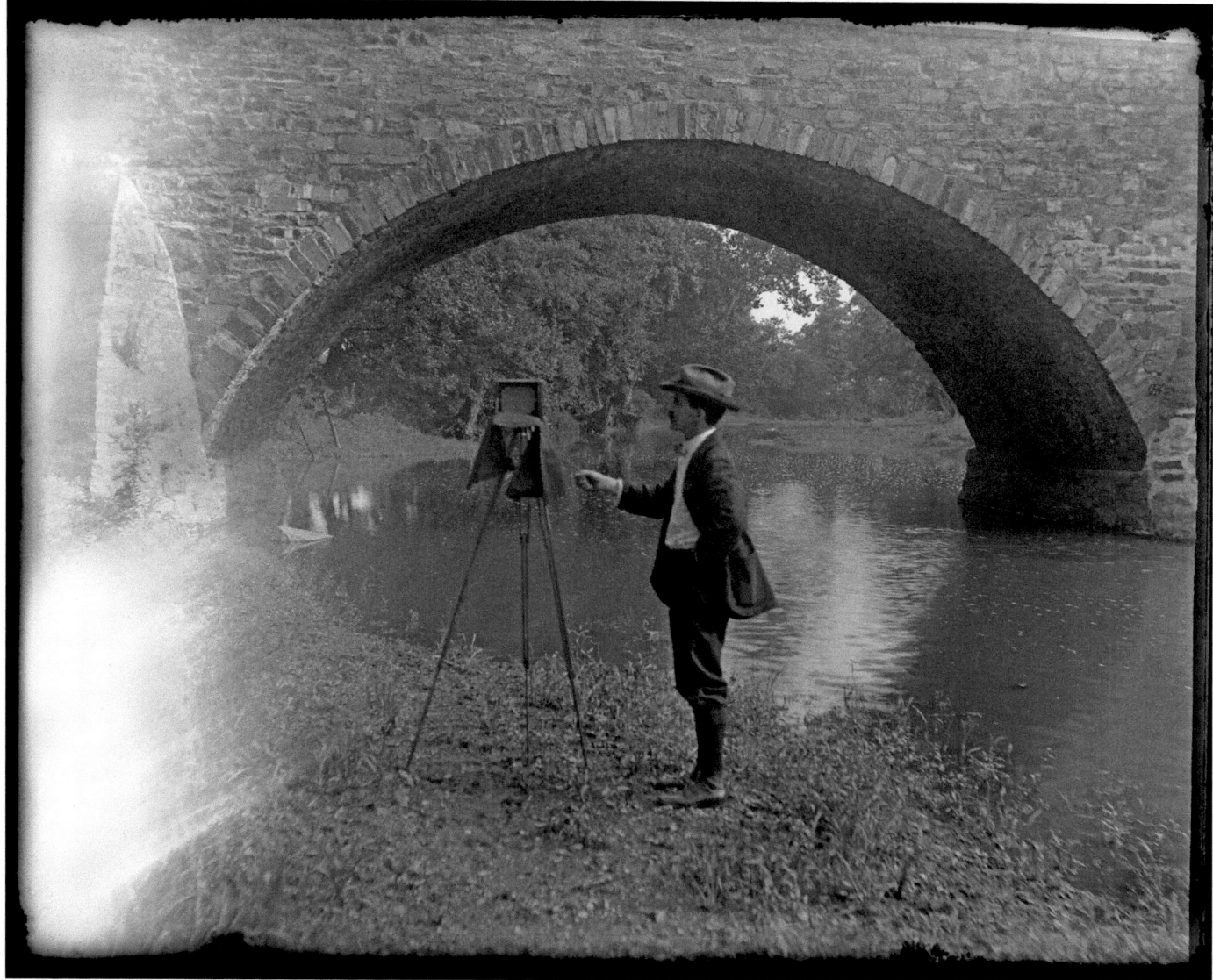

the spring season. In 1898, one of Castner's images of DeCou's Meadows—possibly this one—received high praise at the first annual exhibition of the Trenton Photographic Society. If so, perhaps it drew attention for its unusual composition in which no part of the image is emphasized as the primary subject. Castner may have admired the way that the forms of the grasses in the foreground resemble the branches of the leafless trees in the distance. Since Castner made a lantern slide of his print, he must have valued it as one of his favorites.

A perfect encapsulation of the life of a forgotten New Jersey artist, the self-portrait in **plate 120** is the only known image of Castner with his trusty camera unpacked and at the ready. He carefully composed the shot by placing himself in

Figure 120. Self-portrait of Grant Castner, Stony Brook Bridge, Princeton Township, New Jersey, 1898. Digital positive from 4" x 5" glass plate negative. CH2019.6.515.

profile directly beneath the graceful arch of a stone bridge. The tranquil setting of a tree-lined stream reinforces his love for nature. The photograph was taken in the shadow of one of the two historic stone arch bridges over Stony Brook in Princeton Township. Both bridges are still standing today. One carries Route 206 and the other carries Mercer Road. Once he had framed the shot, Castner probably had a friend or family member take the photo. Self-timers that worked on air pressure were available but not widely in use in 1898.

Notes

1. For the early German immigration to New Jersey, see Theodore Frelinghuysen Chambers, *The Early Germans of New Jersey: Their History, Churches, and Genealogies* (Dover, NJ: Dover Printing Company, 1895); Rudolph J. Vecoli, *The People of New Jersey* (Princeton, NJ: D. Van Nostrand Company, Inc., 1965).

2. Donald Henry Strahle, "Some Early Descendants of Peter Kastner of Elsenz, Germany," last accessed May 30, 2024, https://www.mrlocalhistory.org/wp-content/uploads/2023/07/Kastner_Peter-Castner-family-Liberty-Corner.pdf.

3. I. Alstyne Blauvelt, *A Historical Sketch of the German Reformed Presbyterian Church of German Valley, NJ* (Trenton, NJ: Murphy and Bechtel Steam Book and Job Printers, 1870), 27–28, 53–55; Chambers, *The Early Germans of New Jersey*, 114–117; Amelia Stickney Decker and Ralph Decker, *History of the Newton Presbytery* (Newton, NJ: Newtown Presbytery, 1949), 7, 61–62.

4. *Jeffersonian Republican* (Stroudsburg, PA), May 10, 1843, 2; *Alexandria Gazette* (Alexandria, VA), June 1, 1843, 2; *The Tribune* (New York, NY), August 26, 1843, 2.

5. For the history of the Changewater murders, see Ruth Trask Farrow, *Murders on the Musconetcong: A Tale of Jersey Justice* (Hong Kong: T.F.H. Publications, Inc., 1973); Sharon Meeker and Robert Meeker, *The Changewater Murders* (Budd Lake, NJ: Legacy of America, 1998). Peter W. Parke self-published a pamphlet to protest his innocence in order to raise money to benefit his widow

and three children. See "Protest of Peter W. Parke . . ." (1845), Special Collections and University Archives, Rutgers University, New Brunswick, NJ.

6. "Return of Births in the Town of Belvidere, County of Warren, State of New Jersey, from the First Day of May, 1863, to the First Day of May, 1864," New Jersey State Archives, Trenton, NJ.

7. 1870 U.S. Census, Warren County, New Jersey, population schedule, Belvidere, New Jersey; 1880 U.S. Census, Warren County, New Jersey, population schedule, Belvidere, New Jersey.

8. For the early history of Belvidere, see James P. Snell, *History of Sussex and Warren Counties, New Jersey* (Philadelphia, PA: Everts and Peck, 1881), 532–547. For the history of the Bel-Del Railroad, see Warren F. Lee, *Down Along the Old Bel-Del: The History of the Belvidere Delaware Railroad Company, A Pennsylvania Railroad Company* (Albuquerque, NM: Bel-Del Enterprises, Ltd., 1987). The Bel-Del was eventually absorbed into the Pennsylvania Railroad conglomerate. Lambertville musician J.B. Kline regularly performs his song about the Bel-Del, "Belvidere Line," DangWingnut, April 15, 2024, YouTube video, 4:11, https://www.youtube.com/watch?v=yJT5JS5Kto0.

9. Information about Grant Castner's early life can be found in surviving personal correspondence and ephemera belonging to his descendants John Castner, Jennifer Castner, and Wilden Munsen, hereafter cited as Castner Family Collection. Two issues of Grant Castner's newspaper are known to be extant: *The Starry Flag*, 2.1 (December 1879), Castner Family Collection, and *The Starry Flag*, 2.2 (January 1880), American Antiquarian Society, Worcester, MA.

10. A.P. Berthoud to Grant Castner, September 19, 1884; Decker to Grant Castner, November 24, 1884; McCammon, Miller & Young to Grant Castner, December 8, 1884. Castner Family Collection.

11. 1885 New Jersey State Census, Mercer County, New Jersey, population schedule, Trenton, 3rd Ward; 1900 U.S. Census, Mercer County, New Jersey, Trenton City, 9th Ward; 1910 U.S. Census, Mercer County, New Jersey, population schedule, Trenton City, 10th Ward; *Fitzgerald's Trenton and Mercer County Directory*

Together with a Business Directory of Morrisville, PA, 1885–1934, New Jersey State Library.

12. Portable darkrooms were usually in wagons or tents, but some photographers used a large box on a tripod, one of which was invented by John Carbutt in 1864. William Brey, *John Carbutt: On the Frontiers of Photography* (Cherry Hill, NJ: Willowdale Press, 1984), 12–13. For outdoor views, some camera artists used dry collodion plates, which required long exposures of often five to ten minutes; these negatives, which the photographers either prepared themselves or purchased ready-made, obviated the need for a portable darkroom. However, the vast majority of negatives made from 1850 to 1880 were wet collodion. Adrienne Lundren, "Employing the Preserved Negative: Dry Collodion and the Artists Who Used It," *Topics in Photographic Preservation, Volume Twenty* (Washington, DC: Photographic Materials Group, American Institute for Conservation, 2023), 84–93.

13. Developing and printing services for amateurs' flexible film negatives began with the introduction of the Kodak camera in 1888 and became widespread in the 1890s, but photographers who continued to use glass plates like Castner typically developed their own.

14. Although there are some exceptions, the New Jersey State Museum's collection comprises personal photographs rather than work for hire that he may have done after he began describing himself as a photographer in the 1910s. Castner likely made many more photographs than are currently available.

15. For numerous examples of packed frames, see *Open City: Street Photographs Since 1950* (Oxford, UK: Museum of Modern Art Oxford, 2001).

16. Tom Wolf, *Eva Watson-Schütze: Photographer* (New Paltz, NY: SUNY, 2009); Gary D. Saretzky, "Elias Goldensky: Wizard of Photography," *Pennsylvania History* 64, no. 2 (Spring 1997): 206–272, https://journals.psu.edu/phj/article/viewFile/25383/25152. Last accessed February 22, 2024.

17. Elias Goldensky, "Individuality," *Bulletin of Photography* 3, no. 59 (September 23, 1908): 198, 200. Regarding photographs as

windows, see John Szarkowski, *Mirrors and Windows: American Photography Since 1960* (NY: Museum of Modern Art, 1978).

18. For Lewis Hine's child labor photography, see Vicki Goldberg, *Lewis W. Hine: Children at Work* (Munich et al.; Prestel, 1999). For Lewis Hine's work in New Jersey, see Nicholas P. Ciotola, "From Philadelphia to the Pinelands: The New Jersey Photographs of Lewis W. Hine," *Pennsylvania Magazine of History and Biography*, 137, no. 2 (April 2013): 179–90.

19. The differences between men and women photographers before 1900 is explored in depth in Nicole Hudgins, *The Gender of Photography: How Masculine and Feminine Values Shaped the History of Nineteenth-Century Photography* (London & New York: Routledge, 2020).

20. Milton Meltzer, *Dorothea Lange: A Photographer's Life* (NY: Farrar, Straus, Giroux, 1978), 79.

21. Cartes-de-visite, about 2 1/2 by 4 1/8 inches, were introduced in the United States in 1859. Cabinet cards, about 4 1/4 by 6 1/2, began to be produced in the 1860s and were named in 1866. Tintypes were also made in these sizes for insertion into albums, and there were other less popular card sizes by the 1880s. For more on cartes-de-visite, see Gary D. Saretzky, "A Question of Priority: George G. Rockwood, Charles D. Fredricks and Early Cartes-de-Visite in the United States," revised text of chapter published in *The Daguerreian Annual 2024* (Cecil, PA: Daguerreian Society, 2024), http://saretzky.com/download/2024-annual -saretzky-03_17_25_-revised.pdf.

22. A carte-de-visite in the NJSM collection (CH2019.6.1099) depicts a young girl who is believed to be one of Grant Castner's two older sisters. On the reverse, the carte is marked, "From George K. Marriner's Photograph Gallery, over Currie & Reid's Store, Belvidere, NJ."

23. Merrion Castner paid the Internal Revenue Service for an eight-month license to practice photography in May 1863. Ross J. Kelbaugh, *Directory of Civil War Photographers.* (Baltimore: Historic Graphics, 1991), vol. 2: 78; Ketchledge obituary, *Belvidere Apollo*, October 15, 1914. Born in about 1838, Ketchledge

was a photographer in eastern Pennsylvania before relocating to Belvidere.

24. Gary D. Saretzky with Joseph G. Bilby, "New Jersey Photographers of the Civil War and Postwar Era: John P. Doremus," *New Jersey Studies: An Interdisciplinary Journal*, 8, no. 1 (Winter 2022): 152–223, https://doi.org/10.14713/njs.v8i1.267. Supplemented by *Erratum*, 8, no. 2 (Summer 2022); Gary D. Saretzky, "Gustavus W. Pach: A Nineteenth-Century New Jersey Photographer," *The Daguerreian Annual, 2021* (Cecil, PA: The Daguerreian Society, 2021), 140–159; Frank J. Esposito and Donald Lokuta, *Victorian New Jersey: Photographs by Guillermo Thorn from the Kean University Collection* (Union, NJ: Kean University Press, 2005). Peter Ketchledge stereoviews are rare today. About a dozen different are known. Two are mentioned in *Photographers of the United States of America*, compiled by T.K. Treadwell & William C. Darrah (National Stereoscopic Association, 1994, updated November 28, 2003), https://stereoworld.org/wp-content /uploads/2016/03/US-PHOTOGRAPHERS.pdf. Last accessed February 25, 2024.

25. A collection of views by Graves, one of a number of photographers who photographed the Delaware Water Gap, is at the New York Public Library: "Stereoscopic Views of the Delaware Water Gap and Vicinity," https://catalog.nypl.org/record=b1170 8127, last accessed February 25, 2024. Graves also sold large single views.

26. *U.S. Centennial Commission International Exhibition 1876 Official Catalogue, Part II : Art Gallery, Annexes, and Outdoor Works of Art. Department IV-Art* (Philadelphia: John R. Nagle & Co., 1876).

27. Camera clubs in New Jersey began with the Camerads, which first met at Rutgers in New Brunswick in 1886 in the chemistry rooms under the direction of Professor Peter T. Austen, the uncle of Alice Austen of Staten Island, who has become well known for her street photography. Gary D. Saretzky, "Nineteenth Century New Jersey Photographers," revised text of article published in *New Jersey History*, Fall/Winter 2004, http://www.gary

.saretzky.com/photohistory/resources/photo_in_nj_July_2021.pdf. For the early history of glass positives, including lantern slides, see Kim Timby, "Glass Transparencies: Marketing Photography's Luminosity and Precision," *PhotoResearcher* (European Society for the History of Photography), no. 25 (2016), 7–24.

28. Gernsheim and Gernsheim, 424. For the positioning of the serious amateur members of camera clubs between professional photographers and casual snap shooters, see Ulrich Keller, "The Myth of Art Photography: A Sociological Analysis," *History of Photography* 8, no. 4 (October–December 1984): 249–275.

29. Mary Panzer, *Philadelphia Naturalistic Photography, 1865–1906* (New Haven: Yale University Art Gallery, 1982), 9. Had Castner attended, he likely would have also gone to the lantern slide shows held in the evenings at the society.

30. Emma Kemp opened her Trenton studio in 1888, and Frederick took over the gallery a few years later. In the late 1890s, Frederick brought in Oliver to help him, operating as Kemp & Son. By 1900, according to the U.S. Census for Trenton, Oliver Kemp had become a teacher.

31. The Naars were a prominent Sephardic Jewish family in Trenton for generations. 1900 U.S. Census, Mercer County, New Jersey, population schedule, Trenton City, 2nd Ward; John L. Cleary, "Journalism and Literature in Trenton," in *A History of Trenton* (Princeton, NJ: Princeton University Press, 1929), 779–818.

32. *Trenton Evening Times*, June 9, 1897, 1. The Applegate mentioned was probably George Applegate.

33. *Trenton Evening Times*, May 5, 1898, 2; *Trenton Evening Times*, March 28, 1900, 6; *Trenton Evening Times*, March 8, 1903, 3.

34. According to Census records, Neary began his career as a boatman in Neptune Township, Monmouth County, where his father Hiram W. was a builder. Neary moved to Trenton by 1895. In the 1915 New Jersey Census, he was listed as a steward, and in the 1920 and 1930 U.S. Censuses, as "business manager, State School." Castner's and Neary's remains lie within a few yards of each other at Greenwood Cemetery in Hamilton Township.

35. *Trenton Evening Times*, March 11, 1903, 2; February 1, 1906, 11; February 3, 1907, 3; February 23, 1909, 4.

36. *Illustrated Catalogue of Photographic Equipments and Materials for Amateurs* (New York: E. & H.T. Anthony & Co., 1891 [reprint, Morgan & Morgan, n.d.]).

37. *Trenton Evening Times*, February 8, 1910, 7.

38. *Trenton Evening Times*, May 25, 1904, 2; June 2, 1904, 12; May 27, 1905, 1.

39. Wilson first became well known in photographic circles when he and M.F. Benerman started the journal *Philadelphia Photographer* in January 1864. In 1889, it was retitled *Wilson's Photographic Magazine* and in 1915 *Photographic Journal of America*. Wilson also published the annual *Photographic Mosaics* (1866–1901), the trade paper *The Photographic Times* (1871–1915), as well as, for a time, the U.S. editions of the British *Year-Book of Photography* and *Photographic News Almanac*, among others. See also David Spencer, https://photoseed.com/blog/the-photographic-times-%E2%8E%AF-1871-1915-%E2%8E%AF-definitive-american-photographic-journal/. Last accessed May 23, 2025.

40. Edward L. Wilson, *Wilson's Photographics: A Series of Lessons* (Philadelphia: Edward L. Wilson, 1881.)

41. Sadakichi Hartmann, *The Valiant Knights of Daguerre: Selected Critical Essays on Photography and Profiles of Photographic Pioneers*, eds. Harry W. Lawton and George Knox (Berkeley: University of California, 1978). Between 1898 and around 1920, Hartmann wrote more than five hundred articles for a plethora of photography periodicals, including but not limited to *Bulletin of Photography and the Photographer, The Camera, Kodakery, Photo Era: The American Journal of Photography* (which in December 1916 published one of Castner's photos [plate 116], *Photographic Beacon, Photographic Journal of America, Photographic Times, Wilson's Photographic Magazine*, and *Portrait*, at least some of which would have been known to Castner. Hartmann also wrote for Stieglitz's expensive *Camera Work* to which Castner would not have been likely to subscribe.

42. Peter Buse, "The Photographer as Reader: The Aspirational Amateur in the Photo-magazines," in *Photography Reframed: New Visions in Photographic Culture*, eds. Ben Burbridge and Annebella Pollen (London: I.B. Tauris, 2018), 48–61.

43. Peter Henry Emerson, *Naturalistic Photography for Students of the Art* (New York: E. & F. Spon, 1890).

44. Henry Peach Robinson created sentimental art by cutting up multiple staged photographs and collaging them into what he called a "combination print," which was then photographically reproduced for sale. Robinson's popular manual, *Pictorial Effect in Photography* (1869), which covered a wide range of topics beyond combinations, was regularly reprinted and would have been accessible to Castner. It contained good advice on both portrait and landscape photography. Castner may also have been familiar with Robinson's manual on printing photographs. Henry Peach Robinson and Captain Abney, *The Art and Practice of Silver Printing* (London: Piper & Carter, 1881).

45. The Golden Section, also known as the Golden Ratio, dates back to Euclid and refers to a proportion of about 1.618:1. Dividing a horizontal rectangular photograph in this way creates a square on the longer side and a vertical rectangle on the other. The photographer Henri Cartier-Bresson (1908–2004) used this compositional technique extensively.

46. For oil, bromoil, gum bichromate, and platinotype prints, see Peter C. Bunnell, ed., *Nonsilver Printing Processes: Four Selections, 1886–1927* (New York: ARNO Press, 1973).

47. *The Velox Book* (Rochester: Eastman Kodak Co., n.d.); James M. Reilly, *The Albumen & Salted Paper Book* (Rochester, NY: Light Impressions, 1980); James M. Reilly, "The History, Technique and Structure of Albumen Prints," 1980, https://cool.cultural heritage.org/albumen/library/c20/reilly1980.html. For a discussion of printing on Velox, see Dr. Leo Baekeland, "Some Peculiarities of Velox Paper," *Wilson's Photographic Magazine*, February 1897, 51–53. Baekelend (1863–1944) was the inventor of Velox, a developing-out paper (DOP). Another popular DOP was CYKO, produced by Anthony & Scovill, which changed its name to Ansco in 1907. After exposure to light through a negative, a latent image was formed in the paper's coating, which was then made visible by immersion in a chemical developer. Albumen, the most popular paper from the 1850s to the 1890s, was a printing-out paper (POP) that used physical development (i.e. exposure in the sun) until the

image appeared. Both types of paper needed to be fixed, washed, and toned for stability.

48. Henry G. Abbott, *Modern Photography in Theory and Practice: A Handbook for the Amateur* (New York: George G. Hazlitt, 1898). Dr. L.H. Baekeland invented and began manufacturing Velox paper in 1894.

49. See *The Velox Book*.

50. Janet E. Buerger, *The Last Decade: The Emergence of Art Photography in the 1890s* (Rochester, NY: International Museum of Photography at George Eastman House, 1984).

51. Beaumont Newhall, *The History of Photography From 1839 to the Present* (New York: Museum of Modern Art, 1982), 146.

52. Panzer, 13–14. These Philadelphia salons continued in 1899 and 1900. Whether Castner submitted photographs for judging has not been determined.

53. *Trenton Evening Times*, May 5, 1898, 8. Born in Alabama, William D. Murphy (1834–?) was both a photographer and painter who worked in the South until moving to Philadelphia in 1876. He relocated to New York in 1883 and was active until the early twentieth century. William A. Fraser (c. 1840–1925), a leather merchant, was an avid amateur photographer who, like Murphy and Stieglitz, was an active member of the Camera Club of New York in the late 1890s. He was especially regarded for his lantern slides of urban night scenes. See Christian A. Peterson, *Alfred Stieglitz's Camera Notes* (Minneapolis: The Minneapolis Institute of Arts, 1993), 31–32.

54. Plate 15 in Sarah Greenough and Juan Hamilton, *Alfred Stieglitz: Photographs & Writings* (Washington, DC: National Gallery of Art, 1983). Stieglitz's inclement weather photos probably had a stronger direct influence on John E. Beeby, a professional engraver and librarian of the Camera Club of New York, whose work was published in the *Photographic Times* and other periodicals around 1900. See "Art of the Photogravure," https://photogravure .com/collection/a-dreary-morning/. Last accessed February 22, 2024.

55. Stieglitz could have achieved the soft focus effect by using the Dallmeyer-Bergheim soft focus lens or by printing through a

thin tissue. Regarding the influence of Whistler on photographers, see Kathleen Pyne, *Modernism and the Feminine Voice: O'Keeffe and the Women of the Stieglitz Circle* (Berkeley: University of California Press, 2007), 5–9. For a summary of Stieglitz and the fourth dimension, see Pyne, *Anne Brigman: The Photographer of Enchantment* (New Haven & London: Yale University Press, 2020), 166–167, citing in part, Max Weber, "In The Fourth Dimension from a Plastic Point of View," *Camera Work* 31 (July 1910).

56. See, for example, Archibald Wilberforce, *The Great Battles of All Nations* (New York: Peter Fenelon Collier & Son, 1900), a pictorial work, mostly of paintings, but including fifteen photographs of the Spanish-American War. An early example of a book primarily of text with half-tone illustrations is Willis Fletcher Johnson, *History of The Johnstown Flood* (Philadelphia: J.W. Keeler & Co., 1889), with twenty-four photographs.

57. Mary Panzer, "Eickemeyer Chronology," in *My Studio: Rudolf Eickemeyer Jr. and the Art of the Camera, 1885–1930* (Yonkers: Hudson River Museum, 1986), 97–99. From 1900 to 1905, Eickemeyer was the art manager for the Fifth Avenue celebrity portrait studio of Alfred S. Campbell, the photographic entrepreneur based in Elizabeth, New Jersey. He then became partners with Charles Henry Davis, formerly of Plainfield, New Jersey, after his partner in Davis & Sanford, another high-end gallery, retired. Eickemeyer rejoined Campbell's around 1910. Eickemeyer, who won the gold medal for photography at the St. Louis World's Fair in 1904, also published books of landscape photography, including *Winter* (1903). Numerous contemporary publications by others include work by Eickemeyer, for example Sadakichi Hartmann, *Landscape and Figure Composition* (New York: Baker & Taylor, 1910).

58. The Inter-State Fair was held at the fairgrounds in Hamilton Township, previously used for the New Jersey Agricultural Fair. Much of the site is now the sculpture garden and museum, Grounds for Sculpture, founded by Seward Johnson Jr., which opened in 1992.

59. John Thompson, *Street Life in London* (New York and London: Benjamin Blom, 1969), reprint of 1877 edition, text by

Adolphe Smith; Pierre Mac-Orlan, *Atget Photographe de Paris* (New York: E. Weyhe, 1930). See also John Szarkowski, *The Work of Atget. Modern Times* (New York: Museum of Modern Art, 1985), vol. 4.

60. Jacob A. Riis, *How the Other Half Lives: Studies Among the Tenements of New York* (New York: Charles Scribner's Sons, 1890). Later reprints of *How the Other Half Lives*, notably the Dover edition published in New York in 1971, were illustrated with half-tone reproductions.

61. Sigmund Krausz, *Street Types of Great American Cities* (Chicago & New York: Werner, 1896) reprint of 1891 edition. Unfortunately, Krausz's photos were sometimes accompanied by captions considered racially or ethnically insensitive today. Riis's book also included racial stereotyping typical of his era.

62. Christopher Fulton, ed., *The Social Documentary Photography of Milton Rogovin* (Lexington: University Press of Kentucky, 2019). In his introduction, referencing John Szarkowski, Fulton notes the distinction between subject matter and subject, "the essential theme addressed by the image but not overtly manifest in it" (p. 2).There is an overlap in subject matter between Castner and Rogovin, but there is no evidence that Castner wanted his portraits to promote social change as did Rogovin. Castner's use of photography was also much more varied than that of Rogovin, who almost exclusively did portraits of workers.

63. The Castner collection at the New Jersey State Museum consists almost exclusively of images taken in New Jersey or nearby Pennsylvania. However, the collection does include a small number of negatives and prints of New York locales, including the Brooklyn Bridge, the Hudson River Valley, Rochester, and Niagara Falls.

64. *Trenton Evening Times*, January 26, 1907. 1. It is probable, but not certain, that the earlier Association Camera Club of Trenton and the Trenton Photographic Society were the same organization.

65. For more than three hundred images of women with handheld cameras in the 1890s and the 1900s, see John P. Jacob, ed., *Kodak Girl from the Martha Cooper Collection* (Göttingen, Germany: Steidl, 2011).

66. Quoted in Nelly Bly, "Champion of Her Sex," *New York Sunday World* (February 2, 1896), 10.

67. *Trenton Evening Times*, April 22, 1924, 18; New Jersey automobile licenses, Castner Family Collection.

68. Lee D. Witkin and Barbara London, *The Photograph Collector's Guide* (Boston: New York Graphic Society, 1979), 95–96. Braun excelled at still life photographs of flowers.

69. *Frank Leslie's Illustrated Newspaper*, May 16, 1891, 258.

70. *Trenton Evening Times*, May 6, 1898, 8; *Trenton Evening Times*, April 29, 1923, 10.

71. *Trenton Evening Times*, October 4, 1902, 1.

72. *Trenton Evening Times*, October 3, 1910, 7.

73. *Photo Era: The American Journal of Photography*, 37, no. 6 (December 1916): 270.

About the Authors

Nicholas P. Ciotola has been the New Jersey State Museum's curator of cultural history since 2009. Previously, he was a curator at the Heinz History Center in Pittsburgh (1998–2009). In twenty-five years as a museum professional, he has served as project director, curator, and/or author for numerous exhibitions, books, and articles on American history and material culture.

Gary D. Saretzky, archivist, educator, and photographer, worked as an archivist for more than fifty years at the State Historical Society of Wisconsin, Educational Testing Service, and the Monmouth County Archives. He was the consulting curator of the Grant Castner exhibit at the New Jersey State Museum. As an adjunct professor, he taught history of photography at Mercer County Community College from 1977–2012 and coordinated the Rutgers Public History Internship Program from 1994–2016.